New Age, Neopagan, and New Religious Movements

New Age, Neopagan, and New Religious Movements

Alternative Spirituality in Contemporary America

HUGH B. URBAN

UNIVERSITY OF CALIFORNIA PRESS

University of California Press, one of the most distinguished university presses in the United States, enriches lives around the world by advancing scholarship in the humanities, social sciences, and natural sciences. Its activities are supported by the UC Press Foundation and by philanthropic contributions from individuals and institutions. For more information, visit www.ucpress.edu.

University of California Press
Oakland, California

Library of Congress Cataloging-in-Publication Data

Urban, Hugh B., author.
  New age, neopagan, and new religious movements : alternative spirituality in contemporary America / Hugh B. Urban.
     pages cm
  Includes bibliographical references and index.
  ISBN 978-0-520-28117-2 (cloth : alk. paper) —
  ISBN 978-0-520-28118-9 (pbk. : alk. paper) —
  ISBN 978-0-520-96212-5 (ebook)
  1. Cults—United States.   2. Sects—United States.   3. Occultism—United States.   I. Title.
  BL2525.U73   2015
  299'.930973—dc23   2015008737

Manufactured in the United States of America

24   23   22   21   20   19   18   17   16   15
10   9   8   7   6   5   4   3   2   1

The paper used in this publication meets the minimum requirements of ANSI/NISO Z39.48–1992 (R 2002) (*Permanence of Paper*).

CONTENTS

ILLUSTRATIONS

PREFACE AND ACKNOWLEDGMENTS

New Age, Neopagan, and New Religious Movements is a comprehensive and user-friendly book devoted to the study of alternative spiritual currents in modern America. The text has grown naturally out of my seventeen years of teaching at a major public university, where I have developed and regularly taught such courses as "New Age and New Religious Movements," "New Religious Movements in a Global Context," and "Magic in the Modern World." Thus the book has a distinctly pedagogical focus, centered on key issues and controversies that I have found consistently work extremely well to provoke thoughtful discussion and debate among readers.

I should also say a few words about the approach of this book. For the most part, this book attempts to present these new religious movements in a clear, straightforward, and nonjargony way. For the sake of readability, notes and references will be kept to a minimum, although a list of suggestions for further reading will be included at the end of each chapter. While the book is informed by all of the existing scholarly literature and theoretical approaches to new religions, it seeks to avoid overburdening readers with dense language and long footnotes. Instead, theoretical questions are largely implicit in the body of each chapter and are allowed to emerge naturally out of readers' own engagement with the material. In my experience, when readers engage issues such as the "brainwashing" debate that surrounds new religions such as Heaven's Gate or Peoples Temple, they are usually able to generate the major theoretical approaches to the question on their own, without my having to tell them, "Scholar X says blah blah blah about brainwashing." And once they have generated these interpretations on their own, readers can be directed toward relevant theoretical literature to help nuance and clarify their perspectives. For this reason, the book includes an appendix on theoretical and methodological approaches to new religions for readers who want to delve further into the academic discussions and debates in the study of new religions.

Many chapters include an interview with a contemporary member (or in some cases an ex-member) of each movement, along with suggestions for relevant films and sources for further reading. For those who are using this book in a university setting, there are also suggested classroom exercises and discussion questions.

A great many people have helped me with my work on new religions over the years and deserve my heartfelt thanks. These include colleagues and mentors such as David Bromley, Lorne Dawson, Cathy Gutierrez, Wouter Hanegraaff, Seth Josephson, Jeffrey Kripal, James Lewis, Bruce Lincoln, Thomas Maroukis, Rebecca Moore, Christopher Partridge, Arthur Versluis, and Catherine Wessinger; my editor, Reed Malcolm; and various members of spiritual communities who offered their time and insight, such as Larry Abdullah, Christopher Blythe, Tim Carter, Ivy Chevers, Mike Dangler, Jagannath Dasa, Mustafaa Islam, Nancy Many, Joseph Mauriello, Cindy Riggs, Carla Watson, and Don Webb.

ONE

Introduction

The Rise of New Religions in Modern America

Each fall, my hometown of Columbus, Ohio, hosts the Universal Life Expo, a huge convention for alternative spiritual and religious practices held at our local Veterans' Memorial Hall. Since most central Ohioans come from a mainstream Christian or Jewish background, they are usually amazed to discover that right here, a few blocks from the Ohio Statehouse, we have one of the largest gatherings of New Age and alternative spirituality in the country. Featuring over 330 booths and vendors, the Expo describes itself as a "metaphysical extravaganza" offering "herbs, crystals, jewelry, angels, musical instruments, wholesome food, incense, readings, wellness products, clothing, candles, art, healers, publications, spiritual fulfillment, and something for everybody, even your pets."[1] The various groups and individuals present include both established religious traditions, such as a group of Tibetan monks who create a large sand mandala, and a vast array of newer spiritual arrivals, such as Spiritualists, Scientologists, channelers, Reiki therapists, psychics, crystal healers, and professional ghost-hunters. The interested visitor can consult with a Spiritualist medium, have a tarot card reading, receive a quick "stress test" from the Church of Scientology, have her or his aura photographed, purchase any of the thousands of crystals and other objects on display, and finally relax with a stop by the "Cuddle Party." In many ways, the Expo is a microcosm of religious diversity and of the complex role of spirituality in the contemporary United States, where hundreds of new spiritual groups exist and compete alongside more established religions in a vibrant but at times chaotic marketplace of religious ideas, practices, goods, and services (figure 1.1).

If most Americans are surprised to discover a massive New Age convention in downtown Columbus, they are typically even more astonished to know that the Midwest is also one of the largest hubs of neopagan activity in the United States, with dozens of Wiccan, Druid,

FIGURE 1.1 Aura photography, Universal Life Expo, Columbus, Ohio, 2013. Photo by the author.

and other groups. Just a few weeks after the Universal Life Expo is the neopagan holy day of Samhain (corresponding to Halloween and falling on the autumn equinox). Our own local Druid group, called ADF (Ár nDraíocht Féin, or "A Druid Fellowship"), welcomes the public to attend its major holy days and always performs its major rituals in public spaces such as metro parks, where anyone is invited to attend (figure 1.2).

Even closer to home, I can walk just a few blocks from my campus office down to the Krishna House, the local center for the International Society for Krishna Consciousness (ISKCON). Perhaps the most successful new religious movement to come from India to the United States, ISKCON began in the mid-1960s, and the Columbus Krishna House is one of its oldest centers. The Columbus Krishna House has been visited by such figures as the Beat poet Allen Ginsberg, who had a famous exchange with the ISKCON founder Swami Prabhupada here in 1969. To this day, the Krishna House remains a popular center for spiritual instruction, free food, and high-energy, often ecstatic devotional music, attracting a large crowd of both curious college students and first- and second-generation South Asians.

FIGURE 1.2 Ár nDraíocht Féin (ADF) Druid ritual, Columbus, Ohio, 2013. Photo by the author.

Meanwhile, just two hours to the east lies Prabhupada's Palace of Gold, a large and opulent shrine dedicated to ISKCON's founder in a gorgeous setting surrounded by the West Virginia mountains, flocks of live peacocks, an award-winning rose garden, a major temple, and a cow protection sanctuary (figure 1.3).

This remarkable diversity of new religious life is surely not unique to Columbus, Ohio, where I happen to live (although being in the center of the Midwest, Columbus is typically the ideal test market for virtually everything in America, from new fast-food items to new religious ideas). Rather, this is simply one example of the astounding diversity of alternative spiritual life that exists almost everywhere across the United States, often in the least expected and seemingly most "mundane" spaces. Similar pockets of new religious diversity can be found not just in obvious places such as Northern California but in the farmlands of central Pennsylvania, in the mountains of New York and Massachusetts, on the coasts of Florida, in the forests of Washington, and in the deserts of Arizona, Utah, and Texas.

J. Gordon Melton, one of the most important scholars of new religions, has recently counted over 2,500 religious and spiritual groups in the United States alone; and by his

FIGURE 1.3 Prabhupada's Palace of Gold, West Virginia. Photo by the author.

estimate at least half of them are "non-conventional" or alternative spiritual movements.[2] In other words, in addition to hosting every imaginable form of Christianity and Judaism, as well as various forms of Islam, Hinduism, Buddhism, Jainism, and Sikhism, the United States is home to an incredible array of New Age, neopagan, and new religious movements. These include huge global movements such as Mormonism as well as small and fairly esoteric groups such as the Hermetic Order of the Golden Dawn; high-profile groups that attract celebrity spokespersons such as the Church of Scientology and fairly obscure, low-profile groups such as Heaven's Gate; new forms of Christianity such as the Branch Davidians and various forms of Satanism such as the Temple of Set; movements that emerged in the nineteenth century such as Spiritualism and Theosophy and groups that emerged in the age of cloning technology such as the Raëlians; earth-based forms of spirituality such as neo-paganism and groups based on UFOs from other worlds such as the Aetherius Society; movements based on Eastern religions such as ISKCON and movements rooted in European traditions such as Wicca; and many hundreds of others. Far from marginal or insignificant, New Age, neopagan, and new religious movements are an integral part of the thriving and increasingly eclectic religious landscape of contemporary America.

As we will see in this book, the United States has been from its inception an unusually fertile land for the growth and development of new religions. Indeed, *new religions are arguably quintessentially "American" phenomena*. If Americans have long prided themselves on the values of free speech, freedom of religious expression, individualism, and an entrepreneurial spirit, then *new religions are perhaps the boldest expression of those ideals*. Yet perhaps for these very reasons they also raise some of the most complicated questions surrounding religious diversity, freedom, and privacy in modern America, particularly in a post-9/11 era of government surveillance and scrutiny of religions that fall outside the "mainstream."

NEW RELIGIOUS MOVEMENTS, NEOPAGANISM, AND NEW AGE: THE SCOPE OF THIS BOOK

The book will be organized more or less historically, moving from the mid-nineteenth century to the present, and it will focus on three broad groups of alternative spiritual movements. The first is new religious movements, which we can define as groups that have emerged roughly within the last 150 years and tend to have clear boundaries between insiders and outsiders; they are also usually organized around a charismatic central figure, such as a Joseph Smith, a Madame Blavatsky, an L. Ron Hubbard, or a Jim Jones. Groups in this category include Mormonism, the Theosophical Society, Scientology, Peoples Temple, the Nation of Islam, the Raëlians, and hundreds of others.

The second group is New Age spirituality, which is a far more amorphous, diverse, and decentralized network of beliefs and practices that has roots in the nineteenth century but has become particularly influential since the 1960s and '70s. The broad label "New Age" includes a diverse array of alternative spiritual practices, such as channeling, crystals, astrology, aromatherapy, and various ideas drawn from Eastern religions. But it tends on the whole to be quite "forward looking," that is, looking toward a coming era of spiritual realization and freedom (most famously articulated in the idea of the dawning "Age of Aquarius"). It also tends to be quite individualistic, focused on the optimum physical, psychological, and spiritual development of the individual practitioner, who is free to pick and choose from a wide array of spiritual options.

Although the New Age is a diffuse and "leaderless" phenomenon, there are many high-profile figures in the movement, including self-help gurus such as Deepak Chopra (well known for his appearances on *The Oprah Winfrey Show*), popular channelers such as JZ Knight (the medium for the spiritual entity named Ramtha), and celebrities such as Shirley MacLaine (who helped popularize New Age ideas widely through her best-selling books and TV miniseries). And although the New Age is a decentralized phenomenon, there are many key centers of New Age spirituality around the United States. One of the most famous is Sedona, Arizona, well known for its unique red-rock formations, which are believed by many to be "vortices" or centers of spiritual energy. Sedona is also home to a vast array of alternative spiritual shops, such as the Center for the New Age—a self-described "metaphysical superstore" that offers every imaginable spiritual service and product, ranging from channeling, psychic readings, and UFO guides to crystals, jewelry, incense, and even a "canned vortex" (figure 1.4).

The third group covered in this book is neopaganism, which is a blanket term that covers a broad array of movements that have emerged since the middle of the twentieth century.

FIGURE 1.4 Center for the New Age, Sedona, Arizona. Photo by the author.

In contrast to the New Age, neopagans tend to be "backward looking," that is, looking to an older, usually pre-Christian past that has been long forgotten but is now being rediscovered and revived. And in contrast to new religious movements, neopagans tend to be more fluid and flexible in their communal organization, so that an individual might be a member of multiple covens or involved in a Wiccan circle as well as a Druid group, or be a solitary practitioner. In general, however, neopagans tend to emphasize *praxis,* that is, practical techniques for altering the internal and external world, such as ritual, dance, performance, and magic. Today, there are literally hundreds of neopagan groups in the United States, ranging from well-known groups such as Wicca, to various pagan traditions drawn from a particular region or ethnicity (Celtic, Norse, Slavic, etc.), to gay and lesbian groups such as the Radical Faeries, and countless others.

WHY STUDY NEW AGE, NEOPAGAN, AND NEW RELIGIOUS MOVEMENTS?

Up until the late 1970s, New Age and new religious movements were rarely taken very seriously by scholars and students of religion. For the most part, new religions either were studied by psychologists and sociologists interested in so-called "cult" phenomena or were viewed as relatively insignificant offshoots of the "great traditions," or the world's major religions.

In the last few decades, however, that attitude has changed dramatically, and today not only scholars but also journalists, legal experts, and even politicians and law enforcement agencies have recognized the importance of understanding new religions. The reason for this shift in attitudes is at least threefold. First, these movements give us valuable insight into the *incredible and growing diversity of religious life* in the United States. At the beginning of the twentieth century, many sociologists predicted that religion would gradually wane in significance in the increasingly scientific, rational, industrial, and technological modern world; yet at least in the United States it would seem that quite the opposite has happened, and we now see an incredible proliferation of new spiritual groups in our scientific and technological world. The United States is today arguably the most religiously diverse nation on earth, with new movements proliferating on an almost daily basis, so understanding new religions is critical to understanding this amazing spiritual ferment in modern America. They force us to ask, Why are there now so many new religions? And why particularly in the United States?

Second, new religions raise *key legal, ethical, and political debates* surrounding religion in the contemporary world. As we will see throughout this book, many new religions have become involved in deeply contested legal questions, such as the use of peyote by the Native American Church, the practice of plural marriage by Mormons, the claim to tax-exempt status by the Church of Scientology, and experimentation in human cloning by the Raëlians. Precisely because they are usually small minority groups on the boundary of "mainstream" religion in the United States, new religions highlight the key issues inherent in the First Amendment, the questions of the free exercise of religion, and the problem of just how far that freedom can be pushed before it conflicts with other laws and rights. Although seemingly "marginal" groups, new religious movements have helped in very real ways to *define the boundaries of what counts as "religion" in the United States itself.*

Finally, new religions raise profound questions surrounding *religious freedom and privacy in a new age of terrorism.* At least since the 1990s, following the Oklahoma City bombing of 1995 and even more clearly after the 2001 terrorist attacks, Americans have faced an intense and complicated debate about religious freedom and the rapidly expanding new forms of surveillance wielded by the federal government. We now know that the FBI has been secretly monitoring mosques and other religious establishments, and we have learned that the National Security Agency has been monitoring vast amounts of telephone, Internet, and other communications by American citizens. Particularly toward the end of this book, we will discuss the difficult question of how to balance a commitment to freedom of religious expression and privacy with the need to protect public safety. Where do we draw the line between reasonable government surveillance and real invasions of privacy? How do we negotiate between the long-held American values of religious freedom and privacy and the new technologies of surveillance wielded by the NSA, the CIA, and the FBI that might potentially keep citizens a bit safer?

In other words, New Age, neopagan, and new religious movements are hardly just interesting curiosities for a few people in the academic study of religion. Rather, they raise huge, complex, and critical questions that are of importance to any student in any discipline—from political science to law, from sociology to psychology to business—and really to any thinking citizen who cares about maintaining a healthy, diverse, and vibrant democracy.

"CULT" CONTROVERSIES: NEW RELIGIONS
AND ALTERNATIVE SPIRITUALITY

One of the first problems to grapple with in the study of new religions is the use of the term *cult*. Our English word *cult* is derived form the Latin term *cultus,* and in its simplest meaning it merely refers to a system of religious belief or to a form of religious veneration. Up until the twentieth century, the word *cult* did not really have any particularly negative or derogatory connotations. But in the decades following World War II, as the United States saw the rise of a huge number of new religious communities and alternative spiritual groups, the term *cult* began to be applied in much more specific and usually negative ways to refer to groups that fell outside the dominant American traditions of "Protestant/Catholic/Jew." By the early 1960s, anticult paranoia combined with growing fears about the alleged phenomenon of "brainwashing" during the Cold War. This was particularly the case after the publication of Robert Jay Lifton's widely read book on brainwashing in China, *Thought Reform and the Psychology of Totalism* (1961).[3] Fueled by anticult literature, the fear was now that brainwashing might take place not just in a faraway communist state but within alternative religious groups right here on American soil.[4] And by the 1970s, the fear of new religions had blossomed into a widespread "cult scare" and given rise to a wide array of anticult groups—the Individual Freedom Foundation, Love Our Children, the Citizens Freedom Foundation, the Spiritual Counterfeits Project, Cults Exodus for Christ, the Cult Awareness Network, and many others—dedicated to saving America's youth from dangerous mind-control groups.

Today, some sociologists do continue to use the word *cult* in a nonpejorative way, simply as a means of classifying a small religious community that differs in significant ways from large organized religious institutions and denominations. Following other sociologists, the Canadian scholar Lorne Dawson uses a typology of "church/sect/cult" to distinguish between large religious organizations (such as the Roman Catholic Church or Sunni Islam), smaller denominations or "sects" (such as Pentecostals), and still smaller groups or "cults" (such as Scientology or the Unification Church). In contrast to churches and sects, he suggests, "Cults are more concerned with the satisfaction of individual needs and desires. They usually lay claim to some esoteric knowledge that has been lost, repressed or newly discovered, and they offer their believers some more direct kind of ecstatic or transfiguring experience than traditional modes of religious life."[5] Cults according to this model also tend to have charismatic leaders and are often loosely organized and short-lived, frequently dissolving once the leader has died.

However, most scholars of religion today, and particularly those working in the United States, have abandoned the "cult" label altogether. Since the 1970s, the term has come to have so many negative and often ridiculous associations—brainwashing, mass suicide, baby killing, and so on—that most scholars now see it as too problematic and misleading to be useful for understanding these movements. Some scholars of new religions, such as Catherine Wessinger, even argue that the use of the term *cult* can actually be dangerous, insofar as it can be used to justify aggressive and violent responses to these movements. "It is important," she writes, "that people become aware of the bigotry conveyed by *cult*. The word *cult* dehumanizes the religion's members and their children. It strongly implies that these people are deviants; they are seen as crazy, brainwashed, duped by the leader. When we label people as subhuman, we create a context in which it is considered virtuous to kill them."[6] Wessinger cites the example of the Branch Davidians and the tragic disaster at their ranch in Waco, Texas, when heavily armed agents from the Bureau of Alcohol, Tobacco and Firearms (ATF) raided the community in 1993. Because agencies such as the ATF and the FBI regarded the Branch Davidians as a dangerous cult instead of a legitimate religion, and because they relied for information on highly biased anticult activists, they approached the movement in an overly aggressive and insensitive way that led to a violent shoot-out, a fifty-one-day standoff, and finally the fiery deaths of seventy-six men, women, and children inside the ranch.

Instead, most scholars now prefer to use the more neutral term *new religious movements.* The value of this label is that it highlights the "newness" of these groups while also reminding us to take them seriously as *religions,* that is, as complex systems of beliefs and practices that are profoundly meaningful to those who adhere to them. In other words, they need to be studied and understood on the same terms as the so-called "great" religions of the world, such as Judaism, Christianity, Islam, Hinduism, Buddhism, Jainism, and Sikhism. They also force us to recognize that even the so-called great religions have tremendous internal diversity (from Greek and Russian Orthodox to Pentecostal Christianity, from Sunni and Sufi to Alawite Islam) and vast numbers of new offshoots and variations (from the Branch Davidians and Peoples Temple to the Nation of Islam and al-Qaeda). At the same time, however, calling something a religion rather than a cult surely does *not* mean that we cannot still look at it critically. After all, the fact that we regard the Roman Catholic Church as a religion should not prevent us from looking critically at the history of child sexual abuse and cover-ups within the church. Likewise, the fact that we call the Branch Davidians a religion rather than a cult does not mean that we cannot look critically at the gender and sexual relations within the community, its hostility toward the US government, or its rather violent interpretation of the book of Revelation.

Of course, if we decide to talk about these groups as "new religions" rather than "cults," that raises the question of what exactly we mean by *religion*. There are obviously many, many different ways of defining religion, and our definitions have changed quite a bit over time. For example, prior to the early twentieth century, most forms of Native American belief and practice were not labeled "religion" by scholars or government authorities but were instead called "heathenism," "savagery," or "primitive superstition." Yet today Native American traditions are more or less universally accepted by both scholars and government agencies as "real religions," as complex and sophisticated as any other mainstream tradition. Similarly, when Mormonism first emerged in the mid-nineteenth century it was widely persecuted as a deviant cult or an aberration of Christianity, yet today Mormonism is recognized as one of the largest Christian denominations in the world and even by some as an independent world religion in its own right. Meanwhile, the Church of Scientology had to fight for decades with the IRS and other government agencies in order to finally be recognized as a tax-exempt nonprofit "religion" in 1993, yet Scientology is still not recognized in other nations such as France and Germany, where it is viewed as a *secte* (cult) and a for-profit business. In other words, our definitions of religion not only are highly variable but also change significantly over time. And new religious movements lie at the heart of these debates surrounding the "What is religion?" question.

For the sake of this book, I will follow one of the more useful definitions of religion suggested by the American scholar Bruce Lincoln. While acknowledging the historical contingency of any particular definition and the impossibility of coming up with one that is perfect or universally applicable, Lincoln suggests that we can still use a kind of flexible, provisional, working concept of religion. Rather than a singular thing or essence, he argues, religion is perhaps better understood as a form of discourse that makes a claim to a particular kind of *authority*. Specifically, religious sorts of discourse make a claim to an authority that is believed to "transcend the human, temporary and contingent, and claims for itself a similarly transcendent status." Thus "discourse becomes religious not simply by virtue of its content, but also from its claims to authority. Astrophysicists, for instance, do not engage in religious speech when they discuss cosmogony, so long as they frame their statements as hypotheses and provisional conclusions based on experimentation, calculation, and human reason. . . . But should they ground their views in Scripture, revelation, or immutable ancestral traditions, in that moment their discourse becomes religious because of its claim to transcendent authority."[7] Lincoln then suggests four different features that we typically see in religious phenomena; in addition to their use of *discourse that appeals to a transcendent source of authority*, they also usually involve *a set of beliefs and doctrines* relevant to that transcendent authority; *a set of practices, rituals, and modes of worship;* and finally *an institutional or collective organization* dedicated to the regulation of these discourses, beliefs, and practices.

The advantage of Lincoln's approach is that it leaves *open* the questions of whether religious claims are "true" or "false," whether there really is a transcendent object such as God or the Sacred, and whether some groups are "legitimate" or "illegitimate" religions. Thus, if we follow Lincoln's definition, most of the groups discussed in this book should clearly be approached and taken seriously as religions, even if many of us viewing these groups might personally disagree with them or even find them deeply problematic. Even groups that seem at first to be quite far outside the mainstream or ethically objectionable—such as the Branch Davidians, which involved the stockpiling of illegal weapons and sexual relations with minors—could still be taken seriously as religious attempts to make sense of the universe or find value in human existence. But even if we accept them as religions we can still view them critically and ask serious questions about the role of power, authority, gender, sexuality, or social dynamics in these movements. For ultimately these are the same kinds of critical questions we should be willing to ask of any "mainstream" religion as well, whether it is an Evangelical Christian church, a Hindu community, or a Jewish synagogue.

However, some of the movements discussed in this book—above all, the loose and eclectic category of "New Age"—generally lack the institutional and collective structure that we find in other new religious movements. New Age beliefs and practices tend to be highly individualistic and rarely organized into neatly bounded groups or communities. For this reason, many would call New Age a form of "spirituality" rather than religion—that is, a more individualistic, noninstitutionalized approach to the divine that tends to shy away from organized religious structures (a "religion of no religion," as one scholar, Jeffrey Kripal, put it).[8] According to many recent surveys of religious affiliation, the "spiritual but not religious" category is one of the fastest-growing trends in American culture, so the New Age attitude of spiritual individualism and eclecticism may well be an increasingly visible one in the decades to come.[9]

HOW "NEW" IS THE NEW AGE? THE ADAPTATION OF ESOTERICISM TO THE MODERN WORLD

One of the first questions we need to ask when studying New Age, neopagan, and new religious movements is: Are these groups really "new" at all? Or is this simply a matter of repackaging and dressing up fairly old religious ideas in new outfits with newer and fancier language?

The answer, of course, is both yes and no. While all of the movements discussed in this book are "new" in the sense that they have emerged roughly within the last 150 years, they are also rooted in much older traditions of alternative spirituality. As some scholars have argued, the New Age is in many ways only a modern reinterpretation or reworking of a long current of alternative religious ideas, often referred to as Western esotericism.[10] Derived from the Greek term *esoteros*, meaning "inner" or "hidden," *esotericism* refers to a large body of traditions that date back to the Hellenistic world of the first centuries of the Common Era (CE or AD). These include early forms of Christianity such as Gnosticism that were later branded as heretical by the mainstream church, forms of Jewish mysticism such as Kabbalah, and ancient Greek and Mediterranean traditions such as Hermeticism. A wide array of practices and movements are included under the label of "Western esotericism," including astrology, alchemy, and various forms of magic, as well as secret societies such as Freemasonry and Rosicrucianism. Despite their diversity, however, most of these esoteric traditions share at least four features and themes:

1. *The idea of correspondences.* The entire universe, from the planets and stars in the heavens down to plants, animals, and stones on the earth and every aspect of the human body, is believed to be connected through a complex network of hidden

correspondences or analogies, like a cosmic hall of mirrors. This idea is most famously summarized in the saying "As above, so below" from the early religious and philosophical tradition known as Hermeticism. The correct understanding of these connections is the basis of all forms of magic, astrology, and spiritual healing. This is the underlying logic, for example, of the astrology column in every newspaper still printed today and widely read even by most Americans who know or care nothing about other forms of Western esotericism.

2. *The idea of living nature.* Not only is the entire universe believed to be connected by a network of hidden correspondences, but it is also believed to be a living organism, animated by its own living energy or soul. The correct understanding of this living energy is the key not only to magical practice but also to various forms of spiritual healing. The concept of living nature is similar in many ways to Asian concepts such as the Chinese *ch'i* (as in the practice of Tai ch'i), and the Indian *prana,* which is both breath and a kind of vital energy that flows through not just the body but all of nature. In contemporary literature, the idea of living nature has been partially revived in the Gaia hypothesis, or the view of the earth as a complex self-regulating living system that maintains the conditions for life. And in popular culture, the idea of living nature has found perhaps its most famous form in the *Star Wars* films as "the Force," the vital energy that binds all things and can be harmonized with and/or manipulated by the trained Jedi master.

3. *Multiple, vividly imagined intermediary entities between the human and the divine.* Most Western esoteric traditions include a complex hierarchical view of the universe with a great chain of intermediary entities between the human and the divine, often visualized in highly imaginative forms (as angels, demons, demigods, and other supernatural beings). Through contemplation and spiritual practice, the individual can ascend and descend the complex visionary ladder between this world and the divine. Perhaps the most famous example of this idea is the "tree of life" or tree of the *sephiroth* described in the Jewish mystical tradition known as Kabbalah. Imagined as a series of ten radiant emanations, the *sephiroth* stretch from the infinite abyss of the Godhead down to the divine presence in the physical world. At the same time, the tree of the *sephiroth* represents a visionary ladder that the individual Kabbalist can ascend through contemplation.

4. *The experience of transmutation.* Western esoteric traditions are typically not just a matter of intellectual speculation; they also involve practical techniques for transforming the physical world and the human self. This transmutation may involve the manipulation of the material world through magic or the transformation of the individual subject into a divine or enlightened state. In the tradition of alchemy, for example, the transmutation of metals (such as lead

into gold) can serve as a metaphor for the spiritual transmutation of the individual from a lower to a higher spiritual state.

All of these themes in the Western esoteric tradition can be found in one form or another in the various New Age, neopagan, and new religious movements covered in this book. The entire tradition of neopaganism and modern magic that has flourished since the mid-twentieth century, for example, is based largely on the concepts of living nature and correspondences. Many new religious movements, such as Mormonism, Theosophy, Spiritualism, and the Raëlians, include complex hierarchies of mediations between the divine and human realms, with a variety of supernatural beings such as angels, masters, extraterrestrials, and spirits. And most of the diverse phenomena we call "New Age" are centered primarily on the concept of physical and spiritual transmutation—either healing the mind and body through various techniques, such as energy alignment, aromatherapy, and crystal healing, or transforming the spirit through techniques such as meditation, mediumship, and channeling.

So if we can say that New Age and religious movements have many deep roots in a much longer history of alternative and esoteric spirituality in Western culture, then what if anything is "new" about them? In many cases, what distinguishes new religious movements is less the *content* of their beliefs and practices than the ways in which they *express* or "package" them and uniquely *adapt* them to the modern world. They have, in a sense, been refracted through the lens of modern thought, colored by aspects of modern science, technology, popular culture, and in some cases consumer capitalism.

A good example is the Church of Scientology, which has a great deal in common with older esoteric traditions such as Gnosticism and which draws many elements from Hinduism and Buddhism. Yet from its origins in the early 1950s, Scientology's founder, L. Ron Hubbard, made extensive use of the language of modern science and even developed his own new piece of spiritual technology called the E-meter or Electropsychometer. A science fiction writer himself, Hubbard also incorporated elements from popular culture such as the widespread interest in UFOs, space travel, life on other worlds, and superpowers.

Another good example is the practice of trance channeling, which again has roots that run deep in the history of Western esotericism and alternative spirituality. While communicating very old religious ideas, famous trance channels such as Jane Roberts make frequent use of the language of modern technology, such as radio and television, to describe the way in which they pick up the signal or "channel" of a particular spirit. The contemporary channel JZ Knight makes extensive comparisons to modern science, particularly quantum physics, to explain her spiritual philosophy and the message of her channeled entity named Ramtha. Knight also appeared in a 2004 film *What the Bleep Do We Know?* which was created by followers of the Ramtha movement and which made extensive comparisons between quantum physics and New Age spirituality.

In sum, the "newness" of New Age and new religious movements often lies less in the *message* than in the *medium* through which that message is communicated.

WHY NOW? WHY HERE? REASONS FOR THE RISE OF NEW RELIGIONS IN THE CONTEMPORARY UNITED STATES

If it is true that the United States today has such a tremendous diversity of new religious movements, we have to ask the basic questions: Why here and why now? Why does contemporary America seem to be the land par excellence for the growth and spread of alternative spiritual traditions?

Surely part of the answer lies in this country's unique religious and legal history. Since the arrival of the Puritans, Quakers, and Shakers, the "New World" has long been seen as a refuge for alternative and persecuted religious minorities (even though many of these groups, such as the Puritans, would not turn out to be particularly tolerant of religious difference themselves). Still more importantly, religious diversity in America has a unique history in large part because of the establishment clause of the First Amendment to the US Constitution (that "Congress shall make no law respecting an establishment of religion, or prohibiting the free exercise thereof"). Although this clause has a long and extremely complicated history of legal interpretations, it has meant that American courts and federal agencies have had a fairly "hands off" attitude toward religious groups, at least compared to other modern nations. Indeed, US agencies and courts have generally been reluctant to even define the terms *religion* or *religious organization,* since any fixed definitions would inevitably exclude the beliefs and practices of some faith communities. As the Supreme Court acknowledged as early as 1878 in its discussion of Mormonism, "The word 'religion' is not defined in the Constitution. We must go elsewhere, therefore, to ascertain its meaning."[11] The United States does not register religious groups and has no official hierarchy of religious organizations. This lack of an established state religion and this reluctance by the courts to even define religion has opened the way for tremendous religious experimentation and a kind of "free market" of spiritual innovation and competition. As the historian R. Laurence Moore notes, the growth of a diverse marketplace of religious options was already well under way in the eighteenth century; but the establishment clause of the First Amendment intensified this market rationale and helped foster an environment of competition among denominations, which all had to "make religion popular" amid the many other goods and services of the world.[12] As a result, the United States has become in many ways incredibly fertile soil for the planting and flourishing of a tremendous variety of religious groups over the last two centuries.

In many ways, the rise of New Age and new religious movements can be seen less as a radical shift in American history than as the continuation of a long series of spiritual revivals in the United States dating back to the eighteenth century. The United States has witnessed several periodic upsurges in religious fervor and the proliferation of new forms of worship and ways of relating to the divine.[13] Usually historians describe a First Great Awakening that spread across the American colonies in the 1730s and '40s, followed by a Second Great Awakening in the early nineteenth century. This second resurgence of spiritual life in the 1830s and '40s helped give rise to several of the movements covered in this book, including Mormonism and Spiritualism, which both grew out of the wave of religious revival that began in the northeastern United States.

Some historians also add a Third Great Awakening, which occurred at the end of the nineteenth century and the beginning of the twentieth and helped give birth to new movements such as Christian Science and the Holiness and Pentecostal movements. Still others add a Fourth Great Awakening, which began in the 1960s. In many ways, the period of the 1960s and '70s witnessed the most rapid growth of New Age spirituality and new religious movements. Fueled by the civil rights movement, new forms of feminism, the sexual revolution, experimentation with psychedelic drugs, and anti–Vietnam War protests, these decades gave birth to a wide array of alternative forms of spirituality. At the same time, the new immigration rules signed into law by the Hart-Cellar Act in 1965 opened the door for a new wave of people from South and East Asia to enter the United States, which helped give birth to movements such as the International Society for Krishna Consciousness (aka Hare Krishna) and various new forms of Buddhism. In this sense, the explosion of new religions has been closely tied to the processes of globalization, as people, ideas, and capital have been able to flow ever more rapidly across the planet, interacting with one another in new and creative ways.

Finally, one might well argue that the turn of the millennium and the 9/11 terrorist attacks have ushered in yet another Great Awakening—though perhaps one with darker and more disturbing implications than previous periods of religious resurgence. The years leading up to 2000 clearly witnessed a powerful wave of millenarian and apocalyptic new religious movements, such as the Branch Davidians (who had a tragic showdown with federal agencies in 1993), Heaven's Gate (whose members committed collective suicide in 1997), and Aum Shinrikyo (whose members unleashed sarin gas in Tokyo subways in 1995). Above all, in the wake of the 9/11 attacks, these kinds of new religious movements raise profound and complex questions of religious freedom, privacy, and government surveillance—particularly surrounding the role of government agencies and law enforcement in monitoring religious groups that could be dangerous and/or self-destructive and the extent to which we are willing to allow government surveillance to intrude on basic rights to privacy and religious freedom.

As we will see in the chapters of this book, many new religious movements were also key test cases for the First Amendment, challenging the courts and the American public to think seriously about how far the limits of religious freedom go. Does the nonestablishment of religion mean that Mormon men can marry more than one wife, for example? Does it mean that Native Americans can consume peyote, which is classified as a Schedule I controlled substance? Or that Rastas can smoke marijuana? In other words, not only do new religions represent some of the most remarkable *expressions* of the rich diversity of religious options fostered by the First Amendment, but they also have presented some of the most intense *flash points for debating its meaning and applicability* to specific groups of believers.

To help us dive into the complex issues involved in studying New Age and new religious movements, let's just briefly examine one particular example and then think about various approaches for studying, interpreting, and making sense of it. While there are many possible examples we could focus on here, I would suggest we look at the complex case of the Heaven's Gate movement, thirty-nine of whose members committed mass suicide in 1997. With its rich mixture of Christian apocalyptic ideas, UFO beliefs, and other elements drawn from science fiction and popular culture, Heaven's Gate is not only a striking illustration of many New Age and new religious ideas but also a powerful example of the difficulties we face in trying to study and make sense of these movements.

Heaven's Gate was founded by Marshall Herff Applewhite (1931–97; figure 1.5), who was born the son of a Presbyterian preacher in Spur, Texas. As a young man, Applewhite studied music, briefly served in the military, and then taught music at the University of Alabama and at the University of St. Thomas in Houston. Throughout these years, he also appears to have struggled with his own sexuality, and he was fired from the University of Alabama for having sexual relations with a male student. Eventually Applewhite would have himself hospitalized to try to "cure" his homosexuality, and he later had himself castrated in an attempt to resolve his sexual desires once and for all.

In 1972, Applewhite met Bonnie Lu Nettles (1927–85), a nurse who was very interested in Spiritualist and New Age phenomena such as séances, mediums, fortune-telling, and astrology. Together, Applewhite and Nettles concluded that they had been chosen to fulfill biblical prophecy, eventually calling themselves "the two," referring to the two "witnesses" mentioned in the book of Revelation. Gathering a small group of followers, they began teaching a complex mixture of religious ideas drawn from Christianity (particularly Revelation), UFO beliefs, and elements of popular culture such as *Star Trek*. Heaven's Gate was not, however, the first new religion to incorporate ideas about UFOs into its belief system. Since the late 1940s, there had been widespread speculations about UFO sightings, which also gave birth to many UFO-based religions throughout the United States and Europe (see chapter 14 below).

The basic belief articulated by Applewhite was that two thousand years ago Jesus Christ had come to this world via spacecraft as a "captain" with his "away team" and had delivered his original message. However, that message was misunderstood and corrupted by mainstream Christian churches. Now, however, Applewhite and Nettles were bearing the final message that Jesus would soon be returning, again by spacecraft, and that their followers would have a last chance to exit this world before its final

FIGURE 1.5 Marshall Applewhite.

destruction and renewal. The higher realm from which Jesus had come and to which he would return was called variously the Kingdom of Heaven, the Next Level, or "the Evolutionary Level Above Human" (T.E.L.A.H.), while this world was regarded as a temporary "garden" that would soon be "recycled." According to materials first published in book form and later posted on the Heaven's Gate website:

> Two thousand years ago, the Kingdom Level Above Human appointed an Older Member to send a Representative (His "Son"), along with some of their beginning students, to incarnate on this garden. . . . While on Earth as an "away team" with their "Captain," they were to work on their overcoming of humanness and tell the civilization they were visiting how the *true* Kingdom of God can be entered. . . .
>
> Again an "away team" from the Level Above Human incarnated in the 1970s in the mature (adult bodies) that had been picked and prepped for this current mission.[1]

Nettles died of cancer in 1985, and the group kept a low profile for the next several years. In the 1990s, however, they reemerged with the new name Heaven's Gate and made their home in a large mansion in the San Diego area. During this time they also made their living through a business called Higher Source, which designed websites for various clients in the early days of the World Wide Web.

Members of Heaven's Gate led a highly ascetic and regulated life, similar in many ways to the discipline of a Christian or Buddhist monastic community. Each member was assigned a "check partner" to help monitor her or his behavior throughout the

(continued)

day, and each followed an elaborate list of rules for dress, diet, and comportment, along with a long list of major and minor offenses. Examples of such offenses included: "Taking any action without using my check partner; Trusting my own judgment—or using my own mind; . . . Criticizing or finding faults with my classmates or teachers; . . . Staying in my own head, having private thoughts . . . ; Having likes or dislikes."[2] Sexuality was considered to be especially in need of regulation, and seven other male members of the group would follow Applewhite's lead and have themselves castrated in order to deal with this particular human desire.

The aim of this elaborate regulation of behavior, Applewhite explained, was to overcome and transcend the physical human condition altogether and so prepare members to receive a new, perfect, genderless body that would be part of the Kingdom of Heaven or the "Next Level Above Human." According to Applewhite's instructions, "The student must complete this change to the point of abhorring human behavior before his soul can be a 'match' with a biological body of the *true* Kingdom of God— for that new, genderless body is designed to function at a much more refined level."[3] An image from the Heaven's Gate website depicted how a member of the Next Level might appear: it is a classic popular image of an alien, complete with a large smooth head, black eyes, and a silver space suit.

Demographically, the members of the Heaven's Gate group do not appear to fall into any obvious categories and do not seem to fit the common stereotype of dysfunctional individuals or alienated social misfits. The members were men and women who ranged in age from twenty-six to seventy-three and came from an extremely diverse range of backgrounds. They included a former army paratrooper, a rock musician, a massage therapist, a computer trainer, an oysterman, a farm girl, a nurse, a bus driver, an artist, and a car salesman. Indeed, the occupational, sexual, and racial profile of these individuals does not appear that much different from a sample cross section of the American population as a whole. Moreover, there is no evidence that members were psychologically disturbed, unintelligent, or previously inclined to self-identify as outsiders.[4]

One of the most interesting things about Heaven's Gate is that this was, in many ways, the world's first "cyber-religion." Not only did the members make their living as website designers, but they also used the Internet to advertise their message of the imminent return of Jesus and successfully recruited several new members in this way. Still more significantly, they incorporated the language of computers, cyberspace, and virtual reality into their theology. Thus the articles on the Heaven's Gate website used the language of hard drives and software to describe the relationship between the soul, the brain, and the divine realm: "The soul has its own 'brain' or 'hard drive' that accumulates only information of the Next Level."[5] Members also used technological language drawn from popular science fiction shows such as *Star Trek: The Next Generation*, describing this world, for example, as a "holodeck" where we practice for the "real world," which is the Kingdom of Heaven. As one member put it, "We watch a lot of *Star Trek*, a lot of *Star Wars*, it's just, to us, like going on a holodeck. We've been training on a holodeck. . . . Now it's time to stop. . . . We take off the virtual reality helmet[,] . . . go back out of the holodeck to reality to be with . . . the other members on the craft in the heavens."[6]

On March 19–20, 1997, the Hale-Bopp comet passed within visible range of Earth, and many UFO watchers believed that there was some kind of object—possibly a spacecraft—riding in its tail. Applewhite announced to the group that this was the "marker they had been waiting for" and the sign that a spacecraft was returning to take them back to the Kingdom of Heaven or the Next Level Above Human. To board the craft and ascend to the Next Level, however, they would need to leave behind their physical bodies. In preparation for their departure, Applewhite and members videotaped a farewell message in which they explained their actions—claiming that they were acting completely of their own free will and that this would not be suicide but a journey to a new world. In the video, members are shown dressed in identical black suits with an arm patch identifying them as the "Away Team." On March 24, 25, and 26, thirty-nine members then committed suicide in three groups by consuming phenobarbital mixed with applesauce and washed down with vodka; all but three also had plastic bags over their heads to induce asphyxiation. All of the bodies were found dressed in their identical black Away Team outfits, each wearing black and white Nike sneakers and carrying a five-dollar bill and three quarters (said to be needed for interplanetary tolls).

The Heaven's Gate suicides leave us with a number of extremely difficult methodological and theoretical questions, which are directly relevant to the broader study of new religious movements. How should we go about trying to study this movement, and what methodological approaches would be most useful for trying to make sense of such a complex religious phenomenon? Should we attempt to reconstruct a psychological profile of its founder and members? Should we gather relevant sociological data on the group, examining its demographics and social profile? Should we focus on a textual analysis of the written and digital materials they left behind? Should we try to place the movement in the broader historical and cultural context of America during the 1980s and '90s? Or do we need a mixture of all of the above? And how should we make sense of this movement and its suicides from a theoretical perspective? Is it best understood through the lenses of psychology, or sociology, or sexuality studies, or cultural studies, or comparative religions—or again, through a complex mixture of all of these approaches?

(continued)

Scholars themselves, we should note, do not agree on how to make sense of Heaven's Gate. An entire book was published on the subject, featuring chapters from a wide array of scholars, many of whom argue with one another about the most useful interpretation of this controversial movement. Some argue that Heaven's Gate was not so much a weird "aberration" as a "quintessentially American" religious movement, which creatively synthesized elements of Christian theology, New Age spirituality, elements of popular culture, and other ideas circulating in the American spiritual marketplace.[7] Others, however, describe Heaven's Gate as a kind of "deviant group" creating an atmosphere of "total obedience" that served to cut its members off from the world and ultimately led to self-destructive behavior.[8] And still others argue that we need to approach the movement sociologically, examining the larger cultural, spiritual, and social milieu that leads individuals to join alternative communities like this in the first place.[9]

So readers should be encouraged to disagree, argue, and come up with their own interpretations—not only of Heaven's Gate but of all of the movements discussed in this book. All of these groups should be examined and discussed from multiple perspectives, with different methodologies and different theoretical perspectives, and readers should be encouraged to debate their advantages and disadvantages for the larger project of thinking about religion in contemporary America.

1. See the article "Last Chance to Advance beyond Human," which appeared on the original Heaven's Gate website in 1994 and has been mirrored at www.wave.net/upg/gate/lastchnc.htm. These materials were published as a book entitled *How and When "Heaven's Gate" (The Door to the Physical Kingdom Level Above Human) May Be Entered* (Telah Foundation, 1997).
2. Ibid., sec. 2, p. 9.
3. Ibid.
4. See Hugh B. Urban, "The Devil at Heaven's Gate: Rethinking the Study of Religion in the Age of Cyberspace," *Nova Religio* 3, no. 2 (2000): 268–302; see also George Chryssides, introduction to *Heaven's Gate: Postmodernity and Popular Culture in a Suicide Group*, ed. George Chryssides (London: Ashgate, 2011), 12.
5. "'95 Statement by an E.T. Presently Incarnate," which appeared on the original Heaven's Gate website in 1994 and has been mirrored at www.wave.net/upg/gate/95upd96.htm.
6. Jeffrey Sconce, "*Star Trek*, Heaven's Gate and Textual Transcendence," in *Cult Television*, ed. Sara Gwenllian-Jones (Minneapolis: University of Minnesota Press, 2004), 219.
7. Benjamin Ethan Zeller, "Scaling Heaven's Gate: Individualism and Salvation in a New Religious Movement," in Chryssides, *Heaven's Gate*, 155, 181. See also Zeller, *Heaven's Gate: America's UFO Religion* (New York: New York University Press, 2014).
8. Winston Davis, "Heaven's Gate: A Study of Religious Obedience," in Chryssides, *Heaven's Gate*, 100–102.
9. Robert Balch and David Taylor, "Seekers and Saucers: The Role of the Cultic Milieu in Joining a UFO Cult," in Chryssides, *Heaven's Gate*, 37–52.

HOW TO STUDY NEW AGE AND NEW RELIGIOUS MOVEMENTS: BALANCING RESPECT AND CRITICAL THINKING

The study of new religious movements is in many ways a particularly acute example of the challenges we face in trying to make sense of all religious traditions. Trying to understand any religion—particularly one very different from one's own—involves a complex negotiation between sympathetic understanding and critical distance, between "closeness" and "otherness." But because new religious movements are at once minority communities and also often flash points for larger cultural debates (polygamy, feminism, cloning, use of controlled substances, etc.), they are often particularly difficult cases to analyze and interpret in a sensitive, nuanced way, without dismissing or sensationalizing them.

In this book, I will suggest that we adopt an approach that strives to maintain a careful balance between an attitude of *respect* and an attitude of *critical thinking*. By this I mean that we should first try to take all of these groups seriously on their own terms as legitimate examples of the human desire to find deeper meaning and value in the universe. Here I suggest that we begin by exercising our sympathetic imagination to try as far as possible to see the world from the believer's perspective from the very outset. At the same time, however, this does not mean that we cannot *also* ask difficult critical questions about these groups, such as: What are the implications of this movement for gender relations or the dynamics of power and authority? How are these groups related to broader historical trends or the social, political, and economic contexts of the United States over the last 150 years? In other words, we need to balance our respectful understanding of the beliefs and practices of these groups with a critical and complex analysis of their role in American history and culture as a whole.

Because of the tremendous diversity of new religions in the United States, there is no single "method" for approaching and interpreting them. Some groups might lend themselves particularly well to an ethnographic approach, based on detailed interviews and long-term study of a particular community (for example, an ethnographic study of neopagan festival culture in the United States); but other groups such as Mormonism, which began over a century ago, might lend themselves more to a historical study of their roots in American society and in larger cultural changes over the last 150 years. Still others, such as Spiritualism or Wicca, which offered new forms of authority and leadership to women, might lend themselves to a study of gender and sexuality.

In the chapters that follow, these sorts of theoretical and methodological questions are left largely implicit so that readers can draw their own conclusions through an engagement with the religious movements themselves. However, for those who wish to discuss these theoretical questions more directly, there is also an appendix at the end of the book entitled "Method and Theory in the Study of New Religions." This suggests a variety of methodological and theoretical approaches, ranging from sociology and psychology to feminism and cultural studies. The study of new religions, I will suggest, demands that we assemble a complex and varied "toolbox" of methodologies, as it were. As we examine a wide array of traditions, from the Native American Church and Mormonism to Peoples Temple and the Branch Davidians, I will suggest that we try to examine them from multiple perspectives, through many different theoretical lenses. No one approach can make sense of every religious movement, any more than a hammer can be used to turn screws or a saw used to patch holes. So stocking a good methodological toolbox means that we should be familiar with a variety of methods drawn from psychology, sociology, anthropology, critical legal studies, gender and sexuality studies, media studies, and others. To understand the role of women in contemporary neopaganism, for example, we might want to draw upon contemporary feminist theory; to understand the role of plural marriage in Mormonism, we might want to use a more historical approach, examining the changing role of marriage and family in nineteenth-century America; or to understand the debates surrounding marijuana use by Rastas, we might need to draw upon critical legal studies. By the end of this book, after we have looked at an array of new religions and key issues, we should have a diverse set of theoretical tools that we can use to study not just alternative spiritual groups but really any religions.

HOW TO USE THIS BOOK: KEY ISSUES AND DEBATES IN THE STUDY OF NEW RELIGIONS

The remainder of this book consists of thirteen chapters, each of them covering one specific movement, and progresses more or less chronologically from the mid-nineteenth century to the present. Each chapter also highlights one key issue or controversy related to that movement as a way to spark discussion and debate. For example, the chapter on the Native American Church will highlight the debate surrounding the use of peyote and the complex legal battles that ensued in the late twentieth century as a way of raising larger questions of religious freedom and the law. The chapter on Spiritualism will highlight the new role of women as mediums and spiritual leaders, which raises complex questions about female power, authority, and status in nineteenth-century America. The chapter on the Branch Davidians will highlight the relation of new religions to law enforcement, raising the difficult question of how we should deal with groups that may be engaging in illegal and potentially violent activities.

From the outset, we should emphasize that *we should not and cannot reduce these movements simply to a single issue or controversy.* There is obviously far more to Mormonism than plural marriage, which is no longer even practiced by the vast majority of Mormons. And of course, not all neopagans are feminists or environmentalists. Instead, these key issues should be regarded simply as focal points for thinking more critically about new forms of spirituality and about religion in general. They help us ask key questions, such as: What are the broader legal, social, and political implications of these movements? What role have they played, not just in American religious life, but in American history and culture more broadly? How have they helped shape the boundaries and contours of what we call religions in America (rather than "cults" or "philosophies" or "businesses")? And how, in some more extreme cases, do we deal with groups that engage in illegal or dangerous behavior while still respecting the First Amendment and basic rights to privacy and freedom of religious expression?

In sum, rather than reducing these groups to a particular issue or controversy, the chapters in this book should be used as a means both to explore the larger history of each of these movements and to raise much larger questions about religion in the contemporary United States.

QUESTIONS FOR DISCUSSION AND DEBATE

1. This chapter suggests using Bruce Lincoln's definition of religion as a useful starting point for the study of New Age, neopagan, and new religious movements. But do you find his definition persuasive and adequate? Does it leave anything out? What other definitions could we come up with? And what are the advantages and limitations of each?

2. If we accept the definition of religion outlined in this chapter, does Heaven's Gate meet it? After all, most religions do not typically end in mass suicide. So should we call movements such as Heaven's Gate something else, other than religion? Or does Heaven's Gate tell us something interesting about "religion" itself?

3. This introduction suggests a number of possible reasons for the rapid growth of new religious movements in the United States: (a) the ideal of religious freedom and the interpretation of the First Amendment in US history; (b) the periodic waves of religious "awakenings" in US history from the First and Second Great Awakenings to the 1960s spiritual counterculture; (c) globalization, cultural contact, and rapid social change; (d) the United States as a growing spiritual marketplace with a spirit of experimentation and competition. Which, if any, of these explanations seems most plausible to you? Are there other ways of explaining the rapid growth of new religions in the contemporary United States?

4. Does the United States seem to be unique in this regard—that is, does it seem to be more of a religious hotbed than other nations, or is there simply a global trend toward religious experimentation and proliferation?

SUGGESTED CLASSROOM ACTIVITY

View the Heaven's Gate farewell video (which is widely available online, on YouTube and elsewhere, and is reproduced in many programs, such as the ABC News *Nightline* special "Inside Heaven's Gate"). Discuss, first of all, why such a video would have been made at all, since the members were leaving Earth before it was supposed to be destroyed and "recycled."

What personal, psychological, communal, or spiritual purposes might such a video have served for the group or for their loved ones? Second, how would you begin to analyze these farewell statements themselves? Were they simply "virtual suicide notes," or did they play some larger religious role in this group's complex theology and belief system?

SUGGESTED FILM

"Inside Heaven's Gate." *Nightline,* NBC News, 2007.

SUGGESTIONS FOR FURTHER READING

Chryssides, George D., ed. *Heaven's Gate: Postmodernity and Popular Culture in a Suicide Group.* London: Ashgate, 2011.

Cowan, Douglas E., and David G. Bromley. *Cults and New Religions: A Brief History.* Oxford: Blackwell, 2008.

Daschke, Dereck, and W. Michael Ashcraft, eds. *New Religious Movements: A Documentary Reader.* New York: New York University Press, 2005.

Dawson, Lorne. *Cult Controversies: The Sociology of New Religious Movements.* New York: Oxford University Press, 2006.

Ellwood, Robert S., and Harry B. Partin. *Religious and Spiritual Groups in Modern America.* Englewood Cliffs, NJ: Prentice Hall, 1988.

Gallagher, Eugene V., and W. Michael Ashcraft, eds. *Introduction to New and Alternative Religious Movements.* Westport, CT: Greenwood Press, 2006.

Goodrick-Clarke, Nicholas. *The Western Esoteric Traditions.* New York: Oxford University Press, 2008.

Hanegraaff, Wouter J. *New Age Religion and Western Culture: Esotericism in the Mirror of Secular Thought.* Albany: SUNY Press, 1997.

Kripal, Jeffrey J. *Esalen: America and the Religion of No Religion.* Chicago: University of Chicago Press, 2008.

Lewis, James R., ed. *The Oxford Handbook of New Religious Movements.* New York: Oxford University Press, 2004.

Nova Religio: The Journal of Alternative and Emergent Religions. Berkeley: University of California Press.

Partridge, Christopher. *The Re-enchantment of the West.* Vol. 2. *Alternative Spiritualities, Sacralization, Popular Culture, and Occulture.* London: T. and T. Clark, 2005.

Pike, Sarah M. *New Age and Neopagan Religions in America.* New York: Columbia University Press, 2004.

Tabor, James D., and Eugene V. Gallagher. *Why Waco? Cults and the Battle for Religious Freedom in America*. Berkeley: University of California Press, 1998.

Urban, Hugh B. *The Church of Scientology: A History of a New Religion*. Princeton, NJ: Princeton University Press, 2011.

Versluis, Arthur. *Magic and Mysticism: An Introduction to Western Esoteric Traditions*. Lanham, MD: Rowman and Littlefield, 2007.

Wessinger, Catherine. *How the Millennium Comes Violently: From Jonestown to Heaven's Gate*. New York: Seven Bridges Press, 2000.

Zeller, Benjamin E. *Heaven's Gate: America's UFO Religion*. New York: New York University Press, 2014.

NOTES TO THE INTRODUCTION

1. Program for "One Light: The 22nd Annual Universal Light Expo," October 9–10, 2010, Columbus, OH, 3. The event's name was changed to "Universal Life Expo" in 2013.
2. J. Gordon Melton, *Encyclopedia of American Religions* (Detroit, MI: Gale Research, 1998), 9.
3. Robert J. Lifton, *Thought Reform and the Psychology of Totalism* (New York: Norton, 1961).
4. For examples of such literature, see Walter Martin, *The Kingdom of the Cults* (Minneapolis: Bethany House, 1965); Jan Van Baalen, *The Chaos of the Cults* (Grand Rapids, MI: William B. Eerdmans, 1962).
5. Lorne Dawson, *Cult Controversies: The Sociology of New Religious Movements* (New York: Oxford University Press, 2006), 31.
6. Catherine Wessinger, *How the Millennium Comes Violently: From Jonestown to Heaven's Gate* (New York: Seven Bridges Press, 2000), 4.
7. Bruce Lincoln, *Holy Terrors: Thinking about Religion after September 11* (Chicago: University of Chicago Press, 2003), 5–6.
8. Jeffrey Kripal, *Esalen: America and the Religion of No Religion* (Chicago: University of Chicago Press, 2008).
9. "Nones on the Rise: Religion and the Unaffiliated," *Pew Research*, October 9, 2012, www.pewforum.org/2012/10/09/nones-on-the-rise-religion/. See also Robert C. Fuller, *Spiritual but Not Religious: Understanding Unchurched America* (New York: Oxford University Press, 2001).
10. Wouter Hanegraaff, *New Age Religion and Western Culture: Esotericism in the Mirror of Secular Thought* (Albany: SUNY Press, 1997).
11. Reynolds v. United States, 98 U.S. 145 (1878), 162.
12. R. Laurence Moore, *Selling God: American Religion and the Marketplace of Culture* (New York: Oxford University Press, 1994), 73, 7.
13. See Robert William Fogel, *The Fourth Great Awakening and the Future of Egalitarianism* (Chicago: University of Chicago Press, 2000); Michael McClymond, ed., *The Encyclopedia of Religious Revivals in America* (Westport, CT: Greenwood Press, 2007).

TWO

The Native American Church

Ancient Tradition in a Modern Legal Context

On any given Saturday night throughout the United States, small groups of Native Americans will be gathered for an all-night ceremony that involves drumming, chanting, prayer, introspection, and the consumption of a small, spineless cactus called peyote. Derived from the Aztec term *peyotl*, peyote is a complex plant that contains numerous alkaloids, including mescaline, which has psychoactive effects. Those who participate in the ceremonies describe peyote as a "sacrament" and a "medicine" that brings profound insight, physical healing, and a deep sense of harmony with the community, with the natural environment, and with the divine. Yet from the first contact between Native Americans and Europeans, the use of peyote has been a source of profound misunderstanding, controversy, persecution, and, most recently, an extremely complicated legal battle.

According to archaeological evidence, the ritual use of the peyote cactus can be traced back at least four thousand to seven thousand years. Peyote buttons that appear to have been used for ritual purposes have been found and radiocarbon dated to 5000 BCE; and in south central Texas and northern Mexico rock art images that illustrate peyote rites have been found that are believed to be 3,000 to 4,200 years old.[1] By the time the Spanish arrived in the Americas, peyote was used as a central part of rituals by the Aztec, Huichol, Cora, Tarascan, and other indigenous groups. However, since their initial encounters with the use of peyote, European colonizers, Christian missionaries, and government authorities have been extremely hostile to the practice. Peyote use was repeatedly condemned by the Catholic Church, banned by US government agencies, and later outlawed in fifteen states. It was not until the foundation of the Native American Church (NAC) in 1918 that the peyote movement began to be recognized in the United States as a legitimate form of religion. But even then, the NAC would have to fight a series of legal battles over the use of peyote that went all the way to the US Supreme Court in 1990. Although the use of peyote by members of the NAC is now protected by federal law, the plant continues to be classified as a Schedule I controlled substance, and the legality of its use by non-Native Americans remains an unresolved question.

Today, the peyote movement is the largest indigenous religion among Native Americans, practiced by more than three hundred thousand people in fifty tribes across the United States and existing in many different local variations with complex mixtures of native and Christian themes. In this sense, the NAC is rooted in an ancient tradition, but it has emerged as a new religious movement and as a fusion of Native American and Christian elements that has had to adapt to a modern legal context. While the ritual consumption of the peyote cactus has pre-Columbian roots, its present use has been profoundly shaped by contact and conflict with Europeans, by the incorporation of various Christian elements, and by a long history of legal tangles with the US courts and law enforcement. As such, the NAC raises critical issues of religious freedom and the law that are central to larger debates surrounding many new religious movements in the contemporary United States.

THE PEYOTE CACTUS AND ITS EFFECTS

Peyote (*Lophophora williamsii*) is native to the area that is now north central Mexico and the Rio Grande Valley of southern Texas, growing primarily in desert scrub. The portion of the plant used in the peyote ceremony is the disk-shaped button or crown, which grows above ground and is harvested by being cut carefully from the root. The buttons, which are extremely bitter, are generally dried before being consumed, but they may also be eaten fresh or boiled and brewed into a tea.

The effects of peyote are often divided into two stages, the first primarily physical and often unpleasant, and the second involving mental, perceptual, and emotional changes. It is often said that the hangover precedes the euphoria with consumption of peyote, because the initial symptoms may involve nausea, vomiting, sweating, dizziness, and headaches. The mental changes often involve a sense of heightened visual and auditory acuity, synesthesia or the blending of sensory experiences (for example, sight and sound becoming one, such as "seeing music"), and often a profound sense of identity between self and nonself or a feeling of connectedness with the external environment. An anthropologist named J. S. Slotkin wrote a useful account of his own experience during a peyote ceremony among the Menomini, which contains many of the common themes often described by those who have been through the ritual:

> After midnight, I began to notice the effects of the peyote. There were slight, visual effects: the fire was the most beautifully colored I've ever seen, and the shadows cast by the fire flickered in time to the drumming. Auditory effects: I could hear whispers at the other side of the tipi (sharpened acuity). . . . Suddenly I realized, as I sat with my eyes closed, that the drumming seemed to be coming from inside me.

I paid some attention to this, and discovered that the distinction between my self and non-self disappeared when I closed my eyes.[2]

In addition to these physical and mental effects, peyote users also report a wide range of spiritual effects. These include, for example, a sense of intimate closeness to God or the Creator; a deep sense of humility, serenity, and incommunicable peace; a feeling of sorrow for past misdeeds and a hope for forgiveness; emotional, spiritual, and often physical healing; and a general sense of harmony with both the community and the natural environment. Since the introduction of alcohol to Native American communities and the growing problem of substance abuse on reservations, peyote has been seen by many practitioners as the best means of curing these physical and spiritual ailments. One Winnebago named Albert Kneale summarized the experience of physical illness followed by a sense of spiritual healing through peyote: "When I first used Peyote I became deathly sick. It seemed like I vomited several bottles of whiskey, several plugs of tobacco, and two bulldogs. This accumulation of filth represented all of the sins I have ever committed. With its expulsion I became pure and clean in the sight of God, and I knew that by the continued use of Peyote I would remain in that condition. I was transformed—a new man."[3]

Apart from the initial stage of nausea and physical discomfort, peyote use has never been found to have serious negative effects in either the short term or the long term. There does not appear to be any risk of overdose in humans, and test subjects who were given ten times the typical amount ingested at a peyote meeting suffered no toxic reactions. There is no evidence of chromosome damage, even among Huichol Indians who have a lifelong history of peyote usage (and hundreds if not thousands of years of cultural usage). Nor is there any evidence that peyote is addictive. Indeed, peyote appears to be far less addictive than cocaine, marijuana, alcohol, barbiturates, or opium and its derivatives.[4]

THE MODERN HISTORY OF PEYOTE AND THE BIRTH OF THE NATIVE AMERICAN CHURCH

While the ritual use of peyote in north central Mexico can be dated back thousands of years, and perhaps as long ago as seven thousand years, the spread of peyote beyond its native homeland is a very long and complicated story. Already by the time the Europeans arrived in the fifteenth and sixteenth centuries, peyote was ritually used by numerous tribes in the area that is today northern Mexico and southern Texas; and several of these, such as the Coras, Tarahumaras, and Huicholes, have continued traditional uses of peyote up to the present. For the Huicholes—who are the best-documented traditional users of the cactus—peyote is part of a complex mythological and ritual system at the heart of their religious life. According to Huichol sacred narratives, the oldest of the gods, Grandfather Fire, once led the other male deities on a journey to the homeland of peyote. During their arduous journey, they suffered severe thirst but were offered water by the female deities. When they arrived at the sacred land of peyote, they found and killed a deer. The deer in turn became the source of peyote, which sprouted up from his hooves, antlers, and tail. After making a beverage from peyote, the gods drank it and were healed. Even today, this narrative is reenacted by the Huicholes in an annual pilgrimage, a three-hundred-mile journey to the peyote beds, in which they symbolically "hunt" the peyote with bow and arrow, reenacting the divine hunt for the deer that once restored the gods.

While peyote has been used for millennia by tribes in Mesoamerica, its rapid spread into a wider movement that eventually came to all of the North American tribes took place only in the late nineteenth century. At least three key factors helped transform the use of peyote from an ancient but relatively localized ritual tradition into a powerful pan-Indian new religious movement. The first was the massive relocation of Native Americans from across the United States onto reservations in Oklahoma and Texas. This brought Native peoples from around the country into close proximity to peyote use; many of them were also living in fairly brutal conditions on the reservations, amid rampant poverty and alcoholism, and were often in search of new spiritual alternatives.

The second key factor in the spread of peyote was the building of the railroads throughout the Deep South, which by the 1880s had connected the reservations in Texas and Oklahoma with the rest of the United States. The railroad also ran directly through the peyote lands, making the transport of dried buttons cheap and easy. As a result, the peyote ceremony spread like wildfire and quickly became known throughout the United States and Canada.

Finally, a third key factor in the spread of peyote was the rapid rise and tragic demise of another massive Native American movement, the Ghost Dance. Arguably the largest pan-Indian movement prior to the spread of the NAC, the Ghost Dance was inspired by a Paiute holy man from Nevada named Jack Wilson or Wovoka (1856–1932), who claimed to have had a profound spiritual vision and a meeting with God in heaven. Wilson believed that he had been given a new ritual dance to spread to all Native peoples, the Ghost Dance, which would bring back the dead Native Americans and bring about harmony between Native and white Americans. Although Wilson's original Ghost Dance movement was peaceful and sought harmony rather than violence, it was sometimes given more aggressive interpretations as it spread across the United States. Particularly when it spread to the Lakota Sioux—known as one of the fiercest of the Plains tribes—the Ghost Dance took on a more violent interpretation. Some of the Lakota leaders believed that the Ghost Dance would make participants invulnerable in battle, impervious to white men's bullets, and even capable of eradicating white people from the Americas altogether. The rapid spread of this version of the Ghost Dance among the Lakota was an important factor in the tragic showdown with the US military at Wounded Knee, on the Pine Ridge reservation of South Dakota. Increasingly concerned about rumors of Native Americans dancing and talking about eradicating white men, the government sent a cavalry regiment to intercept and surround an encampment of Lakotas. The confrontation ended on December 29, 1890, in a bloody massacre that left hundreds of Lakota men, women, and children dead.

After the Wounded Knee disaster, the ritual use of peyote spread widely and in many ways filled the gap left by the tragic collapse of the Ghost Dance. While many Native

FIGURE 2.1 Quanah Parker.
Department of Defense.

American dances—including the Ghost Dance, the Sun Dance, and others—were banned following Wounded Knee, the peyote ceremony was far less conspicuous and could be performed in privacy. And while the Ghost Dance had promised a utopian spiritual ideal that was never realized, the peyote ceremony offered immediate effects and perhaps a more tangible way of dealing with the difficulties of Native American life in the white man's world.

Perhaps the most important figure in the modern spread of the peyote tradition was the Comanche leader Quanah Parker (1852–1911; figure 2.1). The son of a Comanche chief and a European American who had been kidnapped and assimilated into the tribe, Parker would become one of the most influential Native Americans of the modern era. After a series of bloody conflicts with the US military, the Comanche surrendered in 1875 and were settled on the Kiowa-Comanche-Apache reservation in the Southwest Indian territories. With his strong leadership skills, Parker was named the chief over all the Comanche on the reservation, respected by Native Americans and whites alike as a powerful and resourceful leader. A shrewd investor, he would also become one of the wealthiest and most influential Native Americans of his generation in the United States. While in Texas, Parker was gored by a bull and suffered severe wounds but was healed by a Mexican *curandera* (healer) with peyote tea. He then helped disseminate the most popular form of the peyote ceremony, the Half Moon ritual, to the Arapaho, Caddo, Cheyenne, Osage, Pawnee, and other tribes. According to a famous quote that is frequently attributed to Parker, peyote offers a far more direct and powerful way to communicate with God than the preaching or sermons found in the white churches: "The White Man goes into his church and talks about Jesus. The Indian goes into his tipi and talks with Jesus."[5]

The second most important figure in the modern movement was John Wilson (1840–1901), a Caddo-Delaware-French medicine man and religious leader. Wilson had spent two weeks in seclusion, consuming large numbers of peyote buttons, during which time peyote "took pity on him" and gave him a profound vision of Christ, along with the outline of the peyote ceremony. As his nephew, George Anderson, recorded Wilson's vision:

> During the two weeks or so of his experimental seclusion, Wilson was continuously translated in spirit to the sky realm where he was conducted by Peyote. In this estate he was shown the figures in the sky and the celestial landmarks which represented the events in the life of Christ, and also positions of the Spiritual Forces, the Moon, Sun and Fire. . . . He was shown the grave of Christ. . . . He was shown, always under the guidance of Peyote, the "Road" which led from the grave of Christ to the Moon in the sky which Christ had taken in his ascent. He was told by Peyote to walk in this path or "road" for the rest of his life.[6]

The first American scholar to begin serious study of the peyote tradition was James Mooney, an anthropologist from the Smithsonian Institute who was also one of the most sympathetic and sensitive ethnographers of his era. Mooney studied the use of peyote at meetings among the Kiowa in Oklahoma, on reservations throughout the Southwest, and among tribes in Mexico. After testifying on behalf of Native American peyote users before Congress, Mooney advised the various tribes to obtain a legal charter to protect their traditions. Thus in 1918, with Mooney's aid, the NAC was officially incorporated. Significantly, the NAC not only described itself as a "church" but also presented itself as "dedicated to teach[ing] the Christian religion with morality, sobriety . . . and right living."[7] While this was not the first peyote organization to incorporate, it was the first to clearly articulate peyote as a "sacrament," with all that the term implies. As we will see below, however, the formation of the NAC did not bring an end to the persecution of peyote use or to the legal debates surrounding this tradition in the United States.

NEW RELIGIONS AND SYNCRETISM? CULTURAL
CONTACT AND NEW SPIRITUAL SYNTHESIS

Like many other indigenous traditions that have survived into the twenty-first century, the NAC is a complex mixture of pre-Columbian traditions and numerous elements drawn from Christianity. When the NAC was established in 1918 it not only labeled itself a "church" that was "dedicated to the teaching of Christian principles" but also incorporated many elements of Christian theology, symbolism, and language. NAC members frequently compare peyote to the body of Christ in the Eucharist, as the sacrament that allows them to commune directly with God. They also often compare it to the Holy Spirit, the "Comforter" from the New Testament that will remain with humankind as a spiritual presence following Christ's resurrection. In the words of Albert Hensley, a Winnebago who was one of the most important defenders of peyote use in the early twentieth century: "To us it is a portion of the body of Christ, even as the communion bread is believed to be a portion of Christ's body by other Christian denominations. Christ spoke of a Comforter who was to come. It never came to Indians until it was sent by God in the form of this Holy Medicine."[8]

However, while many members of the NAC see no tension between Christianity and the peyote tradition, others describe a more ambivalent and critical relationship between the two. Another Winnebago, Reuben Snake, was one of the most important figures in the modern legal debates surrounding peyote use. Snake acknowledges that the NAC has incorporated many Christian elements, and he even makes direct comparisons between Christian theology and the Native American understanding of peyote: "If Jesus was God incarnate in human form, our holy Peyote is God incarnate in plant form."[9] But he also argues that these Christian elements are primarily an "overlay" onto what is a much older indigenous religious system, rather than an essential part of the peyote tradition. "My branch of the Native American Church has incorporated many Christian teachings, including the six days of creation, followed by a seventh day of rest. But this is overlay, superimposed on our original awareness that every day is a holy day."[10] Snake also includes some sharp criticisms of mainstream American Christians, who do not always practice what they preach, and presents the NAC as a far more direct and immediate way of communicating with God than simply sitting in a church pew:

> Instead of looking at the neck of the person in front of us as in Christian churches, we look directly into God's face, his fire. . . .
>
> Christianity teaches that we should love God and neighbor, but I don't see a great deal of love in the so-called Christian society that surrounds us. In the Native American church, sitting inside the tepee, our tabernacle, we are inside our Mother's womb. . . . We can be as God made us, which ultimately is why we feel moved to praise him.[11]

Other practitioners assert that the medicine provides a direct connection to God that makes the sermons of preachers and even the Bible itself unnecessary: "There's no preaching in our ceremony. We get our knowledge directly from the Almighty. We don't need anyone telling us what the word is. That's what the Peyote is for. . . . God will talk to you himself. You don't need a Bible."[12]

In this sense, the NAC is an excellent illustration of the complex blending of religious imagery that often takes place in cases of cultural contact, colonialism, and conquest by foreign powers. Some scholars refer to it as "syncretism"—the merging and combing of elements from different traditions, such as Christianity and Native American traditions, into a new synthesis. However, as we can see in the quote from Reuben Snake and others, the NAC is more than a simple haphazard mish-mash of different religious elements. From the words of Quanah Parker quoted above down to the present day, we can also see a critical element in the language of the NAC, which reinterprets and transforms aspects of Christianity within the framework of a traditional religious system.

THE PEYOTE CEREMONY

The two most widely practiced forms of the peyote ritual today are the Half Moon or Little Moon ceremony, which was spread primarily through the work of Quanah Parker, and the Big Moon or Cross Fire ceremony, which was spread by John Wilson. Taking its name from the crescent shape of the central altar, the Half Moon form is practiced by the majority of peyotists in the United States and Canada. Although it has a number of variant forms among different tribes, the Half Moon ceremony has a fairly consistent general structure that usually proceeds as follows.[13]

The peyote meeting is usually instigated by an individual who wishes to sponsor the ceremony for a particular purpose. The sponsor presents sacred tobacco to the Roadman, who will organize and lead the ritual. Peyote meetings are not held at any specific fixed time or for any one reason but may be organized for a number of different reasons. They may be intended to commemorate a particular holiday such as Christmas or Easter, to celebrate a birth or a wedding, to mourn the loss of a loved one, to heal the sick, or to protect the community from illness or adversity. A time for the ceremony is then agreed upon (often but not always on a Saturday evening). On the afternoon before the ritual, the members erect the teepee that will house the ceremony, with its door facing to the east (figure 2.2). Inside the teepee, a fire hole is dug, and ashes are arranged in a particular symbolic shape, such as an eagle, a water bird, a star, or (in the case of the Full Moon ceremony) a cross. Around the fire pit, a crescent-shaped altar is formed from a mound of earth, and along the top of it a thin line is drawn from one end to the other, symbolizing the "peyote road" that the members will symbolically travel during the ceremony. A large peyote button called the "Grandfather" or "Chief Peyote" is placed at the center of the crescent moon.

The main participants in the ceremony include the Roadman, who is largely responsible for organizing and leading the ceremony; the Drum Chief, who sits to the right of the Roadman and is responsible for the drum (figure 2.3); the Cedar Chief, who sits to the left of the Roadman and is responsible for the cedar incense that is used for blessings throughout the

FIGURE 2.2 Osage peyote teepee, Oklahoma. G. E. E. Lindquist Papers, Burke Library Archives (Columbia University Libraries).

ceremony; and the Fireman, who typically sits on the north side of the doorway and is responsible for tending the fire throughout the night. The ceremony itself is rich with complex symbolism and involves a number of ritual implements with layers of spiritual significance. The primary symbol of the Roadman's authority is an intricately designed staff, which is referred to by various tribes as an "arrow" (Cado), as the "staff of life" (Wichita, Osage), or as the "Moses staff" (Winnebago). The Roadman also carries a sacred fan, typically made from the feathers of eagles and other swift-flying birds, which serves as the messenger that will carry the prayers to the Creator. The drum that is played throughout the service is a water drum that contains a few inches of water and four coals. According to the Kiowa, the drum with its coals and water represents thunder, lightning, and rain.

The service begins with a statement of purpose for the ceremony, after which the Roadman rolls a ceremonial cigarette and passes tobacco and cornhusks clockwise around the circle for each participant to make a cigarette of his or her own. Cedar is burned in the fire and used to purify the peyote; later it will be used to purify the staff, feather, fan, bundle of sage, and rattle. The peyote is then passed around the circle, and each participant uses the bundle of sage to purify his hands and body before ingesting the sacrament. As these make the circle, each participant taps the sage on his head, chest, and other body parts before taking the peyote. The peyote may be consumed in one of several forms: as a dried plant, as a fresh green plant, as finely ground dried plants, or as a tea prepared by steeping the dried plant in water. The Roadman then purifies his staff, rattle, and gourd and sings a series of songs. His staff is passed on to the Drum Chief, who sings a series of songs, and then on to the Cedar Chief for another series. Throughout the ten- to twelve-hour ceremony, the participants sit as quietly and as still as possible, offering prayers for the reasons the meeting has been called.

Around 12:00, the Midnight Water Ceremony occurs, as the Fireman brings a pail of water and places it before the Roadman. Using his eagle bone whistle, the Roadman touches the four quadrants of the surface of the water, honoring the four directions, and flicks water

FIGURE 2.3 Peyote drummer, Oklahoma, 1927. From Edward S. Curtis, *The Indians of Oklahoma* (Seattle: E. S. Curtis, 1930).

in the four directions of the teepee. He then uses the water to bless his own instruments and the Grandfather Peyote and passes the water around the circle. Another round of songs is sung, and the Roadman slips outside the teepee, where he blows four times on his whistle in each of the four directions. According to some traditions, this is intended to notify all things in Creation that a meeting is taking place and to call the Creator to be with participants as they consume the medicine.

The ceremony continues until dawn, following the same pattern. During the night, the Roadman may perform a healing ritual; members may report on the condition of absent ones who need the prayers of the group; and members may make confessions or ask for forgiveness for past misdeeds.

At first daylight, the Water Woman arrives, representing the Peyote Woman who is said in many narratives to have first discovered the sacred medicine. She offers a prayer and brings a pail of water, which is passed around the circle for all to drink. As the sun rises, a meal consisting of four sacred foods (water, corn, fruit, and meat) is brought for the closing ceremony. Finally, the Roadman may offer an inspirational speech to remind them of the purpose of the ceremony and then thanks the participants, who exit the sacred space and greet the new day.

The second most common form of the peyote ritual is the Big Moon or Crossfire ceremony, which was largely developed by the Caddo leader John Wilson. As we saw above, Wilson had been shown in a peyote vision the "Road" that Christ had walked, and it was then revealed to him how to construct the peyote altar and tent. The Big Moon was the form adopted by tribes such as the Wichita, Delaware, Quapaw, Shawnee, Oklahoma Seneca-Cayuga, and Osage.

In general, the Big Moon ceremony shares many features of the Little Moon, including the consumption of peyote, rounds of singing, a ritually maintained fire, and the central authority of the Roadman. The primary differences lie in the shape of the altar—which looks more like a horseshoe or full moon shape—and the prominent role of Christian imagery in the ceremony. Much of the symbolism in the Big Moon ritual and its larger sacred space is given explicitly Christian interpretations. Thus the altar itself, with the coals and ashes separated into two piles during the ritual, has the impression of a face, which is often interpreted as Christ's face. The altar is also often referred to as the empty grave of Christ, while the peyote road that runs from east to west is the path that we follow throughout lives on our way to heaven. And the crossroad, or line traversing the peyote road from north to south, represents the crucifixion. The Big Moon ceremony eliminates the use of tobacco and substitutes the Bible for use in prayer, while Jesus is often referred to in songs, and the Lord's Prayer is recited. In sum, the Big Moon reflects a far more explicit blending of Native American and Christian elements than the Half Moon ceremony.

KEY ISSUES AND DEBATES: THE COMPLEX LEGAL HISTORY OF PEYOTE USE IN THE UNITED STATES

From the first arrival of Europeans to the New World, peyote use was a source of misunderstanding, conflict, and persecution. As early as 1620, the Spanish Inquisition denounced peyote as diabolic and made its use illegal and punishable by torture and death. Ironically, it is worth noting that 1620 was the same year that the Pilgrims landed on Plymouth Rock, seeking refuge from religious persecution in England.

In the nineteenth century, with the spread of the peyote ceremony throughout the tribes on the reservations of Oklahoma, Christian missionaries began lobbying to outlaw the substance. In 1886, peyote use was first reported to the Bureau of Indian Affairs (BIA), who labeled it an intoxicant and issued an order to seize and destroy peyote buttons. In 1909, to deal with Oklahoma's "peyote problem," the BIA appointed a special officer, who raided peyote meetings and destroyed buttons. Throughout the first half of the twentieth century, the BIA worked hard to demonize peyote, dismissing the claim that it was part of a "religion" and arguing that it was a threat to the Indians' "acculturation process."

In 1899, Oklahoma was the first territory to enact laws banning peyote use. Although the Oklahoma law was later repealed, many other states passed laws against peyote use, including Colorado, Nevada, and Utah in 1916–17, Kansas in 1920, Arizona, Montana, North Dakota, and South Dakota in 1923, Iowa in 1924, New Mexico and Wyoming in 1929, Idaho in 1935, Texas in 1937, California in 1959, and New York in 1965.

Peyote's already controversial reputation was only intensified in the 1950s and '60s, when it began to be widely used by non-Native Americans in the United States, England, and Europe, and not always for spiritual purposes. Mescaline, the alkaloid mainly responsible for the psychoactive effects, was synthesized in 1919 and soon began to be used experimentally and recreationally. One of the first notable users and advocates of mescaline was the English writer Aldous Huxley, perhaps most famous for his dystopian novel *Brave New World*. Introduced to mescaline in 1953, Huxley detailed his experiences with the substance in his widely read book *The Doors of Perception*. The title of the book was taken from a poem by William Blake, which reads, "If the doors of perception were cleansed everything would appear to man as it is, infinite." Huxley did not suggest that mescaline was a means to enlightenment or the Beatific Vision, but he described it as closer to what Catholic theologians call a "gratuitous grace" that could be spiritually beneficial: "To be shaken out of the ruts of ordinary perception, to be shown for a few timeless hours the outer and the inner world, not as they appear to . . . a human obsessed with words and notions, but as they are appreciated, directly and unconditionally, by the Mind at Large—this is an experience of inestimable value to everyone."[14] As such, he considered it compatible with religion, even with Christianity, and concluded that the Native American treatment of it as a sacrament was appropriate.

Other notable users of peyote and/or mescaline during the 1950s and '60s included the influential Beat poet Allen Ginsberg, and the popular novelist Ken Kesey. Part of Ginsberg's seminal poem "Howl" (1954) was inspired by a period of peyote-induced visionary consciousness; and Kesey would later recount that his classic novel *One Flew over the Cuckoo's Nest* (1962) was initially inspired by his "choking down eight of the little cactus plants."[15]

These popular accounts of peyote and mescaline from Huxley, Ginsberg, and Kesey would have a tremendous influence on the public perception of peyote—both positively and negatively. On one hand, these books were all key texts for the counterculture and psychedelic movements of the 1960s, influencing not only a generation of hippies but also musicians such as Beatle John Lennon, and Led Zeppelin guitarist Jimmy Page. The American band the Doors also took its name from Huxley's book. Yet at the same time, the increasing recreational usage of peyote outside the Native American community reinforced the perception that this was a dangerous hallucinogenic drug that was a threat to individual health and public safety.

Much of the debate surrounding peyote has centered on how this plant is labeled. For members of the NAC today, peyote is usually called either a "sacrament" or a "medicine" and is regarded as a gift from the divine that brings about spiritual, emotional, and physical healing. For the US government and law enforcement, however, peyote has come to be identified as a controlled substance and a drug, and these conflicting definitions are in large part responsible for the long history of legal debate surrounding its use. In 1970, the US Congress passed Public Law 91–513, the Comprehensive Drug Abuse Prevention and Control Act, which classified peyote and mescaline as Schedule I drugs, defined as substances having a "high potential for abuse" and no accepted medical use in the United States. This class of substances at that time also included opium, LSD, marijuana, and psilocybin.

OREGON V. SMITH: THE LEGAL STORY OF AL SMITH AND PEYOTE USE IN MODERN AMERICA

The most important legal debate surrounding peyote was the Smith case, which centered on a member of the Klamath Nation of Oregon named Alfred Leo Smith. This decision has had the most wide-ranging implications for religious freedom and for the practice of alternative religions both new and old in the United States. As a young man, Smith suffered from alcoholism, but he finally recovered through the help of Alcoholics Anonymous. During his recovery, Smith rediscovered his Native American roots and became an active member of the NAC. Smith was then hired to help develop drug and alcohol rehabilitation programs for Native Americans. In 1984, however, the director of the program learned that Smith and a coworker, Galen Black, were attending NAC services and demanded that they cease doing so, since he considered peyote to be a drug and since the possession of peyote was a felony in the state of Oregon. Smith and Black refused to stop attending, arguing that peyote was not a drug but a "religious sacrament," and they were subsequently fired. As Smith later explained, the primary issue in his opinion was simply a misunderstanding of cultures and languages; while he repeatedly tried to explain that peyote was a "sacrament" and not a "drug," his employer was unable to think about it in any other terms: "They called me into the office on Monday, and asked me if I'd attended the Native American Church ceremony, and I said I did. And they asked me if I ingested that mind altering drug Peyote, and I says no, but I did take the sacrament. . . . And they says you leave us no alternative but we have to terminate you. . . . It's always been a misunderstanding of cultures, misunderstanding of definitions. It's been a language misunderstanding."[16]

Although Smith and Black accepted the loss of their jobs, their denial of unemployment compensation because they had been "terminated for misconduct" in using peyote led the two men to field a lawsuit against the Oregon Employment Division, arguing that they were protected by the Free Exercise Clause of the First Amendment and that they should therefore receive unemployment compensation. Initially, the Court of Appeals reversed the decision of the Employment Board and ruled that both men should be given unemployment compensation, and this ruling then was affirmed by the Oregon Supreme Court in June 1986. David Frohnmayer, the Oregon attorney general, then appealed the decision to the US Supreme Court, which began to hear the case in November 1989.

As the Court began to consider the evidence, several hundred members of the NAC traveled to Washington to offer support for Smith and Black, holding vigils and blessing ceremonies. Shortly before the Court offered its ruling, Smith wrote a letter to members of the NAC community in which he made a poignant argument that this was primarily a battle for religious freedom, particularly for a group that had been historically persecuted and marginalized: "I believe that we have a right to our ceremonies and spiritual ways. I believe that it is wrong to deny any of us our chosen spiritual path. We have been pushed too long, too far, and so, once faced with the threat to my religious freedom, I took a stand."[17] In its ruling, the Court made it clear that this case hinged crucially on the question of religious freedom as stated in the Free Exercise Clause of the First Amendment. As Justice Antonin Scalia wrote, "This case requires us to decide whether the Free Exercise Clause of the First Amendment permits the State of Oregon to include religiously inspired peyote use within the reach of its general criminal prohibition on use of that drug, and thus permits the State to deny unemployment benefits to persons dismissed from their jobs because of such religiously inspired use."[18]

Finally on April 17, 1990, in a difficult 5–4 vote, the Supreme Court ruled against Smith and reversed the lower court's decision. Justice Scalia—well known as one of the most conservative of the justices (and a devout Catholic)—delivered the majority opinion for the court, arguing that religious freedom does not mean that individuals are free to engage in activities that violate existing state laws. Because peyote was classified as a Schedule I drug in the state of Oregon, Smith was not justified in using it or in claiming unemployment benefits after being fired, even if he had been participating in a religious ritual: "We have never held that an individual's religious beliefs excuse him from compliance with an otherwise valid law prohibiting conduct that the State is free to regulate. On the contrary, the record of more than a century of our free exercise jurisprudence contradicts that proposition."[19] Scalia went on to argue that allowing an exemption for using an illegal substance such as peyote in a religious context would open the door to exemption for all kinds of illegal activities. If we allow illegal substances, he reasoned, we would also have to consider allowing all manner of other unlawful activities: in short, it would "open the prospect of constitutionally required religious exemptions from civic obligations of almost every conceivable kind—ranging from compulsory military service to the payment of taxes to health and safety regulation such as manslaughter and child neglect laws, compulsory vaccination laws, drug laws, and traffic laws; to social welfare legislation such as minimum wage laws, child labor laws, animal cruelty laws, environmental protection laws, and laws providing for equality of opportunity for the races."[20]

The Smith decision sent shock waves throughout the Native American community, and many feared that it would have much wider implications not only for the religious rights of Native peoples but for religious freedom in the United States as a whole. In response, the Winnebago leader Reuben Snake formed a coalition from various tribes called the Native American Religious Freedom Project in order to deal directly with Washington. The group helped produce a documentary film called *The Peyote Road*, which explained the history, cultural significance, and religious meaning of the peyote ritual. In Congress, the Project found an ally in Senator Daniel K. Inouye of Hawaii, chairman of the Senate Committee on Indian Affairs, who conducted congressional hearings on the subject. Senator Inouye made an eloquent argument that this was not simply a matter of a few Native Americans whose religious practices might be compromised but a much larger First Amendment issue that threatened the religious freedoms of all US citizens, no matter what ethnicity or religious persuasion:

> The right to freely exercise our religion is a right that millions have sacrificed their lives for. It is a right that is so fundamental to our way of life, no matter whether we are Christian, Jew, Buddhist, or Muslim. Should any of our religious practices be threatened, we join together in defense of our right to exercise our religious beliefs. Except perhaps, when it comes to the religious practices of the Native People of this country. These are the religious practices that are little understood and which in recent years, the rulings of the courts have systematically undermined. We should

all feel threatened, when the religious rights of Native people are challenged. For today it may be their rights . . . that are discouraged, but tomorrow it may well be ours.[21]

With Inouye's leadership, Congress passed the Religious Freedom Restoration Act, which was intended to reaffirm the rights of Native Americans to practice traditional rites. As President Clinton put it, upon signing the act into law in 1993, "The signing of [today's] legislation . . . assumes a majestic quality because we affirm the historical role people of faith have played in our country, and the constitutional protections those who profess their faith have historically enjoyed." These protections, he concluded, "will not be complete until traditional Native American religious practices have received the protection they deserve."[22]

The Religious Freedom Restoration Act was a landmark piece of legislation. However, it did not entirely resolve the peyote question, since it did not specifically mention peyote or the case of the NAC.[23] Thus in 1994 a new bill called the American Indian Religious Freedom Amendments, which explicitly protected the use of peyote, was proposed and passed. According to the amendments, "The use, possession, or transportation of peyote by an Indian for *bona fide* traditional ceremonial purposes in connection with the practice of a traditional Indian religion is lawful and shall not be prohibited by the United States or any state. No Indian shall be penalized or discriminated against on the basis of such use."[24] This federal law effectively did away with the patchwork of individual state laws in which twenty-eight states had an exemption for peyote and twenty-two considered it a felony. However, the amendments placed two key conditions on the use of peyote: (1) it could only be used by an Indian (defined here as a member of a federally recognized tribe), and (2) it had to be part of a *"bona fide"* religious ceremony.

While the passage of the 1994 Amendments was a major victory for the Native American Church, it raised a number of profound legal and religious questions. Perhaps the most important of these was whether an individual needed to be of Native American descent in order to participate in the peyote ceremony—and thus the larger and more complex question of whether *race and ethnicity* should be determining factors in the exercise of religious freedom. For example, the NAC of North America—a coalition of church organizations in the United States, Mexico, and Canada—requires that its members be one-quarter or more "Native American blood" and either belong to a federally recognized tribe, be a member of the First Nations of Canada, or be a member of a traditional people of Mexico to participate in the ceremony.[25] But does this mean that freedom of religious expression is in some cases dependent on one's *bloodline and racial identity?*

This question has come up several times in the courts. For example, in 1990, a non-Native American named Robert Boyll was charged with unlawfully importing peyote through the US mail and possessing peyote with intent to distribute it. In his defense, Boyll argued that, although not a member of a federally recognized tribe, he was a practicing member of the NAC and therefore could not be prevented from exercising his religious freedom simply on the basis of race. The judge in this case agreed with Boyll, ruling that such a prohibition would violate both the First Amendment right to free exercise of religion and the Fourteenth Amendment right to equal justice under the law: "It is one thing for a local branch of the Native American Church to adopt its own restrictions on membership, but it is entirely another for the government to restrict membership in a religious organization on the basis of race. Any such attempt to restrict religious liberties along racial lines would not only be a contemptuous affront to the First Amendment guarantee of freedom of religion but also to the 14th Amendment right to equal justice under the law."[26]

More recently, two similar cases have come up in Utah and Arizona. The first involved James Warren "Flaming Eagle" Mooney, the founder of the Oklevueha Earth Walks Native American Church of Utah. In 2000, Mooney was charged with a dozen counts of distributing peyote to non-Native Americans, and fifteen thousand peyote buttons in his possession were confiscated. While the use of peyote is permissible for Native Americans in the state, both Mooney's own Native heritage and the legality of peyote use by non-Native Americans were unclear. While Mooney claimed membership in the Oklevueha band of Yamasee Seminoles, this is not a federally recognized tribe, and Mooney himself had been disavowed by the official body of the NAC. More controversial, however, was the charge that Mooney had been distributing peyote to other non-Native Americans.

While the prosecuting attorney did acknowledge that peyote use is allowable for Native Americans, he argued that it is not, according to the wording of the law, permissible for anyone who is not a member of a federally recognized tribe. Mooney in turn cited the 1991 Boyll case, which concluded that allowing some groups to use peyote and disqualifying others because of race would be a violation of the First Amendment's Free Exercise Clause. Once again, in 2004, the Utah Supreme Court ended up siding with Mooney, dismissing the case and the charges against him. Ironically, however, the fifteen thousand peyote buttons remained in custody. The US Attorney's Office did return the "Peyote Chief" button, which holds center stage in the peyote ceremony, but it held on to the remaining fifteen thousand, once again citing its doubt that Mooney was himself a genuine member of a federally recognized tribe. So in spite of the Utah court's ruling, the fate of peyote's legality in this case hinged once again on a question of ethnicity.

Meanwhile, a similar case came up in Arizona, where a group of non-Native Americans called the Peyote Way Church has been practicing its own unique form of the peyote ceremony since 1978. A complex mixture of Native American traditions and elements of Mormonism, mainstream Christianity, and other traditions, the Peyote Way Church teaches that the sacrament of peyote should be open to everyone regardless of race or religious background. In this case, the Peyote Way Church filed suit against the state of Texas and the federal government, challenging the requirement that one be at least 25 percent Indian blood in order to buy peyote. Yet despite the decision in favor of Boyll, the district court and then the US court of appeals rejected the Peyote Way Church's claims. According to the judgment of the appeals court, the exemption for peyote use applies only to members of the NAC and not to other religious groups, "no matter how sincere these other religious groups are in their beliefs."[27]

In both of these cases, a central question is whether race and tribal identity should be a requirement to practice this particular religious rite. Those sympathetic to Mooney and to the Peyote Way Church argue that religious freedom should extend to everyone, regardless of blood or tribal affiliation. More critical observers, however, worry that this would open the floodgates to non-Native Americans using peyote—thus further endangering this species of cactus and potentially watering down or cheapening this ancient Native American tradition.[28]

QUESTIONS FOR DISCUSSION AND DEBATE

1. Is there a difference between a religious experience that comes from consuming a plant such as peyote and a religious experience that comes through other means, such as prayer, meditation, or chanting? Or are all of these just different spiritual techniques for achieving altered states and/or communion with the divine?

2. The NAC uses many elements of Christianity, particularly in the Big Moon form of the ritual. Yet many NAC members, as we saw above, are also critical of aspects of Christianity and claim to have roots that go back thousands of years before Jesus's birth. So should we call the NAC "Christian"? Or should we call it something else? And what is at stake, or what difference does it make what we call it?

3. Why were Europeans and then the US government so hostile to peyote use? If it does not appear to be a particularly addictive or dangerous substance, why has it been the focus of intense scrutiny, persecution, and legal debate for hundreds of years? If alcohol appears to be a more dangerous and addictive drug, why hasn't the sacramental use of wine by Christian denominations been subject to the same kind of persecution?

4. How would you resolve the debate surrounding groups such as Mooney's Oklevueha Native American Church or the Peyote Way Church? Should bloodline or membership in a federally recognized tribe be a requirement to use peyote? If so, does that mean that religious freedom in this case is dependent on one's race and ethnicity? If not, wouldn't that open the floodgates to all sorts of non-Native uses of peyote, bringing all the problems that critics fear?

SUGGESTED CLASSROOM ACTIVITY

Depending on the size of the class, students could be divided up into three to five groups and each assigned a particular party to represent in a classroom debate over the legality of peyote use. The groups could include, for example, members of the Native American Church, federal law enforcement agents, Supreme Court justices, religious studies scholars, scientists who have studied the effects of peyote, and non-Native American citizens who are in favor of peyote use for everyone regardless of religious or ethnic identity. Give each group time to prepare evidence drawn from the actual cases such as the Smith case, Justice Scalia's opinion, and other texts and then to formulate a persuasive argument. The debate should be more complex than a simple "either/or," "legal or not-legal" dispute. It should engage more difficult questions such as "Legal for whom?" (only for members of the NAC, only for Native Americans, only for individuals of a certain age?) and "Legal in what contexts?" (only in the context of an NAC ceremony, only on reservations, only when not operating vehicles or heavy machinery?). What are the implications of making race and ethnicity a requirement for use of peyote? Should children be allowed to use peyote? Also, what about environmental concerns such as overharvesting and endangerment of this species?

SUGGESTED FILM

Cousineau, Phil, and Fidel Moreno, directors. *The Peyote Road: Ancient Religion in Contemporary Crisis.* Kifaru Productions, 1994.

SUGGESTIONS FOR FURTHER READING

Anderson, Edward. *Peyote: The Divine Cactus.* Tucson: University of Arizona Press, 1996.

Maroukis, Thomas C. *The Peyote Road: Religious Freedom and the Native American Church.* Norman: University of Oklahoma Press, 2010.

Smith, Huston, and Reuben Snake. *One Nation under God: The Triumph of the Native American Church.* Santa Fe, NM: Clear Light, 1996.

Stewart, Omer C. *Peyote Religion: A History.* Norman: University of Oklahoma Press, 1993.

Sullivan, Winnifred Fallers. *The Impossibility of Religious Freedom.* Princeton, NJ: Princeton University Press, 2007.

Swan, Daniel C. *Peyote Religious Art: Symbols of Faith and Belief.* Jackson: University Press of Mississippi, 1999.

NOTES TO CHAPTER 2

1. Thomas C. Maroukis, *The Peyote Road: Religious Freedom and the Native American Church* (Norman: University of Oklahoma Press, 2010), 14–15.
2. J. S. Slotkin, *Menomini Peyotism* (Philadelphia: American Philosophical Society, 1952), 569.
3. Albert H. Kneale, *Indian Agent: An Autobiographical Sketch* (Caldwell, ID: Caxton, 1950), 212.
4. Edward F. Anderson, "Pharmacology, Legal Classification, and the Issue of Substance Abuse," in *One Nation under God: The Triumph of the Native American Church,* ed. Huston Smith and Reuben Snake (Santa Fe, NM: Clear Light, 1996), 109–13.

5. Phil Cousineau and Gary Rhine, "The Peyote Ceremony," in Smith and Snake, *One Nation*, 91.

6. Quoted in Daniel C. Swan, *Peyote Religious Art: Symbols of Faith and Belief* (Jackson: University Press of Mississippi, 1999), 30–31.

7. David Chidester, *Patterns of Power: Religion and Politics in American Culture* (Englewood Cliffs, NJ: Prentice Hall, 1988), 133.

8. Albert Hensley, quoted in Omer C. Stewart, *Peyote Religion: A History* (Norman: University of Oklahoma Press, 1987), 157.

9. Reuben Snake, quoted in Maroukis, *Peyote Road*, 29.

10. Reuben Snake, introduction to Smith and Snake, *One Nation*, 17.

11. Ibid., 20–21.

12. Anonymous, in Smith and Snake, *One Nation*, 42.

13. This brief summary is based on the descriptions of the ceremony in Swan, *Peyote Religious Art*; Maroukis, *Peyote Road*; and Smith and Snake, *One Nation*.

14. Aldous Huxley, *The Doors of Perception and Heaven and Hell* (New York: Harper and Row, 1963), 73.

15. John Clark Pratt, introduction to Ken Kesey, *One Flew over the Cuckoo's Nest*, rev. ed. (New York: Penguin, 1996), xvii.

16. Al Smith, quoted in Edward Anderson, *Peyote: The Divine Cactus* (Tucson: University of Arizona Press, 1996), 202.

17. Al Smith to NAC, April 13, 1990, quoted in Maroukis, *Peyote Road*, 205.

18. Justice Antonin Scalia, "Opinion of the Court," Employment Division, Department of Human Resources of Oregon v. Smith (No. 88–1213), 875, https://www.law.cornell.edu/supremecourt/text/494/872#writing-USSC_CR_0494_0872_ZO.

19. Ibid., 879–80.

20. Ibid., 888–89.

21. Sen. Daniel Inouye, chairman of the Select Committee on Indian Affairs, Portland, OR, 1992, quoted in Phil Cousineau, ed., *A Seat at the Table: Huston Smith in Conversation with Native Americans on Religious Freedom* (Berkeley: University of California Press, 2006), 103.

22. Bill Clinton, quoted in Smith and Snake, *One Nation*, 146.

23. In a later case in 1997, the Supreme Court ruled that the act itself was unconstitutional, since Congress had no power to override the Court's own interpretation of the Constitution. See Winnifred Fallers Sullivan, *The Impossibility of Religious Freedom* (Princeton, NJ: Princeton University Press, 2007), 28.

24. American Indian Religious Freedom Act Amendments of 1994, Public Law 103–344, 108 Stat. 3124.

25. Maroukis, *Peyote Road*, 210.

26. Judge Juan Burciaga, "Memorandum of Opinion and Order," United States of America v. Robert Lawrence Boyll, US District Court for the District of New Mexico, Criminal no. 90–207-JB, 1991.

27. Peyote Way Church of God, Inc., v. Richard Thornburgh, Attorney General of the United States, et al., No. 88–7039, US Court of Appeals for the Fifth Circuit, 922 F.2d 1210, February 6, 1991.

28. On this point, see Maroukis, *Peyote Road*, 210ff.

THREE

Mormonism and Plural Marriage

The LDS and the FLDS

The history of the Native American Church was in many ways the story of an ancient tradition that faced intense persecution but narrowly managed to survive into the twenty-first century by adapting to a modern legal context. The history of Mormonism, on the other hand, is the story of a new religious movement that not only survived a period of intense persecution but actually flourished and thrived in the modern world. Like other forms of Christianity that emerged in the mid-nineteenth century, Mormonism claimed to be rooted in the Old and New Testaments and in fact to be the true restoration of primitive Christianity, which had been lost and misinterpreted after Jesus's death. Yet this was also in many ways a "new" religious movement that offered its own scriptural revelation called the Book of Mormon, along with a concept of continuing prophecy that differed from the beliefs of most other American denominations and, most controversially, the practice of plural marriage, which was a key part of the Mormon community from the 1840s to the 1890s. Like the Native American Church, Mormonism faced intense criticism from the surrounding American society, as well a series of complex legal battles surrounding the practice of plural marriage. Yet today Mormonism is by all estimates one of the most prosperous, successful, and vibrant Christian denominations in the world. The largest Mormon organization, the Church of Jesus Christ of Latter-day Saints (LDS), now claims 14.7 million members and over eighty thousand missionaries worldwide, making it by far the most successful new religious movement of the last 150 years and what some would consider an independent "world religion" in its own right.

However, Mormonism also seems to hold a kind of dual and ambivalent place in the American popular imagination. On the one hand, Mormons are widely perceived as exemplary models of clean-cut, American values, well known for their virtuous lifestyle and commitment to family. The famous Mormon Tabernacle Choir still performs every Sunday morning, with 325 men and women singing a mix of Christian hymns and patriotic American tunes. Dubbed by President Ronald Reagan "America's choir," the Mormon Tabernacle Choir has been broadcast weekly over the CBS radio network since 1920, making it the longest-running feature in American radio history.

Yet on the other hand, Mormonism has from its inception been ridiculed and persecuted by the surrounding American society. The early Mormon movement was forced to move repeatedly, and its founder Joseph Smith was killed by an angry mob in 1844. Anti-Mormon propaganda and satires of the church were pervasive in nineteenth-century America and in many ways continue to this day. Thus Mormonism has been satirized on television shows such as *South Park* (2003) and has even been the subject of a major Broadway musical satire, *The Book of Mormon* (2011). Although the mainstream LDS Church has rejected plural marriage for over 120 years, most Americans today still associate Mormonism with polygamy. And small splinter movements such as the Fundamentalist Church of Jesus Christ of Latter-day Saints (FLDS) have kept this stereotype alive by continuing the practice of plural marriage in areas such as Utah, Texas, and Colorado. In 2008, an FLDS community was raided by the Texas Child Protective Services, who removed 439 children from the ranch and sparked an intense debate over the issues of religious freedom, state law, and child safety.

One of the clearest examples of this dual image of Mormonism—as both a clean-cut, "all-American" religion and a strange and suspicious "cult"—was the presidential campaign of Mitt Romney. When he ran in the Republican presidential primaries in 2004 and won the nomination in 2008, Romney seemed to many supporters to be the ideal conservative candidate: a successful business entrepreneur, devoutly religious, and a dedicated family man. Yet his Mormon faith was a serious problem for many in the Republican Party, particularly for some Evangelicals who do not consider Mormonism "real Christianity." In 2007, Romney felt compelled to give a special televised speech entitled "Faith in America," which was largely an attempt to reassure the American public that he was in fact a real Christian and not a member of some strange cult.[1]

Thus, even though Mormonism has flourished and grown into one of the largest Christian denominations in the United States and now in the world, it continues to hold a controversial place in the American religious landscape. As we will see in this chapter, much of this controversy continues to center on the practice of plural marriage, which still informs the popular perception of Mormonism even a hundred years after it was discontinued in the main LDS community. Obviously it would be a mistake to reduce the history of Mormonism to the controversies surrounding polygamy, since there is a great deal more to this rich, complex, and successful religious movement. Nonetheless, the practice of plural marriage was a key part of Mormonism's early history and its place in the American spiritual landscape; it raises critical issues of religious freedom and the law, which have enormous implications for American religious life more generally; and the practice still continues among several Mormon splinter groups, such as the FLDS, which have recently generated even more questions about religious freedom, privacy, and law enforcement in the twenty-first century.

FIGURE 3.1 Early portrait of Joseph Smith by unknown painter, circa 1842. On display at the Community of Christ headquarters, Independence, Missouri.

THE BIRTH OF MORMONISM IN THE BURNED-OVER DISTRICT OF THE NORTHEASTERN UNITED STATES

Mormonism emerged out of the rich and tumultuous religious activity that swept across the United States during the period of the Second Great Awakening in the early nineteenth century. The area in which the movement first developed—western New York State—was at the heart of a region often called the "burned-over district" because of the many waves of intense religious enthusiasm that swept over it like wildfire in these years. The church's founder, Joseph Smith, was born in Sharon, Vermont, in 1805 but grew up in Palmyra, New York, in the very midst of this new blaze of spiritual excitement (figure 3.1). As Smith recalled his early life, he had been deeply conflicted about organized religion and distressed by the many competing denominations swirling all around him during these decades. He was, in short, profoundly troubled by the very problem of religious diversity as it was rapidly expanding in nineteenth-century America.

In 1820, at the age of fourteen, Smith claimed to have a divine vision in which God told him that his sins were forgiven and that all contemporary churches had turned aside from the Gospel (figure 3.2). Therefore, he "must join none of them, for they were all wrong," and "All their creeds were an abomination in his sight."[2] Three years later, in 1823, Smith had a second vision in which he was visited by an angel named Moroni, who directed him to seek out a set of golden plates stored in a stone box and buried in a nearby hillside. The golden plates were written in an ancient hieroglyphic language—identified by Smith as "reformed Egyptian"—and it was another four years before Smith set about the work of making sense

FIGURE 3.2 Joseph Smith's first vision of God the Father and God the Son, stained-glass window by unknown artist, circa 1913. Museum of Church History and Art, Salt Lake City, Utah.

of them. Although Smith could not read the script himself, he was able to translate the plates using a technique involving two "seer stones"—small white and chocolate-colored stones—that were placed into a stovepipe hat in order to reveal the meaning of the plates, which was then dictated to several scribes. The text that resulted was first published in 1830 as *The Book of Mormon: An Account Written by the Hand of Mormon upon Plates Taken from the Plates of Nephi*. Although its structure and language bear some resemblance to the Old Testament of the King James Bible, the Book of Mormon tells the story of a religious civilization that existed in the Americas between 600 BCE and 432 CE. This civilization was established by a prophet named Lehi, who came from Jerusalem to the Americas in 600 BCE and became the forefather of two nations called the Nephites and the Lamanites. The pivotal moment in the Book of Mormon is the appearance of Jesus, who revealed himself to the Nephites after his death and resurrection. As the Book of Nephi (11:8–11) describes the encounter,

And behold, they saw a Man descending out of heaven; and he was clothed with a white robe; and he came down and stood in the midst of them; and the eyes of the whole multitude were turned upon him, and they durst not open their mouths, even one to another, and wist not what it meant, for they thought it was an angel that had appeared unto them. And it came to pass that he stretched forth his hand and spake unto the people, saying: "Behold, I am Jesus Christ, whom the prophets testified shall come into the world. And behold, I am the light and the life of the world; and I have drunk of that bitter cup which the Father hath given me, and have glorified the Father in taking upon me the sins of the world."

The history of the Nephites was later compiled in the fourth century CE by the prophet Mormon, who inscribed the golden plates and entrusted them to his son, Moroni. One thousand four hundred and forty years later, Moroni would return as an angel to reveal them to Joseph Smith.

Surely one of the main reasons for both the tremendous popularity and the intense controversy surrounding the Book of Mormon was its claim to be a fulfillment of biblical prophecy. On the one hand, the text was extremely attractive to many Americans of the nineteenth century, who were still steeped in a belief in the literal truth of prophecy and who found the idea of a uniquely American chapter in the history of Christianity deeply compelling. In a sense, the Book of Mormon is the ultimate self-fulfilling prophecy: it claims to be an ancient record promising that a book will one day appear, while at the same time itself being the very book that has been promised. Yet at the same time, Smith's claim to a form of ongoing prophecy or "continuing revelation" was regarded with tremendous hostility by many other Christians, who saw Smith's new additions to scriptural canon to be heretical and fraudulent.

In addition to the revelation that culminated in the Book of Mormon, Smith had several other revelations that claimed to be the fulfillment of biblical prophecy. In 1830, he had a vision that led him to believe that the text of the Bible itself had been corrupted over time and needed to be dramatically revised. This resulted in his Book of Moses, which added large portions to the text and nearly tripled the length of the first five chapters in Genesis. In 1835, Smith also produced a text called the Book of Abraham, which he claimed was based on Egyptian papyri that he had purchased from a traveling mummy exhibition. These two books were later canonized as part of the Pearl of Great Price, a compendium of Smith's writings that is one of the foundational scriptures for contemporary Mormonism.

The first church founded by Smith was called the Church of Christ. However, the movement soon relocated to Kirtland, Ohio, and in 1834 took the new name of the Church of Latter-day Saints. Here the movement grew rapidly, winning the conversion of over one hundred members of the Disciples of Christ congregation and then quickly swelling to two thousand members by 1835. Because of internal tensions and pressures from the surrounding Ohio society, Smith moved the center of the LDS to Jackson, Missouri, where it assumed another new title, the Church of Jesus Christ of Latter-day Saints (LDS), the name held by the majority of Mormons today.

The growing numbers and influence of the LDS community aroused growing suspicion and hostility from the local Missouri residents, which in turn led to even fiercer resistance from the Mormons. In 1838, Smith and his followers surrendered to 2,500 armed state troops, and Smith was arrested for treason. However, while being escorted to Boone County, Smith escaped custody and fled to Illinois. Here Smith and his followers established a new city called Nauvoo (from the Hebrew word meaning "to be beautiful"), which became a virtually autonomous Mormon city, complete with its own army, the Nauvoo militia. The church continued to face internal and external problems, however, and in early 1844 a group of Mormon dissidents set up a rival church and began to criticize Smith through its newspaper, the *Nauvoo Expositor*. Fearing an uprising, the Nauvoo council ordered the destruction of the newspaper's press and eventually declared martial law. A detachment of Illinois state militia was sent in, and Smith and his brother Hyrum were arrested for inciting a riot. While in custody in the Carthage jail, Joseph and Hyrum were attacked by an angry mob and killed on June 27, 1844.

At the time of Smith's death, there was no clear successor to the leadership of the church. Foremost among his twelve apostles was Brigham Young, who would lead the largest group of Mormons from Illinois in 1845, taking them all the way across the country to the Great Salt Lake Valley in Utah. However, Brigham Young's leadership was challenged by Sidney Rigdon, who formed his own Church of Christ, and by Smith's own son, Joseph Smith III, who stayed behind with a group of loyal followers and formed the Reorganized Church of Jesus Christ of Latter-day Saints (RLDS) in 1860. Today, *Mormonism* refers to a wide array of related churches, of which the LDS is surely the largest and most recognized but by no means the only denomination.

MORMON COSMOLOGY AND THEOLOGY: A RESTORED CHRISTIANITY OR A NEW RELIGIOUS MOVEMENT?

When Joseph Smith began to circulate the Book of Mormon and gather followers, he did not claim to be starting a "new" religion; rather, he believed that he was restoring the true form of Christianity, which had been misinterpreted and corrupted over the centuries. Likewise, most Mormons today will self-identify as "Christian" and not as members of a new religious movement. However, many aspects of Mormon theology, cosmology, and practice depart so significantly from other mainstream forms of American Christianity that many scholars would classify this as a "new religion" in its own right.

As we have already seen, Mormonism was initially controversial in the United States because of the idea of continuous revelation, or the belief that God and his agents did not cease to communicate with humankind at the end of the New Testament but still speak to chosen prophets to this day. Not only Smith himself but later church leaders and others are believed to utter divinely inspired truths when moved by the Holy Ghost. Indeed, even non-Mormon texts such as the US Constitution are believed to be divinely inspired documents.

A second key theological difference between Mormonism and most other Christian denominations is its understanding of God. Mormonism holds to non-Trinitarian theology, in which the Father, the Son, and the Holy Ghost are not of one substance but rather are three separate beings. Moreover, Mormonism holds not only that Jesus the Son had a physical body but also that God the Father has a perfected, glorified physical body, which was seen by Ezekiel, Moses, Jacob, Stephen, John, and other biblical figures. Thus the human body is regarded not as a source of sin but rather as a source of joy and exaltation, made in God's image and intended to become more and more like him.

Critics of Mormonism often make a great deal out of the idea of "Kolob"—a name that appears in Smith's Book of Abraham and refers to the star or planet that is the heavenly body closest to the throne of God. In the satirical *Book of Mormon* Broadway musical today, this is referred to as God's "own planet." However, Mormon scholars disagree as to whether Kolob is a literal heavenly body, perhaps at the center of our own galaxy, or simply a metaphorical reference to Jesus Christ as the spiritual center of our universe.

Perhaps the most unique aspect of Mormon theology, however, is its view of human existence, both past and future. Mormons believe that all human beings existed before this particular life on earth as spirits or intelligences in the presence of God. God offered them each a plan whereby they could choose to live on earth, taking on an earthly body and experiencing suffering in order to progress toward their own godhood. Most spirits accepted this plan, but a third of them, led by Satan, rejected it. The central part of the plan is Jesus Christ's atonement, which paid for the sins of the entire world and allows us to become redeemed even though we inevitably make mistakes and fall into sin.

The Mormon view of the afterlife also departs significantly from that of most other Christians in being more complex than simply the two alternatives of heaven and hell. After death, souls first move on to the spirit world, where those who accepted the Gospel of Christ dwell temporarily in a spirit paradise, while those who rejected it because of either ignorance or arrogance dwell in a kind of spirit prison. However, the latter souls still have a chance to accept the Gospel and be redeemed. Finally, after the Last Judgment and resurrection, all souls will move on to an eternal state: the most wicked of the wicked will be cast into a state of eternal damnation called the Outer Darkness, while the remaining souls will dwell in one of three kingdoms. The Telestial Kingdom is reserved for the basically "bad" people who still do not accept Jesus as Savior; the Terrestrial Kingdom is for those who led good lives and accepted Jesus but were halfhearted or complacent in their devotion; and the Celestial Kingdom is reserved for those who not only accepted Christ as Savior but also continuously strove to do the Lord's work.

However, perhaps the most striking aspects of the Mormon view of the afterlife are the concepts of "exaltation" and "eternal progression" toward God. Rather than simply enjoying an individual afterlife in the presence of God, Mormons look forward to the possibility of becoming like God themselves (exaltation) and believe that although they are saved from physical and spiritual death individually, they are exalted as families: individuals must be married through the sealing power of the Mormon priesthood to be exalted, and their sealing (and the automatic sealing to them of any children born within the marriage) allows families to stay together in the afterlife. As the *Encyclopedia of Mormonism* explains this doctrine, "Exaltation is a state that a person can attain in becoming like God—salvation in the ultimate sense. Latter-day Saints believe that all mankind (except the sons of perdition) will receive varying degrees of glory in the afterlife. Exaltation is the greatest of all the gifts and attainments possible. . . . This exalted status, called eternal life, is available to be received by a man and wife. It means not only living in God's presence, but receiving power to do as God does, including the power to bear children after the resurrection."[3]

Because of these key theological differences, many scholars have argued that Mormonism should be regarded not simply as one more denomination of Christianity but rather as a new religious movement in its own right. As the historian Jan Shipps suggests, Mormonism emerged out of nineteenth-century Christianity in much the same way that early Christianity emerged out of its Jewish context. Just as early Christians claimed to possess the fulfillment of Jewish biblical prophecy but quickly diverged from Jewish tradition and established a "new religion," so too Joseph Smith's followers claimed to possess the fulfillment of biblical prophecy but quickly "embarked on a path that led to developments that now distinguish the tradition as surely as early Christianity was distinguished from its Hebraic context."[4] Of course, most Mormons today would respond by saying that Mormonism did not introduce anything "new" into Christianity but simply restored the faith to its true origins after centuries of misinterpretation.

MORMON CHURCH ORGANIZATION, PRIESTHOOD, AND MISSIONARY WORK

The organization and hierarchy of Mormonism also differ considerably from those of other Christian denominations. The highest office within the LDS Church is the president, who is regarded as holding the same authority as that vested in the disciple Peter by Christ. Beneath that are the priesthood of Aaron and the priesthood of Melchizedek (modeled on the biblical figures Aaron and Melchizedek), and then within each of these priesthoods several suboffices. Boys within the LDS are made deacons in the Aaronic priesthood at age twelve, teachers at age fourteen, and priests at age sixteen. The Melchizedek priesthood is a higher order for boys eighteen and older and has its own hierarchy of offices such as elder, high priest, patriarch, seventy, and apostle. Those who hold the priesthood have the authority to administer the Mormon sacraments, such as baptizing and laying on hands, blessing the sacrament for the Lord's Supper, conferring priesthood, performing marriages for eternity, and anointing the sick.

At present, women do not hold any priesthood roles within Mormonism; however, they do have some other roles and organizations within the church, such as the Relief Society, Young Women, and the Primary Association, which emphasizes activities for children. More recently, a few more radical women's movements have emerged within the modern LDS Church that have called for more active roles and even ordination within Mormonism, such as the group "Ordain Women." In 2014, one outspoken Mormon woman, Kate Kelly, was excommunicated from the church for advocating gender equality, bringing the question of women's ordination into the national spotlight.[5] Of course, the debate over women's ordination in Mormonism is not very different from the debates surrounding women in Catholicism, Orthodox Judaism, or other mainstream religious communities that reserve primary religious roles for men.

One of the main reasons for the global success of Mormonism has been its missionary program. Young men between the ages of eighteen and twenty-five are strongly encouraged to undertake a two-year, full-time period of missionary work, which involves proselytizing, humanitarian aid, and community service. Although it is not required for continued church membership, missionary work is often described as a "rite of passage" for young Mormon men entering adulthood. Women may also undertake missionary work after age nineteen for an eighteen-month period. All of the missionaries work as volunteers, receiving no salary, and typically finance their service themselves or with help from their families. As of 2013, the LDS reported having eighty thousand missionaries at work in every nation on earth, a feature that has surely been a large part of Mormonism's rapid global spread in the twentieth and twenty-first centuries.

Mormon ritual life involves a series of "ordinances" or sacred rites and ceremonies through which the individual forms a covenant with God. These are performed by the priesthood and are roughly analogous to sacraments in other Christian denominations. Some of these are considered "saving ordinances," which are required for exaltation, such as baptism, confirmation, and ordination to the Aaronic or Melchizedek priesthoods; others are considered "nonsaving ordinances," which are not required for exaltation, such as the sacrament (similar to the Eucharist in other Christian denominations) and naming and blessing a child. Finally, some are "temple ordinances," which can be performed only in one of the Mormon temples; these include the endowment ceremony, in which the individual is washed, anointed, clothed in a temple garment, and instructed in the principles of salvation, and the sealing ceremonies, in which spouses are sealed to one another and children sealed to their parents for all eternity as a family unit. Currently the LDS has 143 temples worldwide, including the most famous temple in Salt Lake City, which serve as dedicated houses of God and sacred spaces for the performance of these key ordinances.

One of the more unique aspects of the Mormon ordinances is that they include rites performed not just for the living but also for the dead. Because baptism and sealing are necessary for salvation, Mormons believe that these can be performed by proxy for the deceased—including non-Mormons. In fact, the LDS has engaged in a massive effort to digitize every genealogical record in existence so that baptisms and sealings can be performed for as many of those who have ever lived as possible. Perhaps not surprisingly, however, some groups have complained about this practice. Many Jews, for example, have taken issue with the fact that that their ancestors—including Holocaust victims—are now being baptized by Mormons.[6]

From its origins, Mormonism was the object not only of violent attack but also of satire, parody, and ridicule in American popular culture (figure 3.3). While many Americans attacked Mormonism as a dangerous threat, others saw it as silly and nonsensical. One of the most scathing reviews of the Book of Mormon came from the great American novelist and humorist Mark Twain in his 1872 book *Roughing It.* Twain showed little patience for either the contents or the tedious prose of the text, which he described as an unusually dull and rather silly attempt to mimic the prose of the King James Bible:

> The book is a curiosity to me, it is such a pretentious affair, and yet so "slow," so sleepy; such an insipid mess of inspiration. It is chloroform in print. If Joseph Smith composed this book, the act was a miracle—keeping awake while he did it was, at any rate. If he, according to tradition, merely translated it from certain ancient and mysteriously-engraved plates of copper, which he declares he found under a stone, in an out-of-the-way locality, the work of translating was equally a miracle, for the same reason.
>
> The book seems to be merely a prosy detail of imaginary history, with the Old Testament for a model; followed by a tedious plagiarism of the New Testament. The author labored to give his words and phrases the quaint, old-fashioned sound and structure of our King James's translation of the Scriptures; and the result is a mongrel—half modern glibness, and half ancient simplicity and gravity.[7]

Parodies of the Book of Mormon have continued well into the twenty-first century, as we see in the episode "All about Mormons" on the animated TV satire *South Park* (2003). In the *South Park* episode, a new family of Mormons moves into town, and, as they are asked questions about their faith, the story breaks off into the narrative of Joseph Smith and the discovery of the golden plates. The character Stan is outraged by the numerous logical flaws in the Mormon founding story and ends up shouting at the family for believing such ridiculous ideas without proof—and also for being so nice all the time.

The creators of *South Park,* Trey Parker and Matt Stone, later worked with composer and lyricist Robert Lopez to create an award-winning Broadway musical satire entitled *The Book of Mormon* in 2011. The Broadway version contains an even more ruthless satire of the faith, telling the story of two young Mormon missionaries sent to a village in Uganda where a brutal warlord is threatening the local population. The songs in the show parody Mormon beliefs with dramatic musical crescendos and sweeping choruses, as the young missionaries sing about their unshaken—and apparently unreflective and unsubstantiated—faith in the more unusual aspects of Mormon theology and cosmology:

> I believe: that God has a plan for all of us
> I believe: that plan involves me getting my own planet

FIGURE 3.3 "The Mormon Octopus Enslaving the Women of Utah," from
J. H. Beadle, *Polygamy: Or the Mysteries and Crimes of Mormonism*
(Philadelphia: National Publishing, 1904).

And I believe: that the current president of the church, Thomas Modson, speaks
    directly to God
I am a Mormon, and dang it! A Mormon just believes!
. . .
I believe: that God lives on a planet called Kolob
I believe: that Jesus has his own planet as well
And I believe: that the Garden of Eden was in Jackson County, Missouri
You can be a Mormon: you'll feel it
And you'll know it's all true: you just feel it
You'll be a Mormon
By gosh! A Mormon just believes![8]

Interestingly enough, the official LDS response to the *Book of Mormon* musical was quite
measured overall. Rather than threatening lawsuits or organizing protests, the church
issued a statement saying simply that "the production may attempt to entertain audiences
for an evening, but the Book of Mormon as a volume of scripture will change people's lives
forever by bringing them closer to Christ."[9]

While many American religious groups have been the subject of parody and satire (particularly on shows such as *South Park,* which makes a point to mock everything), it does
seem that Mormonism has often been singled out for special ridicule. So we should reason-
ably ask why that is the case: Why has Mormonism been so much more often a target of satire than, say, the Theosophical Society or the Nation of Islam? One reason, as we have

already seen, is the Mormon idea of continuing revelation, which to many Americans seems not only to be heretical but also to open the door to all manner of strange new "revelations." A second and probably deeper reason, however, is surely the size, rapid growth, and political power of the church. In the competitive spiritual marketplace of American religious life, a church that grows as quickly as Mormonism and attains as much political power in states such as Utah will naturally be perceived as a threat. As one critic, J. H. Beadle, put it in 1904, "Scattered throughout the nation Mormonism would be the weakest of all religions; collected in one State, and ruling there with almost absolute power, they present a painfully interesting problem."[10]

KEY ISSUES AND DEBATES: PLURAL MARRIAGE AND THE LAW

However, probably the number one reason why Mormonism is still a target of satire in contemporary America today is the practice of plural marriage. The mainstream LDS Church abandoned the practice over 120 years ago, and most ordinary Mormons today know little about the history of plural marriage and generally downplay its role in the development of the church. Nonetheless, plural marriage was a central and important part of the early growth of Mormonism in the nineteenth century, helping to define and in some ways sustain this movement in a hostile American spiritual environment. At the end of the nineteenth century, when it was debated by the Supreme Court, plural marriage highlighted critically important questions of religious freedom and the law. And in the twenty-first century, plural marriage continues to be practiced by several Mormon splinter groups, generating new debates about First Amendment freedom and the protection of underage girls in some Mormon communities.

The debate surrounding plural marriage begins with Joseph Smith and his first wife, Emma, with whom he had a deeply loving but often conflicted relationship. It is unclear precisely when Joseph first began to develop the idea of plural marriage or when he engaged in his first polygamous relationship, which may have been during the early 1830s. Smith was accused of having a relationship with his serving girl Fanny Alger, and many accounts consider this to have been a plural marriage. However, the relationship was quickly terminated by Emma Smith, and Fanny left the community to marry another man in November 1836.

The practice of plural marriage was officially sanctioned on April 5, 1841, when Joseph was married to Louisa Beaman. Eventually, over the next two and a half years, Joseph would marry at least thirty additional women, ten of them already married to other men. The practice was initially kept secret—even from Emma herself, who would never know the full extent of her husband's polygamous activities. The relationship between Emma and Joseph was indeed complex, and while she clearly loved her husband intensely, she was never entirely comfortable with the idea of plural marriage and fought against it on multiple occasions.

One of the most important moments in the early development of plural marriage occurred on July 12, 1843, when Joseph dictated a revelation on plural and celestial marriage while his secretary William Clayton recorded his words. Joseph's brother Hyrum took the revelation to Emma, believing that he could now convince her of the necessity of plural

Christopher was a particularly interesting person to interview because he is both a Mormon convert and a scholar who, at the time of the interview, was doing his doctoral work in religious studies at Florida State University. As such, he has thought a great deal about the challenges of critically studying a controversial religion of which one is a practicing member.

I was raised in an Episcopalian family but was baptized into the largest branch of Mormonism, the Church of Jesus Christ of Latter-day Saints, when I was thirteen years old. I was the only member of my family to convert, although they were always very supportive. At the age of twenty-three, I went on a two-year mission to West Virginia. When I returned home, I began a master's degree under the first Mormon studies chair, Philip Barlow, at Utah State University. Two years later, I started my doctoral work at Florida State University.

The academic study of religion can definitely make you stop and pause about your beliefs; however, my beliefs and level of practice have stayed largely consistent. Being a believing Latter-day Saint studying Mormonism means that my informants trust me. I speak their language. I know the ins and outs of the culture. Because my first interest in Mormonism was completely personal, I spent a decade immersed in primary sources before I even realized I wanted to be a scholar. I am convinced that the insider scholar can—if he operates with the understanding that religion is the study of people, not truth claims—use any methodological or theoretical models he chooses.

I tend to follow Jan Shipps's model of considering Mormonism a New Judeo-Christian tradition. When teaching any form of alternative Christianity, I introduce the idea that the scholar's role is not to force a title onto a tradition. The label of Christianity is for adherents to wrestle over. Thus we speak of Christianities. I root Mormonism in other American forms of new religious movements rooted in the nineteenth century. In my American religious history courses, I tend to use Mormonism as both an example of antebellum new religious movements rooted in utopian thought and millenarianism. It allows us to examine broader trends of innovation throughout American religion.

I suspect Mormonism has continued to bear such scrutiny and satire because of three major issues: the intensity of its missionary work, its regional dominance in the American West, and its intersections with politics in the past decade. There is a long history of Mormon-themed satire. I don't think we should classify all such products as "persecution." Much of it is intolerant, a good share is mean-spirited, but it often conjures a sense that Mormons are bizarre but not dangerous. I do think we should acknowledge Bill Maher, for example, as a bigot of the same quality as other anticult

(continued)

fundamentalist Christians. However, many popular representations are designed to poke fun more than warn against the menace of one's Mormon neighbors.

I think Mormons appear exotic to many Americans because many Americans are limited in their knowledge and experience with both their own traditions and others. Those who would see the bizarre or seemingly impossible elements in another's faith usually don't look for the same in their own. On one hand, I think this is not changing. Many Americans probably left the *Book of Mormon* musical with an idea of Mormonism itself as very exotic, with one memorable song reciting all of Mormonism's strangest ideas. On the other hand, the fact that Mitt Romney was able to gain so many American votes suggests something significant about the current place of Mormonism in American culture. This is true even though his candidacy highlighted the various misunderstandings and prejudices of many Americans. I read an important Pew survey which suggested that there was a decrease in the number of Americans who thought Mormonism was starkly different from their own religion following the election.

Plural marriage was a crucial component of Mormon identity in the second half of the nineteenth century. Even if it was only practiced by about one-third of the population, all were affected by the practice. It was the defining trait of what made Mormons so unusual from other Americans. Some governmental leaders were more concerned about a Mormon theocracy in the West than they were about deviant marital practices, but this is what raised the hackles of the average American. The initial Republican Party platform pointing against the twin pillars of Barbary—slavery and polygamy—stressed the importance of how such a position could be mobilized for political gains.

To discuss all the Latter-day Saint justifications for plural marriage would require a volume, but we can point to a few. I think the answer for the introduction of Mormon plural marriage is by and large a theological one. Joseph Smith believed in a restoration of Old and New Testament religion. When he first presented a revelation on plural marriage, he referred to the practice as "the works of Abraham." It linked nineteenth-century Mormons with the ancient practices of the patriarchs. Smith also taught the need to be ritually "sealed" to one another. By linking individuals to himself in "celestial marriage," he was trying to enact a utopian—heavenly—society on earth.

When plural marriage was repudiated, then Mormon prophet Wilford Woodruff explained the decision as a means to stave off persecution. He cited the separation of imprisoned fathers from their families, the absence of church leaders who were in hiding, and the danger of losing property rights over temples and other church buildings. By ending plural marriage, the attention on the Latter-day Saints as a criminal body came to an end. Eventually the church was able to make greater strides in evangelization, Utah was recognized as a state, and gradually Latter-day Saints were thought of as a less subversive body. There was a decade in which some plural marriages continued to be solemnized, but the church clarified their position in 1904 and all subsequent polygamists were excommunicated. The Mormons faced a dilemma between whether to continue plural marriage or to have success in bringing the rest of their message to a broader public. They selected the latter. Instead of a focus on plural marriage, modern Mormons focus on missionary work.

marriage. Portions of the revelation are in fact directed specifically to Emma and address Joseph's immediate problems with her, for example: "Let my handmaid, Emma Smith, receive all those who have been given unto my servant Joseph, and who are virtuous and pure before me." The revelation also declared that Joseph would receive "an hundredfold of this world, of wives" if Emma did not obey. The sanction to follow plural marriage is here attributed directly to God, and the punishment for denying the practice is made quite clear; "If any man have a wife . . . and he teaches unto her the law of my priesthood, as pertaining unto these things, then she shall believe and administer unto him, or she shall be destroyed, saith the Lord your God."[11] Emma at times resigned herself to the idea of multiple wives and at times rejected it, even threatening to divorce Joseph. Nonetheless, the two remained, at least in outward appearance, a warm and loving couple until Joseph's death.

Plural marriage continued in the main body of the LDS community under the leadership of Brigham Young and the Twelve Apostles, seven of whom had also taken plural wives. Young himself married a total of fifty-five wives and fathered fifty-seven children. At its peak in the 1850s, over 40 percent of the Mormon population was engaged in plural marriage.[12] However, the practice became an increasing point of tension with the US federal government throughout the second half of the nineteenth century. Plural marriage was one of the driving factors behind the Utah War, an armed confrontation between US forces and Mormon settlers in 1857–58; and in 1862 Congress passed the Morrill Anti-bigamy Act, which banned plural marriage in the US territories. Mormons, however, continued to practice polygamy up through the 1880s, believing it to be protected by the Free Exercise Clause of the First Amendment.

The debates surrounding plural marriage in the nineteenth century raised key questions of constitutional law that have in many ways shaped our modern American understanding of religious freedom and the separation of church and state.[13] From the Mormons' perspective, the practice of plural marriage was based on the ideals of religious freedom and local self-government. From the antipolygamist critics' perspective, however, plural marriage represented a new form of *slavery,* only now involving white women in Utah rather than black men and women in the southern states. Moreover, many argued, the Mormons in Utah were creating a dangerous kind of theocratic society that threatened the separation of church and state that is central to American democracy.

In 1878, the issue went all the way to the US Supreme Court in the case of *Reynolds v. United States*. George Reynolds served as a secretary in the office of the church president and was charged with bigamy because of his marriage to two wives. Appealing to the First Amendment, Reynolds argued that it was not simply his religious freedom but his religious duty to practice plural marriage. In this case, the Court acknowledged that, under the First Amendment, Congress could not pass laws that prohibited the free exercise of religion; however, it concluded that there was a key distinction between religious *belief* and religious *action*. While Congress could not pass laws relating to beliefs, it could pass laws relating to actions, and the practice of plural marriage had been prohibited since the time of King James I in English law, upon which US law was based. The Court reasoned that if we allowed plural marriage on the basis of the First Amendment, someone else could argue that we should allow human sacrifice, as well, since this could also be construed as the free exercise of religion.

> Laws are made for the government of actions, and while they cannot interfere with mere religious belief and opinions, they may with practices. Suppose one believed that human sacrifices were a necessary part of religious worship; would it be seriously contended that the civil government under which he lived could not interfere to prevent a sacrifice? . . .
>
> So here, as a law of the organization of society under the exclusive dominion of the United States, it is provided that plural marriages shall not be allowed. Can a man excuse his practices to the contrary because of his religious belief?
>
> To permit this would be to make the professed doctrines of religious belief superior to the law of the land, and, in effect, to permit every citizen to become a law unto himself. Government could exist only in name under such circumstances.[14]

Like the legal debates surrounding the use of peyote, the *Reynolds* decision has had profound implications for religious freedom and constitutional law. In many ways, the legacy of the *Reynolds* decision is one that we still grapple with today when we discuss the question of religious freedom: Americans may be free to *believe* whatever they like, but they are not always free to *act* on those beliefs.

However, the mainstream LDS Church did not formally abandon plural marriage until 1890. Under increasing pressure from the federal government, church president Wilford Woodruff issued a manifesto that officially ended the practice (though it did not dissolve existing plural marriages). Subsequently, relations with the federal government markedly improved, and Utah was admitted into the union as a state later that same year. While some Mormons in the church continued to marry multiple wives, church president Joseph F. Smith disavowed the practice before Congress and issued a second manifesto in 1904, calling for all plural marriages to cease.

Although it may seem exotic to most Americans today, the early Mormon practice of plural marriage was really part of a wider experimentation with alternative family and marriage practices during the nineteenth century. The early 1800s were a period of rapid social, economic, and religious change, with the proliferation of many new forms of spiritual practice, a transition from a largely agrarian to an increasingly urban industrial economy, and a shift in communal and domestic life. During this same period, a variety of new religious movements emerged that experimented with alternative sexual practices and domestic arrangements. The Shakers (or United Society of Believers in Christ's Second Appearing) practiced celibacy, establishing a series of highly successful asexual communities across the eastern United States. The Spiritualists (whom we will meet in chapter 4) advocated the idea of Spiritual Affinity—or what was called "Free Love" by critics—arguing that marriage should be based not on economic need or family arrangements but on an inner, spiritual attraction. And still others, such as the Oneida community in New York State, practiced a form of "complex marriage," according to which every male member was married to every female member and exclusive relationships were discouraged.

But if plural marriage was indeed an important part of Smith's life and teachings, and a key aspect of the early Mormon movement, the question is why? How was the practice justified, and why did it last for nearly sixty years within the main body of the Mormon community? The first and perhaps most obvious reason is scriptural. After all, if Joseph Smith hoped to restore the primitive church, based not simply on the New Testament but on all the dispensations going back to Adam, then he surely would have wondered why so many of the ancient prophets had more than one wife. As early as 1831, Smith seems to have asked why Abraham, Isaac, Jacob, and Moses had two or more wives simultaneously—which could only have been, he reasoned, if it was "commanded by God."[15]

Second, plural marriage was closely tied to Mormon theology and to its unique understanding of the spiritual role of marriage. According to Smith's teachings, the highest form of marriage is not simply an affair for this lifetime on earth, a matter of "till death do us part"; rather, earthly marriage can and should be made eternal through a special sealing ceremony that allows the union to continue permanently after death. Men and women who are not married for eternity will inhabit the lowest class in the afterlife, as solitary "ministering angels" who are unable to progress further in the postmortem state. But men whose marriages are sealed for eternity can progress toward "godhood," becoming patriarchs and exploring new worlds. And if a monogamous marriage sealed for eternity could offer a man a kind of godhood in the afterlife, then plural marriage could make his eternal descendants "as numerous as the stars in the sky," just as God had promised Abraham in the book of Genesis (26:4).

Finally, in addition to theological and scriptural reasons, plural marriage may have played an extremely important sociological role in the early Mormon community. As the historian Lawrence Foster has argued, the early Mormon community faced a series of crises as it was forced to move repeatedly in the wake of intense persecution during its first decades. In this context, plural marriage helped to create large and complex kinship networks among the members of the community that provided tremendous strength, resilience, and economic resources to the young Mormon movement. A single individual could be related to hundreds of others, providing a real form of communal and economic strength at a time when Mormons faced intense hostility from the surrounding American society. At the same time, they were able to establish a highly autonomous society and political system that operated largely outside the scrutiny of US state and federal law until the late nineteenth century:

> Not feeling able to achieve redress of their grievances from the larger society, Mormons, in attempting to create their "new Israel," increasingly turned in on themselves and depended on family and kinship ties to secure loyalty to the group. Polygamy could make possible a far greater extension of such ties than could monogamy. For example, by the time of his death at age eighty-eight, the Mormon patriarch Benjamin F. Johnson was related by blood or marriage to more than eight hundred people and presumably had greater power and security than those with less extensive kinship networks. The Mormon concern for extending family ties and for controlling their own marriage practices was part of a larger effort to establish an autonomous, self-sufficient organization separate from an evil and corrupt world, an effort to create a "political kingdom of God."[16]

Other scholars have noted that plural marriage was also a means of addressing real economic problems of the nineteenth century. As historian Kathryn M. Daynes suggests, plural marriage helped redistribute scarce resources in the early Utah territory by allowing poor and even destitute women to become wives of more affluent men.[17] In this sense, plural marriage was not so much an exotic cult practice as a practical part of social and economic life during this period of American history.

PLURAL MARRIAGE IN CONTEMPORARY MORMON COMMUNITIES

While the mainstream LDS Church discontinued the practice of plural marriage in the late nineteenth century, several other smaller Mormon groups have continued the practice to this day. It is estimated that roughly thirty thousand to thirty-five thousand individuals are involved in plural marriages in the United States. The largest group still practicing plural marriage is the Fundamentalist Church of Jesus Christ of Latter-day Saints (FLDS), which is based mainly in Colorado City and Hildale, Colorado, and has roughly eight thousand to twelve thousand members. The FLDS maintains that its practice of plural marriage is based on the authority and injunction of the third Mormon president, John Taylor (d. 1887). Other Mormon churches that continue the practice of plural marriage include the True and Living Church in Manti, the Latter-day Church of Christ centered along the Wasatch Front in Utah, and the Apostolic United Brethren Church located near Salt Lake City.

The continuing practice of plural marriage in the contemporary United States became the subject of huge media attention in 2005 and again in 2008 amid investigations of sexual assault and child endangerment among FLDS communities. In May 2006, the leader of the

FLDS, Warren Jeffs, was placed on the FBI's most wanted list for unlawful flight to avoid prosecution on Utah state charges. Alleged to have arranged illegal marriages between his adult male followers and underage girls, Jeffs was arrested in August 2006 in Nevada and taken to Utah for trial. Then in 2007 the state of Arizona charged him with eight further counts, including sexual conduct with minors and incest. Although the Utah conviction was later overturned because of incorrect jury instructions, Jeffs was extradited to Texas, where he was again convicted of sexual assault of children and sentenced to life in prison.

In the midst of the ongoing Warren Jeffs trials, the FLDS also became the center of media attention when its Yearning for Zion (YFZ) Ranch near Eldorado, Texas, was raided by state authorities.[18] The YFZ Ranch had been established in Texas by FLDS members who left Utah and Colorado because of increasing scrutiny from the media and law enforcement. On March 29, 2008, Texas Child Protective Services received phone calls from individuals who claimed to be abused children. It later turned out that one or more of these calls was actually fake and had been placed by Rozita Swinton, a Colorado Springs resident who had been masquerading as a YFZ Ranch resident. Swinton had been arrested for previous hoax calls, in which she had also pretended to be an abused young girl.

The calls triggered a large raid led by law enforcement officers and child welfare officials beginning on April 3. Armed with automatic weapons, the officers removed nearly all the children and placed them in state custody, arguing that they were either real or potential victims of sexual abuse. In all, the officers removed 468 children aged seventeen and younger and held them in child protective services. More than one hundred women volunteered to leave the ranch in order to stay with the children; however, only children under the age of four were allowed to stay with the mothers until DNA testing was completed, and after the testing only children under eighteen months were allowed to stay with their mothers. The children were then placed in sixteen different foster homes and group shelters.

The authorities initially claimed that thirty-one of the girls aged fourteen to seventeen either had children or were then pregnant. However, a report by the Texas Department of Family and Protective Services in December 2008 concluded that only twelve of the girls had been "spiritually married" between the ages of twelve and fifteen, and only seven of them had children. According to Texas law, children under the age of seventeen cannot consent to sex with an adult, and sex with a child under fourteen is considered aggravated assault.

The FLDS, meanwhile, argued that the removal of children—some of them very young or infants—was simply inhumane and unnecessary. The church also argued that this was a form of religious persecution, likening it to a witch hunt, in which FLDS members were being unfairly targeted simply because of their nonmainstream beliefs and lifestyle.[19] Finally, on May 28, an appeals court ruled that there was insufficient evidence that the children were in any immediate danger to justify keeping them in state custody, and all of the children had to be returned to their family's care.

However, many adult male members of the FLDS ranch were eventually convicted of sexual assault and bigamy in 2009 and 2010. Seven men were charged with sexual assault of girls under seventeen, receiving fines of up to $10,000 and prison sentences of up to thirty-three years.

The raid on the FLDS ranch raises profound questions for the study of new religious movements and the balance between religious freedom and law enforcement in the twenty-first century. Defenders of the FLDS community have argued that state law enforcement clearly overstepped its boundaries by raiding a religious community with heavily armed agents and then removing small children from their families. Critics of the church, however, argue that many FLDS members were in fact violating state laws regarding sexual relations with minors and that these children were in real danger.[20] This is yet another case where the balance between First Amendment freedoms and the need to protect public safety—particularly that of minors—is not clearly defined and requires an ongoing, perhaps always unresolved, critical debate.

QUESTIONS FOR DISCUSSION AND DEBATE

1. Why do you think Mormonism has been by far the most successful of all American new religious movements in terms of numbers? What is it about Mormon theology, scripture, practices, or missionary outreach that has allowed it to become almost an independent world religion in its own right, even as many other new religions have waned and almost disappeared with time?

2. Of all the controversial aspects of Mormonism (its theology, its view of revelation, its view of the afterlife), why do you think plural marriage has been the one issue that most Americans, journalists, and lawmakers have focused on as the primary point of debate? Why was the idea of plural marriage so controversial in the nineteenth century? And do you think it is still as controversial today as it was 150 years ago? We have many states that now accept same-sex marriage but none that accept plural marriage. Why is that? Why would same-sex marriage appear more acceptable than marriage to multiple partners—even heterosexual ones?

3. Why do you think Mormonism seems more "exotic" and strange to most Americans even today? Is it simply the practice of plural marriage, or are there other reasons for the ongoing stereotypes, suspicion, and satire of Mormons in mainstream culture?

4. Where do you stand on the debate over the raid on the FLDS ranch in 2008? Were state officials and law enforcement agents justified in undertaking the raid and removing the children? Or is the FLDS Church correct in saying that this was an unjust persecution of a minority religion? Are there other ways law enforcement could have handled the case that would have both ensured the safety of the children and respected the rights of the community?

SUGGESTED CLASSROOM ACTIVITY

Critically examine the representation of Mormonism in popular culture by looking at one or more of the following examples: the *South Park* episode "All about Mormons," the Broadway musical *The Book of Mormon,* or the TV series *Big Love.* Discuss the ways in which this representation of Mormon life helps or hinders the understanding of Mormon religious life in general and the FLDS community in particular. If other religions were represented in this way, would we find it more or less offensive?

SUGGESTED FILM

"The American Experience: The Mormons." *Frontline,* PBS, 2007.

SUGGESTIONS FOR FURTHER READING

Bushman, Richard Lyman. *Mormonism: A Very Short Introduction.* New York: Oxford University Press, 2008.

Bushman, Richard Lyman, and Claudia L. Bushman. *Building the Kingdom of God.* New York: Oxford University Press, 2001.

Daynes, Kathryn M. *More Wives Than One: Transformation of the Mormon Marriage System, 1840–1910.* Urbana: University of Illinois Press, 2001.

Fluhman, J. Spencer. *A Peculiar People: Anti-Mormonism and the Making of Religion in Nineteenth-Century America.* Chapel Hill: University of North Carolina Press, 2012.

Gordon, Sarah Barringer. *The Mormon Question: Polygamy and Constitutional Conflict in Nineteenth-Century America.* Chapel Hill: University of North Carolina Press, 2002.

Shipps, Jan. "Is Mormonism Christian? Reflections on a Complicated Question." In *Mormons and Mormonism: An Introduction to an American World Religion,* edited by Eric A. Eliason, 76–98. Chicago: University of Illinois Press, 2001.

———. *Mormonism: The Story of a New Religious Tradition.* Urbana: University of Illinois Press, 1987.

Van Wagoner, Richard S. *Mormon Polygamy: A History.* Salt Lake City, UT: Signature Books, 1992.

NOTES TO CHAPTER 3

1. "Transcript: Mitt Romney's Faith Speech," National Public Radio, December 6, 2007, www.npr.org/templates/story/story.php?storyId=16969460.

2. Richard T. Hughes, "Soaring with the Gods: Early Mormons and the Eclipse of Religious Pluralism," in *Mormons and Mormonism: An Introduction to an American World Religion*, edited by Eric A. Eliason (Chicago: University of Illinois Press, 2001), 25.

3. "Exaltation," *Encyclopedia of Mormonism*, 2014, http://eom.byu.edu/index.php/Exaltation.

4. Jan Shipps, *Mormonism: The Story of a New Religious Tradition* (Urbana: University of Illinois Press, 1987), ix–x.

5. Peggy Fletcher Stack, "After Excommunication Kate Kelly Hurting but 'Joyful,'" *Salt Lake Tribune*, July 10, 2014, http://www.sltrib.com/home/1399797-155/kelly-church-ordain-women-blog-excommunicated.

6. Mark Oppenheimer, "A Twist on Posthumous Baptisms Leaves Jews Miffed at Mormon Rite," *New York Times*, March 2, 2012, www.nytimes.com/2012/03/03/us/jews-take-issue-with-posthumous-mormon-baptisms-beliefs.html?_r=0.

7. Mark Twain, *Roughing It* (Ithaca, NY: Cornell University Press, 2009), 127.

8. Trey Parker, Robert Lopez, and Matt Stone, "I Believe," in *The Book of Mormon: Original Broadway Cast Recording* (New York: Ghostlight Records, 2001).

9. "*Book of Mormon* Musical: Church's Official Statement," *Newsroom*, February 7, 2011, www.mormonnewsroom.org/article/church-statement-regarding-the-book-of-mormon-broadway-musical.

10. J. H. Beadle, *Polygamy: Or, the Mysteries and Crimes of Mormonism* (Philadelphia: National Publishing, 1904), 5.

11. Lawrence Foster, *Women, Family, and Utopia: Communal Experiments of the Shakers, the Oneida Community and the Mormons* (Syracuse, NY: Syracuse University Press, 1992), 156.

12. Richard Lyman Bushman, *Mormonism: A Very Short Introduction* (New York: Oxford University Press, 2008), 186.

13. For an excellent discussion of these issues, see Sarah Barringer Gordon, *The Mormon Question: Polygamy and Constitutional Conflict in Nineteenth-Century America* (Chapel Hill: University of North Carolina Press, 2002).

14. Reynolds v. United States, 98 U.S. 145 (1878), 98–99.

15. Kathryn M. Daynes, *More Wives Than One: Transformation of the Mormon Marriage System, 1840–1910* (Urbana: University of Illinois Press, 2001), 20.

16. Foster, *Women, Family, and Utopia*, 128.

17. Daynes, *More Wives Than One*, 91–140.

18. For an overview of these events, see "Timeline of Raid on FLDS-Owned YFZ Ranch," *Deseret News*, May 23, 2008, www.deseretnews.com/article/700228439/Timeline-of-raid-on-FLDS-owned-YFZ-Ranch.html.

19. John Quinones, "Willie Jessop: Purported Frontman at Texas Polygamy Compound," ABC News, April 18, 2008, http://abcnews.go.com/2020/story?id=4684344&page=1.

20. For a good discussion of these complex issues, see "ACLU Statement on the Government's Actions Regarding the Yearning for Zion Ranch," ACLU.org, May 2, 2008, https://www.aclu.org/religion-belief/aclu-statement-governments-actions-regarding-yearning-zion-ranch-eldorado-texas.

FOUR

Spiritualism

Women, Mediums, and Messages from Other Worlds

In the fall of 2005, I took a small group of Ohio State University students to the Guiding Light Spiritualist Church, located in a small former retail space in an aging strip mall on the outskirts of Columbus, Ohio. The Guiding Light community is just one of many spiritualist groups in the central Ohio area, which also include the Christian Spiritualist Temple, the White Lily Chapel, Light in the Woods, and a dozen or so others, some dating back over one hundred years. Despite its humble appearance, the Guiding Light Church was lively and well attended that Sunday morning, attracting a group that was impressively diverse in age, race, and social background. The service was led by Reverend Joseph Mauriello (a medium who claims to have been in contact with the spirit realm since early childhood), accompanied by his mother (also a spirit medium) and his wife (then a medium in training). Mauriello is also the author of several books on Spiritualism and the afterlife, including *Ghost Psychology 101* and *Your Departed Loved Ones and Spirit Guides Are Only a Thought Away*. During the service, the reverend skillfully mixed prayers, healing ceremonies, and serious discussions of Spiritualist philosophy with some very funny jokes and anecdotes (after welcoming our OSU group, for example, he turned and whispered to his wife, "Did you tell them about the human sacrifices?").

In the very middle of the service, however, the reverend's wife suddenly stood up and interrupted, declaring that the spirit of a deceased individual was in the room with us at that moment. After some consultation, the reverend and his wife determined that it was the spirit of a young man who had died in a car accident who was not yet ready to move on in the afterlife and had accompanied someone in the congregation to the service. They then asked if anyone in the room knew someone who had recently died in an accident, and, sure enough, one of the students in our group had a friend who had been killed in a collision not long before. Unfortunately, the deceased friend was female, not male, which led to further consultation between the reverend and his wife. Finally, they decided that, whoever the spirit might be, they would lead the congregation in prayers to help guide it to a more restful state in the afterlife.

Although Spiritualism is not well known to most Americans today, it was a huge and popular movement from the middle to the end of the nineteenth century and has had a formative influence on virtually all later forms of New Age spirituality. As a new religious movement, American Spiritualism was born in the same general context as Mormonism, emerging out of the "burned-over district" of New York State in the early nineteenth century and spreading rapidly throughout the United States. Unlike Mormonism, however, Spiritualism was always a more loosely organized and decentralized movement, depending not on a strong institutional structure but rather on the charismatic power of mediums and their ability to communicate with spirits in other realms. And unlike Mormonism, Spiritualism was as much a popular form of entertainment as a religious movement. Much of its popularity came from the spectacle of mediums—many of them attractive young women—entering into trance states, communicating with the dead, and offering commentary on religious, metaphysical, and often broader cultural issues.

Historically, Spiritualism was also important not simply as a religious phenomenon but as a key part of several larger social movements in the nineteenth century, most importantly the abolitionist and early women's rights movements. Spirit mediums in the nineteenth century had a unique new form of religious authority and a popular platform to speak from, which allowed them not only to discuss new religious ideas but also to speak critically about key social issues such as slavery, gender equality, and marriage. Because females were believed to be naturally more "open" to the influences of the spirit realm, the movement also offered new roles for women to become religious authorities and to have a public voice that was rarely if ever available to them in nineteenth-century American society. As such, Spiritualism went hand in hand with the early women's rights movement in the nineteenth century and helped dramatically alter the broader landscape of gender and religion in the United States.

One of the key debates surrounding nineteenth-century Spiritualism is the prominent role of women as spiritual mediums and religious authorities. On the one hand, Spiritualism offered women unusual new forms of authority and a new kind of public voice, which allowed them to speak out on many social issues such as abolition and women's rights. Yet at the same time, this authority was largely based on the nineteenth-century belief that women were more passive, childlike, and receptive to the voices of the spirits, who spoke through them while they were in unconscious trance states. So we might well ask whether and to what degree Spiritualism helped "empower" women in the nineteenth century by giving them new roles as religious mediums and leaders. Was Spiritualism even a kind of "protofeminism"? Or did Spiritualism only repeat and reinforce traditional gender stereotypes, such as the view of women as weak, women as childlike, women as passive vehicles for the voices of others in a still largely male-dominated society?

Although Spiritualism gradually declined in the twentieth century, it influenced other new religious movements that we will discuss briefly in this chapter. Perhaps the most important is the Theosophical Society, founded by the Russian mystic Helena Petrovna Blavatsky and her American partner Henry Steel Olcott in New York City in 1875. Although Blavatsky later became critical of the Spiritualist movement, she helped popularize some of its most important ideas and herself claimed to be in contact with an array of spiritual beings from other realms. Together, Spiritualism and Theosophy became two of the most important influences that would later give birth to the broader phenomenon of New Age spirituality in the 1960s and '70s.

THE BIRTH OF SPIRITUALISM IN NINETEENTH-CENTURY AMERICA

The origins of American Spiritualism as a widespread popular phenomenon are often dated to the 1840s, particularly to the same part of the northeastern United States that gave birth to Mormonism and to many other new movements. However, the roots of Spiritualism really lie much deeper and can be traced back well into the history of the Western esoteric traditions that we discussed in chapter 1.

Probably the most important forefather of modern Spiritualism was the Swedish philosopher, theologian, and scientist Emanuel Swedenborg (1688–1772). Up until the age of fifty-three, Swedenborg had been a highly respected inventor and scientist, well known for his numerous engineering innovations and for his investigations into anatomy and physiology. However, in 1741 he also began to have a series of intense mystical experiences, dreams, and visions, claiming that he had been called by God to reform Christianity and introduce a new church. According to his interpretation, the Last Judgment had already taken place, occurring in a spiritual rather than physical sense, while the Second Coming had occurred through the revelation of an inner spiritual sense of the Word of God, transmitted through Swedenborg himself.

In the course of his mystical experiences, Swedenborg believed that his spiritual eyes had been opened, allowing him to journey to heaven and hell—which he described vividly—and to converse with angels, demons, and spirits. His most famous work, *Heaven and Hell* (1758), contains an astonishingly detailed description of the afterlife, recounting in minute particulars the appearance, homes, and activities of the angels, as well as the intermediate World of Spirits. Thus he provides an elaborate account of angels' dwellings, which are like those on earth but far more radiant and perfect:

> Whenever I have talked face to face with angels, I have been with them in their dwellings. Their dwellings are just like the dwellings on earth which we call homes, except that they are more beautiful. They have rooms, suites, and bedrooms, all in abundance. They have courtyards and are surrounded by gardens, flowerbeds and lawns. . . . I have been allowed to go walking through them, to sightsee, and on occasion to enter homes. This has happened to me when I was fully awake, when

my inner sight was opened. I have seen palaces of heaven so noble as to defy description. The higher parts glowed as if they were made of gold, the lower as though made of precious gems; each palace was more splendid than the last.[1]

Swedenborg's vast body of writings had a tremendous impact on many new religious movements of the next two centuries, becoming part of a larger spiritual revival in Europe, England, and the United States. Above all, his idea of heaven as a realm filled with spirits that we can visit and communicate with would influence virtually all later forms of mediumship in the nineteenth and twentieth centuries. Although organized groups such as the Swedenborg Foundation are relatively few today, his teachings on the spiritual realm were immensely influential and have continued well into contemporary New Age spirituality. Even today, many practicing Spiritualists, such as Reverend Mauriello of the Guiding Light Church in Ohio, cite Swedenborg as their greatest spiritual forefather.

However, when historians today talk about Spiritualism as a widespread popular movement in the United States, they often trace its origins to a small farmhouse in Hydesville, New York, and to a group of sisters named Leah, Margaret, and Kate Fox. In March 1848, the two younger sisters Kate and Margaret (then aged twelve and fifteen) claimed that they heard a series of mysterious rappings and knockings coming from the house. Kate eventually challenged the noise-making entity to repeat the snapping of her fingers, which it allegedly did, and the girls were then able to work out a code by which they could communicate with it. The girls initially referred to the entity as "Mr. Splitfoot," a nickname for the Devil, but the entity later stated that it was in reality the spirit of a peddler named Charles R. Rosma, who had been murdered in the farmhouse five years before. A few pieces of bone were allegedly dug up in the cellar, and the news of this contact with the spirit world spread like wildfire across the area. Kate and Margaret soon became hugely famous as mediums, appearing at public séances before crowds of hundreds throughout the 1850s.

The Fox sisters, however, were just a small part of a much broader Spiritualist movement that swept across the eastern United States during these decades. As a new religious movement, Spiritualism had a profound philosophical aspect, complete with a compelling new view of God and the universe, as well as a popular side, providing new forms of entertainment and spectacle for ordinary American consumers.

SPIRITUALISM AS A NEW RELIGIOUS MOVEMENT: A RADICAL ALTERNATIVE TO MAINSTREAM CHRISTIANITY

As a new religious movement, Spiritualism was in many ways an attractive alternative to the mainstream Christian denominations of nineteenth-century America. In contrast to the many other options that emerged during this vibrant period of religious awakening, Spiritualism offered the unique promise of direct contact with the spiritual realm and departed loved ones, without the need for scripture, clergy, or other institutional intermediaries. In contrast to most mainstream Christian denominations, Spiritualism painted a far rosier

Reverend Mauriello is a minister at the Guiding Light Spiritualist Church in Columbus, Ohio. The son of a Spiritualist minister, he recalls that he has been able to see and talk with spirits since he was a child, and he has written two books on how to communicate with deceased loved ones. In this interview, he talks about his own background, the origins of Spiritualism as a religious movement, and what goes on at a typical Spiritualist service.

My mother was a Spiritualist minister. When I was about five, she left Catholicism and started searching for something different, and she found Spiritualism. But frankly, I was communicating with spirits my whole life, since before I could talk physically. So a lot of the answers she was starting to find made sense to me, even at five. Then my mother found a church she really liked. And basically you become a minister within a church you are attending. There are classes you have to take, and you have to be able to achieve certain goals, such as being able to be a psychic reader, a healer, and to be able to teach the religion. So she started her own church once she became ordained. Pretty much my whole life, I knew where I was heading, so as I got older I started doing more and more in the church until I got ordained.

As a child, communicating with spirits was fantastic. But I didn't know any differently. I had done it all my life. To give an example: my dad's parents and my mom's father had all passed away before I was born, but they were still part of my life. They would show up for special events or whatever was going on, and I would talk with them and get to know them. A lot of what you perceive goes on in the mind. It is possible to see spirits outside your mind and to see them as clearly as you can a physical person. But spirits—and everything—operate on energy. Spirits are energy that your mind interprets, and you kind of see it in your mind. I've been working since 1985 to explain the difference between your own thoughts and spirit communication, and it's almost impossible. You have to experience it. The best I can do is to say there's a feeling of it coming into you instead of just being created in your own mind. You hear their words, see their images. And it's not limited to that—I've smelled cookies baking. All the senses can be used by spirits. I've done it every single day of my life. I can talk to the other side as easily as I can talk to you. I've always been able to do that.

Anybody can learn to communicate with spirits. As a matter of fact, I would say most people do it to some degree. They get hunches about a situation, they don't know where it came from; they get a feeling about somebody—like maybe someone is lying to them and not trustworthy, and there's nothing outwardly indicating that, but they just get this sense suddenly, "Don't trust that person." A lot of that is communication; spirits are trying to let you know: "Be aware of that person."

(continued)

The spirits are moving on in the afterlife, to a certain degree. Life goes on, on the other side. The only spirits who don't move on are what we call ghosts. Really they don't accept the fact that they've died. But all the other spirits, like your family members, are coming back because they're family. They want to visit, share good times with you, share bad times with you, to be there with you. We also teach about spirit guides. Spirit guides are specially trained spirits on the other side who are there to help guide you in life. We believe that everybody has at least one that we call a main guide or guardian guide, who was with you from before you were born and will stay with you through your physical life and then help you cross over. Some people call them guardian angels. And they're always there for you. As you grow spiritually and are able to communicate better, other spirits will come in to work with you.

We believe in God, and we believe in an all-powerful, all-knowing, all-good, all-present God. We don't believe in heaven or hell. We believe that by your actions you create heaven or hell in your life here and now. We believe that God exists everywhere, so it's not possible to ever be out of God's presence, and everybody receives God's guidance in some form. Belief in reincarnation is left up to the individual Spiritualist—some believe in it, some don't. I happen to, and most of the people who come to our church do. We believe that you are an immortal soul. We believe that you exist in a physical body, an etheric body, and an aura body. When death occurs, what actually happens is that just the physical body dies. Your soul continues to exist in the etheric and aura bodies. The etheric and aura realms exist in parallel with the physical realm. Basically you just continue existing, but now you're in the etheric body, and you're aware of the etheric realm.

If you go back into very ancient times you'll find a lot of what we teach being practiced—healing, spirit communication. It's really a very basic spiritual concept, and the idea of the immortality of the soul is the basis of all religions, as far as I know. So in that context, the ideas of Spiritualism are maybe as old as mankind.

Modern Spiritualism, as it's called, started sometime in the 1700s among the scientific community of Europe. Emanuel Swedenborg was one of the first. He was a scientist—that was one of the keys. He had a very Christian background; his father was a minister. Mediumship was already around, but he began a scientific investigation of it, and that's when a lot of people claim modern Spiritualism started. It's a scientific study into the nature of life.

Most of our beliefs are based on our own experience. We don't have a scripture, which is why, when you go to a Spiritualist church, you'll see them teaching from all kinds of scriptures. If there's a Truth, there's a Truth—why not use it? Spiritualism is a bit of an odd sort of religion. We don't have a prophet you can look back to, we don't have a single text you can learn from, and we don't believe in blind faith. We don't say:

"You have to believe this." Spiritualism's approach is the idea that "here's what we believe; now gather evidence and decide for yourself." It's sort of the scientific approach, and that's because it was mostly scientists that started it in the modern version.

A lot of Spiritualist churches follow somewhat of a similar format. We'll often start out with an opening song, an opening prayer. After that, we do healing, where our trained healers stand up in front of the church, and anyone who wants healing can come up and receive laying on of hands. After that portion of the service, we have teaching, where I or one of the other ministers will get up and teach something to the congregation. And the last part of the service is what we call the message service, where our psychic mediums or ministers will get up and give maybe a two- or three-minute message to people in the congregation. And usually it ends with a closing prayer.

Our congregation is very diverse. Spiritualist churches tend not to be neighborhood churches. We pull people from all over the city. We have every age show up—little babies on up are in the service—and just as diverse as you can imagine. We have people of every background and education level. If it were legal to perform same-sex marriages, Spiritualist churches would be doing it. Sexual orientation, everything we accept. Spiritualists are people who are searching, who are looking for things. They may not always have higher education diplomas, but they do thirst for knowledge and are constantly searching. That is one of the draws of Spiritualism. It is a religion that has you study and learn for yourself and grow. But you're still expected to do most of it yourself. I can help you communicate with spirits, but you've got to do the actual work.

picture of the afterlife, rejecting the ideas of a punishing deity or an eternal hell and imagining instead a God of pure love and an afterlife of endless spiritual progress. In such a worldview, with no concept of original sin, predestination, or eternal damnation, even the person of Jesus Christ ultimately became unimportant for the sake of spiritual advancement.

Perhaps the most important spokesman for the American Spiritualist movement was the clairvoyant and medium known in the popular media as the "Poughkeepsie Seer," Andrew Jackson Davis (1826–1910; figure 4.1). In his autobiography, Davis recalls attending a Dutch Reformed church as a child, where he engaged in a theological dispute with his Sunday school teacher, arguing with him about the idea of eternal punishment. Concluding that "a God of Love and Wisdom is TOO GOOD to create anybody to suffer in hell forever," Davis left the church and began to teach his "Harmonial Philosophy" based on a God of pure love and a universe of inherent, harmonious goodness.[2] Throughout his writings, Davis was extremely critical of those who claimed to be Christian while engaging in the most hypocritical and self-righteous condemnation of their fellow men: "My whole soul shrinks from contact with sectarian Christians. . . . Christians, so styled in the newspapers, are the most stupid in spiritual principles, and the most unmistakable materialists I have yet met with in

FIGURE 4.1 Andrew Jackson Davis. From *The Magic Staff: An Autobiography of Andrew Jackson Davis* (New York: J. S. Brown, 1859).

society. Infidels, on the contrary, are accessible and decently fraternal. They can and will *think*."[3] Ultimately, Davis concluded that the liberal and positive ideals of Spiritualism were fundamentally at odds with the pessimism and intolerance of mainstream Christianity: "To be a consistent Christian is to be illiberal. On the other hand, to be consistently liberal is to be an illegitimate Christian."[4]

Davis recalled having intense spiritual and clairvoyant experiences from childhood and began entering into trance states from age seventeen. In March 1844, he claimed to have encountered the spirit of Emanuel Swedenborg, whose influence can be seen throughout his later writings. In contrast to Swedenborg's, however, Davis's teachings about the spirit world departed much more dramatically from Christian theology. Rejecting the very idea of hell, Davis described the afterlife as encompassing not just the two alternatives of salvation or damnation, but rather a series of seven increasingly spiritual spheres through which the soul progressed toward ever-greater degrees of perfection. He compared these seven spheres to a great "Tree of Immortal Life," which consisted successively of the germ, roots, body, branches, buds, blossoms, and fragrance. Thus, beyond the first sphere of the natural world, there was the second or spiritual sphere, followed by the third or celestial sphere, the fourth or supernatural sphere, the fifth or superspiritual sphere, and the sixth or supercelestial sphere. Each of these first six realms also had its own subdivisions, dwelling places, and various spiritual inhabitants. Finally, there was the seventh realm called the Divine Foundation or the eternal sun-sphere of the divine Father and Mother, resting at the "positive attractive

Center" of the universe, to which all spiritual beings were drawn.[5] Davis saw the entire cosmos as a harmonious organism, in which every part was connected to and corresponded with every other, like the cells and limbs of a single body. Like the notes in a musical composition, all the individual parts of the universe were orchestrated by the infinite love of God, who lay at the center of all things like the animating soul within the body of the cosmos:

> The structure of the universe and all its living beauties, together with the Divine Essence that gives it life and animation, presents an indestructible basis of hope and faith, and a corresponding foundation of human action. It is a mirror in which are reflected all corresponding beauties yet uncreated, but proved to be in embryo by the universal teachings of natural law. The whole is as one body, and God the Soul and Father of all living and unliving things. Everything is perfect in its way and state of being; everything is necessary, everything is pure, even celestial and divine; everything teaches harmony and reciprocity. . . . Everything is of, in, through, and unto the Divine Mind; all things are parts of Him, as of one whole— even Nature, Man, and Heaven.[6]

In sum, Davis's view of God and the universe was exceptionally optimistic, rejecting the very idea of hell and damnation for an ideal of an ascending journey through progressively more sublime spheres toward the infinite love of the Divine Center of all things.

This narrative of growing up in a Christian faith and then abandoning it for the more liberal beliefs of Spiritualism was a common one in the nineteenth century. Another of the most important Spiritualist writers of the time was Mary Fenn Love (1824–66), who would later become Davis's wife. Born into a Baptist family in western New York State, Love agonized over the idea that God might condemn so many souls to eternal damnation and hold such a bleak view of the natural world. Finally, upon converting to Spiritualism, she embraced a vision of a natural universe of inherent beauty that was permeated by divinity, overseen by a God of infinite love who consigned none to eternal punishment: "When at last I dared to gaze into the opening Heavens, the tempest and darkness, the shroud and pall all vanished, and I saw only angels, with their deep calm eyes, so full of beauty and tenderness. Then like the gushing of mighty waters came over my soul a sense of harmony and glory and of the all-pervading love of the Infinite Father. . . . None, *none* in the vast Universe of God were lost to him."[7] Such an optimistic vision of an all-loving deity and the hope of an ultimate salvation for all souls was surely a large part of Spiritualism's appeal to many Americans in the nineteenth century.

SPIRITUALISM AS A POPULAR PHENOMENON: SÉANCES AND OUIJA BOARDS

In addition to the metaphysical views of authors such as Andrew Jackson Davis, Spiritualism spread rapidly as a popular movement, as a lively form of entertainment, and even as a consumer product. Spiritualist gatherings were very often a form of popular spectacle, providing not only insight into the afterlife but also an entertaining show in an era long before the advent of radio, television, and movies. Spiritualist events attracted skeptics as much as true believers, and, for many, part of the fun was surely the hope of uncovering a fraud as much as experiencing real contact with the spirit realm.

At the same time, however, Spiritualism was also a kind of "domestic" religious movement, one that could be practiced in the living rooms of ordinary Americans. Because trance mediums were not ordained by any official religious body, and because spirit phenomena could take place in an ordinary farmhouse as much as in a church, Spiritualism became a movement that could be practiced by virtually anyone in their own homes. Séances became not just mass public affairs for famous mediums such as the Fox sisters but gatherings that could be held with friends and family in the parlor. And by the 1850s and '60s, there was a thriving market of Spiritualist devices that could be inexpensively purchased and used by anyone to make contact with the spirit world.

The first widely popular device was the planchette, from the French word meaning "little plank," which was a small heart-shaped or shield-shaped flat piece of wood with castors and a hole at the top to hold a pencil. First developed by the educator and later founder of the movement of "Spiritism" in France, Allan Kardec, the planchette was intended to help facilitate communication with the spirit realm by allowing the spiritual energy to flow through the medium's hand and guide the rolling pencil to deliver a particular message. In 1858, planchettes came to the United States where they became hugely popular in the 1860s as consumer items sold widely in toyshops and bookstores. The most successful manufacturer of planchettes was Kirby & Company, which claimed to have sold over two hundred thousand units in the first year alone.

The planchette in turn became the chief inspiration for an even more popular device used in occult communication, the Ouija board. First introduced in the 1890s and still mass produced by the Parker Brothers company to this day, the Ouija board typically used a small triangle that could be guided over an alphabet and a simple "yes" or "no" in order to spell out answers from the spirit world. Together, the planchette and the Ouija board helped introduce spirit communication to a much broader audience of ordinary consumers, muddying the boundary between spiritual phenomena and popular commodities to be enjoyed in middle-class living rooms and opening the door for a new mass audience to begin experimenting with mediumship. At the same time, these popular devices transformed the ordinary family home into a new kind of spiritual space that blurred the boundary between religion and domesticity, between contact with the dead and good fun entertainment.

A final reason for the general popularity of Spiritualism was its apparent fit with many new scientific technological developments of the nineteenth century. Above all, the phenomenon of electricity and the newly invented technology of the telegraph provided ideal metaphors for instantaneous communications with spirits in distant worlds beyond the five senses. Many Spiritualists noted the parallels between the instantaneous communication of messages over long distances through the physical telegraph and what many called the "spiritual telegraph," or the ability of spirit mediums to communicate messages between this world and the afterlife. Some even referred to electricity as "God's principle at work."[8] As one Spiritualist author named Hudson Tuttle put it, when "a sympathetic cord is established" between two spirits, "thoughts flow on it, from mind to mind, as electric fluid on the telegraphic wire."[9]

SPIRITUALISM AND SOCIAL REFORM

One of the most important aspects of nineteenth-century American Spiritualism was its complex and influential role in the seemingly "nonspiritual" domains of society, politics, and gender. Because mediums were believed to channel the voices of otherworldly spirits and great figures from the past, they were endowed with a special kind of authority that often allowed them to speak out on more "this-worldly" topics such as race, slavery, gender, marriage, and social institutions. For example, one of the great radical events of the mid-nineteenth century was the Rutland Free Convention of 1858. Held in central Vermont, the convention was a key site for the discussion of major progressive social issues of the day, such as abolition, marriage reform, and women's rights. Many of the speakers were Spiritualists, including Mary Fenn Davis, who argued that Spiritualism not only went hand in hand with these sorts of progressive social reforms but was perhaps even the "door" that could open the way to a more radical kind of freedom in other aspects of life.[10]

Another influential but today little-known nineteenth-century Spiritualist was a mixed-race medium and author named Paschal Beverly Randolph (1825–75). Born to a white father and a mother of English, French, German, Native American, and Malagasy background, Randolph was raised as a free black in New York City. After being orphaned at the age of seven, he ran away from his foster parents as a teenager to travel the world and explore a wide range of religious movements. Returning to the United States in the 1850s, Randolph earned a reputation as a Spiritual medium, particularly for the more "reform-minded spirits." Beginning in 1853, Randolph claimed to have received a series of messages from the spirit realm, which included communications from a being called the Angel Mother, the Persian prophet Zoroaster, and the French philosopher Blaise Pascal. Like many Spiritualists in the years just before and during the Civil War, Randolph was an outspoken leader in the abolitionist movement and in the debate over the enlistment of black soldiers in the Union army. In October 1864, he attended the National Convention of Colored Men as one of New York City's delegates and there delivered a powerful and often-cited speech, championing the black cause and the racial future of America:

> Here we are met, not to hear each other talk, not to mourn over the terrible shadows
> of the past; but we are here to prove our right to manhood and justice and to
> maintain these rights not by force or mere appeal . . . but by the divine right of
> brains, of will, of true patriotism, of manhood, of womanhood, of all that is great
> and worth striving for in human character. We are hear to ring the bells at the door

of the world; proclaiming to the nations, to the white man in his palace, the slave in his hut, kings on their thrones, and to the whole broad universe, that WE ARE COMING UP.[11]

While figures such as Randolph were by no means the only voices in the abolitionist movement, they did lend the cause a source of otherworldly and transcendent authority that, for many audiences, was more persuasive than a merely "human" voice (particularly that of a mixed-race man in mid-nineteenth-century America).

SPIRITUALISM, MARRIAGE, AND WOMEN'S RIGHTS

In contrast to their contemporary Christian churches, the Spiritualist groups offered powerful new roles to women as mediums, leaders, and even commentators on social and political issues. At a time in nineteenth-century America when the right of women to speak in public was hotly contested, trance mediumship offered a powerful way for women to find an authoritative voice and a public stage to speak out on both religious and social issues. Because Spiritualism was very much a religion of the home and the domestic space, it naturally became tied to the authority of women. In contrast to the male-dominated space of the church, Spiritualism was in many ways a religion of the "women's sphere," where participants gathered around parlor tables rather than before altars and in pews.

Women, moreover, were widely viewed as the most natural and appropriate mediums for spirit communication. Ironically, the very qualities that were believed to make women appear weak, passive, and vulnerable—at least according to nineteenth-century American views of the sexes—also made them the most suitable mediums and the most "receptive" to the movements of the spirit realm: "Women in the nineteenth century are physically weak and declining," as one Spiritualist author put it, but if "the functions depending on force and muscle are weak ... the *nerves* are intensely sensitive. ... Hence sickness, rest, passivity, susceptibility, impressionability, mediumship, communication, revelation!"[12] Once given the voice to speak publicly, female mediums were able to articulate powerful statements about not only an array of religious ideas but also social concerns such as women's rights and abolition.

Of the many famous nineteenth-century female mediums, one of the most popular and controversial was Cora Hatch (born Cora Scott, 1840–1923; figure 4.2). Although her parents were initially Presbyterians from New York State, they moved to the Hopedale community in Massachusetts, a planned community that was dedicated to the ideals of abolitionism, socialism, and nonviolence. There in early 1852, at the age of twelve, Cora first began to enter into trance states and transmit messages that appeared to be from other worlds. Already by the age of fifteen, Cora had become one of the most famous mediums of the era, known for her ability to speak with supernatural eloquence on any subject—theological, metaphysical, or scientific.

FIGURE 4.2 Cora L. V. Hatch.

However, Cora was at least if not more famous for her physical beauty and her innocent, yet mysteriously seductive, adolescent charm. Described in the newspapers of the day as "a fair and slender girl, on whose flowing ringlets seventeen summers sit with light and easy grace," she was clearly an attraction not only because of the philosophical content of her message but also because of the spectacle of a very pretty and colorfully dressed woman entering into unconscious states. A popular photo of the young Hatch from this period highlights her flaxen ringlets flowing over bare shoulders, suggesting an air of both remarkable beauty and childlike innocence. As the popular media portrayed her, "She remains seated with upraised eyes fixed in an expression of intense yet confident invocation. As the questions to be discussed are started, an indescribable change steals over her face. It is a look of rapt entrancement, such as our fancy would depict for the Pythoness or Sybil of classic faith."[13] Even while still in her teenage years, Cora was the subject of heated and intensely divided public opinion. While some regarded her as "the intellectual wonder of the age" who put forth "an eloquent exposition of the principles of Christianity," others dismissed her teachings as "a horrible attack on religion" and "a sacrilegious assault on the Church!"[14] On the one hand, she was described in some publications as an amazing young woman, whose brilliant intellect matched her refined beauty. As one periodical, *The Banner of Light*, put it in 1857,

> Mrs. Cora L. V. Hatch . . . is one of the most remarkable women the world has ever produced. She is seventeen years old, of medium height, delicately formed and possessed of an ethereal beauty, which may not at once attract but enlists the admiration of the beholder by its deep absorbing *spiritualle*. In ordinary circumstances, she

is simple and childlike to a charming degree, but on the stage, when laboring under what she believes to be the spirit agency, her flights of eloquence are bold, lofty, sublime, and beautiful beyond description.

Having never attended school since she was ten years of age, it cannot be supposed that her education is of the most thorough character; nevertheless, she will discourse by the hour upon the most profound sciences, never lacking a word, never making a mistake, and never repeating what she has said before. . . .

Philosophers have heard her with astonishment, and orators have listened to her declamations with boundless enthusiasm. She has carried New Yorkers by storm, and every one of her lectures in that city have been attended by wondering thousands.[15]

Yet on the other hand, many critics—including some of the more prominent advocates of women's rights in the nineteenth century—were shocked and outraged by her appearance. As key figures in the early women's movement such as Susan B. Anthony complained, these sorts of beautiful, scantily clad female mediums were doing more harm than good to the women's cause, simply reinforcing the dominant stereotypes of the weak and sexualized female body: "Nobody who dressed as she did could represent the earnest, solid, hardworking women of the country for whom they were making the demand of equal rights."[16]

Among her other spiritual teachings, Cora claimed that there was a divine feminine in addition to a divine masculine aspect of God—a Divine Mother in addition to and *co-equal with* God the Father. As she put it in her book *Psychosophy,* "All ancient religions symbolized the Infinite in the Unknown yet Perfect Sphere of Omniscience; yet all ancient religions considered the first expression of Deity as twofold. The terms Divine Maternity and the Great Mother Nature are synonymous with the feminine name of the deity."[17] Likewise, Cora taught that every era or dispensation had its own Messiah or world-teacher, that every Messiah had both a male and a female expression, and that Christ himself had a female aspect (which was worshipped as the Virgin Mary in the Catholic Church). In the future, as humanity advanced spiritually, Messiahs would be even more "feminized" and gender balanced: "The feminine expression of the Christs will be more prominent than in the past. In this coming dispensation the expression will be dual, there will be man and woman, the typical Christ, the perfect humanity."[18]

With her famous childlike beauty and her ability to expound on the most complex metaphysical issues such as the female nature of God, Cora Hatch is a particularly striking example of the ambivalent role of gender in nineteenth-century Spiritualism. On the one hand, Cora in many ways embodied the worst stereotypes of femininity in nineteenth-century culture, such as the idea that women are weak, childlike, innocent, passive, and subject to external influences. Yet at the same time Cora was able to turn that seeming "weakness" into a tremendous asset, emerging as one of the most celebrated mediums of her age and writing numerous influential books that helped promote a powerfully "feminine" interpretation of religion.

SPIRITUALIST CRITIQUES OF MARRIAGE

In addition to their powerful challenge to nineteenth-century Protestant religious beliefs, the Spiritualists directly attacked key social institutions supported by those beliefs, including the institution of marriage. For the Spiritualists, marriage as it existed in the nineteenth century was a "body and soul-destroying institution," a system based primarily on economic concerns and male lust, though sanctioned by the Christian churches.[19] In place of the "brutality and dullness of marriage," Spiritualists such as Andrew Jackson Davis advocated a form of love based on "spiritual affinity" and deep complementarity of male and female, which ultimately superseded the bond of legal marriage.

One of the most poignant examples of the Spiritualist view of marriage was Mary Fenn Love herself. When Mary Fenn Love had her life-changing vision of God as an all-loving being and left mainstream Christianity, she also made a decision to leave her husband and what she felt to be an oppressive, loveless marriage. Later in 1855, she found true love with Andrew Jackson Davis and embraced an ideal of marriage based on spiritual affinity rather than economics, social pressure, or family obligation. However, she also struggled for a decade to try to regain custody of her children, whose loss turned out to be the price she paid for her true love and for her freedom. Mary Fenn Davis subsequently became one of the many fierce critics of the institution of marriage as it existed in the nineteenth century, which she and others saw as more akin to legalized prostitution than to a form of love: "The law gives the husband a right to the person of his wife and from this has grown up the system of legal prostitution, to the gratification of lust."[20]

One of the most common criticisms of Spiritualists in nineteenth-century America was that they were advocates of "free love." For opponents of the movement, this charge implied that Spiritualists were sexually immoral, promiscuous, and advocates of indiscriminate relations with multiple partners outside marriage. Spiritualists themselves did not often use the phrase "free love" but instead preferred to speak of the ideal of "spiritual attraction" or harmony between man and wife as the true basis of marriage rather than economic need or carnal desire. Indeed, they were the first proponents of the modern idea of "soul mates," or the belief that two partners should have a deep spiritual bond, more profound than physical desire or social pressures. As the *Plain Guide to Spiritualism* put it, "All marriages and all sexual cohabitings [are] false and infernal unless they are based on spiritual affections and are under the purer influences of celestial harmony."[21]

One of the most remarkable cases of the "free love" debate centered on the mixed-race American Spiritualist Paschal Beverly Randolph. As we saw above, Randolph was one of the most outspoken advocates of abolition during the mid-1800s; but he was also an outspoken advocate of women's rights and female sexuality, including the importance of female orgasm for a healthy marital relationship. However, Randolph's writings on marriage and sexuality soon generated suspicion from the surrounding Victorian American society. In 1872, he was arrested and put on trial for the charge of disseminating dangerous "free love" literature and spreading all manner of sexual indecency among the public. Although he was never proven guilty of any illegal activities, Randolph published his own highly entertaining fictionalized account of the affair, which he dubbed "the Great Free Love Trial." In the account, Randolph makes it clear that he does not advocate free love in the sense of sexual promiscuity, only love that is freely chosen by a spiritually attuned and faithfully committed husband and wife within the bonds of holy matrimony. In the end, Randolph concluded that the prosecuting attorney was unable to prove anything more against him than that he "encouraged women to think of themselves as equals to men."[22]

KEY ISSUES AND DEBATES: FEMALE EMPOWERMENT OR REINFORCEMENT OF GENDER STEREOTYPES?

One of the most complicated questions surrounding nineteenth-century Spiritualism is how exactly to make sense of the role of women in this movement. On the one hand, it does appear that Spiritualism offered women a rare opportunity to speak publicly and to be given authority, respect, and an audible voice during a time in American history when such opportunities were rare. Trance mediumship gave women such as Cora Hatch and Mary Fenn Davis a chance not only to be accepted as religious teachers but also to speak out on key social and political issues such as abolition, women's rights, and marriage.

On the other hand, the way in which women performed spirit mediumship was typically not particularly "empowering"—at least not on the face of it. Women could gain a voice as a medium, but only by becoming unconscious, entering into trance states, and serving as the passive voice of another being. The very principle of mediumship rested on highly stereotyped gender roles, in which women were seen as childlike, innocent, and passive and thus as more open to the movements of the spirits. Many of the most famous mediums such as Hatch dressed in exaggeratedly "feminine" ways, wore scandalously revealing dresses, and appeared publicly in ways that shocked other advocates of women's rights. As we saw above, even key figures in the early women's movement such as Susan B. Anthony were outraged by the flimsy dress, childlike passivity, and sexual display of these female mediums. In this sense, even if Spiritualism helped support the early women's movement, it would be difficult to describe it as feminist in any modern sense of the term.

In her study of nineteenth-century Spiritualism, the American historian Ann Braude has argued for a more complex and nuanced approach to the question. As Braude suggests, mediumship in nineteenth-century Spiritualism was clearly tied to the stereotypical view of women as passive, childlike, and weak. And yet, precisely because they were imagined as being receptive and passive, women were also believed to be more naturally open to the inspirations of supernatural beings. Ironically, this gave them a new kind of voice and authority to speak publicly, at a time in American history when they had few opportunities to do so. Because of their newly found voice as mediums transmitting messages from higher authorities, women were able to speak about an array of contemporary topics, including not only spiritual ideas but also social issues such as abolition and women's rights. Thus, Braude suggests, Spiritualism offered nineteenth-century American women a new space and a public audience, allowing them to speak out with a new kind of authority that simply had not been possible or even imaginable in mainstream American religion:

> Spiritualism helped a crucial generation of American women find their voice. It produced both the first large group of female religious leaders and the first sizable group of American women to speak in public. Whether one views the medium's voice as inspired by an external intelligence or by some remote region in her own mind, the trance state liberated it. . . . More women stepped beyond conventional female roles because of Spiritualism than they would have without it. In mediumship and in its inherent individualism, Spiritualism held up a model of women's unlimited capacity for autonomous action to the men and women of nineteenth-century America.[23]

Thus, while it might not be accurate to describe these female mediums as feminist in any modern sense of the term, they were in many ways key figures in the long struggle for women's rights in modern America, helping to lay the groundwork for later women's movements that would come along in the twentieth century.

THE DECLINE OF SPIRITUALISM AND THE CHALLENGE FROM OTHER MOVEMENTS SUCH AS THEOSOPHY

While Spiritualism was a huge and widespread popular movement throughout the second half of the nineteenth century, its numbers rapidly declined in the twentieth century. While Spiritualist churches still exist throughout the United States, England, and Europe, the movement is nowhere nearly as prominent as it was at its height in the nineteenth century. Part of the reason for this decline was a growing skepticism among the American public, particularly after certain key Spiritualist figures were accused of or confessed to being frauds. Margaret Fox herself confessed in 1888 that she and her sister had secretly made the rapping sounds by cracking their toe and finger joints. She then issued a strong condemnation of Spiritualism as an "absolute falsehood from beginning to end."[24]

However, perhaps a more basic reason for the eventual decline of Spiritualism was probably also one of the main reasons for its early popularity—namely, its radically individualistic and antiauthoritarian nature. Because it placed so much emphasis on the power of the individual to interact with the spirit world, independently of priests or churches, Spiritualism generally lacked the organization, hierarchical authority, and centralization of mainline Christian churches, or even of other new religious movements such as Mormonism. Thus it was less able to adapt to the rapid social and demographic changes of modern America. Despite the powerful alternative it offered to mainstream churches of the day, Spiritualism quickly declined as a major religious presence in the United States during the twentieth century.

At the same time, Spiritualism began to draw criticism from other new religious movements that were emerging as powerful rivals in the teeming marketplace of American

FIGURE 4.3 Madame Blavatsky and Colonel Olcott, 1888. From the Theosophical Society of America Archives.

spirituality. One of the most important alternatives was the Theosophical Society, founded by the enigmatic Russian mystic Helena Petrovna Blavatsky (aka Madame Blavatsky or HPB, 1831–91; figure 4.3), who drew much of her early inspiration from Spiritualism but also later voiced some of the strongest criticisms of the movement. Born to a noble family in what is now the Ukraine in 1831, Blavatsky was married at age seventeen to the vice-governor of Erevan, a much older man. Fleeing the marriage, she traveled the world and visited the Middle East, Europe, the Americas, India, and (possibly) Tibet. In the course of her travels she claimed to have met a mysterious "Master" or Mahatma (the Sanskrit term for a "great souled being") named Morya. Together, Master Morya and his companion Master Koot Hoomi were said to run a school for adepts adjacent to the great Buddhist monastery of Tashi Lhunpo in Tibet.

Blavatsky was a powerful, charismatic, and striking figure, who was memorable as much for her appearance and personality as for her spiritual message. With her eastern European features, her exotic clothing, her foreign accent, and her idiosyncratic mannerisms, she radiated an aura of mystery, concealed knowledge, and hidden power. One of the more colorful early descriptions of Blavatsky in America was provided by Elizabeth Holt, a young school-teacher who stayed in the same tenement house occupied by Blavatsky. As Holt recalled many years after the encounter, Blavatsky was rather outlandish in her dress and personal habits, wearing strange, garish clothing and constantly smoking hand-rolled cigarettes, but she was also a person of undeniable charisma and even "Stalin-esque" power:

> She was like a magnet, powerful enough to draw round her everyone who could possibly come. I saw her day by day, sitting there rolling her cigarettes and smoking incessantly. She had a conspicuous tobacco pouch, the head of some fur-bearing animal, which she wore round the neck. She was certainly an unusual figure. . . . She had a broad face and broad shoulders; her hair was lightish brown and crinkled. . . . Her whole appearance conveyed the idea of power. I read somewhere lately an account of an interview with Stalin; the writer said that when you entered the room you felt as if there was a powerful dynamo working. You felt something like that when you were near H.P.B.[25]

Like Spiritualist mediums such as Cora Hatch, Blavatsky was a powerful female figure who held unusual spiritual authority for a woman in nineteenth-century America. Yet unlike pretty young mediums such as Hatch, Blavatsky's charisma as a spiritual figure derived not from her childlike innocence and beauty but rather from her exotic appearance, her strange accent, her travels throughout the mysterious Orient, and her alleged contact with a secret order of Masters.

Blavatsky returned to the United States in 1873, at the height of the new interest in Spiritualism and psychical research. While investigating Spiritualist phenomena at the Eddy farmhouse in Chittendon, Vermont, Blavatsky met Henry Steel Olcott, a successful lawyer who was also intensely interested in Spiritualism. The two became close friends and founded the Theosophical Society in New York City two years later. Meaning "divine wisdom," Theosophy claimed to embody the ancient spiritual truth that lay at the heart of all the world's religious and philosophical traditions and had been passed down by masters and sages throughout the ages of human civilization. An ambitious synthesis of European esoteric traditions such as Kabbalah, Gnosticism, and occultism with Asian traditions such as Hinduism and Buddhism, Theosophy was one of the first attempts to unite Eastern and Western religions and so became a primary influence for virtually all later New Age spirituality.

Initially, Blavatsky was quite supportive of Spiritualism, which she saw as a useful vehicle to prove the validity of nonmaterial ideas and so awaken humanity from its spiritual lethargy. She too participated in séances and even claimed to have been in contact with a spiritual entity named John King. "In this wondrous outburst of phenomena that the Western world has been seeing since 1848," she wrote, referring to the famous incident of the Fox sisters in New York, "is presented such an opportunity to investigate the hidden mysteries of being as the world has scarcely known before. . . . Theosophy, with its design to search back into historic records for proof, can be regarded as the natural outcome of phenomenalistic Spiritualism or as a touchstone to show the value of its pure gold."[26]

However, Blavatsky soon turned away from Spiritualism, which she increasingly saw as a naive and often fanatical movement. In her view, the so-called "spirits" of the Spiritualist mediums were not the souls of the dead but rather what she called "elementary spirits" or "shells," which were more like the psychic debris of the dead and could at best imitate their former personalities.[27] Rather than communing with mere spirits, Blavatsky claimed to be in contact with a great brotherhood of Masters who represented the ancient wisdom of all religious traditions that had been passed down secretly throughout human history. This brotherhood included not only Masters Morya and Koot Hoomi but also teachers such as the Masters Serapis Bey, Tuitit Bey, and many others.

Inspired by the Masters, Blavatsky, Olcott, and their students set out to create a far more ambitious synthesis in Theosophy, which brought together not only elements of modern Spiritualism but also the much longer tradition of Western esotericism and Eastern traditions such as Hinduism and Buddhism. Blavatsky's first major work, *Isis Unveiled* (1877), begins with a critique of modern Western science—particularly Darwinian evolutionary theory—and then takes a long foray into comparative religion and expounds esoteric

Buddhism as the ancient wisdom within which science and religion can be reunited. Her second major work, *The Secret Doctrine* (1888), is an even more ambitious work that claims to explain both the origin of the universe and the complete history of mankind. Synthesizing Hindu and Buddhist ideas such as karma and reincarnation with elements drawn from Kabbalah, Gnosticism, Hermeticism, and other Western esoteric traditions, Theosophy became widely attractive in a late nineteenth-century global context as Americans were increasingly coming into contact with and trying to make sense of the world's many religious traditions. All of this made Theosophy a serious competitor to Spiritualism in the late nineteenth-century marketplace of alternative religions.

Today, both Theosophy and Spiritualism are relatively small movements in terms of actual numbers, yet each has had a huge and lasting influence on virtually all later forms of New Age and alternative spirituality in the United States. As we will see in chapter 11, Spiritualism's fundamentally optimistic view of the universe and its emphasis on individual empowerment would later become central elements in New Age spirituality during the 1960s and '70s; and its belief in the ability of individual mediums to speak with spiritual entities would later be reworked in New Age practices such as channeling. The prominent role of women in Spiritualist practice would be continued in various New Age and new religious movements, from Wicca and neopaganism down to the work of contemporary female channels such as Jane Roberts, JZ Knight, and many others.

Theosophy, meanwhile, was one of the first movements to articulate a rich synthesis of Eastern and Western traditions that has become more or less a basic feature of New Age spirituality since the 1960s. The term *New Age* itself was first used in the modern sense by the Theosophist Alice Bailey to refer to the transition from the astrological sign of Pisces to the sign of Aquarius—a transition in the heavens that was believed to reflect a larger historical shift from an age of violence, war, and suffering to a new era of spiritual growth and harmony.[28] This belief in the "Aquarian Age" would become a central part of New Age and alternative spirituality throughout the late 1960s and '70s. Likewise, the Theosophical belief in an ancient lineage of Masters or Mahatmas has been a recurring theme throughout most later New Age spirituality and has reappeared in the work of various twentieth- and twenty-first-century channels who have claimed to be in contact with ancient masters, such as Ramtha, Seth, Merlin, and others.

In sum, despite their small numbers today, both Spiritualism and Theosophy have transmitted a profound legacy to contemporary New Age and new religious movements.

QUESTIONS FOR DISCUSSION AND DEBATE

1. How would you compare Spiritualist mediumship with religious phenomena in other traditions such as spirit possession in Afro-Caribbean religions or glossolalia in Christian Pentecostalism? In what ways are they similar or different in terms of spiritual practice, theology, and social function? If you see

similarities between these different phenomena, how would you explain or interpret them?

2. Does the fact that Spiritualist mediums often used their trance states to address social and political issues seem to enhance or undermine their credibility as "religious" figures, in your opinion? In other words, does it seem as though the platform of mediumship was simply being used to give a higher authority to these secular issues? Or would you say that most religious leaders use their spiritual platform as a way to address broader social and religious issues? Give examples.

3. What is your view of the role of women in nineteenth-century Spiritualism? Does Spiritualist mediumship seem to have been empowering for women during this period? Or did it instead reinforce stereotypical views of women as passive, weak, and submissive to external authority? Or was it more complicated than either of these views? Would you say that Spiritualism was feminist in any modern sense of the term? Or perhaps protofeminist? Or was it in some ways an obstacle to the early women's rights movement in the United States?

SUGGESTED CLASSROOM ACTIVITY

Closely examine one example of Spiritualist mediumship, either from this chapter or from a film clip. Then brainstorm as a group and generate as many possible ways as you can think of to interpret and make sense of the phenomenon of mediumship. How might trance states and communication with spirits be interpreted from the perspectives of comparative religions, theology, psychology, sociology, gender studies, neurology? Then debate as a group which of these perspectives seems most persuasive in this particular case and for understanding Spiritualism more broadly.

SUGGESTED FILM

"Spiritualism—The Fox Sisters." *Enigma.* VisionTV, Canada.

SUGGESTIONS FOR FURTHER READING

Blavatsky, Helena Petrovna. *The Key to Theosophy.* London: Theosophical Publishing House, 1968.

Braude, Ann. *Radical Spirits: Spiritualism and Women's Rights in Nineteenth-Century America.* Boston: Beacon Press, 1989.

Cox, Robert S. *Body and Spirit: A Sympathetic History of American Spiritualism.* Charlottesville: University of Virginia Press, 2003.

Davis, Andrew Jackson. *Death and the Afterlife*. Whitefish, MT: Kessinger, 2010.

———. *The Harmonial Philosophy*. Whitefish, MT: Kessinger, 2010.

Deveney, John Patrick. *Paschal Beverly Randolph: A Nineteenth-Century American Spiritualist, Rosicrucian and Sex Magician*. Albany: SUNY Press, 1997.

Goodrick-Clarke, Nicholas, ed. *Helena Blavatsky*. Berkeley, CA: North Atlantic Books, 2004.

Gutierrez, Cathy. *Plato's Ghost: Spiritualism in the American Renaissance*. New York: Oxford University Press, 2009.

Owen, Alex. *The Darkened Room: Women, Power and Spiritualism in Late Victorian England*. Chicago: University of Chicago Press, 2004.

Richmond, Cora J. V. (Scott). *Psychosophy, in Six Parts*. Chicago: Regan Printing House, 1915.

Sears, Hal. *The Sex Radicals: Free Love in High Victorian America*. Lawrence: Regents Press of Kansas, 1977.

Swedenborg, Emanuel. *Heaven and Hell*. New York: Swedenborg Foundation, 1976.

Urban, Hugh B. *Magia Sexualis: Sex, Magic, and Liberation in Modern Western Esotericism*. Berkeley: University of California Press, 2005.

NOTES TO CHAPTER 4

1. Emanuel Swedenborg, *Heaven and Hell* (New York: Swedenborg Foundation, 1976), 123.
2. Andrew Jackson Davis, *The Magic Staff: An Autobiography of Andrew Jackson Davis* (London: Forgotten Books, 2012), 162.
3. Andrew Jackson Davis, *Death and the Afterlife* (Whitefish, MT: Kessinger, 2010), 10.
4. Davis, *Magic Staff*, 446.
5. Davis, *The Harmonial Philosophy* (Whitefish, MT: Kessinger, 2010), 159–79.
6. Ibid., 159.
7. Mary Fenn Love, quoted in Ann Braude, *Radical Spirits: Spiritualism and Women's Rights in Nineteenth-Century America* (Boston: Beacon Press, 1989), 42.
8. Braude, *Radical Spirits*, 5.
9. Quoted in Robert S. Cox, *Body and Spirit: A Sympathetic History of American Spiritualism* (Charlottesville: University of Virginia Press, 2003), 88. See Cathy Gutierrez, *Plato's Ghost: Spiritualism in the American Renaissance* (New York: Oxford University Press, 2009), 50.
10. Quoted in Braude, *Radical Spirits*, 71.
11. H. H. Bell, *Minutes of the Proceedings of the National Conventions* (New York: Arno Press, 1969), 21–22.
12. *Banner of Light*, November 10, 1866, 2.
13. "Miss Cora Hatch, the Eloquent Medium of the Spiritualists," *Frank Leslie's Illustrated Newspaper*, May 9, 1857, 358.
14. Ibid.
15. "A Remarkable Young Lady," *Banner of Light*, October 24, 1857, 5.

16. Ida Husted Harper, *The Life and Work of Susan B. Anthony* (Indianapolis: Hollenbeck Press, 1898), 72.
17. Cora J. V. (Scott) Richmond, *Psychosophy, in Six Parts* (Chicago: Regan Printing House, 1915), 16.
18. Ibid., 100.
19. See Braude, *Radical Spirits*, 117–19.
20. Mary Fenn Davis, quoted in *Banner of Light*, February 21, 1863, 8.
21. Uriah Clark, *A Plain Guide to Spiritualism: A Handbook for Sceptics, Inquirers, Clergymen, Believers, Lecturers, Mediums, Editors . . .* (Boston: William White, 1863), 121.
22. Joscelyn Godwin, *The Theosophical Enlightenment* (Albany: SUNY Press, 1994), 256. See Paschal Beverly Randolph, *P. B. Randolph: The "Learned Pundit" and "Man with Two Souls": His Curious Life, Works and Career: The Great Free-Love Trial* (Boston: Randolph, 1872); and Hugh B. Urban, *Magia Sexualis: Sex, Magic, and Liberation in Modern Western Esotericism* (Berkeley: University of California Press, 2005), 71–76.
23. Braude, *Radical Spirits*, 201.
24. Reuben Riggs Davenport, *The Death-Blow to Spiritualism: Being the True Story of the Fox Sisters* (CreateSpace, 2014), 76.
25. Elizabeth Holt, quoted in John Symonds, *The Lady with the Magic Eyes: Madame Blavatsky, Medium and Magician* (New York: T. Yoseloff, 1959), 31–33.
26. Helena Petrovna Blavatsky, "The Drift of Western Spiritualism," *Theosophist*, October 1879, www.blavatsky.net/blavatsky/arts/DriftOfWesternSpiritualism.htm.
27. Nicholas Goodrick-Clarke, ed., *Helena Blavatsky* (Berkeley, CA: North Atlantic Books, 2004), 24, 43.
28. Alice Bailey, *Discipleship in the New Age* (New York: Lucis, 1944), 74.

FIVE

The Nation of Islam and the Five Percenters

Race, Religion, and Hip-Hop

On March 24, 2005, hip-hop artist RZA (aka Robert Fitzgerald Diggs, b. 1969) appeared on the popular comedy/news show *The Daily Show with Jon Stewart* to promote his new book, *The Wu-Tang Manual*. As Stewart observed in the interview, RZA's book not only highlights key themes in the music of his band, the Wu-Tang Clan, but also contains a complex mixture of religious and philosophical ideas drawn from Buddhism, Christianity, martial arts, and popular cultural forms such as comic books, film, and novels. "It's literally the only book I've seen where Picasso and Walt Whitman are quoted, as well as 'Tricky,'" Stewart joked, referring to the English hip-hop musician and writer. However, one theme that did not come up in the *Daily Show* interview but that *does* appear very prominently in RZA's *Wu-Tang Manual* is the influence of the Nation of Islam (NOI) and the Five-Percent Nation on his work. The book clearly explains it, even breaking down their influence on specific songs. Yet even with this explicit analysis provided by the artists themselves, the influence of religious movements such as the NOI on hip-hop remains largely unknown to most Americans.

Founded in Detroit in 1930, the NOI is a new religious movement that combines elements of traditional Islam with a uniquely American message, focused on racial politics and African American rights. The movement emerged into national prominence in the 1960s as a more radical alternative to the civil rights movement, particularly through the work of the hugely influential member Malcolm X (born Malcolm Little, 1924–65) and current leader Louis Farrakhan (b. 1933). From its origins, this has been a controversial and polarizing movement. While the stated aims of the NOI are to uplift and improve the spiritual, social, and economic conditions of African Americans, critics of the movement have described it as a black supremacist organization rooted in antiwhite and anti-Semitic rhetoric.

Perhaps even more controversial—if far less well known—than the NOI is the offshoot group called the Five-Percent Nation, also known as the Five Percenters or the Nation of Gods and Earths (NGE). Founded in Harlem in 1964, the NGE teaches that the true God is none other than the "Asiatic black man" himself and that the true Earth is the black woman. Meanwhile, only a small fraction of humankind (the 5 percent) are able to see the truth accurately, while the vast majority (the 85 percent) are blind and manipulated and a powerful minority (the 10 percent) use their wealth and influence to deceive the ignorant masses. The NGE is also unique in its use of a complex esoteric system of number and letter symbolism (called the Supreme Mathematics and Supreme Alphabet) to transmit its teachings in a coded way, while making clear distinctions between insiders and outsiders, those who are in the know and those who are not.

However, although the NOI and the NGE are relatively small in numbers of followers, their influence has been remarkably widespread through popular media such as rap and hip-hop music. In addition to all the members of the Wu-Tang Clan, many other prominent hip-hop artists have been involved with the NOI and the NGE, often making extensive use of both explicit and subtly coded references in their music. NOI and NGE imagery has appeared in best-selling records since the 1980s, with hugely successful groups such as Public Enemy, Brand Nubian, Big Daddy Kane, Gang Starr, and myriad others making hip-hop the single most powerful medium for the transmission of these often esoteric ideas to a mass public audience.

Thus the NOI and the NGE raise profound questions for the study of new religions in the United States. The first question—and one that my Muslim students always want to ask—is, Should these groups should be classified as "real" or "genuine" Islam or as something else (such as a heretical form of Islam or a new religion that simply incorporates some references to Islam)? And if we decide that the NOI and the NGE are not "real Islam," what do we do with other alternative forms of Islam such as Sufism or even—in the eyes of conservative Sunni Muslims—forms of Shi'a Islam? Where do we draw the line between legitimate and illegitimate Islam, and, more importantly, who gets to make such a decision? Scholars? Muslim clerics and authorities? And which ones?

A second key question raised by the NOI and the NGE—and also by several other movements discussed in this book—is why music is such a powerful medium for the spread of new and alternative religious ideas. What is it about sound, rhythm, lyrics, and performance that seems to make this such an effective way to disseminate spiritual ideas that tend to go outside the boundaries of mainstream religions? And how is the use of music in these new religions similar to or different from the use of music, hymns, and sacred performance in more conventional religious traditions?

THE MOORISH SCIENCE TEMPLE

The NOI was not the first new religious movement inspired by Islam that made a direct appeal to African Americans. One of the most important predecessors of the NOI was the

Moorish Science Temple, founded in New Jersey in 1913 by a figure calling himself the Prophet Noble Drew Ali. He was born Timothy Drew in North Carolina in 1886, and his biographical background is somewhat unclear: some sources describe him as the son of two slaves who was adopted by the Cherokees, while others describe him as the son of a Moroccan Muslim father and a Cherokee mother. Drew claimed to have traveled the world as a young man, in the course of which he met with a high priest of Egyptian magic. In some versions of Drew's biography, the priest regarded him as the reincarnation of various religious prophets, including Jesus, Buddha, and Muhammad, and subsequently revealed to him a lost section of the Koran (Qur'an).

The text revealed to Drew was first published as *The Holy Koran of the Moorish Science Temple of America* and is popularly known as the "Circle 7 Koran" (because of the red number 7 inside a blue circle that lies on its cover).[1] Much of Drew's *Holy Koran* seems to have been inspired by an earlier book called *The Aquarian Gospel of Jesus Christ* by Levi Dowling, which claimed to reveal portions of Jesus's life not found in the canonical Gospels, including his travels to India and Egypt. According to Drew's *Holy Koran*, Jesus had actually been "Asiatic"—a term that he uses to refer to all dark-skinned peoples, including not just Africans but also Moors (who are identified with the biblical Moabites), Egyptians, Arabs, Japanese, Chinese, Indians, and even South Americans. All of these Asiatic groups are contrasted with the pale-skinned Europeans:

> The key of civilization was and is in the hands of the Asiatic nations. The Moorish, who were ancient Moabites, and the founders of the Holy City of Mecca. The Egyptians, who were the Hamathites, and of a direct descendant of Mizraim. The Arabians, the seed of Hagar, Japanese and Chinese. The Hindoos of India, the descendants of the ancient Canaanites, Hittites, and Moabites of the land of Canaan. The Asiatic nations of North, South, and Central America. The Moorish Americans and Mexicans of North America, Brazilians, Argentinians and Chilians in South America. Columbians, Nicaraguans, and the natives of San Salvador in Central America, etc. All of these are Moslems. The Turks are the true descendants of Hagar, who are the chief protectors of the Islamic Creed of Mecca; beginning from Mohammed the First, the founding of the uniting of Islam, by the command of the great universal God—Allah. (45:2–7)

Jesus, who was dark-skinned and of Asiatic blood himself, was unjustly subjected to pressure from "the pale skin nations of Europe" and was then crucified by the Romans (46:2–3).

Another key influence on both the Moorish Science Temple and the later NOI was the work of the charismatic black nationalist leader Marcus Mosiah Garvey (1887–1940). One of the most influential black writers of the early twentieth century, Garvey taught a message of racial unity, solidarity, and separatism that inspired a number of black new religions that followed in his wake (including Rastafari, as we will see in chapter 6). Born in Jamaica,

Garvey lived in both the United States and England and eventually founded the Universal Negro Improvement Association. Garvey's ambitious goals were to establish a worldwide confraternity of the black race, to develop Africa from a backward colonial enclave into a self-supporting giant, to create Africa as a nation to which blacks could return, to develop black educational institutions, and to uplift black people everywhere. For Garvey, and for many religious movements that came after him, Africa was not simply a geographic region but a powerful symbol of the past greatness and the future glory of black people all over the world. In his words, "When Europe was inhabited by a race of cannibals, a race of savages, naked men, heathens, and pagans, Africa was peopled with a race of cultured black men . . . who, it is said, were like gods."[2]

Garvey's influence on black new religions in the United States would be difficult to over-estimate. In fact, Drew Ali's *Holy Koran* even invokes Marcus Garvey by name, calling him the forerunner and herald of Noble Drew himself: "In these modern days there came a forerunner of Jesus, who was divinely prepared by the great God-Allah, and his name is Marcus Garvey, who did teach and warn the nations of the earth to prepare to meet the coming prophet; who was to bring the true and divine Creed of Islam, and his name is Noble Drew Ali" (48:3).

In addition to its complex reinterpretation of biblical and racial history, much of Drew's message was about fostering pride and self-improvement among African Americans, calling upon his followers to reject labels such as "black," "negro," and "colored" in favor of "Asiatic" and to become more productive and successful citizens. Like the later NOI, the Moorish Science Temple encouraged African Americans to build up their own businesses and communities, thereby becoming successful members of American society without giving up their own unique racial and cultural identity. Particularly after their relocation to Chicago in 1925, Drew and his followers became well respected in the business community and collaborated with several African American politicians in the city.

Drew's Moorish Science Temple incorporates many basic elements of traditional Islam, while reinterpreting and transforming them within a twentieth-century American context. Thus followers are instructed to accept Allah as God, to pray five times a day facing east, and to regard Friday as their holy day. Yet they are also instructed to accept Drew himself (rather than Muhammad) as their Prophet, and services incorporate many hymns from black Christian churches. As is the case with the NOI, many traditional Muslims therefore do not consider the Moorish Science Temple an authentic form of Islam but rather an aberration or adulteration of the religion.

Like several of the leaders of the NOI, Drew Ali died in mysterious circumstances. When a series of murders took place within the movement in 1929, Drew Ali was taken into police custody for questioning and died shortly thereafter. Some speculate that he died as a result of police beatings, while others believe that he was assassinated or "made to disappear" by the FBI. The Moorish Science Temple itself has declined significantly since its peak of membership in the 1930s, though it continues to have a small but influential presence in twenty-first-century America.

WALLACE FARD MUHAMMAD, ELIJAH MUHAMMAD, AND
THE BIRTH OF THE NATION OF ISLAM

During the 1930s, another black Muslim movement emerged in the United States, initially known as the Lost Found Nation of Islam and later simply as the Nation of Islam. Its founder was a mysterious figure named Wallace D. Fard—also known as Wallace Fard Muhammad—who was born sometime between 1877 and 1893. There is much uncertainty as to Fard's exact identity, origins, and even ethnicity, and it remains unclear whether he was Arab, Turkish, or African American. Fard himself claimed to have come from the holy city of Mecca. According to some historians, Fard was involved with the Moorish Science Temple beginning in 1929 and even claimed to be Noble Drew Ali's successor; however, there is also debate over this part of his life, and the NOI today denies that he had any involvement in Ali's movement.[3]

Whatever his background, Fard moved in 1929 to Detroit, a city that, like other booming industrial cities in the North, had become an important refuge for many blacks in the years between the two world wars as they fled lynchings, blatant racism, and poverty in the South. Fard began teaching from door to door, spreading the message that the black man's true religion was Islam, that his original language was Arabic, and that his original identity had been stolen from him by the white man. The message spread quickly, as Fard attracted a growing following among the city's large and mostly poor African American population, drawing as many as eight thousand members in Detroit alone by 1933. In 1932, however, Fard became implicated in a murder committed by one of his followers and, though never charged with the crime, was eventually forced into hiding in 1934.

Before his departure, Fard named one of his close disciples, Elijah Muhammad, as his successor and head of the NOI (figure 5.1). Born Elijah Poole in 1897, the son of a Baptist lay preacher from Georgia, Elijah Muhammad was really the architect of the NOI and its guiding influence for the next forty years until his death in 1975. According to Elijah Muhammad's interpretation, Wallace Fard had been the Mahdi—the prophesied redeemer in Muslim theology, who will, together with Isa (Jesus), combat evil and rule the world before the Day of Judgment. Indeed, Fard was none other than Allah himself appearing in human form and directly intervening in this world.

CONTROVERSIAL BELIEFS OF THE EARLY NATION OF ISLAM:
THE YAKUB STORY AND THE MOTHER PLANE

Under the leadership of Fard and then of Elijah Muhammad, the NOI adopted an aggressive and often controversial attitude toward racial and religious identity. While Noble Drew Ali had taught a message of racial pride and tolerance for non-Muslim religions, Fard was far less compromising in his attitude toward whites and toward Christianity, which he regarded as the religion of the white man and a tool to control the minds of black people. Rather than simple black pride, Fard taught a form of black supremacy and introduced the idea that whites were not just different but in fact "devils."[4]

FIGURE 5.1 Elijah Muhammad, 1964. *New York World-Telegram and Sun* staff photographer.

One of the most controversial aspects of NOI belief is a complex narrative of human racial origins that centers on a mysterious figure called Yakub (also spelled Yacub or Yacob). The story first appeared in Fard Muhammad's teachings called the "Lost-Found Lessons," a kind of catechism presented in question-answer format, and was then developed in more detail by Elijah Muhammad in his 1965 book *Message to the Blackman in America*. As Elijah Muhammad explains, Yakub was an evil scientist who lived 6,600 years ago and was responsible for creating the white race as a race of "devils." According to this complex and rather convoluted narrative, Yakub engaged in a practice of selective breeding or "grafting" while living on the island of Patmos (where St. John was said to have been exiled when he received the vision that culminated in the book of Revelation). Through his experiments in selective breeding, Yakub took the pure black stock of mankind and progressively created a white race by systematically weeding out and destroying all the dark-skinned babies and preserving the light-skinned ones. Finally, he made a race of men with white skin and blue eyes whose evil spread not only among themselves but to others as well:

> In the days of Yakub's grafting of the present white race, a new and unalike race among the black nation for 600 years, his law was—that they should not allow the birth of a black baby in their family, but the white [devils] should mix their blood with the black nation, in order to help destroy black; but, they should not allow the black to mix with their blood. . . .
> The Yakub made devils were really pale white, with really blue eyes; which we think are the ugliest of colors for a human eye. They were called Caucasian—which

means, according to some of the Arab scholars, One whose evil effect is not confined to one's self alone, but affects others.[5]

The Yakub story probably strikes many American readers today as not only strange and implausible but quite offensive. However, if we place it in the broader context of comparative religions and also the context of twentieth-century American politics, it becomes a bit more intelligible. Many religious traditions have complex historical and mythological narratives to explain the origin of a given group of people: we need only think of God's covenant with Abraham, who was promised that all of his offspring would inherit the Promised Land of Israel; or we could look to the Mormon narrative of Lehi sailing from Jerusalem to the Americas to found the lineage of the Nephites, who would receive Jesus's message after his resurrection. Moreover, Elijah Muhammad's Yakub story was published in 1965, at the height of racial tensions and racial violence in the United States, when the KKK and other white racist groups were still very active, and the lynching and murder of blacks was still disturbingly common. Similar kinds of pseudoscientific narratives of racial origins had been disseminated by the Nazis and Fascists in Europe and by the American Nazi Party and other Far Right groups in the United States to try to prove the primacy and superiority of whites. So it is not entirely surprising that Elijah Muhammad would create a counternarrative that claimed the supremacy of blacks. At a time when African Americans were still victims of legal and often violent discrimination, the critique of white people as "devils" seemed accurate to many black Americans. And the idea of blackness as a source of pride rather than shame was directly appealing to many men and women during these decades.

Another aspect of Elijah Muhammad's teachings that strikes many non-NOI Americans as unusual is his interpretation of the vision of the biblical prophet Ezekiel. In the biblical text, Ezekiel's famous vision describes a windstorm of flashing lightning and brilliant light, within which there were four half-human/half-animal creatures, each surrounded by swirling wheels within wheels that spun in all directions. In Elijah Muhammad's interpretation, however, Ezekiel's vision of the whirlwind and the wheels refers to a great "Mother Plane," a huge divine ship in outer space that has the power to destroy the entire planet. As he wrote in his 1965 book *Message to the Blackman,*

> The present wheel-shaped plane known as the Mother of Planes is one half mile by a half mile and is the largest mechanical man-made object in the sky. It is a small human planet made for the purpose of destroying the present world of the enemies of Allah. The cost of such a plane is staggering! The finest brains were used to build it. It is capable of staying in outer space six to twelve months at a time. . . . It carried fifteen hundred bombing planes with the most deadliest explosions. . . . The very same is to be used in the destruction of the world. . . .
> This is only one of the things in store for the white man.[6]

Elijah Muhammad went on to warn that the great "battle in the sky" between Allah and the devils was dangerously close. In his reinterpretation of the Koranic and biblical accounts, Allah would return in the person of Master W. Fard Muhammad as the Mahdi to wage a war to end all wars. Finally, the white devils would be destroyed and Allah's chosen ones, the black people, would be "put on top of civilization."[7]

As the current NOI leader Louis Farrakhan later commented on the Mother Plane in a 1996 speech, this enormous spaceship is what most Americans have described as a UFO. It has been imaginatively depicted in countless science fiction stories and also in various government cover-ups:

> The white man writes in his above top secret memos of the UFOs. He sees them around his military installations like they are spying.
>
> That Mother Wheel is a dreadful-looking thing. White folks are making movies now to make these planes look like fiction, but it is based on something real. The Honorable Elijah Muhammad said that Mother Plane is so powerful that with sound reverberating in the atmosphere, just with a sound, she can crumble buildings.[8]

Again, this mixture of biblical visions with UFOs, racial politics, and apocalyptic speculation probably strikes many Americans today as fairly strange. But when we put it in its historical context of the United States during the mid-1960s, it begins to seem a good bit less bizarre. Similar kinds of UFO mythologies were common from the late 1940s onward, just as the arms and space race with the Soviet Union began to escalate, appearing in a variety of new movements such as Heaven's Gate and Scientology (which we have already discussed), the Raëlians (discussed in chapter 14), the Aetherius Society, and numerous others. We should also keep in mind that Elijah Muhammad published this text in 1965—just three years after the Cuban missile crisis, at the height of Cold War anxiety, when many Americans feared the imminent end of the world. And again, this narrative of racial conflict and the destruction of the white man appeared at the height of the civil rights movement, amid intense and often violent racial conflict. In this sense, Elijah Muhammad's idea of the Mother Plane seems less like a strange aberration than a reflection of the many political, social, racial, and religious changes taking place in 1960s America.

The NOI, however, was not simply a belief system offering a new spiritual and racial identity for black Americans but also a whole new way of life with implications for social relations, business, dress, diet, and daily interactions. Demographically, NOI members in the early years came from a wide range of social and economic backgrounds. Some who were poor and had been involved in either crime (like Malcolm X) or drug abuse found in the NOI a way to transform their lives from poverty and vice into moral stability and financial success. But many came from middle-class backgrounds, including bus drivers, teachers, lawyers, insurance brokers, and blue-collar workers. One of the major thrusts of Elijah

Muhammad's early message and its success was his call for black-owned businesses, black schools, and other black institutions. NOI members established barbershops, bakeries, clothing stores, and restaurants, many of them highly successful and lifting both the pride and the economic status of many black Americans, particularly in urban areas.

Like many new religious movements, the NOI placed special emphasis on disciplining and transforming the physical body, particularly through diet. In the 1950s, Elijah Muhammad began to recommend "permitted" and "prohibited" foods (in a way somewhat similar to the concepts of halal and haram in traditional Islamic law, though with many specific differences). Permitted foods, according to his early recommendations, included small navy beans, string beans, white cabbage, cauliflower, eggplant, okra, carrots, mustard greens, turnips, spinach, white potatoes, whole wheat bread, white fish, trout, bass, and salmon. Red meat was also on Elijah Muhammad's list of permitted foods, though he encouraged members to avoid it as much as possible. Prohibited foods, on the other hand, included lima beans, butter beans, cornbread, carp, catfish, crustaceans, mollusks, rabbit, squirrel, coon, and above all pork. Many of these prohibited foods were forbidden in part because they were associated with "slave culture," which had to be overcome on the path of spiritual and moral development.[9] Elijah Muhammad also outlawed illegal drugs, liquor, and tobacco as harmful to both the body and the soul of his people. This list of permitted and prohibited foods from the 1950s is no longer followed today, but NOI members do still avoid the basic substances of pork, shellfish, alcohol, drugs, and tobacco (a set of prohibitions that, we should note, is very similar to traditional halal dietary laws in mainstream Islam).

FRACTURES AND REFORMS WITHIN THE NATION: MALCOLM X, WALLACE MUHAMMAD, AND LOUIS FARRAKHAN

In the 1960s and '70s several important transformations took place within the NOI. The first was the rise of Malcolm X, who quickly became the most powerful voice in the NOI and one of the most influential figures in American history (figure 5.2). Born Malcolm Little in Omaha, Nebraska, he lost his father at the age of six, and rumors circulated that his father had been murdered by white racists. Seven years later, his mother was placed in a mental hospital, and he grew up in a series of foster homes. At the age of twenty, Little was sent to prison for larceny and breaking and entering, and it was during his prison years that he encountered the NOI. Here he assumed the new name Malcolm X (the X signifying that his old surname had been a white slave master's name and that his true African name could never be known). After his release in 1952, he quickly emerged as one of the leading figures in the movement and its most eloquent public voice.

Serving as the national representative of the Honorable Elijah Muhammad for the next twelve years, Malcolm X spoke throughout the United States and abroad about the status of blacks in America. With his message of black self-determination and separation from whites, Malcolm X offered a powerful alternative to the more moderate civil rights movement of the 1960s. Indeed, he would chastise Martin Luther King Jr. and other leaders of the

FIGURE 5.2 Malcolm X, 1964. *U.S. News and World Report* Magazine Photo Collection, Library of Congress.

movement as self-hating Uncle Tom Negroes who had been duped by the illusion of integration. An inspiring, articulate and engaging speaker, Malcolm X was interviewed by Mike Wallace in 1959 on the CBS show *News Beat* for a television documentary on the NOI called "The Hate That Hate Produced." As we see in this powerful speech delivered in Detroit in November 1963, Malcolm X was critical both of mainstream Christianity and of the civil rights movement itself, which talked about "revolution," but only in weak, nonviolent, and wholly inadequate terms:

> You don't have a turn-the-other-cheek revolution. There's no such thing as a nonviolent revolution. The only kind of revolution that is nonviolent is the Negro revolution. . . . It's the only revolution in which the goal is a desegregated lunch counter, a desegregated theater. . . . That's no revolution. . . .
>
> Revolution is bloody, revolution is hostile, revolution knows no compromise, revolution overturns and destroys everything that gets in its way. . . . Whoever heard of a revolution where they lock arms . . . singing "We Shall Overcome"? You don't do that in a revolution. You don't do any singing, you're too busy

swinging. It's based on land. A revolutionary wants land so he can set up his own nation.[10]

By 1964, however, Malcolm X had grown disillusioned with the NOI and its leader, Elijah Muhammad. He also grew critical of the racism and black supremacy of the movement, finally repudiating its teachings. Eventually, Malcolm X embraced traditional Sunni Islam and made a life-changing pilgrimage to Mecca, which he described as a moment of revelation when he realized that Islam in its true meaning is a religion of racial harmony that solves the race problem. As he recalled in his *Autobiography*,

> America needs to understand Islam because this is the one religion that erases from its society the race problem. Throughout my travels in the Muslim world, I have met, talked to and even eaten with people who in America would have been considered "white"—but the "white" attitude was removed from their minds by the religion of Islam. I have never before seen *sincere* and *true* brotherhood practiced by all colors, together, irrespective of their color. . . .
>
> During the past eleven days here in the Muslim world, I have eaten from the same plate, drunk from the same glass, and slept in the same bed . . . while praying to the *same* God—with fellow Muslims, whose eyes were the bluest of blue, whose hair was the blondest of blond, and whose skin was the whitest of white. And in the *words* and in the *actions* and in the *deeds* of the "white" Muslims, I felt the same sincerity that I felt among the black African Muslims of Nigeria, Sudan, and Ghana.[11]

However, not long after his public rejection of the NOI, Malcolm X received a series of death threats and then was assassinated during a speech in Manhattan on February 21, 1965. Three members of the NOI were arrested and convicted of the murder, though a number of alternative theories continue to circulate that blame the FBI or others for the death of Malcolm X.

A second major split within the Nation occurred after Elijah Muhammad's death in 1975. The chosen successor as supreme minister of the movement was Elijah's fifth son, Wallace Muhammad, who quickly turned things in a much more traditionally Sunni Muslim direction. Renaming the movement the World Community of al-Islam in the West (later the American Society of Muslims), he rejected the extreme black supremacist views of his father and began accepting white members. He also began to use the Arabic term *masjid* for the Nation's mosques and Arabic script for their décor instead of the old slogans that had denounced white America. Taking the name Warith Deen Muhammad (meaning, in Arabic, "the inheritor of the religion of Muhammad"), he also began to build links with traditional Muslim leaders and communities. Finally, in 1985, Warith Deen announced that his followers were no longer to be identified by any separate name at all but were simply Muslims and part of the worldwide body of Sunni Islam.

Mustafaa Islam is the imam at the An-Nur Islamic Center in Springfield, Ohio. He joined the Nation of Islam in the early 1970s and then followed W. D. Muhammad when he led the movement toward a transition to mainstream Islam. In this interview, he discusses the reasons for his interest in Islam and why he chose to follow traditional Islam rather than Farrakhan's new Nation of Islam today.

I was born in Springfield in 1948, a Christian in the Methodist Church. I attended school in Redwood High School here in Springfield. I went away to college to Brown University, graduated, and then came back here to Springfield in 1971. In 1973, I joined the Nation of Islam under the leadership of the Honorable Elijah Muhammad. When he passed away, I transitioned into the community that was led by his son Imam Warith Deen Muhammad, and I have been a Muslim ever since.

When I joined Nation of Islam I was in college, and it was a very tumultuous time in this society. It was the '60s. I graduated high school in 1966, so '66–'70 was my time in college, and a lot of things were going on in this country. The Vietnam War and a lot of riots and different things were happening. So I guess I was searching. I looked at a lot of different organizations. I began to read about the Nation of Islam. A little after I graduated, I joined in 1973, and it seemed like it was the best thing out there. There were some things I wasn't completely comfortable with, but out of the things that were available, it seemed that it was the best way to go. I wasn't really comfortable with the idea that the white man is the devil, because I'd had enough life experience to know that there were good and bad people in all races. My mother basically taught me that. But still I can see from the history of our country and slavery that there were reasons why that statement was made. So I went and joined. When the honorable Elijah Muhammad passed away, his son came into leadership, and I listened to him speak. And as he began to transform the community from the more nationalist and racist teaching to the more universal teaching, that appealed to me more. It was pretty easy for me to transition, because as I said I was getting uncomfortable with the state of things.

The biggest difference between the Nation of Islam and traditional Islam is the concept of God. The Nation of Islam portrayed Farad Muhammad as God in person. But still there were things that the Honorable Elijah Muhammad said in prayer, and one of the main prayers is "Surely I have turned my self to thee, being upright to him who originated the heavens and the earth." Now we know that Farad didn't originate heaven and earth, because he was a man. And this is a prayer that comes from the Koran. But this is a prayer that was said in the Nation of Islam. . . . So that is leaning toward or actually pointing to the true Islamic faith. So there were things existing that

(continued)

would give hints that the community was going to move that way. I think what Farad brought was intended to only be temporary and not permanent and would eventually give birth to true Islam.

At one point, Minister Farrakhan and Imam Muhammad came together at a Savior's Day Observance of the Nation of Islam. They had always been friends. They didn't always agree on everything. Imam Muhammad transformed the community to universal Islam, so there were obviously things that the Nation of Islam wasn't following. I think Minister Farrakhan knew that he would eventually have to transform the community to universal Islam. I believe they are trying to move in that direction, and I think that's good.

Initially, when I began to pursue Islam, my family initially had raised eyebrows. But after they saw that I was sincere, I was serious, and again up close and personal, they could see that it was not a bad thing, it was a good thing: "I want to tell you that I am now the person that you wanted me to be."

Very simply put, al-Islam respects your intelligence. It respects rational thinking. It presents the religion very simply, that there is a Creator, a God, all-powerful, and then there is his creation. There is nothing or no one as intermediary or go-between. You have a direct connection with your Creator. You are responsible and held accountable for your actions. There is no one like a savior to take responsibility for you or take responsibility off of you. It is for all people. Its biggest ritual is the Hajj. I made Hajj in 2003. Going there and experiencing it personally, I could see that there were people from all different countries, all different continents. It just gave the feel of an international body of the human family. Those would be some points I could say that would be attractive to converts.

The Islamic Center where I'm the imam is for the most part American-born converts who are of African American descent. There is another *masjid* here that is a large community and is mostly Pakistani, Indian, and Arab; most of them are immigrants, though many are citizens now. A lot of them are doctors or engineers. We interact some, mostly around Ramadan and Eid.

The imam is responsible for teaching the religion and officiating weddings and funerals, but basically teaching. It doesn't have to be a do-all and be-all. There are other roles that other people can take on, and the imam may advise the proper religious slant they may take, but the imam is basically to teach the religion and lead the prayers. . . . Every ritual in Islam can be performed by a common person. A common person can do the prayers—they can even do the funerals and the weddings.

To be an imam, the first qualification is to have a good moral character. He should be the most knowledgeable in the religion in his group. He doesn't necessarily have to go to seminary schools. You have to be able to speak on teaching the religion, you have to be able to lead the prayers, perform the funerals and weddings. There is no formal school you have to go do, and usually the community is the one that says they want someone to be the imam. They can do what you might call a ratification. No one is supposed to seek to be the imam. If they do, then that's not the person you choose. You choose the person who's not seeking after it. It's not a political thing.

We didn't experience anything after 9/11. We didn't have much of a problem. One of the reasons for that is that we have made an effort to have good relations with the people, with our neighborhood, and with the city government. We had Imam W. D. Muhammad (who passed away in 2008) in Springfield on three occasions at least. He came to Memorial Hall early on in his leadership; he came to Wittenberg University right after 9/11; and then he came back again in 2008 early in the year. So we've had a good relationship, and I think the people in the city have seen that their up close and personal relationships with Muslims have shown them that we're not a violent community. We're not a people who are blowing up each other, blowing up other people's places of worship. That's not what we're about, and that's not what Islam is about.

Not all of the movement's followers were happy with the shift that took place under Wallace Muhammad's leadership, however. In 1981, another of Elijah Muhammad's close disciples, Louis Farrakhan, announced the revival of the NOI and the continuation of its original teachings. Farrakhan's new NOI is essentially a Black Power movement dedicated to the old separatist ideal of establishing an independent nation. However, the movement has also been actively engaged in efforts to improve urban neighborhoods, by cleaning up drug-infested areas and addressing the economic and social problems of inner-city blacks. In fact, Farrakhan was the key figure in the growth of the NOI during the 1980s and '90s, particularly among young black men and college students, helping it to expand to over 130 temples and an estimated fifty thousand members throughout the world. Perhaps the height of Farrakhan's national prominence occurred in 1995, when he helped organize the Million Man March in Washington, D.C., a massive event intended to promote African American unity and family values.

Since the 1990s, Farrakhan has made some efforts to "Islamicize" the NOI and bring it somewhat more into alignment with traditional Islam (though never going as far as Warith Deen Muhammad by merging it completely into Sunni Islam). Thus attendance at Friday prayers is strongly encouraged, as are strict codes in diet and dress. However, most NOI members still do not typically pray five times a day, and their racial attitudes are still widely at variance with the traditional Muslim view that all human beings are equal in the eyes of God.

Like Elijah Muhammad, Farrakhan has been a controversial figure, particularly because of various racial comments he has made over the years. During the 1980s, Farrakhan generated outrage for allegedly referring to Judaism as a "gutter religion" or "dirty religion," and in response Nathan Perlmutter, the chair of the Anti-Defamation League, referred to Farrakhan as the "Black Hitler."[12]

THE FIVE-PERCENT NATION OF GODS AND EARTHS

In Harlem in 1963, a former member of the NOI named Clarence 13X formed a new black Muslim movement called the Nation of Gods and Earths (NGE) or Five Percenters. Born Clarence Ernest Smith (1928–69) in Virginia, Clarence 13X had been a student of Malcolm X in New York. However, Clarence left the NOI after a theological disagreement, rejecting the idea that W. Fard Muhammad was God or Allah. Instead, Clarence 13X ("later known as Allah the Father") taught that every black man is God and that every black woman is an embodiment of Earth, the planet on which God produces life (hence the name "Nation of Gods and Earths"). Thus Clarence 13X rejected the idea of God as a mystical being and instead identified God as the Asiatic Black Man, whose proper name is "Allah" (an acronym standing for arm, leg, leg, arm, head—in other words, the human body).

Members of the NGE are also known as Five Percenters because of their belief that only 5 percent of humankind really know the truth about the world and are able to enlighten the rest; 10 percent of humankind are the powerful elites who know the truth but choose to keep it hidden in order to deceive and manipulate the remaining 85 percent of humankind who live in ignorance and oppression. The term *Five Percenter* itself is derived from Clarence 13X's interpretation of the key NOI text the "Lost-Found Lessons." A kind of NOI catechism, the Lost-Found Lessons were instructions given by Fard to Elijah Muhammad in a question-answer format, which first laid out the basic idea of the 5 percent:

14. Who is the 85%? ANS. The uncivilized people; poison animal eaters; slaves from mental death and power; people who do not know the Living God. . . .

15. Who is the 10%? ANS. The rich slave-makers of the poor, who teach the poor lies—to believe that the Almighty, True, and Living God is a spook and cannot be seen by the physical eye. Otherwise known as bloodsuckers of the poor.

16. Who is the 5%? ANS. They are the poor righteous teachers who do not believe in the teachings of the 10% and are all-wise and who know who the Living God is; and Teach that the Living God is the Son of man, the supreme Being, the (Black man) Asia.[13]

The NGE makes elaborate use of esoteric symbolism to transmit its ideas, mostly orally by word of mouth and through music. In many ways, its use of symbolism is reminiscent of that of secret societies and initiatic orders such as the Freemasons or the Sufis, using esoteric knowledge both to transmit spiritual ideas in subtle ways and to distinguish between those inside and those outside the community. Thus the key symbol of the NGE is the Five Percent flag, which consists of the number 7 (representing G for God, the seventh letter of the alphabet); a sun (symbolizing truth, knowledge, and the black man); a crescent moon (symbolizing wisdom and the black woman); and a five-pointed star (symbolizing knowledge and children). This use of esoteric symbolism is further developed in "the Supreme Mathematics" and "the Supreme Alphabet," which give deeper philosophical meanings to each number and each letter of the alphabet. According to the Supreme Mathematics, the number 1 stands for knowledge and the male; the number 2 stands for wisdom and the female; the number 7 stands for God and perfection and also refers to the seven colors of the rainbow and to the seven notes of the musical scale; and so on. According to the Supreme Alphabet, the letter A stands for Allah, the rightful name of man (as arm, leg, leg, arm, head). B stands for be or born, to bring into existence either physically or mentally; C means to "see" or understand; I stands for Islam, which is an acronym for "I-Self-Lord-And-Master"; and so on. In addition to the Supreme Mathematics and Supreme Alphabet, NGE members must memorize 120 questions and answers, beginning with the first question, "Who is the original man?" (to which the correct answer is "the Asiatic Black Man").[14] One can be tested by other members at any time.

The NGE spread rapidly among young black men in Harlem and Brooklyn (called "Mecca" and "Medina" in NGE's modified Islamic language), and later to other areas such as New Jersey ("New Jerusalem"), Detroit ("D-Mecca"), and Chicago ("C-Mecca"). From its origins, the reputation of the NGE has been mixed and ambivalent; while their admirers regard them as a positive force that has helped rebuild black identity and community in urban areas, some critics regard them as essentially a gang and a dangerous, often criminal presence in American cities.

THE NATION OF ISLAM, FIVE PERCENTERS, AND HIP-HOP

While both the NOI and the Five Percenters remain fairly small movements in terms of numbers, they have had a tremendous cultural influence, above all through music. Since the early 1990s, NOI and Five-Percent themes have spread widely through hip-hop, inspiring a huge number of groups with powerful socially conscious and politically charged themes drawn from Malcolm X, Louis Farrakhan, and Clarence 13X. Prominent artists who either belong to the NOI or are sympathetic to Farrakhan's movement have included Ice Cube, Public Enemy, Kam, Professor Griff, and Paris. For example in the track "Party for Your Right to Fight" from their 1998 album *It Takes a Nation of Millions,* the hugely influential band Public Enemy lays out a fairly explicit account of NOI philosophy, including a direct invocation of Elijah Muhammad:

> It was your so-called government
> That made this occur
> like the grafted devils they were. . . .
> Word from the honorable Elijah Muhammad
> Know who you are to be black
> To those that disagree it causes static

For the original Asiatic Black Man
Cream of the earth
And was here first
And some devils prevent this from being known.[15]

However, perhaps even more hip-hop artists have been members of or sympathetic to the Five Percenters, including all members of the Wu-Tang Clan, Big Daddy Kane, Busta Rhymes, Guru of the group Gang Starr, Mobb Deep, and many others. One of the more striking examples of this mix of hip-hop and Five-Percent imagery is the group Brand Nubian, which is well known for its politically charged songs and its black Muslim inspiration. Their 1993 song "Allah U Akbar" (God is great) even begins with the traditional Islamic call to prayer, which is overlaid by a powerful hip-hop drumbeat and then fairly explicit lyrics. This is a remarkable juxtaposition of sounds: for most orthodox Muslims, it is absolutely forbidden (haram) to set the call to prayer to music and drums, since the call is only to be "recited" and since music and recitation are two distinct categories that should remain separate. The Brand Nubian track, on the other hand, blends the call to prayer smoothly with more mainstream hip-hop language and imagery:

Wake up in the morning at the hour of God and make beats
Later hit the street for some forty-fifth sweets
So y'all been told, black youth essential
God damn right, l-o-r-d j-a-m-a-r
Says peace and Allah u Akbar
Back like a motherfucker to crack
Brand Nubian tracks are filled with black facts.[16]

Some of the most complex and interesting uses of NOI and Five Percenter themes in hip-hop are found in the work of the Wu-Tang Clan. RZA, the key member of the Wu-Tang Clan, actually explains the role of NOI, Five Percenter, and other religious themes in the band's material in his popular book *The Wu-Tang Manual*. Here RZA recalls how he was first taught by fellow Clan member GZA, who had him memorize the Five Percenters' 120 questions and answers, beginning with "Who is the original man?" By the time he was twelve in 1982, RZA had memorized all 120.[17] In his *Wu-Tang Manual*, RZA walks the reader through the basics of NOI and Five Percenter philosophy, including the Supreme Mathematics and the Supreme Alphabet, and provides detailed commentary on Wu-Tang Clan lyrics and specific references to religious themes. However, as the text makes clear, the Wu-Tang Clan combines this NOI and Five Percenter imagery with spiritual, philosophical, and political references to everything from Taoism to Christianity to the martial arts.

Wu-Tang Clan songs also often take NOI or Five Percenter themes and give them a significantly new interpretation. For example, the 1997 song "Wu Revolution" from the number one album *Wu-Tang Forever* contains a fairly explicit account of Five Percenter philosophy, including references to the Asiatic Black Man and the battle between God and the devil; however, it also reworks these themes in interesting new ways—for example, by identifying the "devil" not as the white man (in the NOI sense) but rather as the "mental devil" of drugs, guns, and alcohol that are destroying minds and ruining lives. Heaven and hell are thus not literal places in some afterworld but the lives we create for ourselves here and now on earth:

It's time to rise, and take our place
So we can inherit the universe
The planet earth belongs to God
Every square inch of it. . . .
We are the original man, the Asiatic black man
The maker, the author, the cream of the planet earth
Father of civilization and daughter of the universe. . . .
Arise you gods, 'cause the time for the revolutional war
That's the mental war
That's the battle between God and devil
Take the devil off your plane
Take him off your mental mentality
Take him off your brain
Leave all the cigarettes and guns
The alcohol and everything
That's the mental devil that exists within your body
That's destroying and decaying your mind
Don't look toward the sky
Cause there's no heaven above
Don't look down beneath your feet
There's no hell below
But heaven and hell exist within
Heaven is what you make it and
Hell is what you're going through.

Meanwhile, in the background, a second voice sings, "The revolution will be televised" and "Malcolm X, Malcolm X!" The song concludes with a fairly straightforward presentation of Five Percenter ideas, combined with a creative reading of American history and the slave trade. Here the 85 percent refers to the majority of humankind who are "mentally enslaved," while the 10 are the slave masters who deceive and exploit them. Finally, the 5 are the "righteous teachers" who will awaken, enlighten, and uplift those who are enslaved:

It was a hundred percent of us
That came on the slave ships
Eighty-five percent of us was uncivilized.

. . .

They're slaves of the mental powers
They don't know who the true and living God is
And their origins in the world.

. . .

And now you got the 10 percent who are rich slave makers of the poor
Who teach the poor the lies that make the people believe
That the all mighty true and living God is a spook in the sky
And you can't see him with the physical eyes
They're also known as bloodsuckers of the poor
And then you got the 5 percent.
Who are the poor righteous teachers
Who do not believe in the teachings of the 10 percent
Who is all wise and know who the true and living god is
And teach that the true and living god is the supreme being black man from Asia.[18]

This use of explicit Five Percenter imagery has continued well into the twenty-first century. Thus in 2006 Lord Jamar, a founding member of Brand Nubian, released an entire two-disk recording entitled simply *The Five Percent Album,* whose cover features the NGE flag, in dazzling black, gold, and orange. As we see in his track "I.S.L.A.M.," Lord Jamar combines clear references to NGE philosophy with references to jihad and a vaguely Eastern-sounding sitar melody laid over a hip-hop beat:

I be the Arm Leg Leg Arm Head
Here to drop bombs on the mentally dead
Islam'll keep you properly fed
And to the four devils, I'll be choppin' yo head
"Well how you be God?"
I be all wise and civilized
Deliver truth while the 10 percent deliver lies
His devilishment has been solidified
I be the Five Percent, epitomized. . . .
All praise due to the Most High
I blaze you with my four-five
This is Jihad music, see the God do it
Allah U Akbar, Lord Jamar's the truest.[19]

In addition to these explicit references, however, Five Percenter ideas would eventually work their way more subtly and implicitly throughout hip-hop culture, language, and lyrics—often in ways that most casual listeners would not notice. For example, even the "G" in the common phrase "What up, G?" originally referred not to "gangsta" but to God in the Five

Percenter sense of the term. Similarly, the common affirmation "Word" comes from Five Percenter teachings, and the phrase "dropping science" originally referred to sharing knowledge of Five Percenter ideas such as the Supreme Alphabet and the Supreme Mathematics. NOI and NGE themes are also often woven subtly into album covers, packaging, and artwork, often in ways that are quite esoteric. For example, Gravediggaz's 1997 recording *The Pick, the Sickle and the Shovel* is modeled on a tenth-century Persian bowl, around the periphery of which runs Arabic calligraphy that reads: "He who believes in God's mercy is generous. . . ."

The fact that many of these references are not immediately recognizable to non-Five Percenters or to those who don't know much about hip-hop is probably intentional. Among other things, the subtle use of Five Percenter terminology is part of a complex code language that helps distinguish between insiders and outsiders, between "those who know" and those who do not, between the true 5 percent who have grasped the truth and the 85 percent who need to be progressively awakened by real knowledge.

KEY QUESTIONS AND DEBATES: IS THE NATION OF ISLAM "REAL" ISLAM?

One of the most common debates surrounding the Nation of Islam is the basic question: Is this "real" Islam? Or is it a sort of pseudo-Islam that simply borrows elements of the faith in order to further a race-based and largely American political agenda? Not long after its emergence, the NOI was condemned as either fake or heretical Islam by most mainstream Muslim groups. Thus in 1972 the Islamic Party of North America published an article accusing NOI members of heresy, stating that they were "not Muslim according to the Qur'an and Sunnah [tradition of the Prophet Muhammad]" and instead labeling them a "polytheistic racial cult" that did not follow the five pillars of Islamic practice.[20] The most common reasons that more orthodox critics consider the NOI to be non-Islamic are: (1) According to the first pillar of Islam, only Allah can be called divine, while the NOI claims that Fard was a divine being. This is considered an act of *shirk* or association with God, the greatest sin one can commit. (2) Most Muslims believe that Muhammad was the last prophet and final messenger of Allah, so the NOI's claim that Elijah Muhammad was a prophet of Fard is likewise regarded as heretical. (3) Finally, most Muslims see all human beings as equal in the eyes of God, so the NOI's racial views and depiction of whites as "devils" are also heretical.

Other sympathetic scholars, however, have argued for a more complex historical view of the NOI and of Islam as a whole. As Edward Curtis has argued, Islam itself is not a simple, homogeneous, or static tradition; rather—like every religion—it is extremely diverse, heterogeneous, and quite variable over time. From its origins and as it spread throughout the Arab world, Africa, South Asia, Southeast Asia, and then the entire world, Islam had to continuously adapt to new social, cultural, and historical contexts, assuming a wide variety of different forms that varied widely from sub-Saharan Africa to India, from eastern Europe to Indonesia. In addition to the major divisions of Sunni and Shi'a, Islam gave birth to a wide array of small, marginal, and seemingly "heterodox" forms of Islam beyond the standard Sunni-

Shi'a divide. These include many forms of Islamic mysticism or Sufism—some of which were persecuted and regarded as heretical by more conservative Muslims—and small sects such as the Druzes and the Alawites.

Throughout the broader Muslim world, as Islam spread to new cultures and new communities it often blended in complex ways with local traditions. For example, when Islam spread to Pakistan, it gave birth to a whole new tradition of mystical devotional song called Qawali, even though mainstream Islam typically prohibits this sort of music. Similarly, when Islam spread to northeast India and Bangladesh, it gave birth to a whole "Islamic syncretistic tradition" that fused elements of Sufi mysticism with Hindu yoga, meditation, and Tantra. In this sense, the NOI should be regarded, not as "fake Islam" or mere heresy, but rather as one of many unique appropriations of Islam in a new cultural context—what some scholars call the complex process of "Islamicization" in a new historical period.[21]

A second related question surrounding the NOI and the Five Percenters is the role of popular music in the dissemination of these movements. Historically, the role of music in traditional Islam has been widely disputed by Muslim scholars and jurists; many Muslim jurists have argued that music is forbidden by both the Koran and the *hadith* (the authoritative sayings of the Prophet), while others have argued that music is permissible under certain conditions, and only if it does not encourage sinful behavior. In any case, setting the call to prayer to music is generally forbidden throughout most of the Muslim world. Yet music—including music accompanying the call to prayer—has been a huge part of the spread of the NOI and the Five-Percent Nation in the United States since the 1980s. Again, this raises the question of whether this represents an "adulteration" of Islam or simply another adaptation to a new cultural and historical context—much like Qawali Sufi music in contemporary Pakistan. Moreover, conservative Muslims would probably argue that hip-hop lyrics encourage a great many acts that would be considered forbidden or haram by traditional Islamic law (consumption of intoxicants, illicit sexual activity, violence, and so on). Can this side of hip-hop be reconciled with traditional Muslim beliefs, or is this finally pushing outside the limits of what can legitimately be called "Islam"?

QUESTIONS FOR DISCUSSION AND DEBATE

1. As we saw in this chapter, many non-NOI Muslims who come from more traditional Sunni or Shi'a backgrounds do not accept the NOI as "real" Islam but instead regard it as an aberration or a heresy. But can we draw a line between those who are "really" members of a religion and those who are not? For example, couldn't we ask the same question about whether Mormons are really Christians, or whether Hare Krishnas are really Hindus? Who gets to decide questions like this? Scholars? Religious leaders? And does it really matter whether we call the NOI "real Islam" or not? What is at stake?

2. How would you compare the role of race in the NOI with the role of race in the Native American Church? How has the history of racism in America played out in the emergence of these two groups, and how have they used racial language and/or requirements to respond to and survive within the dominant white society? Does the fact that race is so central to the NOI make this movement seem less "legitimately religious" to you? Or is that simply a facet like any other of this complex new religious movement?

3. Elijah Muhammad's narrative of the evil scientist Yakub, who created the white race through selective breeding, probably seems strange to many non-NOI readers today. But how would you compare this narrative to other religious narratives about the origin of human beings and the cause of human misfortune? Why might it seem stranger to many Americans than other such religious narratives?

4. Even if it seems odd to many readers in the twenty-first century, why would the Yakub narrative have been compelling for many black Americans in the 1960s?

5. Why has there been such a close fit between NOI and Five Percenter ideas and hip-hop music? What is there about these religious teachings that would be particularly attractive to hip-hop artists and audiences? And in turn, why has hip-hop been such an effective medium for transmitting these ideas, rather than other musical genres?

SUGGESTED CLASSROOM ACTIVITY

Critically examine the representation of the NOI in popular films such as Spike Lee's *Malcolm X* (1992) and Michael Mann's *Ali* (2001). How are these films each portraying the NOI for the screen, positively and negatively, and why? Who do you think their intended audiences were? And was their representation of the NOI more or less respectful than the representation of other new religious movements discussed so far, such as Mormonism? Why? (And why don't we see satires of the NOI the way we do of LDS?)

SUGGESTED FILM

"Malcolm X: Make It Plain." *The American Experience,* PBS Video, 1994.

SUGGESTIONS FOR FURTHER READING

Ali, Noble Drew. *The Holy Koran of the Moorish Science Temple of America.* Hunlock Creek, PA: E World, n.d. [1927].

Curtis, Edward E. *Black Muslim Religion in the Nation of Islam, 1960–1975*. Chapel Hill: University of North Carolina Press, 2006.

Essien-Udom, E. U. *Black Nationalism: The Search for an Identity*. Chicago: University of Chicago Press, 1995.

Farrakhan, Louis. "The Divine Destruction of America: Can She Avert It?" *Final Call*, 2013. www.finalcall.com/artman/publish/Minister_Louis_Farrakhan_9/article_7595.shtml.

Malcolm X. *The Autobiography of Malcolm X: As Told to Alex Haley*. New York: Ballantine Books, 1987.

Miller, Monica. *Religion and Hip-Hop*. New York: Routledge, 2013.

Miyakawa, Felicia. *Five Percenter Rap: God Hop's Music, Message and Black Muslim Mission*. Bloomington: Indiana University Press, 2005.

Muhammad, Elijah. *How to Eat to Live: Book No. 2*. Newport News, VA: National Newport News and Commentator, 1972.

———. *Message to the Blackman in America*. Chicago: Hammad Mosque of Islam No. 2, 1965.

Muhammad, Fard. *The Supreme Wisdom Lessons by Master Fard Muhammad: To His Servant, the Honorable Elijah Muhammad for the Lost-Found Nation of Islam in North America*. CreateSpace, 2009.

RZA. *The Wu-Tang Manual*. New York: Penguin, 2005.

Smith, Jane I. *Islam in America*. New York: Columbia University Press, 1999.

Turner, Richard Brent. *Islam in the African-American Experience*. Bloomington: University of Indiana Press, 2003.

NOTES TO CHAPTER 5

1. Noble Drew Ali, *The Holy Koran of the Moorish Science Temple of America* (Hunlock Creek, PA: E World, n.d. [1927]). Citations to this work are given parenthetically in the text by chapter and verse.
2. Marcus Garvey, *Philosophy and Opinions* (London: Frank Cass, 1967), 57.
3. For his possible connections with the Moorish Science Temple, see E. U. Essien-Udom, *Black Nationalism: The Search for an Identity* (Chicago: University of Chicago Press, 1995), 35; Richard Brent Turner, *Islam in the African-American Experience* (Bloomington: University of Indiana Press, 2003), 92.
4. Master Fard Muhammad, *The Supreme Wisdom Lessons by Master Fard Muhammad: To His Servant, the Honorable Elijah Muhammad for the Lost-Found Nation of Islam in North America* (CreateSpace, 2009), 16.
5. Elijah Muhammad, *Message to the Blackman in America* (Chicago: Hammad Mosque of Islam No. 2, 1965), 155, 116.
6. Ibid., 291.
7. Ibid., 294.

8. Louis Farrakhan, "The Divine Destruction of America: Can She Avert It?" excerpts from a June 9, 1996, speech, *Final Call*, 2013, www.finalcall.com/artman/publish/Minister_Louis_Farrakhan_9/article_7595.shtml.

9. Edward E. Curtis, *Black Muslim Religion in the Nation of Islam, 1960–1975* (Chapel Hill: University of North Carolina Press, 2006), 98. See Elijah Muhammad, *How to Eat to Live: Book No. 2* (Newport News, VA: National Newport News and Commentator, 1972).

10. George Breitman, ed., *Malcolm X Speaks: Selected Speeches and Statements* (New York: Grove Press, 1994), 9.

11. Malcolm X, *The Autobiography of Malcolm X: As Told to Alex Haley* (New York: Ballantine Books, 1987), 347.

12. "Minister Farrakhan Rebuts Fraudulent 'Judaism Is a Gutter Religion' Canard," NOI.org, 2013. www.noi.org/judaism-religion/.

13. Fard, *Supreme Wisdom*, 26–27.

14. Clarence 13X, *Supreme Lessons of the Gods and Earths: A Guide for Five Percenters* (African American Bookstore Publications, 1993).

15. Public Enemy, "Party for Your Right to Fight," from *It Takes a Nation of Millions* (Def Jam, 1988).

16. Brand Nubian, "Allah U Akbar," from *In God We Trust* (Elektra Entertainment, 1992).

17. RZA, *Wu-Tang Manual*, 43.

18. Wu-Tang Clan, "Wu-Revolution," from *Wu-Tang Forever* (Loud Records, 1997). See also Lakim Shabazz, "The Lost Tribe of Shabazz," from *The Lost Tribe of Shabazz* (Tuff City Records, 1999): "Ten percent of us can help but don't feel a need / They love greed, and this really bothers me / Eighty-five percent of us are totally ignorant / Walking around with the nigger mentality / Five percent of us are ready to die for the cause / Of course, the source is Elijah / Knowledge of self is what you need to stop the war / If you don't get it, I'm held responsible / Rhymes I make are designed to reach the youth / I gotta teach, that's why I speak the truth."

19. Lord Jamar, "I.S.L.A.M.," from *The Five Percent Album* (Babygrande, 2006).

20. Curtis, *Black Muslim Religion*, 5.

21. Ibid., 13–14.

SIX

Rastafari

Messianism, Music, and Ganja

On November 2, 1930, Emperor Haile Selassie I was crowned "King of Kings, Conquering Lion of the Tribe of Judah," in Addis Ababa, Ethiopia (figure 6.1). An event that generated enormous international attention, Haile Selassie's coronation was featured in news media across the world, including two issues of *National Geographic* and two issues of *Time* magazine, which also named him *Time*'s "Person of the Year" in 1935. Born Lij Tafari Makonnen and later known as Ras Tafari Makonnen, he had already generated intense international attention before being crowned emperor, leading Ethiopia into the League of Nations in 1923, and serving as the first Ethiopian leader to travel to Europe.

For many blacks around the world, the coronation was seen as an event of tremendous historical, political, and spiritual significance. In the tiny Caribbean island of Jamaica, the coronation of Haile Selassie and his title as "Lion of Judah" was in fact regarded by some as the sign of the return of Christ and the fulfillment of the book of Revelation. This belief became one of the basic tenets of the Rastafari movement, first established by Leonard Percival Howell and others in the Kingston area in the early 1930s. Combining elements of traditional African religions with Christian messianism, Old Testament law, and even some themes drawn from the many Indian Hindus working on the island under the British Empire, Rastafari emerged as a uniquely hybrid new religious movement. But Howell combined this spiritual message with a powerful ideal of political and racial liberation, criticizing the brutal history of slavery, colonialism, and oppression of poor blacks on the island and looking to Africa as the symbol of both the past and future black homeland. Not surprisingly, the movement became increasingly popular and increasingly controversial in a Jamaica still ruled by the British crown.

Although a little-known religious movement confined primarily to Jamaica up until the mid-1960s, Rastafari suddenly emerged into international attention through the power of

FIGURE 6.1 Emperor Haile Selassie, 1923. G. Eric and Edith Matson Photograph Collection, Library of Congress.

music—above all, through the new genre of reggae and through the work of hugely popular artists such as Bob Marley, Peter Tosh, Burning Spear, and many others. Like other Jamaican musicians in the mid-1960s, Marley was deeply committed to issues of social, political, and racial justice, and he found in the Rastafari faith an inspiring message of spiritual hope and liberation. Growing dreadlocks and formally adopting the religion, Marley began to incorporate Rastafari themes throughout his music, which became known worldwide through hit songs such as "Buffalo Soldier," "Exodus," and many others. While most Americans today associate Rastafari only with dreadlocks and marijuana, the music of Marley and others made the spiritual and political message of the religion available in at least an indirect form to whole new generations of listeners around the world. And in the twenty-first century, a new wave of musicians such as Sizzla Kalonji have taken up Rastafari and reggae, remixing it with a variety of other musical and cultural styles for a new global audience.

With its complex mixture of messianism, popular culture, and social resistance, the Rastafari movement has generated a number of controversies since its very origins, both in Jamaica and in the United States. Like the Native American Church, Rastafari has generated debates over the use of an illegal substance, ganja (marijuana, *Cannabis sativa*), as part of its religious lifestyle. Given the far greater availability and recreational usage of marijuana, this raises even more complicated questions of the law and religious freedom than the peyote controversy did.

A second question raised by the Rastafari movement in the United States is the popularization of Rasta imagery—often in a superficial way—through the dreadlocks, reggae music, and ganja use that permeate American youth culture. Many have questioned whether this sort of casual borrowing of Rasta features has anything legitimately to do with "Rastafari" as a religion, or whether this might be regarded as an offensive misappropriation of the tradition that transforms its revolutionary message into an entertaining commodity.

BACKGROUND: MARCUS GARVEY AND THE BACK TO AFRICA MOVEMENT

Like the Moorish Science Temple and the Nation of Islam in the United States, the early Rastafari movement drew powerful inspiration from the teachings of the Jamaican-born activist Marcus Garvey. As we saw in the previous chapter, Garvey was one of the most important black intellectuals of the early twentieth century, inspiring a variety of new social, political, and spiritual movements. But his influence was particularly profound in his homeland of Jamaica, where he gave voice to generations of blacks who had suffered poverty and racism under British rule. Although slavery had been abolished on the island since 1834, Jamaica remained a colony of the British Empire until 1962, with a large and very poor black population dominated by a small and often racist white minority. Marcus Garvey was one of the first Jamaican intellectuals to really begin to awaken the political consciousness of the people, bearing a message of black racial pride and the vision of Africa as the original past homeland and future nation for black people from all over the world.

Like other black leaders of the early twentieth century, Garvey made specific references to Ethiopia as a symbol of both the past greatness and the future glory of blacks. Because of its place in the Bible, Ethiopia had come for many blacks of the New World to stand for Africa as a whole and for the hope of another world, separate from the slavery, oppression, and racism of the white world. And just as whites have traditionally seen God through white eyes, Garvey suggested that it was now time for blacks to see God with black eyes, as the God of Ethiopia: "We, as Negroes, have found a new ideal. Whilst God has no color, yet it is human to see everything through one's own spectacles, and since the white people have seen God through white spectacles, we have only now started out (late though it be) to see our God through our own spectacles. . . . We Negroes believe in the God of Ethiopia, the everlasting God—God the Son, God the Holy Ghost, the God of all ages. That is the God in whom we believe, but we shall worship him through the spectacles of Ethiopia."[1] Finally, certain prophetic statements were also attributed to Garvey that were later given profound significance by the early Rastafari community. In 1916, Garvey reportedly declared, "Look to Africa for the crowning of a Black King, he shall be the redeemer"—a statement that many Jamaicans took to mean the crowning of Haile Selassie in 1930.[2]

THE FIRST RASTAS: FROM HINDU HOLY MEN TO
CHRISTIAN MESSIANIC MOVEMENT

The founding fathers of the Rastafari movement were a group of young men who began preaching in Jamaica during the early 1930s. Foremost among them were Joseph Nathaniel Hibbert, Henry Archibald Dunkley, and, most importantly, Leonard Percival Howell. Joseph Hibbert had migrated to Jamaica from Costa Rica in 1911 and then traveled to Panama, where he joined an Afrocentric brotherhood called the Mystic Order of Ethiopia. When he returned to Jamaica and heard of the coronation of the new Ethiopian emperor, he began to proclaim the divinity of Ras Tafari. Dunkley, meanwhile, had traveled widely as a sailor for the United Fruit Company and then disembarked in Jamaica in 1930. Like Hibbert, he began to preach the message of Ras Tafari's divinity and to gather followers to the growing movement.

However, the most important figure in the birth of the Rastafari movement and its public face during the early period was Leonard Howell, who was born in Clarendon Parish in Jamaica in 1898. Although born in an Anglican family, he left home as a young man to travel the world, journeying as far as Africa, where he served in the Ashanti War and learned several African languages. He also visited the United States, spending time in New York City in 1923, where he witnessed severe racial discrimination and was exposed to the ideas of Marcus Garvey. Upon returning to Jamaica in 1932, he began to develop the unique spiritual and social vision that would become the early Rastafari movement. Like other Jamaicans influenced by Garvey's work, Howell saw the crowning of the Ethiopian emperor as the sign of the Messiah returned to earth and the dawn of a new age for black people everywhere.

Howell's religious ideas were a complex mixture of several different traditions. One of the most interesting but today least well known of these is the influence of Hinduism, which was present in Jamaica through the many Indian laborers who had been brought over by the British in the mid-nineteenth century as part of the global network of the empire. Up to the mid-twentieth century, there were as many as twenty-five thousand Hindus on the island, though most of them later converted to Christianity. Much of the very early Rastafari movement bears the mark of influence from Hindu holy men called *sadhus* or *sannyasins* (renunciants), who typically wear their hair in long dreadlocks and are also known for their use of *Cannabis sativa*, which was first brought to the New World from India. Indeed, the Rastafari term for cannabis, *ganja*, is itself a Hindi term.

Howell himself would even assume the title of "Gangunguru Maragh," an adaptation of the Sanskrit words *jnana* (knowledge), *guna* (virtue), *guru* (spiritual teacher), and *maharaja* (great king). Like others in black America and the Caribbean, Howell had a certain amount of "Hinduphilia" and later had children by an Indian woman. A great admirer of Gandhi, he had particular respect for the Mahatma's understanding of the power of common people to refuse and resist colonial exploitation through the methods of nonviolent resistance. Moreover, the Hindu belief that God can assume an incarnation or descent (*avatar*) in human form had an especially close resonance with the Rastafari view of Haile Selassie. As Joseph Hibbert, Howell's companion in the early movement, later recalled: "After learning about the Hindu God-incarnates Rama, Krishna, and Buddha [Howell] was convinced that every nation had its own God—Jesus for the whites, Rama, Krishna, Buddha for the Indians, and someone in Africa . . . for the Africans." And according to Hibbert, when Ras Tafari was crowned, Africans realized that "his title, given to him by the whole world, makes him a God, just like Ashoka, Buddha, Rama, Krishna."[3] Although few if any Rastas today are aware of the Hindu influence, it can still be seen in the dreadlocks and ganja smoking that remain central features of the movement to this day.

The early Rastafari movement took shape in Kingston during the early 1930s through the work of Howell, Hibbert, Dunkley, and others. As the movement grew, however, Howell's message took on a more radical and even revolutionary tone, with a more explicitly racial and antigovernmental agenda. His teachings during this phase emphasized the belief that Haile Selassie was the Supreme Being and only ruler of black people; that the black race was superior to the white; and that blacks should separate themselves from white society and return to Africa.

Not surprisingly, given the increasingly radical nature of his ideas in the context of Jamaica under British colonial rule, Howell was arrested and imprisoned for sedition in 1934. While in prison he wrote his first book, *The Promised Key* (under the name G. G. Maragh), in which he identified Emperor Haile Selassie as the Messiah and blacks as God's chosen people. Following his release, he left Kingston to form a commune called Pinnacle up in the hills about twenty miles away. A secretive community, Pinnacle could be reached only on foot, and its entrance was known only to members. Nonetheless, the police found and raided the group in 1941 and then again in 1954, finally destroying the commune and forcing its members to relocate to the slums of Kingston. In turn, Rastafari began to develop an intense hatred for the government establishment in all its forms—which became known as "Babylon"—and especially for the police.

Tensions between the Rastas and the surrounding Jamaican society continued to mount in the late 1950s as the movement became both more numerous and more visible. To help address the situation, Dr. Arthur Lewis, head of the University of the West Indies, asked three of his best scholars to study the doctrines and conditions of the Rastas and then to make a recommendation to the premier. The three scholars produced a remarkably sensitive, nuanced, and sympathetic description of the Rastafari movement, explaining both its socioeconomic conditions and its spiritual aims to the Jamaican public. The report also included a set of recommendations to the government, which included sending a mission (which would include Rastas) to African countries to arrange for the immigration of Jamaicans; advising the Jamaican public to recognize the majority of Rastas as peaceful, hardworking citizens; asking the police to cease persecuting Rastas; building low-rent housing and cooperatives for poor members to live in; and helping Rastas to establish cooperative workshops for their employment.[4] Although these recommendations were not taken very seriously when first published in 1960, they did help give Rastafari a fair public hearing in which it was taken seriously as a religious movement rather than dismissed as a criminal organization or social nuisance.

A key turning point for the movement occurred on April 21, 1966, when Haile Selassie himself visited Jamaica. Over one hundred thousand Rastas from all over the island turned out to greet him, filling the air with a cloud of ganja smoke. The emperor was unexpectedly gracious to the Rastas, meeting with several Rasta elders and remaining respectful of their beliefs—including the belief that he was the Messiah. The date of his visit is celebrated by Rastas worldwide as Grounation Day, the second holiest day in their calendar after the emperor's coronation day, November 2.

RASTAFARI RELIGION: BELIEFS AND PRACTICES

Like the movement's origins and history, the Rastafari belief system is a complex melding of various elements drawn from Christianity, African religions, and twentieth-century racial politics. The core elements of the early Rastafari faith include the following ideas: Haile Selassie is the living God; the black person is the reincarnation of ancient Israel; the white person is inferior to the black person; the Jamaican situation is a hopeless hell; Ethiopia is heaven; and one day soon black people will be repatriated to Ethiopia. A manuscript by the early Rasta Samuel Brown entitled *Treatise on the Rastafarian Movement* summarizes the core beliefs as follows:

> We are the vanguard of 144,000 celestial selectors who shall in turn free 468,000 millions particularly and the world at large. We are the disciples of Rastafari, who have walked with God from the time when the foundation of creation was laid. . . . We now stand as the fulfillers of prophecy; we knew before that when a king should be crowned in the land of David's throne, that individual would be Shiloh, the anointed one, the Messiah, the Christ returned in the personification of Rastafari. . . . The scriptures declare God hangs in motionless space surrounded by thick darkness; hence a black man.[5]

The Rastas regard the Bible as a holy book, though they read the text in a very particular way. In the Rastafari view, the Bible was originally composed in the Amharic language of Ethiopia and was later corrupted over time in order to enhance the power of the slave masters and colonizers. Different Rastafari groups read the text in different ways, some as a collection of symbols to be contemplated and some as a source for various religious practices. For example, in support of wearing dreadlocks, Rastas point to passages such as Leviticus

21:5, "They shall not make baldness upon their head, neither shall they shave off the corner of their beard," and in support of their strict dietary rules, they often cite the Nazirite vows described in Numbers 6:1–21.

The most important ceremonial meeting is called the Nyabinghi, which is held to commemorate various events that are sacred to the Rastafari. The term *Nyabinghi* is derived from a religious and political resistance movement in colonial Uganda that emerged at the end of the nineteenth century. Today, however, it refers to the Rastafari meetings, also known as "groundation," that are held monthly or on special occasions such as the coronation of Haile Selassie. The meetings involve drumming, chanting, smoking herb, and singing hymns drawn from Christianity.

One of the unique features of Rastafari religion is its complex use of symbolism and language. Perhaps the most immediately noticeable symbol of Rastafari is the wearing of dreadlocks or "natty dreads," which—like hairstyles in many religious traditions—carry complex layers of cultural and spiritual meaning. Rastas themselves use biblical references to explain the wearing of dreadlocks, citing the story of Samson or the image of the lion of Judah with its powerful mane. However, the wearing of long, matted hair also clearly carries profound cultural significance, particularly in the context of Jamaican society, where hair has long been a sign of social differences. Traditionally in Jamaica, fine silky hair was considered "good" or socially desirable, while wooly, kinky hair was seen as "Negro" and frowned upon; thus the Rastafari practice of deliberately adopting long, matted dreadlocks was clearly a rejection of these outward markers of social status and an embrace of "African-ness" and blackness. At the same time, Rastas adopted the aura of freedom, power, and defiance that comes with such rejection of mainstream values. Significantly, when the police began to crack down on Rastafari in the early years of the movement, one of their first responses was to cut off the Rastas' hair—in effect, symbolically emasculating and disempowering them. Thus the wearing of dreadlocks became the focus of intense symbolic and social-political struggle. Bob Marley would highlight these various layers of symbolism in his hugely successful 1974 album, *Natty Dread*.

In addition to elaborate symbolism and imagery, Rastafari involves its own unique kind of language. Typically called *Iyaric* (a combination of *Iya*, meaning "higher," and Amharic, the language spoken by Haile Selassie), *livelect* (from *live* and *dialect*), *dread-talk*, or *I-talk*, this is a mixture of Jamaican English and spiritual ideas drawn from Rastafari belief. Most commonly, the pronoun *I* replaces *me*, to emphasize the fact that the individual is a subject and not an object; the phrase *I and I* is used in place of *we* or *you and I* to emphasize that all humans are one and that God is within us all, the whole world united under love of Jah. The *I man* is the inner, true person or spiritual self within each Rastafari, *Idren* refers to the oneness of Rastafari believers, and so on.

Many Rastas also follow a diet called Ital (from *vital*), based on the consumption of foods designed to increase one's *livity* or living, physical, and spiritual vitality. The Ital diet is not uniform among Rastas: it is required in one of the Rasta mansions (subgroups), the Nyabinghi, but not in others such as Twelve Tribes. The specifics of Ital also vary, but they often include a strict vegetarian diet and in some cases veganism; most Rastas avoid any foods that have been touched by modern chemicals, as well as alcohol, coffee, and flavored beverages; and virtually all Rastas avoid products from pigs, which are considered scavengers of the dead, as are crabs, lobsters, and shrimp. As in other aspects of Rastafari practice, the Ital diet bears the influence of several different religious traditions, including Hindu vegetarianism, a Jewish *kashrut* or kosher diet, and Ethiopian Christianity.

Perhaps the most widely recognized and—as we will see below—controversial Rastafari practice is the smoking of ganja or "herb," which has been a core part of the movement's ritual since the early days at the Pinnacle commune. Widely used by Hindu holy men in India for centuries, ganja came to have profound spiritual and sociopolitical meanings for the early Rastafari religion. On the one hand, part of its significance has always been a matter of social protest, a rejection of mainstream values and an assertion of the Rastas' freedom from the laws that govern Babylon society. It is, literally, an expression of the Rastas' desire to "think differently" and cultivate a consciousness that is separate from that of the establishment. Yet at the same time, the smoking of ganja is also a ritual and often a communal act that is believed to be part of an attitude of meditation and worship. As one Rasta put it, in words that are reminiscent of the Native American Church's views of peyote, "The Rastafarian sees ganja as part of his religious observance. He sees ganja as the smoother of mental imbalances and as a meditatory influence. Ganja is really used to bring forth a peaceful and complacent aspect within man. We do not believe in excessive use of ganja. . . . It is not a drug."[6] At least in its Jamaican context, smoking of herb typically follows a ritual pattern: a package of herb is produced and either made into a cigarette called a spliff or packed into a pipe. Before it is lit, a prayer is recited: "Glory be to the Father and to the maker of creation. As it was in the beginning is now and ever shall be, World without end. Jah Rastafari. Eternal God Haile Selassie."[7] Several pulls of smoke are taken, and the pipe or spliff is passed to the next person.

THE ORGANIZATION OF RASTAFARI

As Rastafari became more established as a religious movement, it eventually branched out into three main sects called "mansions" or "houses." The oldest and largest of these is the House of Nyabinghi, whose name is derived from a legendary queen who was said to have possessed a Ugandan woman and inspired a resistance movement against the colonial authorities in the nineteenth century. Subscribing to the more militant ethos of the early Rasta movement, the Nyabinghis are also fairly patriarchal, subjecting women to male authority and excluding them from the circle of males during the smoking of ganja.

The next mansion to emerge was the Bobo Ashanti, founded in 1958. *Bobo* means "black," and *Ashanti* refers to the Ashante peoples of Ghana, from whom many of the original Jamaican slaves descended. The key distinction of the Bobo Ashanti is its worship of the sect's founder, Emanuel Charles Edwards (1898–1981), who is regarded as the reincarnation of Jesus Christ and as part of a holy trinity together with Haile Selassie and Marcus Garvey.

Bobo Ashanti members are also marked by wearing tightly wrapped turbans around their dreadlocks and adhering closely to aspects of Jewish law, such as the observance of the Sabbath from Friday sundown until Saturday sundown. Following a more rigid discipline than the Nyabinghis, Bobos typically practice a frugal lifestyle based on subsistence farming and making brooms to sell. They are also a highly patriarchal community, branding women as distracting to men's spiritual pursuit and relegating them largely to the background of religious life.

Finally, the most recent mansion to be established is the Twelve Tribes of Israel, founded in 1968. The founder, Vernon Carrington, claimed to be the reincarnation of God and one of the twelve sons of Israel. Often called Christian Rastas, the Twelve Tribes accept Jesus as the one true savior and regard Haile Selassie not as the Messiah but simply as a representative of Jesus and as a divine king in the line of David. Members of the mansion each belong to one of twelve tribes or houses, which are determined by their birth month and are associated with particular colors, body parts, character traits, and apostles. Unlike other Rastas, members of the Twelve Tribes do not have to wear dreadlocks or headgear; and unlike the early Rastafari movement, the Twelve Tribes reject the idea of black supremacy and anti-white sentiment, accepting members from any race. Thus the Twelve Tribes have spread widely around the world and now represent the largest Rastafari group in the United States, Europe, New Zealand, and Africa.

RASTAS IN NORTH AMERICA

Through the combined influence of reggae music and the steady stream of Jamaican immigrants to the United States and Canada, Rastafari has had an increasingly visible presence in North America since the 1980s. Initially, Rastas in North America gathered in small circles of like-minded believers to edify and inspire one another; then gradually they began to replicate the various formations of Rastafari that emerged in Jamaica. Today in the United States and Canada, we find circles of Rastas identifying themselves as Nyabinghi, Twelve Tribes, and Bobo Ashanti, some with more regular congregational gatherings. However, many Rastas simply practice independently or gather informally. As one American convert to Rastafari, Ivy Chevers, notes, much of the North American Rasta culture tends to center on reggae festivals and concerts, which become major hubs of community even when there are no established Rasta houses in the area.[8]

Perhaps the most organized Rasta community in the United States is the Church of Haile Selassie I. Formed in 1987 by Ammanuel Foxe (aka Abuna Foxe) in the Bedford-Stuyvesant area of Brooklyn, the Church of Haile Selassie I holds regular weekly services, including congregational meetings and Sunday school. Unlike other branches of Rastafari, the Church of Haile Selassie I developed a form of "Temple Worship" that is in many ways closer to the liturgy of the Ethiopian Orthodox Church than it is to the Nyabinghi rites of other Rasta communities. In fact, the church has often been critical of Twelve Tribes, Bobo Ashanti, and other Rasta houses that simply, in their view, "use the jargon of Rastafarianism but practice a skewed creed" and lack a structured liturgy.[9] Today, the Church of Haile Selassie I has spread outside the United States and has a strong presence in London, Jamaica, Trinidad, Belize, and elsewhere.

RASTAFARI AND REGGAE

Probably the single most important factor in the transformation of Rastafari from a small Jamaican movement into a global religious tradition was reggae music. Beginning in the late 1960s, reggae swept Jamaica and then spread quickly throughout America, England, and Europe, combining infectious rhythms, danceable beats, and beautiful melodies with spiritual and political ideas drawn heavily from Rastafari religion. The term *reggae* itself is derived from the Jamaican English word *rege* or *rege-rege*, meaning both "rags or ragged clothing" and "a quarrel or argument." However, as a musical term it was first used to refer to the 1968 song by the band the Maytals entitled "Do the Reggay."

Musically, the roots of reggae can be traced back through a number of different influences that came together in Jamaica during the 1960s, including the Nyabinghi drumming of the Rastafari movement. A form of ritual drumming used in Rastafari meetings, Nyabinghi was carried over into other early Jamaican popular musical forms, such as ska, rocksteady, and then reggae. A classic example of the early ska style is the 1963 hit single "Simmer Down" by Bob Marley's band, the Wailers, recorded before their turn to reggae and Rastafari. The song contains the key features of ska, such as the emphasis on the offbeat (or the second and fourth beats of a four/four time signature), scratchy guitar chops on the offbeat, and a walking bass line. All of these elements were carried over into classic examples of reggae music, such as Bob Marley's well-known song "Stir It Up." In many ways, "Stir It Up" closely resembles "Simmer Down," but it is much, much slower. It features the same offbeat rhythm, walking bass line, and guitar chop on the second and fourth beats, but it is played at only about 74 bpm as opposed to the 124 bpm of "Simmer Down."

Like other musicians in the early rise of reggae, Bob Marley became a committed Rastafari in the mid-1960s and soon became its most important, eloquent and globally popular spokesperson for the next decade (figure 6.2). Both spiritual and political themes began to emerge much more explicitly in his recordings of the early 1970s, perhaps most famously in the 1973 song "Get Up, Stand Up," which remains a classic anthem of spiritual freedom and sociopolitical resistance. Here Marley offers a clear critique of the idea of God as some kind of otherworldly being and heaven as some otherworldly place in the sky; instead, he emphasizes the very "this-worldly" dimension of spirituality, which is about standing up for and winning rights on the ground in real-life social and political struggle:

> Preacher man, don't tell me,
> Heaven is under the earth.
> I know you don't know
> What life is really worth.

Ivy Chevers became involved with Rastafari in the 1970s, first in Chicago and then during her work for the Peace Corps in Jamaica. She later wrote her dissertation at Ohio State University on Rastafari in the United States, focusing on the complex question of American appropriations of Rasta culture. In her interview she talks about how she was first drawn to Rastafari and the role of reggae in Rasta culture in the United States.

I got interested in Rasta in about 1977–78. I remember visiting my sister, who worked at the Institute of Positive Education in Chicago, Illinois. That's run by Haki Madhubuti, who ran Third World Press out of Chicago. I visited her in the mid-'70s, and when I went, there was some type of festival going on at the Institute of Positive Education. There were a lot of dreadlocked people there, and I was like, "Oh my God, what is this?" I had never seen dreadlocks before. And my sister had just started growing her dreadlocks. After I left Chicago, I started visiting a record shop in Cincinnati. I was at the University of Cincinnati at the time, and I start buying reggae albums. And that was it for me; I started researching Rasta. But to be honest, I didn't learn a lot about Rasta until I went to Jamaica in 1981–82. After I left undergrad school I joined the Peace Corps, and that is when I fully immersed myself into Rastafarian culture.

I didn't find any problem with being accepted by Rastafarians. The funny thing is, I was in the Peace Corps, and there were two other African American women. One of them was from California, and she had dreadlocks. I had dreadlocks at the time, because as soon as I left Chicago I started growing my dreadlocks. So we would be walking down the streets—the three of us with some white Peace Corps volunteers— and people would stop and tell us, "Don't walk around with these white people, because they're from the CIA!" And we would just look at each other and say, "We're Peace Corps volunteers too." But there was not any problem. At the time, there were some Rasta sisters working with a group of Rasta women, and we were invited to those meetings. There was no problem; we were accepted wholeheartedly.

The main belief of Rastafarians is that His Imperial Majesty Haile Selassie is God. That is the main belief. Other beliefs might include a back to Africa movement and an Ital diet. Ital might mean no salt, pure vegetables and fruit, and natural foods. But a lot of people don't see Rastafari as a religion; they see it more as a philosophy or a way of life.

In Jamaica smoking marijuana is like a sacrament. So when Rastas get together and they have Nyabinghi, prayers are being said before the pipe is lit up. It's not just a recreational thing. And I have met Rastas here who deal with herb the same way. It's something sacred. I would say that it's comparable to the use of wine in the Catholic Church or the use of peyote by the Native American Church.

I don't think that people in America really understand what Rasta is. If you go to Jamaica, and you ask somebody on the street they will have a better understanding of what Rasta is, whereas here people might just look at the hair and the music and smoking marijuana and think that's all there is to Rastafari. I don't think they know anything about how Rastas identify with Africa and with His Imperial Majesty. To me it's more of a reggae thing than it is a cultural heritage thing.

But what I also found in dealing with that question is that the reggae music really brings together a lot of people—brings together a lot of Caribbean people, a lot of African people—and those reggae concerts become a space for people to network, people to talk about their heritage, to be together. Those reggae spaces are really a place for African people of the diaspora to come together. I did come to the conclusion that music does act as a type of social movement. During the '60s, '70s, and '80s that positive message of reggae music really brought people together.

It's not all that glitters is gold;
'Alf the story has never been told:
So now you see the light, eh!
Stand up for your rights. Come on!
Get up, stand up: stand up for your rights!
Get up, stand up: don't give up the fight!
. . .
Most people think,
Great god will come from the skies,
Take away everything
And make everybody feel high.
But if you know what life is worth,
You will look for yours on earth:
And now you see the light,
You stand up for your rights. Jah!
Get up, stand up! (jah, jah!)[10]

One of the most important challenges for the Rastafari movement was the loss of its own messiah. During the 1970s, Ethiopia was torn by revolutionary unrest and turmoil, which resulted in a military coup and the arrest of Haile Selassie in late 1974. The deposed emperor would die less than a year later in August of 1975, after which a Marxist government took power. The sudden and irreverent dethroning of the emperor, followed by his physical death, sent the Jamaican Rastafari community into a deep meditation. But ironically, it would emerge in many ways stronger than ever before, and now moving onto a global stage. The

FIGURE 6.2 Bob Marley in concert in Dalymount Park, July 6, 1980. Photo by Eddie Malin. Creative Commons Attribution 2.0 Generic License.

very same year that Haile Selassie died also saw the release of one of the most important and widely acclaimed reggae songs ever recorded: Bob Marley's "Jah Live." In many ways Marley—and with him the broader reggae movement—helped carry, continue, and revive the Rastafari movement at the very moment when it seemed in danger of collapsing with the death of the Messiah. And it is arguably reggae—along with fusion forms of reggae now mixed with rock and hip-hop—that has helped spread Rastafari to a global audience in the twenty-first century. Largely through the power of reggae, the movement rapidly transformed from a small religious group on the tiny island of Jamaica to a global phenomenon that is now recognizable in some form everywhere from America to Australia.

While Bob Marley was surely the most famous and influential musician to refer to Rastafari ideas in his music, other Jamaican musicians embraced the tradition even more explicitly and in far more detail. One of the most important reggae artists to emerge in the wake of Marley was Burning Spear (aka Winston Rodney, b. 1945), who was deeply influenced by the ideas of Marcus Garvey and began to incorporate Rastafari themes throughout his records from the mid-1970s onward. In 1975 he recorded his third album, *Marcus Garvey*, which, despite its seemingly esoteric and intellectual title, was a huge commercial success. In the title track, he expresses the sorrow of the poor and oppressed, along with the Rastafari hope for spiritual justice:

Marcus Garvey's words come to pass,
Can't get no food to eat,
Can't get no money to spend, Woo-oo-oo
Can't get no food to eat,
Can't get no money to spend, Woo-oo-oo
Come, little one and let me do what I can do for you
And you and you alone
Come, little one, woo-oo-oo
Let me do what I can do for you and you alone, woo-oo-oo
He who knows the right thing
And do it not
Shall be spanked with many stripes,
Weeping and wailing and moaning,
You've got yourself to blame, I tell you.
Do right do right do right do right do right,
Tell you to do right, Woo-oo-oo.[11]

Following Marley's death, the power of reggae began to wane in Jamaica during the 1980s and '90s, when it was increasingly displaced by new movements such as dancehall. Using faster rhythms and more electronic instruments, dancehall tended to be accompanied by a lifestyle of drugs, guns, and "slackness" (vulgarity). However, in the late 1990s and early 2000s a new resurgence of reggae and Rastafari themes began to emerge, often mixing classic reggae with elements of dancehall, rock, and hip-hop, and continuing to weave in key Rastafari themes and references. One of the most outspoken contemporary Rasta reggae artists is Sizzla Kalonji (b. 1976), who was born to devout Rastafari parents and has himself been a member of the Bobo Ashanti branch of the movement since the 1990s. Sizzla has used extensive and explicit references to Rastafari ideas throughout his recordings, such as *Praise Ye Jah* in 1997, *Bobo Ashanti* in 2000, and his album dedicated to Haile Selassie, *The Messiah*, in 2013. But Sizzla is also known for his rich mix of older reggae elements with hardcore dancehall music and influences from R&B, rock, jazz, and hip-hop. Sizzla's work shifts freely from explicit and sexually charged lyrics such as the "Pump Her Up Pum Pum" to songs full of Rastafari spiritual reverence, such as "Praise Ye Jah." A recurring theme throughout his lyrics is the call to defend the poor and the meek and to raise up the down-trodden youth. As such, he is widely regarded as a key bridge between the older generation of Rastafari elders and a new generation of young people, more used to hip-hop than to Nyabinghi. However, when he uses religious imagery, many of Sizzla's songs, such as the 2000 track "Whether or Not," sound almost like a Rastafari catechism, articulating the central beliefs surrounding Haile Selassie, the evils of the Babylon establishment, the suffering of the poor, and the past and future greatness of black people, who will one day be returned to Africa:

Yea burn away the anger and the fury, oy
Hail king Selassie I, his praise and glory

Whether or not, yo from them dis king Selassie I
Babylon goin' collapse
Whether or not, ey from yuh dis Emmanuel
Babylon me know yuh heart goin' stop
Whether or not, yo from yuh dis the Black woman
Me know yuh glory it goin' drop
Whether or not, from yuh nah love Rastafari
That means say yuh doh love the Black

. . .

True Rastaman ah pray pon the mountain peak
Fi protect and care fi the poor and the meek
Doh dis the order, wake up on the east
'cuz poor people gone Babylon waan thief
poor people farm Babylon waan reep
Them nah give the ghetto youth one thing fi eat
So nah bother dis the Rastafari ey nah bother do it
Babylon ah kill the ghetto youth inna the street
Mi say fi rise and live bongo nah go repeat
Repatriation I nah go retreat,
Babylon, gonna sink yuh inna the deep.[12]

Interestingly enough, the crossover appeal of Rastafari and reggae has drawn some converts from the hip-hop world. In 2012, after a trip to Jamaica, the American rapper Snoop Dogg (b. 1971) embraced Rastafari and adopted a new title, Snoop Lion. This resulted in the release of a reggae album, *Reincarnation*, along with a documentary film about his Jamaican experience in 2013. Featuring songs such as "Here Comes the King" Snoop Lion mixes hip-hop beats with reggae melodies and themes, calling on his audience to embrace "One king, one faith, one religion, and if you hear me, come and join the revolution."[13]

KEY ISSUES AND DEBATES: GANJA AND WHITE RASTAS

Like the Native American Church (NAC), the Rastafari movement has been controversial from its very origins because of its use of the plant *Cannabis sativa* (known in Jamaica by its Indian name *ganja* and called "herb" by practitioners). The Rastas were growing and using the plant from the earliest days of the Pinnacle compound in the 1930s, and suppression of the movement was often linked to its use of the plant, which was widely perceived as a dangerous intoxicant and was also subject to prohibitions and regulations as a drug in the United States from the 1920s and '30s onward. In many ways, the use of marijuana raises several of the same issues of religious freedom and federal law that we encountered in chapter 2 with the NAC—and as we will see, many Rastas have made direct comparisons between their use of the plant and the NAC's use of the cactus. Yet at the same time, the case of marijuana is in many ways more complex and ambiguous than the peyote case in the NAC. For example, marijuana is far, far more widely available and widely used as a recreational drug than peyote, heavily used by vast numbers of Americans for nonreligious purposes. Marijuana is neither an endangered species nor difficult to cultivate, making it even more easily accessible to vast numbers of users. Moreover, while peyote use remains largely restricted to ritual use in the setting of the NAC, marijuana is used by millions of casual smokers who have no connection to any particular religious, ritual, or ethnic tradition.

The legality of cannabis came up in federal courts in 1991, when a Rasta named Ras Iyah Ben Makahna (born Benny Guerrero) was arrested for possession and importation of marijuana seeds at an international airport in the US territory of Guam. Makahna had been returning from a trip to California to his home in Guam when he was charged with importing a controlled substance. Raising complex issues of religious freedom and federal law, the case eventually attracted the attention of the American Civil Liberties Union, which offered him legal assistance.

In his defense, he argued that he was required by his religion to use the plant sacramentally and that it was based on divine commandments according to the Rasta interpretation of the Bible. Not to use herb, he claimed, would be a sin in the eyes of God. Quoting the books of Genesis and Revelation, Makahna argued that he "was told by Rastafari Elder, Ras DaSilva, chairman of the Rastafari Centralization Organization, that Rastafari are required to use cannabis. . . . JAH/GOD commands us to use all herb-bearing seed (Genesis 1:11, 29). The cannabis plant has also been identified as the Tree of Life, whose leaves will be for the Healing of the Nation (Revelation 22:2)."[14]

In September 2000, the Superior Court of Guam decided in Makahna's favor, dismissing the charges even before the trial. To apply marijuana laws to Rastafari, the court decided, was a violation of both Guam's own territorial constitution and the federal Religious Freedom Restoration Act, which we discussed in chapter 2. As in the case of peyote and the NAC, the ruling hinged primarily on the question of the free exercise of religion and the unconstitutionality of laws that prohibit that freedom.

However, the prosecution appealed to the Ninth Circuit Court, which heard the case in late 2001 and early 2002. This time the court determined that Makahna might not have been guilty of *possession* of cannabis but that he could still be tried on charges of *importing* the plant. Significantly, the court in its decision made a direct comparison to the case of Al Smith and peyote, noting that in neither case does religious freedom mean that one can import controlled substances: "The parallels of Smith to this case are striking. Like Smith, Guerrero used a controlled substance in the practice of his religion, and Guam has a neutral, generally applicable law proscribing the importation of such controlled substance. Under Smith, then, Guam may constitutionally punish Guerrero for importing a controlled substance, even if doing so substantially burdens his ability to practice his religion."[15] In July 2002, Makahna in turn appealed the court's decision, arguing that his religious faith required him not only to possess and use the plant but also to travel with it when necessary. Makahna himself also made a direct comparison to the NAC's use of peyote (and like the NAC, to the Catholic Church's sacramental use of wine), which might also require practitioners to travel with the substance: "Rastafari is required to possess, cultivate and travel with cannabis for medicinal and religious reasonings. . . . Much the way the Native American Indian Church travel with their medicinal-sacramental peyote or the Christian use wine and bread. Would you leave your Holy Bible at home when you went to gather for services?"[16] While the fate of Makahna's appeal regarding importation remains uncertain, his case has set an important precedent for the religious use of marijuana. Because of this decision, Rastafarians may now legally smoke cannabis for religious purposes on any federally owned lands, which include forests, national parks, and lands held by the Bureau of Land Management.

Finally, in Jamaica itself, the question of the legalization of ganja has been directly addressed by the government and courts. In 2000, the Jamaican government appointed the National Commission on Ganja, which was chaired by Barry Chevannes, a scholar of Rastafari and dean of the Social Sciences Department at the University of the West Indies at Mona. After careful deliberation, the commission recommended that ganja be decriminalized and subjected to new rules to ensure safe, responsible use. They concluded that the relevant laws should be amended so that ganja is decriminalized for private personal use of small quantities by adults and also decriminalized for use as a "sacrament for religious purposes." They urged the government to establish a Cannabis Research Agency to investigate the health and other effects of the plant and to work with other countries to reexamine its legal status. Initially, the Jamaican government indicated its support for the commission's recommendations; however, strong opposition from churches and from the US government pushed the issue from the nation's legislative agenda, and it was never implemented.[17]

A second key debate surrounding Rastafari in the United States—and tied in many ways to the ganja debate—is the appropriation of Rastafari culture, symbolism, and practices by non-Rasta audiences. Today, actual gatherings of faithful Rasta for a Nyabinghi ceremony are fairly rare and certainly not very visible in the United States, yet dreadlocks, marijuana, reggae music, and posters of Bob Marley can be found in every college dorm across the country. In most cases, these non-Rastas will have little knowledge or understanding of the religious symbols and practices they are appropriating. Hence, many critical observers have argued that this is a kind of violation of Rastafari traditions, even a kind of "cultural theft" that uproots these religious symbols and rituals from their original context and transforms them into just another set of commodities to be bought and sold in the American shopping mall of cultures. Thus some argue that this appropriation of Rastafari symbols is a tragic loss of the original revolutionary power of this tradition. When reggae, dreadlocks, and ganja are taken up by suburban white kids, they argue, these cultural objects become transformed from images of resistance against oppression into simple commodities and forms of entertainment. As one scholar, Obiagele Lake, put it, "While Diaspora Africans are grooving to the reggae beat, capitalist industries continue to prosper once again—using Africans as human capital."[18]

In 2007, a group called the Ethio-Africa Diaspora Union Millennium Council issued a statement condemning the appropriation of Rastafari cultural symbols by non-Rastafari individuals who have exploited them for commercial profit. As they concluded their statement: "Non-Rastafari individuals and organisations that continue to exploit Rastafari culture, symbols, artifacts, music, art and religious marks and fail to recognise the authority of the Rastafari community to protect and preserve same and to benefit financially from same, will be regarded as hostile to the Rastafari community and will be treated accordingly."[19] While the council does not specify exactly how they planned to treat individuals who exploit Rastafari culture, their statement does demonstrate that many in the community perceived this exploitation as a real problem.

Other more sympathetic observers, however, have argued that the diffusion of Rastafari has its own kind of power to transform American culture. Even if young Americans don't really understand the history behind Rastafari music and symbols, they may still be inspired by these "unfamiliar" objects to look critically at their own "familiar" culture and think about alternative ways of living in the world. As George Lipsitz notes, while "it is important to document the harm done by uncomprehending appropriations of cultural creations," we should acknowledge that consumers of these cultural creations can still find a transformative message in them in new social and historical contexts: "Many of these commodities have drawn the investment and engagement of consumers because their moral and political messages have gained even more power when applied to a new situation. . . . Even when listeners and readers have been ignorant of the exact original and local meanings of reggae . . . they have often displayed advanced understanding about how they could use resonances of an 'unfamiliar' culture to 'defamiliarize' their own culture and then 'refamiliarize' themselves and others with it on the basis of the new knowledge and critical perspectives made possible by cultural contrast."[20] Thus, even if a white teenager wearing dreadlocks and listening to Bob Marley doesn't understand the entire history and meaning behind the music, he or she might be motivated to look more deeply into Jamaican and African history and might be inspired to think more critically about issues of race, poverty, oppression, and spiritual freedom in contemporary America.

QUESTIONS FOR DISCUSSION AND DEBATE

1. It seems that there are clearly elements of Hinduism in early Rastafari, yet few if any Rastas today would acknowledge any South Asian or Hindu influence. Why do you think this is the case? Are there other examples of this sort of "historical forgetting," in which religious groups forget or reject certain influences in their past in favor of others?

2. Particularly in its early development, Rastafari was a black separatist movement and quite critical of white society. Yet the religion was embraced by musicians such as Bob Marley, who advocated a message of universal love, and its music became hugely popular worldwide with white as well as black listeners. How do we explain this fact? Is it a contradiction or simply a natural evolution of the religion as it spread beyond the historical and cultural boundaries of Jamaica?

3. Compare the legal debates surrounding the use of marijuana by Rastas with those surrounding peyote use by the NAC. Is it essentially the same debate and the same basic issue of religious freedom? Or is it far more complicated, given the widespread availability and use of marijuana as a recreational drug, the fact that cannabis is not an endangered species, and so on?

SUGGESTED CLASSROOM ACTIVITY

Critically examine the appropriation of Rasta imagery and culture by white non-Rastas in the United States (in popular music, film, or daily life). Discuss the negative reaction of many Rastas, who find this to be an offensive and exploitative "theft" of their religious and cultural traditions. Conversely, discuss the views of scholars such as George Lipsitz, who argue that these sorts of cultural appropriations might still have positive effects, such as "defamiliarizing" individuals from their own cultures and "familiarizing" them with the lives and struggles of other cultures. Which of these perspectives seems most persuasive? Why?

SUGGESTED FILM

Rebel Music: The Bob Marley Story. Palm Pictures, 2001.

Barnett, Michael, ed. *Rastafari in the New Millennium: A Rastafari Reader*. Syracuse, NY: Syracuse University Press, 2012.

Barrett, Leonard E., Sr. *The Rastafarians*. Boston: Beacon Press, 1988.

Chevers, Ivy. "Study of Rastafarian Culture in Columbus, Ohio: Notes from an African-American Woman's Journey." PhD diss., Ohio State University, 2008.

Cushman, Thomas. "Rich Rastas and Communist Rockers: A Comparative Study of the Origin, Diffusion and Defusion of Revolutionary Musical Codes." *Journal of Popular Culture* 25, no. 3 (1991): 17–61.

Edmonds, Ennis B. *Rastafari: A Very Short Introduction*. New York: Oxford University Press, 2012.

Garvey, Marcus. *Philosophy and Opinions*. London: Frank Cass, 1967.

Howell, Leonard P. (aka G. G. Maragh). *The Promised Key: The Original Literary Roots of Rastafari*. Hunlock Creek, PA: E World, 2001.

Lake, Obiagele. *Rastafari Women: Subordination in the Midst of Liberation Theology*. Durham: University of North Carolina Press, 1998.

Lee, Helene. *The First Rasta: Leonard Howell and the Rise of Rastafarianism*. Chicago: Chicago Review Press, 2004.

Lipsitz, George. *Dangerous Crossroads: Popular Music, Postmodernism and the Poetics of Place*. London: Verso, 1997.

Murrell, Nathaniel Samuel. *Chanting Down Babylon: The Rastafari Reader*. Philadelphia: Temple University Press, 1998.

Smith, M. G., with Roy Augier and Rex M. Nettleford. *Report on the Rastafari Movement in Kingston, Jamaica*. Kingston, Jamaica: Institute of Social and Economic Studies, 1960.

NOTES TO CHAPTER 6

1. Marcus Garvey, *Philosophy and Opinions* (London: Frank Cass, 1967), 34. "The Universal Negro Improvement Association represents the hopes and aspirations of the awakened Negro. Our desire is for a place in the world, not to disturb the tranquility of other men, but to . . . rest our weary backs and feet by the banks of the Niger and sing our songs and chant our hymns to the God of Ethiopia" (120).
2. Quoted in Leonard E. Barrett Sr., *The Rastafarians* (Boston: Beacon Press, 1988), 67.
3. Joseph Hibbert, quoted in Helene Lee, *The First Rasta: Leonard Howell and the Rise of Rastafarianism* (Chicago: Chicago Review Press, 2004), 101.
4. M. G. Smith, with Roy Augier and Rex M. Nettleford, *Report on the Rastafari Movement in Kingston, Jamaica* (Kingston, Jamaica: Institute of Social and Economic Studies, 1960), 38.

5. Samuel E. Brown, "Treatise on the Rastafarian Movement," *Journal of Caribbean Studies* 6, no. 1 (1966): 1.
6. Barrett, *Rastafarians*, 130.
7. Ibid., 131.
8. Ivy Chevers, "Study of Rastafarian Culture in Columbus, Ohio: Notes from an African-American Woman's Journey" (PhD diss., Ohio State University, 2008).
9. "A Defiant Message from the Church of Haile Selassie I," *Gleaner*, September 8, 2013, http://jamaica-gleaner.com/gleaner/20130908/news/news8.html.
10. Bob Marley and the Wailers, "Get Up, Stand Up," from *Burnin'* (Island Studios, 1973).
11. Burning Spear, "Marcus Garvey," from *Marcus Garvey* (Island, 1975).
12. Sizzla Kalonji, "Whether or Not," from *Bobo Ashanti* (X Terminator Productions, 2000). Perhaps the clearest example of this mix of dancehall rhythms and Rasta imagery is his 1997 album *Praise Ye Jah*, whose title track combines praise of Jah with reflections on black history and a critique of mainstream Christianity.
13. Snoop Lion, "Here Comes the King," from *Reincarnated* (Bernhane Sound System, 2013).
14. Reverend Damuzi, "Legal Herb for Rastas?" *Cannabis Culture*, January 6, 2003, www.cannabisculture.com/articles/2661.html.
15. People of Guam v. Benny Toves Guerrero, US Court of Appeals, Ninth Circuit, No. 00–71247, May 28, 2002, http://caselaw.findlaw.com/us-9th-circuit/1355714.html.
16. Damuzi, "Legal Herb for Rastas?"
17. Ennis B. Edmonds, *Rastafari: A Very Short Introduction* (New York: Oxford University Press, 2012), 50–51.
18. Obiagele Lake, *Rastafari Women: Subordination in the Midst of Liberation Theology* (Durham: University of North Carolina Press, 1998), 125.
19. Quoted in Chevers, "Study of Rastafarian Culture," 11–12.
20. George Lipsitz, *Dangerous Crossroads: Popular Music, Postmodernism and the Poetics of Place* (London: Verso, 1997), 161.

SEVEN

The Church of Scientology

New Religions and Tax Exemption

On October 8, 1993, the current head of the Church of Scientology, David Miscavige, delivered a triumphant speech before ten thousand cheering Scientologists in the Los Angeles Sports Arena. The occasion for this celebration was the announcement that, one week before, the US Internal Revenue Service had issued letters that formally recognized Scientology and all of its related organizations as fully tax-exempt "religious" entities. This decision by the IRS, in fact, marked the end of a decades-long and complex battle between Scientology and the agency, which had stripped all Scientology entities of tax exemption in 1967. This was a battle that involved not just literally thousands of lawsuits but also an array of illegal activities, such as Scientology operatives infiltrating IRS and other federal offices through an audacious program of espionage during the 1970s. In Miscavige's words, this 1993 IRS decision marked the end of the biggest challenge ever faced by the Church of Scientology and an event of far more than legal significance: "The war is over!" he declared. ". . . What exactly does this mean? My answer is: everything. The magnitude of this is greater than you may imagine."[1] Among other things, Miscavige argued that this decision by the IRS in America would help the church with its struggle for recognition as a "religion" in other nations, particularly in France and Germany, where it has been consistently labeled a "cult" and a for-profit big business.

Scientology's war with the IRS is just one example of the long history of controversy and contestation that has surrounded this new religious movement. Founded in 1953 by former science fiction author L. Ron Hubbard (1911–86; figure 7.1), Scientology quickly emerged as one of the wealthiest and most powerful new movements in postwar America. Best known in the media for its cast of high-profile celebrity spokespersons, such as Tom Cruise, John Travolta, and Kirstie Alley, Scientology has been widely attacked by journalists, anticult

FIGURE 7.1 L. Ron Hubbard
with E-meter. Getty Images.

groups, and various government agencies as a brainwashing cult and a greed-driven business. In the words of Cynthia Kisser, former director of the Cult Awareness Network, "Scientology is quite likely the most ruthless, the most classically terroristic, the most litigious and the most lucrative cult the country has ever known. No cult extracts more money from its members."[2]

Over the last sixty years, Scientology has been at the center of a number of larger debates surrounding alternative spiritual groups in the United States, among them the role of secrecy in new religious movements, the often vast amounts of wealth generated by some new spiritual movements, the question of copyright and trademark for confidential religious materials (particularly on the Internet), and perhaps most importantly the basic question "What is religion?" In other words, it has raised the fundamental question of whether new movements such as Scientology are best described as "religions" or as something else, such as self-help therapies or for-profit corporations.

Historically, US government agencies and courts have been reluctant to lay out any explicit definitions of the terms *religion* or *religious organizations*. Indeed, because of the reli-

gion clause of the First Amendment, it would be unconstitutional for the federal government to apply a strict definition of these terms, since any fixed definition would inevitably
exclude the beliefs and practices of some faith communities. As the Supreme Court acknowledged as early as 1878 in its discussion of Mormonism, "The word 'religion' is not defined
in the Constitution. We must go elsewhere, therefore, to ascertain its meaning."[3] Unlike
some nations, the United States does not register religious groups and has no official hierarchy of religious organizations. Yet federal income tax law *does* provide exemption for religious organizations, and, therefore, there must be *some* means to determine whether a
group claiming to be religious is "genuine" for purposes of tax-exempt status. Ironically, this
means that in some ways the most important decision made on this question—at least in the
United States—is that of the tax authorities.

In this sense, the Church of Scientology is not only a complex, fascinating, and multifaceted example of a new religious movement emerging in post–World War II America; it also
raises more profound questions about what the very label of "religion" means, who gets to
make that designation, and what exactly is at stake in a group being called a religion rather
than a cult or a form of therapy or a commercial business. Although this case has been settled for Scientology in the United States since the 1990s, it continues to be debated in other
nations throughout the world and therefore raises equally difficult questions about many
other new spiritual movements today.

L. RON HUBBARD: "THE MAN WHO SOLVED THE RIDDLE OF THE HUMAN MIND" OR "THE GREATEST CON MAN OF THE CENTURY"?

At the heart of the mystery and controversy that surrounds Scientology is its enigmatic
founder, L. Ron Hubbard (1911–86). Portrayed in the church's literature as at once an engi-
neer and scientist, a bold world explorer, and a philosopher who "solved the riddle of the
human mind," Hubbard has also been described by his critics as a liar, a madman, and even
"the greatest con man of the century."[4] Indeed, it is extremely difficult to write the story of
Hubbard's life, since there are at least two very different versions of that narrative.

On one side, according to his own accounts and official church biographies, Hubbard
was an adventurer who set out to explore not just the farthest ends of the earth but also the
infinite reaches of the human mind—as much a daredevil barnstormer, a master mariner,
and a Far East explorer as the founder of a revolutionary new philosophy. As a young man,
Hubbard claimed to have been initiated into the secrets of the Blackfoot Indians, then to
have become the nation's youngest Eagle Scout, and later to have traveled to Asia, where he
learned the esoteric teachings of various Eastern sages: "Among the first westerners . . .
admitted into traditionally forbidden lamaseries," he delved into the "dread mysteries
of India," studied with Buddhist priests, and met "the last remaining magician for
Kublai Khan's court."[5] Back in the United States, Hubbard claimed that he had mastered
the sciences, studying engineering and atomic physics at George Washington University.
At one point, Hubbard claimed to have been "one of the first nuclear physicists in the

United States"—an assertion that appeared on the cover of his book *All about Radiation.*[6] During World War II, Hubbard served as a naval lieutenant, commanding several vessels in various theaters. Scientology publications have made various claims about his military achievements, some stating that he was awarded as many as twenty-nine decorations. Hubbard also claimed that the war had left him blind and a hopeless cripple but that he had healed himself using the techniques that later became the basis of his new science of Dianetics.

On the other side, however, virtually every detail of Hubbard's biography has been the subject of debate, and many critics argue that most if not all of this narrative is a fabrication. As Hubbard's own son, L. Ron Hubbard Jr., put it, "Better than 90 percent of what my father has written about himself is untrue."[7] Skeptics have pointed out, for example, that most of Hubbard's academic credentials are fictional. Hubbard, the alleged "nuclear physicist," had merely enrolled in one introductory course on molecular and nuclear physics at George Washington University, receiving a grade of F, while his PhD turned out to be the product of a sham diploma mill called Sequoia University. Far from a decorated war hero, Hubbard was actually investigated for firing on an uninhabited island in Mexican waters and was judged by Rear Admiral F. A. Braisted to be "not qualified for command or promotion."[8] There is also no evidence that Hubbard was ever wounded in battle, much less that he healed himself.

Thus Hubbard's autobiography is perhaps best understood not as an accurate historical chronicle but rather as a kind of "hagiographic mythology"—that is, an idealized narrative composed self-consciously of mythic themes.[9] In this sense, it is comparable to the highly elaborated and often imaginative narratives of other new religious leaders, such as Madame Blavatsky, Joseph Smith, or Anton LaVey (and arguably the biographies of the founders of mainstream religious traditions as well).

Both critics and admirers of Hubbard do agree, however, that he was a tremendous storyteller and an incredibly prolific writer. During the 1930s and '40s, Hubbard was among the most widely published authors of the Golden Age of science fiction, churning out hundreds of sci-fi, fantasy, and adventure tales. He wrote not only in many different styles but under the pseudonyms of many different identities, revealing a literary multiple personality that assumed the various names of Winchester Remington Colt, Lt. Jonathan Daly, Bernard Hubbel, René Lafayette, Kurt von Rachen, Lt. Scott Morgan, and Legionnaire 14830, among others. Among Hubbard's myriad titles from the period are "The Battle of Wizards," "The Dangerous Dimension," "Man-Killers of the Air," "Tomb of the Ten Thousand Dead," "Cargo of Coffins," and "Death Waits at Sundown." More than one observer has pointed out that there are numerous continuities between Hubbard's science fiction tales of the 1930s and '40s and the elaborate cosmology of his early Scientology writings of the 1950s and '60s.

Hubbard's first encounter with the spiritual realm is described in an unpublished manuscript entitled "Excalibur," composed in 1938. According to Hubbard's account, the manuscript was the result of a near-death experience that he had during an operation while under heavy anesthesia. Passing through the curtain of death, Hubbard had a rare glimpse into the "secret of life" and heard a voice cry out, "Don't let him know!" Upon returning to his body, Hubbard immediately sat down at his typewriter and hammered out the ten-thousand-word "Excalibur" manuscript.[10] This manuscript is said to be so profound that it has never been published in full. His literary agent at the time, Forrest Ackerman, also recounts this story, noting that Hubbard claimed that whoever read the manuscript "either went insane or committed suicide."[11] At present, only brief excerpts of the manuscript are available on Scientology websites.

DIANETICS: THE NEW SCIENCE OF THE HUMAN MIND

In May 1950, Hubbard published his "new science of the mind" called Dianetics in an issue of the popular magazine *Astounding Science Fiction* (figure 7.2). Derived from the Greek *dia* and *nous,* meaning "through the mind," Dianetics claimed to be a revolutionary new breakthrough for humankind, comparable to "the discovery of fire and superior to the wheel and the arch."[12] On the basis of his experimentation with a wide array of philosophical, psychological, and spiritual ideas, Hubbard believed that he had unlocked the secret to the working of the human mind, the cause of all physical and psychological problems, and the means to achieving an optimal state of well-being called "Clear." In an issue of *Marvel Science Studies* in 1951, Hubbard presented Dianetics as the path to transcend the state of *Homo sapiens* and become a *"Homo superior"* or superman. Published in book form later in 1950, *Dianetics* became surprisingly successful and went to the top of the *New York Times* best-seller list for twenty-eight weeks. The "Dianetics craze," as it was known at the time, spread like wildfire across America, and many small grassroots Dianetics clubs sprouted up throughout the country.

The beliefs of the early Dianetics movement focused primarily on Hubbard's understanding of the human mind and the cause of suffering in this lifetime. Hubbard saw the mind as having two main parts: the reactive mind—which is roughly analogous to Freud's idea of the unconscious—and the analytical mind—which sees the world accurately like a flawless computer. Throughout life, individuals have negative experiences of pain and unconsciousness that become burned in the reactive mind in the form of what Hubbard called "engrams" or negative memory traces, which cause us both physical and psychological problems. To remove these engrams, Hubbard developed a unique form of therapy called auditing (from the Latin *auditus,* to hear). The practice involves a trained counselor (the "auditor") who works with an individual to help identify the painful memory traces or engrams that have been burned into the reactive mind. Through auditing, the individual can relive these experiences—some going back to infancy and even the prenatal state—and then clear them from the reactive mind. Once all of the negative engrams have been removed, the individual experiences a state of optimal psychological, emotional, and physical well-being called "Clear." As Hubbard described the Clear individual: "His physical vitality and health are markedly improved, and all psychosomatic illnesses have vanished. . . . His ability to seek and experience pleasure is great. His personality is heightened, and he is

A STREET AND SMITH PUBLICATION

Astounding

SCIENCE FICTION

JUNE

BRITISH 1/- EDITION

THE HELPING HAND
BY POUL ANDERSON

"Dianetics"
A new science of the mind

FIGURE 7.2 The original
version of Dianetics in
Astounding Science Fiction,
1950.

creative and constructive. His vigor, persistence, and tenacity are much higher than anyone has thought possible."[13]

To aid in the auditing process, Hubbard began to use a device called the E-meter (electro-psychometer). The first versions of the E-meter were developed by Volney Mathison, a chiropractor and author of paranormal and science fiction books. After a falling-out with Mathison in 1954, Hubbard devised his own modification of Mathison's E-meter, which has undergone various upgrades and is still used to this day. The E-meter works somewhat like a lie detector, operating as a skin galvanometer that measures fluctuations in the passage of a trickle of electricity through the body. The primary component of the meter is an instrument called the Wheatstone Bridge, which measures changes in electrical resistance. The individual undergoing auditing holds two cylinders that are connected by wires to the meter, while the auditor asks a series of questions in order to identify where specific engrams lie.

Once the engram has been identified and cleared from the reactive mind, the needle of the meter is supposed to "float," an indicator that the individual no longer reacts to that painful memory.

Although initially extremely popular, the early Dianetics movement proved to be a short-lived phenomenon and faltered just a year or two after its birth. The movement suffered a series of embarrassments in the media and growing tensions between Hubbard and early supporters such as John Campbell and Joseph Winter. Already in financial difficulties by April 1951, Hubbard's movement underwent voluntary bankruptcy in 1952.

THE CHURCH OF SCIENTOLOGY: SPIRITUAL SELVES, PAST LIVES, AND SUPERPOWERS

From the ashes of early Dianetics, however, Hubbard soon created a new and more ambitious movement called the Church of Scientology, which was now presented not just as a science of the mind but in fact as a "religion" in its own right (figure 7.3). The reasons for the failure of the early Dianetics movement and the shift to the religion of Scientology were several. First, throughout the early 1950s, practitioners of Dianetics were being scrutinized by the Food and Drug Administration and by various state medical boards because of their claims to physical as well as psychological healing. Between 1951 and 1953 several individuals were arrested for practicing medicine without a license, and in 1958 the FDA seized and destroyed a consignment of twenty-one thousand tablets of Hubbard's anti-radiation sickness drug Dianezene, claiming that they were falsely labeled for treatment of real illness. In response, Hubbard began to argue that the aim of his new therapy was not *physical* healing but rather *spiritual freedom* and thus that it was not subject to FDA scrutiny. Hubbard himself would later reflect that this was one of the main reasons "why Dianetics fell out of use" as a form of "healing" and why Scientology as a means to "spiritual freedom" took its place.[14]

At the same time, practitioners of Dianetics had begun to report memories from past lives in the course of auditing. This led Hubbard to explore the idea of an immortal spiritual self, which he called the "thetan," and a belief in past lives going back thousands and even millions of years.

On April 10, 1953, Hubbard wrote a letter to Helen O'Brien, then the head of the Dianetics movement in Philadelphia. In it, he suggested that they should consider pursuing what he called the "religion angle," since the current Dianetics movement "couldn't get worse public opinion than we have had or have less customers with what we've got to sell."[15] Finally, in December 1953, Hubbard incorporated the Church of Scientology along with two other churches in Camden, New Jersey. This was followed by the opening of a church in California in 1954 and the incorporation of the Founding Church of Scientology in Washington, D.C., in 1955.

While Hubbard's early Dianetics had been a primarily nonreligious form of self-help therapy, his new Church of Scientology began to incorporate much more explicitly religious

FIGURE 7.3 Scientology center in Los Angeles. Photo by the author.

ideas that extended well beyond the individual human mind and this particular lifetime. As he argued in lectures of the early 1950s, Scientology has much in common with Eastern religions, particularly Hinduism and Buddhism, which are its closest spiritual kin. During this period, Hubbard introduced the idea of the "Eight Dynamics," or the urge that all beings have to survive on eight levels of existence, which are symbolized by the eight points of the Scientology cross. These include the desire to survive as an individual, as a family, as a group, as a species, as all life forms, as the physical universe, as a spiritual entity, and finally as Infinity, God, or the Supreme Being. However, Hubbard had little to say about this eighth dynamic of Infinity or the Supreme Being, leaving it largely up to the individual to make up his or her mind about its exact nature.

Hubbard did have quite a lot to say, however, about the thetan, its past history, and its ultimate potential. In its original form, the thetan was an inherently infinite and even "god-like celestial entity" that originally had its own "Home Universe" created by its own free will.[16] But the thetan has become mistakenly trapped in this present universe of matter, energy, space, and time (MEST). The thetan has had countless past lives in this universe, including numerous life forms on earth—such as clams, birds, sloths, apes, and so on. But it has also had numerous adventures on other planets among various alien life forms— what Hubbard called "space opera." While most Scientologists today downplay these space opera themes, they are pervasive throughout Hubbard's early lectures of the 1950s. On the basis of his extensive auditing, Hubbard believed that he had reconstructed the "Whole Track" or the entire history of the universe and the thetans' various adventures from the time they first "hit the time track" sixty million years ago. These include space opera episodes not only among ancient civilizations on Earth (such as Atlantis and ancient Egypt) but also on various other planets and among alien civilizations such as Arsclycus (a "city in space"), the Marcab Confederacy, and so on.[17]

As Scientology grew and expanded during the 1960s, Hubbard added more and increasingly esoteric levels of training and organization. Beginning in 1966, he revealed a series of auditing levels called Operating Thetan (OT), in which the thetan or spiritual self is believed to achieve ever-greater freedom from the material world and ever-greater spiritual powers. These OT levels were intended to be highly confidential and released only to Scientologists who had passed through the required levels of auditing—although they were all eventually leaked to the media and now circulate widely on the Internet. The church lists fifteen OT levels in its current road map of the Scientology path, "The Bridge to Total Freedom," though only eight of these appear to have been completed by Hubbard before his death.

Despite the intense secrecy surrounding them, the OT levels eventually became part of the court record in two lawsuits during the 1980s and were leaked first to the media and then onto the Internet, where, despite numerous legal battles, they now circulate freely. Perhaps the most infamous material in these advanced grades is contained in OT level III (which was also savagely mocked on the animated TV show *South Park*). The basic outline of the story runs as follows: seventy-five million years ago, there was a Galactic Confederacy consisting of seventy-six planets and ruled by a dictator named Xenu (or Xemu in some versions). To solve the problem of overpopulation in his confederacy, Xenu brought billions of people to Earth (then called Teegeeack) and placed hydrogen bombs in Earth's volcanoes to destroy them. The thetans from these individuals, however, survived and eventually adhered to the bodies of modern human beings. Thus each one of us today has a mass of "extra-body thetans" stuck onto ourselves, which are causing us pain and unhappiness in this lifetime.[18]

Although the media have made a great deal of the Xenu story, it is important to note that it is a relatively small part of the larger Scientology belief system and not a concern for most ordinary Scientologists. Moreover, the Xenu story is really quite unremarkable when compared to the more elaborate space opera narratives contained in Hubbard's publicly available lectures from the early 1950s.

As the Scientologist passes through these confidential OT levels, he or she is also believed to experience ever-greater freedom as a thetan and greater mastery over the MEST universe. Ultimately, the thetan is believed to acquire various "superpowers," such as telepathy, clairvoyance, physical healing, and "remote viewing" or seeing things at great distances—a paranormal ability that was actively being explored by the CIA during this time. Hubbard also wrote extensively about the thetan's ability to "exteriorize" or leave the physical body and travel at will throughout the universe, which has much in common with the concept of "astral travel" discussed by many in the Theosophical Society and other new religions of the late nineteenth and early twentieth centuries.[19] At the Scientology center in Clearwater, Florida, the church has begun construction of a huge "Super Power Building" adjacent to its Fort Harrison Hotel. According to Scientology's *Source* magazine, the Super Power Building is "an entirely New Universe" and ideal in every detail: "Expanding on technology developed by NASA astronauts, it's now combined with everything else they never conceived of in terms of space." Photos of the interior of the building feature space age–looking rooms with large shiny orbs and a GyroSpin device.[20]

SCIENTOLOGY'S ORGANIZATION

The organization of the Church of Scientology has a long, convoluted, and complicated history. The early Dianetics movement was first organized as the Hubbard Dianetic Research Foundation (HDRF). However, the HDRF went bankrupt in 1952 and was replaced by the Hubbard Association of Scientologists (HAS) and then by the Hubbard Association of Scientologists International (HASI). In 1981, the Church of Scientology International (CSI), also known as the Mother Church, was formed; and this was followed in 1982 by the Church of Spiritual Technology (CST), which owns all copyrights on the estate of L. Ron Hubbard, and then by the Religious Technology Center (RTC). While the RTC claims only to be the "holder of Dianetics and Scientology Trademarks," it is the most powerful executive organization within the church, and its current chairman, David Miscavige, is widely recognized as the effective head of the movement.

Today, what we call Scientology is in reality a remarkably complex network of ostensibly independent but clearly interconnected corporate entities. These include not only the many individual churches (or "outer orgs") but also publishing houses, such as Bridge Publications and Golden Era Productions, as well as various groups and services, such as World Institute of Scientology Enterprises (WISE), Scientology Missions International (SMI), the Citizens' Commission on Human Rights (CCHR), and the Foundation for Religious Freedom (FRF), as well as drug and criminal rehabilitation programs such as Narconon and Criminon, among many, many others. As such, the Church of Scientology is perhaps best understood not simply as a "religion" but as a complex, multifaceted multinational corporation of which religion is simply one aspect.[21]

In 1968, Hubbard created the Sea Organization or Sea Org, which is the elite, innermost, dedicated core of Scientologists. Modeled on a naval organization, the Sea Org was initially formed to accompany Hubbard on his vessel, the Apollo. Members of the Sea Org sign a "billion-year contract," vowing to come back lifetime after lifetime to assist in Hubbard's mission to spread Scientology and ultimately to create a new civilization on this planet. Indeed, the Sea Org was presented in Scientology publications as the only means to save the human race from nuclear war and "the terror of total destruction."[22]

Today, the Sea Org is largely a land-based order centered in Clearwater, Florida, and there is currently only one working vessel, the *Freewinds*. But Sea Org members continue to wear naval uniforms and maintain strict military discipline. According to the Church of Scientology, the tight discipline of the Sea Org is analogous to that of a Christian or Buddhist monastic order. In the eyes of critics and many ex-members, however, the Sea Org is a manipulative cult that controls, surveils, and manipulates members in a way that borders on brainwashing. Perhaps the most controversial aspect of the Sea Org is its disciplinary program called the Rehabilitation Project Force or RPF. The RPF began aboard Sea Org ships in the late 1960s, when members who needed discipline were assigned to clean the filthier parts of the ship; eventually RPF centers would be established at Scientology complexes in Los Angeles, Clearwater, London, and Copenhagen. According to the Church of Scientology

Most of the other interviews in this book are from current members of new religions. For a different perspective, and to raise a different set of methodological questions, this chapter includes an interview with an ex-member. Nancy Many was a longtime member of Scientology who served in a variety of very high-level positions, including head of the church's Celebrity Centre in Hollywood, California. After leaving Scientology, she published a memoir entitled My Billion-Year Contract. *In this interview she explains how she first became involved with Scientology, her views of L. Ron Hubbard, and why she eventually left the movement and returned to her Roman Catholic roots.*

I first became involved in Scientology as a teenaged college student. I had been raised Roman Catholic—Irish Catholic. This was during the '70s, when Vatican II was creating strong changes in the church; I drifted away from the weekly mass or involvement with a parish community. I still held onto my Christian/Catholic beliefs, but these were not an important part of my life at this time. I was interested in social justice issues, and my heart's desire was to become a practicing social worker.

My introduction to Scientology was not as a religion but as a practical philosophy— and if it was a religion it was nondenominational. This was a "group of people who were making the world a better place." That was my goal as well—to make the world a better place. I read the book *A New Slant on Life,* which is a collection of essays by L. Ron Hubbard. I found them to be appealing, with the exception of a few on the "place of women."

I was interested in Scientology for a couple of compelling reasons: (a) This was a group of people who were "making the world a better place" that I could join. I was promised that I could be practicing as a social worker in less time than my college program. (b) No drugs. The main spiritual aspect of Scientology that I was interested in was the recalling of past lives. This was a belief I held, and Scientology was my first encounter with a "method" to help people remember their past lives. I wanted to remember my own past lives.

When I first joined Scientology I thought about L. Ron Hubbard as this older man who was a writer. He had lived a lot of life, and through his experiences he put together this practical philosophy. I knew several people who personally worked with him. Through their stories of Hubbard's nature I knew him as a man with the faults and foibles of a man. I felt he was very intelligent and recognized in him an ability to write about complicated matters in a simple, easy-to-understand way. When I worked within the organization, Hubbard's attentions became something I both craved and feared. The man was mercurial, and organizational snafus would often have him on a tirade leaving

(continued)

multiple bodies in his wake. Now I feel that he was a sociopath. I think that L. Ron Hubbard created a criminal, human-trafficking, human rights–abusing money tree.

Scientologists believe that man is a spirit who has a body. They believe that we have lived before and will live again. Scientologists believe that a person is completely responsible for whatever situation he finds himself in. The individual person is ultimate cause. Bad things only happen to a person when they themselves have done something bad (shameful and secretive). Should a Scientologist find himself suffering from cancer, the Scientologist will work to uncover all their hidden deeds, misdeeds, or thoughts that caused this cancer to come to them.

The daily life of a staff member is a 24/7 involvement with Scientology. A Scientology staff member is expected to devote their lives to the expansion of Scientology. Anything (or person) that draws their attention away from the expansion of Scientology is considered "Dev-T." Dev-T is short for "developed traffic": it basically means anything which takes time or attention away from the focus of the group. Dev-T could include the illness of your child, having to spend time helping another staff member on their job, or any one of a myriad of bumps in the road to being a 100 percent devoted worker bee.

I had two major breaks with Scientology. The first was in 1982 when I left the Sea Organization. The Sea Organization is the part of Scientology that runs the entire administration of Scientology. Members of the Sea Organization work, live, and eat within the organization. I was part of the higher-level international management arm. My husband and I had a young son (three years old) who was not well cared for. The child care facilities were sub par. One day my husband and I were removed from our management positions and ordered to join the Rehabilitation Project Force. The Rehabilitation Project Force is a labor camp where members are kept under guard. We were taken to their location in the basement by guards and separated from our son. We did not know where our son was, and were told we would not be able to see him for several weeks, and then only if "we were good."

We escaped the next morning, recovered our son, and left the Sea Organization. This was extremely difficult, as we had nothing. We had no money; we had no place to live and no jobs. Through the assistance of former Sea Org members who had left before us we were able to find jobs, an apartment, and even a low-cost car. Without this network of extremely supportive ex-members, I have no idea what we would have done. This is an informal network that continues today.

This leaving of the Sea Org was not my final break from Scientology. I attempted to remain a member as a "public." Scientology had little control over my day-to-day life as a public person. The only control Scientology could have had during my time as a "public Scientologist" would have been with other members. If I left while working for another member of Scientology, I would have been fired. At the time that I left Scientology for the final time, I did not work for a Scientologist, thus I only lost "friends."

During my time as a public Scientologist I made my way back to the Catholic Church, and my membership remains today. My view of Scientology today is similar to what it was when I joined. Scientology is a business that uses the "religious cloak" to enjoy the legal and financial benefits of a religion. Scientology enhanced my understanding and abilities in the business world. I learned sales techniques, I learned how to manage staff and multiple organizations, and much more. Scientology is a self-serving organization that preys on the good nature and good hearts of people.

and to more sympathetic scholars, the RPF is comparable to a "monastic retreat" in Christian communities and simply involves periods of work and church counseling.[23] Critics, however, claim that the RPF is less like a monastic retreat than a "Chinese ideological re-education center" and that it involves forcible confinement, physical maltreatment, demanding chores, poor diet, and inadequate medical care—in short, serious human rights violations.[24]

In part because of these allegations of mistreatment and abuse, a number of high-ranking Scientologists have recently left the church and spoken out quite critically about the current leadership. Some of the strongest criticism has come from Marty Rathbun, who served as the inspector general of the Religious Technology Center and as a close associate of David Miscavige. Still loyal to Hubbard's legacy, however, Rathbun has called for a "Scientology Reformation" that would clean up the corruption in the church and restore the original message of its founder.[25]

THE WORLD'S MOST CONTROVERSIAL NEW RELIGION: SCIENTOLOGY, CELEBRITIES, AND THE MEDIA

By the 1970s, Scientology had emerged as one of the most successful but also most controversial new religions in the world, attracting both tremendous media attention and numerous attacks by journalists, anticult groups, and various government agencies both in the United States and overseas. The church also began to attract a wide array of celebrities, who have since served as influential spokespersons, advocates, and defenders of the church. Plans to attract celebrities had been suggested as early as the mid-1950s, but in the early 1970s the church began to build a number of opulent Celebrity Centres in Hollywood and around the world specifically catering to actors, musicians, artists, and entertainers. The church's more prominent celebrity advocates have included actors Tom Cruise, John Travolta, Kirstie Alley, and Nancy Cartwright; musicians Isaac Hayes and Chick Corea; and (formerly) director Paul Haggis.

Cruise, in particular, has been one of the church's most outspoken but also controversial supporters. First becoming involved with Scientology in 1986 through fellow actress Mimi Rogers, he claims that Hubbard's technology helped him overcome dyslexia and that Narconon is the only successful drug rehabilitation in the world. Indeed, he made headlines in 2005 when he launched into an intense critique of psychiatry and prescription drug use during a heated interview with Matt Lauer on NBC's *Today* show. A close friend of current head David Miscavige, Cruise has done a great deal of promotional work for the church, including a confidential—and quite controversial—video that was leaked to YouTube in 2008.

After Cruise, Scientology's most prominent celebrity spokesperson has been John Travolta, who was first introduced to Dianetics in 1975 while working on his first film. According to his own testimony, it was because of Hubbard's methods that he landed a leading role on the sitcom *Welcome Back Kotter* and had a string of successful films. In addition to his major service and contributions to the church, Travolta was closely involved with and starred in the 2000 film *Battlefield Earth*, based on Hubbard's epic science fiction saga.

At the same time that Scientology began to attract a number of celebrity spokespersons, however, it began to acquire a far more negative reputation in the American media. Since its origins, Scientology has had a tense and at times hostile relationship with journalists, who have regularly described it as either a silly fad or a dangerous cult. The early Dianetics movement was often dismissed as a kind of "ersatz psychiatry" and a "hoax," while the later Church of Scientology was dubbed the "Thriving Cult of Greed and Power" by *Time* magazine in 1991.[26]

In turn, the church has often responded fiercely to its critics, by launching numerous lawsuits and in some cases using extralegal measures. The most infamous formulation of this doctrine was a practice called "fair game," according to which enemies of Scientology could be fought using any and all means at one's disposal. As Hubbard put it in a letter in October 1967, those who are designated "fair game" may be "deprived of property or injured by any means by any Scientologist without any discipline of the Scientologist. May be tricked, sued or lied to or destroyed."[27] For example, when the journalist Paulette Cooper published a damning critique of the church in 1971, she became the target of a plan by the church's intelligence branch or Guardian's Office (GO) called Operation Freakout. According to a document from 1971, the primary object of the operation was to get Cooper "incarcerated in a mental institution or jail," and it was later found that the GO had devised a plot to frame Cooper for terrorism against various government officials—including Henry Kissinger himself.[28] Similarly, after the 1991 *Time* magazine article on "the Cult of Greed," the church launched a massive $416 million libel suit against Time Warner; meanwhile, the article's author, Richard Behar, brought his own countersuit against the church, claiming that he had been the target of various legal and extralegal attacks, including the efforts of a swarm of lawyers and private detectives to "threaten, harass and discredit" him.

Finally, in addition to its various battles with journalists in the print media, Scientology has been enmeshed in a number of major battles in cyberspace over the dissemination of its confidential Operating Thetan materials. Since the dawn of the Internet, critics and ex-

Scientologists have been circulating the confidential OT documents on various websites, and the church has in turn launched a series of lawsuits against online groups. In 1993, for example, ex-Scientologist Larry Wollersheim began posting OT materials on his website FACTNet ("Fight Against Coercive Tactics Network"), which was designed to spread information about what he regarded as abusive cults. In 1995, a federal court ordered a raid on his home and the confiscation of all of Wollersheim's computers and files, which sparked a complex legal battle that dragged on for several years until a settlement was reached in 1999.

In many ways, the fight over the circulation of Scientology's confidential materials in cyberspace really highlights a tension within the First Amendment itself. From the church's perspective this is a matter of *free exercise of religion* and its right to maintain control over the dissemination of its confidential materials. The OT materials, the church argues, are not only copyrighted and trade secrets but also religious texts that should be respected. From the perspective of critics and ex-members, conversely, this is a matter of *free speech* and their own rights to speak openly about Scientology in order to spread what they feel is much-needed information about this controversial group.[29]

KEY ISSUES AND DEBATES: TAX EXEMPTION AND THE DEFINITION OF "RELIGION" IN THE UNITED STATES

Of all the many debates surrounding Scientology, perhaps the one with the most complex and wide-ranging implications is the debate over its status as a religion and specifically over its claims to tax exemption as a nonprofit religious organization in the eyes of the US Internal Revenue Service (and other government agencies in other nations).

One of the main reasons that Scientology has been so controversial in the United States and other countries is that it charges a great deal of money for its auditing services and has rapidly grown into one of the wealthiest religious organizations in the world. In the eyes of many critics, Scientology is thus better understood as a for-profit "business" than a religious or charitable organization. Scientology auditing was always rather expensive, but it became increasingly more so as the church expanded in the 1960s, '70s, and '80s. In particular, the advanced Operating Thetan levels became quite costly, some running into the thousands and tens of thousands of dollars. Today, the total cost of OT training will vary depending on the amount of auditing an individual Scientologist requires. However, conservative estimates are that rising to the basic level of "Clear" costs at least $128,000 and that ascending to the most advanced level of OT VIII requires a minimum of $300,000 to $400,000.[30] As of 1993—the last year the church had to declare income before receiving tax exemption—the assets of the worldwide church were $398 million, while the amount it earned that year alone from investments, counseling fees, and book sales totaled $300 million. Not surprisingly, these large amounts of money attracted the attention of the IRS and raised a much larger debate surrounding religious organizations and tax exemption.

The church's battle with the IRS—dubbed "THE WAR" by current Scientology head Miscavige—first began in the late 1950s. Hubbard's movement initially had little trouble winning tax-exempt status, which was awarded to Scientology churches in California and Washington, D.C., in 1956 and 1957. Just a year later, however, the IRS sent the Washington church a letter withdrawing its tax-exempt status, stating that the tenets and practices of Scientology did not constitute an exclusively religious or educational activity. When the church in turn appealed to the US Court of Claims, the court ruled that exempt status was rightly withdrawn because Hubbard and his wife were personally benefiting financially from the church beyond reasonable remuneration. In short, Scientology was found to be a "business, a profit-making organization run by Hubbard for his personal enrichment."[31]

In 1966, facing mounting pressure from governments in the United States, the United Kingdom, and Australia, Hubbard decided to transfer all of Scientology's worldwide assets to a hitherto minor entity called the Church of Scientology of California (CSC). The CSC had also been given tax-exempt status in 1957 and had apparently flown under the IRS radar up to this point. By placing all of Scientology's global assets under the tax-exempt CSC umbrella, the church could bypass all of the various problems it had faced in the United Kingdom and other countries where their tax exemption was still in question. However, this move to shift all of Scientology's finances under the CSC was also short-lived in its success. Just a year later, in 1967, the IRS decided to strip the CSC of its tax-exempt status, along with all other related Scientology organizations. The Founding Church of Scientology promptly sued, claiming to be exempt from federal income tax on the grounds that it was a corporation organized "exclusively for religious purposes."[32] The courts, however, remained unconvinced, concluding that Scientology's revenue was still primarily benefiting private individuals such as Hubbard and his family. In fact, the IRS undertook a mammoth audit of the church for the years 1970 through 1974 and determined that "the Church's activities were akin to a business" and not to a religious organization.[33] This in turn sparked a massive, twenty-five-year war between the church and the IRS, which eventually resulted in thousands of lawsuits.

At the same time that Scientology was enmeshed in this battle with the IRS, Hubbard began to strongly assert the "religious" nature of the church. In what the Los Angeles Times called Scientology's "most sweeping religious makeover," Scientology franchises became "missions," and the display of clerical collars and crosses became strictly enforced.[34] As Hubbard wrote in a policy letter from February 1969 entitled simply "Religion," all staff were directed to make certain to display overtly religious paraphernalia such as crosses, clerical collars, and the Scientology Creed: "Visual evidences that Scientology is a religion are mandatory. . . . Any staff who are trained at any level as auditors . . . are to be clothed in the traditioned [sic] ministerial black suit, black vest, white collar, silver cross for ordinary wear. Creed of the Church is to be done big and plainly posted in public areas."[35]

But perhaps the most bizarre episode in the church's war with the IRS was its covert operation carried out against the IRS and other government offices during the mid-1970s. The plan, dubbed Operation Snow White, was launched by Hubbard's wife, Mary Sue, and the church's intelligence bureau, the Guardian's Office. Devised in early 1973, Operation Snow White involved GO agents infiltrating offices of the IRS and other government agencies in order to steal thousands of documents relating to Scientology. GO agents also wire-tapped IRS offices during meetings in which Scientology was discussed. When the operation was uncovered in 1977, the FBI launched the largest raid in the Bureau's history, sending 134 agents into Scientology offices in Washington, D.C., and Los Angeles and confiscating over two hundred thousand documents and other materials. Mary Sue and eleven other Scientologists were arrested, tried, and convicted, while Hubbard was named an unindicted coconspirator and spent the remainder of his life in hiding.

Interestingly enough, in that same year of 1977, the IRS introduced new guidelines in its determination of what counts as a tax-exempt "religious" organization. The service developed a set of general criteria and a list of thirteen points it uses to judge the validity of a group's claim to religious status. The points include a distinct legal existence, a recognized creed and form of worship, a distinct ecclesiastical government, a formal code of doctrine and discipline, a distinct religious history, a membership not associated with any other church, a complete organization of ordained ministers selected after prescribed courses of study, regular congregations, regular religious services, Sunday schools for the instruction of the young, and schools for the preparation of ministers.[36] It is probably no accident that the year the IRS introduced these guidelines was the very same year that Scientologists working for the GO were arrested for their covert operations against the IRS. And this was also during the height of Scientology's efforts to reemphasize its religious profile through the display of crosses, clerical collars, and religious titles. Thus the legal battles between the church and the IRS have been central to the shifting definition of religion itself as the service has attempted to sort out what is and is not "religion." In turn, Scientologists have tried to fit themselves into whatever definitions of religion have been operative at given moments, adapting creatively to the shifting definition of religion in contemporary America.

The church's war with the IRS, meanwhile, was not resolved until 1993, following a private meeting between Miscavige, Marty Rathbun, and IRS head Fred T. Goldberg Jr. Although the precise details of this agreement have never been fully revealed, the church agreed to pay back taxes of $12.5 million in exchange for an impressive blanket tax exemption of all Scientology-related entities in the United States. This blanket exemption, remarkably, includes not only religious entities within the Scientology network but also seemingly quite "secular" entities that have nothing to do with religion, such as Galaxy Press, which reprints Hubbard's science fiction and fantasy stories. As Miscavige triumphantly proclaimed to an audience of Scientologists shortly after the decision, "the war" was over, and now other governments around the world would have to take note of the IRS's recognition of this "American religion": "We will waste no time carrying news of this new breakthrough to all foreign countries. Those battles have been being held in place by suppressive governments just quoting the IRS. The line has been: 'You are an American religion. If the IRS doesn't recognize you, why should we?' The answer is—'They do. And now, you better as well!'"[37] Shortly after the church's victory with the IRS, in fact, the US State Department began to recognize Scientology in its annual reports on religious freedom and to criticize other governments such as Germany for their harsh treatment of the church.[38]

But despite its triumph in the United States, Scientology has continued to face numerous challenges in many other countries, particularly in France, Germany, Russia, Australia, and the United Kingdom. Scientology was the subject of scathing government reports in both Australia and the United Kingdom in the 1960s and '70s, and it continues to be viewed with intense suspicion in France and Germany. French courts, which regard Scientology as a *secte* (cult) and not as a religion, convicted Scientology of fraud in October 2009; and as recently as 2007, German federal and state interior ministers undertook a move to ban the church.

In sum, while Scientology has won the right to be labeled a "religion" in the United States—at least in the eyes of the IRS and the State Department—it is still regarded as something else—as a cult, a business, or a secular therapy—in many other nations. Thus it forces us to think hard not only about the question "What is religion?" but, more importantly, about the questions "Who gets to *decide* what counts as a religion?" and "*What is at stake* in calling something a religion?"

QUESTIONS FOR DISCUSSION AND DEBATE

1. The most frequently asked question about Scientology is simply, Is it a religion? But think about what that simple question implies . . . Do we all agree on what a religion is? Does our idea of religion never change? Why does anyone care if we call it a religion or a cult or a business or whatever? What's really at stake? Are there any potential risks in *not* calling Scientology a religion (for example, a slippery slope toward rejecting other marginal groups, such as Mormons, Rastas, and others)?

2. Much of the debate surrounding Scientology has focused on whether this particular religious group should have tax exemption. But we could also ask the question of whether *any* religious groups should have tax exemption. After all, Pat Robertson and other Christian televangelists make a huge amount of money too. What are the reasons for tax exemption for religious groups, and do we think they're still valid in twenty-first-century America? If not, what is the alternative?

3. This chapter includes an interview with Nancy Many, who was formerly a high-level member of Scientology but now has left the church and is very critical of L. Ron Hubbard. What are the positive and negative, problematic and beneficial implications of using an interview from an ex-member of a new religious movement? Should we read her view of Scientology more critically than that of a current member of the church? Or less critically? Or should we read and examine every account of a new religious movement with an equally critical eye?

Hold an in-class debate on the question of new religions and tax exemption, using Scientology as a test case. Again, try to avoid reducing this to a simplistic "yes or no" or pro versus con debate. Consider including representatives not just from Scientology and the IRS but from other marginal religious groups who might be affected (Mormons, Jehovah's Witnesses, NAC, Rastas, etc.) as well as from government agencies in other nations (France, Germany, etc.) where Scientology is not recognized as a religion. Perhaps the most complex decision facing the class might be: Who should really decide and be the "highest" authority? The IRS, the Supreme Court, scholars of religious studies?

SUGGESTED VIDEO

"The Church of Scientology." *20/20*, ABC News, 2007.

SUGGESTIONS FOR FURTHER READING

Behar, Richard. "The Thriving Cult of Greed and Power." *Time*, May 6, 1991, 50–57.

Brill, Ann, and Ashley Packard. "Silencing Scientology's Critics on the Internet: A Mission Impossible?" *Communications and the Law* 19 (1997): 1–23.

Christensen, Dorthe Refslund. "Inventing L. Ron Hubbard: On the Construction and Maintenance of the Hagiographic Mythology of Scientology's Founder." In *Controversial New Religions*, edited by James R. Lewis and Jesper Aagaard Petersen, 227–58. New York: Oxford University Press, 2005.

Church of Scientology International. *Scientology: Theory and Practice of a Contemporary Religion*. Los Angeles: Bridge Publications, 1998.

Dawson, Lorne L., and Douglas E. Cowan, eds. *Religion Online: Finding Faith on the Internet*. New York: Routledge, 2004.

Friends of Ron. *L. Ron Hubbard: A Profile*. Los Angeles: Bridge Publications, 1995.

Hubbard, L. Ron. *Dianetics: The Modern Science of Mental Health*. Los Angeles: Bridge Publications, 2007.

———. *Scientology: A History of Man*. Los Angeles: Saint Hill Organization Worldwide, 1968.

———. *Technique 88: Incidents on the Track before Earth*. Los Angeles: Golden Era Publications, 2007.

Kent, Stephen A. "Scientology—Is This a Religion?" *Marburg Journal of Religion* 4 (1999): 1–23.

Lewis, James R., ed. *Scientology*. New York: Oxford University Press, 2009.

Many, Nancy. *My Billion-Year Contract: Memoir of a Former Scientologist*. Bloomington, IN: Xlibris, 2009.

Melton, J. Gordon. *The Church of Scientology*. Salt Lake City, UT: Signature Books, 2000.

Rathbun, Mark Marty. *The Scientology Reformation: What Every Scientologist Should Know*. Pancho 'n' Lefty Publishing, 2012.

Reitman, Janet. *Inside Scientology: The Story of America's Most Secretive Religion*. New York: Houghton Mifflin, 2011.

Urban, Hugh B. *The Church of Scientology: A History of a New Religion*. Princeton, NJ: Princeton University Press, 2011.

Wallis, Roy. *The Road to Total Freedom: A Sociological Study of Scientology*. New York: Columbia University Press, 1976.

Whitehead, Harriet. *Renunciation and Reformulation: A Study of Conversion in an American Sect*. Ithaca, NY: Cornell University Press, 1987.

Wright, Lawrence. *Going Clear: Scientology, Hollywood, and the Prison of Belief*. New York: Knopf Doubleday, 2013.

NOTES TO CHAPTER 7

1. David Miscavige, "International Association of Scientologists Speech," October 8, 1993, www.cs.cmu.edu/~dst/Cowen/essays/speech.html.
2. Cynthia Kisser, quoted in Richard Behar, "The Thriving Cult of Greed and Power," *Time*, May 6, 1991, 50–57.
3. Reynolds v. United States, 98 U.S. 145 (1878), 162.
4. "L. Ron Hubbard: Founder of Scientology," Aboutlronhubbard.org, 2006. www.aboutlronhubbard.org/eng/wis3_1.htm; Martin Gardner, *Fads and Fallacies in the Name of Science* (New York: Dover, 1957), 263.
5. L. Ron Hubbard, *Hymn of Asia* (Los Angeles: Golden Era Productions, 2009), n.p.
6. L. Ron Hubbard, *The Technical Bulletins of Dianetics and Scientology*, vol. 3 (Los Angeles: Scientology Publications, 1976), 49.
7. Dennis Wheeler, "Son of Scientology," *News-Herald*, July 7–13, 1982, www.lermanet.com/scientologynews/newsherald-DeWolfe07–82.htm.
8. Quoted in Jon Atack, *A Piece of Blue Sky: Scientology, Dianetics and L. Ron Hubbard Exposed* (New York: Carol, 1990), 79–80.
9. See Dorthe Refslund Christensen, "Inventing L. Ron Hubbard: On the Construction and Maintenance of the Hagiographic Mythology of Scientology's Founder," in *Controversial New Religions*, ed. James R. Lewis and Jesper Aagaard Petersen (New York: Oxford University Press, 2005), 227–58.
10. Church of Scientology International, "Excalibur by L. Ron Hubbard," 2014, www.ronthephilosopher.org/phlspher/page08.htm.
11. Channel 4 Television (UK), *Secret Lives: L. Ron Hubbard*, November 19, 1997.
12. Harriet Whitehead, *Renunciation and Reformulation: A Study of Conversion in an American* Sect (Ithaca, NY: Cornell University Press, 1987), 52.

13. L. Ron Hubbard, *Dianetics: The Modern Science of Mental Health* (Los Angeles: Bridge Publications, 2007), 227.

14. Stephen Kent, "Scientology's Relationship with Eastern Religions," *Journal of Contemporary Religion* 11 (1996): 21–36.

15. L. Ron Hubbard to Helen O'Brien, April 10, 1953, in Hugh B. Urban, *The Church of Scientology: A History of a New Religion* (Princeton, NJ: Princeton University Press, 2011), 65.

16. David Bromley, "Making Sense of Scientology: Prophetic, Contractual Religion," in *Scientology*, ed. James R. Lewis (New York: Oxford University Press, 2009), 91.

17. See L. Ron Hubbard, *Scientology: A History of Man* (Los Angeles: Saint Hill Organization Worldwide, 1968), *Secrets of the MEST Universe* (Los Angeles: Bridge Publications, 1990), and *Technique 88: Incidents on the Track before Earth* (Los Angeles: Golden Era Publications, 2007).

18. For a discussion of this narrative, see Mikael Rothstein, "'His Name Was Xenu. He Used Renegades . . .': Aspects of Scientology's Founding Myth," in Lewis, *Scientology*, 365–88.

19. See L. Ron Hubbard, *Dianetics and Scientology Technical Dictionary* (Los Angeles: Publication Organizations, 1975), 279; Urban, *Church of Scientology*, 112–15.

20. "An Entirely New Universe—In Every Detail," *Source* 194 (2007): 40–41.

21. Stephen Kent, "Scientology—Is This a Religion?" *Marburg Journal of Religion* 4 (1999): 1–23.

22. Urban, *Church of Scientology*, 124; see Nancy Many, *My Billion-Year Contract: Memoir of a Former Scientologist* (Bloomington, IN: XLibris, 2009).

23. Juha Pentikäinen, Jurgen F. K. Redhardt, and Michael York, "The Church of Scientology's Rehabilitation Project Force," CESNUR Center on New Religions, 2002, www.cesnur.org/2002/scient_rpf_02.htm.

24. Gerry Armstrong, "Gerry Armstrong Describes Experience on the RPF," Scientology Lies.com, 1999, www.scientology-lies.com/gerryarmstrong5.html. See Stephen Kent, "Brainwashing in Scientology's Rehabilitation Project Force," 1997, www.skeptictank.org/his/brainwas.htm; Susan Raine, "Surveillance in a New Religious Movement: Scientology as a Test Case," *Religious Studies and Theology* 28 (2009): 63–94.

25. Mark Marty Rathbun, *The Scientology Reformation: What Every Scientologist Should Know* (Pancho 'n' Lefty Publishing, 2012).

26. Albert Q. Maisel, "Dianetics, Science or Hoax?" *Look*, December 5, 1950, 85; Behar, "Thriving Cult."

27. L. Ron Hubbard, "Penalties for Lower Conditions," *HCO Policy Letter*, October 18, 1967; see Roy Wallis, *The Road to Total Freedom: A Sociological Study of Scientology* (New York: Columbia University Press, 1976), 144.

28. Sentencing Memorandum, United States v. Jane Kember, 487 F. Supp. 1340 (D.D.C. 1980), No. 78–401 (2) & (3), 23–24.

29. See Ann Brill and Ashley Packard, "Silencing Scientology's Critics on the Internet: A Mission Impossible?" *Communications and the Law* 19 (1997): 1–23; Urban, *Church of Scientology*, chap. 5.

30. See Urban, *Church of Scientology*, 135–37.

31. Atack, *Piece of Blue Sky*, 142–43.

32. Church of Scientology of California v. Commissioner of Internal Revenue Service, No. 3352–78 (D.D.C., 1984), 386.

33. Ibid., 451.

34. Joel Sappell and Robert W. Welkos, "Shoring Up Its Religious Profile," *Los Angeles Times*, June 25, 1990, www.latimes.com/news/local/la-scientology062590a,0,3090542.story.

35. L. Ron Hubbard, "Religion," *HCO Policy Letter*, February 12, 1969, reprinted in his *Organization Executive Course*, vol. 6 (Los Angeles: American Saint Hill Organization, 1969), 119.

36. Bruce Hopkins, *The Law of Tax-Exempt Organizations* (Hoboken, NJ: John Wiley and Sons, 2003), 237.
37. Miscavige, "International Association of Scientologists Speech."
38. US Department of State, "Germany Human Rights Practices, 1993," January 31, 1994, www .usask.ca/relst/jrpc/article-scientology.html.

EIGHT

Wicca and Neopaganism

Magic, Feminism, and Environmentalism

For over thirty years, thousands of witches, Druids, Heathens, Radical Faeries, and other neopagans have gathered each July for a huge, multiday festival of drumming, chanting, bonfires, workshops, lectures, ritual performances, and magic called Starwood. Now the largest neopagan festival in North America, Starwood began in Pennsylvania in 1981 and has since been held at various locations in New York and Ohio, typically attracting between 1,400 and 1,600 people. Like other neopagan festivals held across the United States, Starwood includes a wide array of workshops on spiritual topics, various forms of political activism, performance of pagan rituals, and numerous vendors selling an array of food, drink, clothing, jewelry, and ritual implements—all of this in a lively, friendly, party-like atmosphere. Attendees arrive in every manner of attire, ranging from Druid robes and witches' hats to wildly colorful costumes, exotic belly-dancer outfits, and ordinary jeans and T-shirts. Starwood also has a "clothing-optional" policy, and it is not uncommon for participants to appear "skyclad," or naked. As the festival's organizers described the event held in the hilly woodland of southeast Ohio in July 2014, "Starwood is a seven-day exploration of mind, body and spirit, of creativity and possibilities, features over 20 performances of music, drumming, dance and theater. . . . It's a multiversity featuring over 150 classes, workshops and ceremonies offered by prominent teachers from many fields, disciplines, traditions and cultures. It's a family-friendly camping event with tenting and hiking, food vendors, co-op child care, swimming, hot showers, a Kid Village and multimedia shows. Starwood is also a social event with costume parades, jam sessions, merchants, parties, giant puppets, all-night drumming and much more, including our huge and infamous Bonfire!"[1] Although Starwood is the largest of its kind, it is just one of dozens of pagan festivals held across the United States—often in quite unexpected locations, such as Hawkfest Drum and Dance in

FIGURE 8.1 Ár nDraíocht Féin (ADF) Druid ritual, Columbus, Ohio, July 2013. Photo by the author.

Georgia, Prometheus Rising in Pennsylvania, Women's Gathering in Indiana, Moondance in Alabama, Summerland Spirit Festival in Wisconsin, the Midwest Witches' Ball in Michigan, the Pagan Unity Festival in Tennessee, and California Witchcamp, to name but a few (figure 8.1).

This lively and eclectic festival culture reflects the vitality, breadth, and diversity of neopaganism as a religious phenomenon in the contemporary United States. Today, the United States has hundreds of neopagan groups, which include not only well-known organizations such as Wicca but also various Druid groups, which look back to ancient European Druidic traditions; Dianic groups, which focus primarily on the goddess; Heathen groups, which draw upon Germanic traditions; the Church of All Worlds, which focuses on Gaia or the Earth Goddess; gay and lesbian groups such as the Radical Faeries; and many others.

Despite their tremendous diversity, these various neopagan movements do share at least a few features. First, in contrast to New Age spirituality and to many new religious movements, neopagan groups typically look not to a future new era but rather *backward* to an

FIGURE 8.2 Gerald Gardner.
Photographer unknown.

ancient, usually pre-Christian past that they wish to either recover or draw inspiration from in the modern world. Second, neopagan groups tend to be more loosely organized than other new religious movements; rather than drawing rigid boundaries between insiders and outsiders, they tend to be organized in more fluid, flexible communities (such as covens), and individuals may be involved in multiple groups or may simply practice on their own. Third, neopaganism tends to be a very practice-oriented movement, typically with a stronger emphasis on ritual performance and magic than dogmatic belief systems. As a "religion without the middle man," it empowers individuals to engage in magical practice themselves rather than relying on priests or other religious authorities.[2] Finally, as we will see in this chapter, most forms of neopaganism emphasize either women's roles or gender equality; and most have some form of deep environmental ethic, regarding the natural world as sacred or infused with the divine.

Although all of these groups look back to much older sources, they are all "neo-" or "new" movements in the sense that they have all emerged (or some would argue "reemerged") in America and Europe in relatively recent times, basically since the 1950s and '60s. The most important figure in the revival of modern paganism was the eccentric British author Gerald Gardner (figure 8.2), who claimed to have been initiated into an ancient coven of witches that had secretly survived the millennia of Christian rule and was now resurfacing in the twentieth century. But Gardner's new Wicca movement quickly spawned a tremendous array of new forms of paganism, first in England and then in Europe and the United States from the 1950s onward.

One of the most important reasons—though surely not the only reason—for the success of neopaganism in the United States has been its close association with two other social and political movements: feminism and environmentalism. Neopaganism entered the United States in a huge way in the 1960s, at the height of the American counterculture movement, amid the rise of new forms of feminism and a new environmental awareness. At the same time that modern witchcraft was spreading through San Francisco, New York, and other major American cities, radical theologians such as Mary Daly were publishing influential feminist works such as *The Church and the Second Sex* (1969). And at the same time that American neopagans began to invoke the Earth Goddess, environmentalists such as Rachel Carson were publishing *Silent Spring* (1962) and other influential books that helped spark the modern environmentalist movement. In short, just as the Spiritualist movement had gone hand in hand with powerful new social movements such as abolition and women's rights, so contemporary neopaganism has often gone hand in hand with new social movements such as post-1960s feminism and environmentalism.

Because of the tremendous diversity of contemporary neopaganism, this chapter will focus primarily on early Wicca as it developed in England and then began to influence feminist witches in the United States such as Starhawk and Z Budapest. Combining paganism and goddess worship with women's rights, political activism, and environmentalism, Starhawk in particular has developed an earth-based spirituality that works toward both environmental sustainability and social justice. Perhaps the most famous neopagan author in North America, Starhawk has also begun to be taken seriously in the academic study of religion—for example, delivering a lecture at the Harvard Divinity School in 2013.

As we will see in this chapter, however, the role of feminism and environmentalism in contemporary neopaganism raises complicated questions and debates. For example, by associating women with "the Goddess" and with "the earth," are neopagans such as Starhawk actually challenging gender stereotypes and patriarchal traditions? Or are they in some ways ironically reinforcing traditional gender stereotypes (such as the association of women with nature, the earth, the body, and reproduction)? At the same time, they raise the question of whether we need spiritual movements such as neopaganism to help us address the many environmental crises that we face today or whether these appeals to the supernatural are a distraction from and an impediment to real action on serious environmental issues.

GERALD GARDNER AND THE BIRTH OF MODERN WICCA

While many neopagans trace their origins to ancient, pre-Christian, and even Paleolithic times, the birth of neopaganism as a modern religious movement really begins in the late nineteenth and early twentieth centuries. Interest in pagan traditions and in ancient Greek and Roman religions had been a growing trend in England throughout the nineteenth century, appearing in romantic poetry, novels, and artwork. At the same time, there was a fresh revival of the Western esoteric traditions of Kabbalah, Hermeticism, and magic, which we discussed in chapter 1, giving birth to new ritual magical groups such as the Hermetic Order of the Golden Dawn in the late 1880s.

In many ways the forefather of modern neopaganism was the British occultist and magician Aleister Crowley (1875–1947). Although Crowley was demonized in the popular press as "the wickedest man in the world" and a "drug fiend," he was one of the most important figures in the development of modern magic as a whole (as well as the development of rock 'n' roll and heavy metal in the 1960s and '70s). Crowley spelled *Magick* with a *k* in order to distinguish it from mere stage magic and parlor tricks. As he defined it, Magick is the "science and art of causing change to occur in conformity with will." It is a science in the sense that it works by natural laws and can be tested and replicated; and it is an art in the sense that it involves a great deal of beauty, art, symbolism, and theatrical performance. Although many neopagans today disavow Crowley because of his controversial reputation, his basic definition of magic is still widely used by many practitioners. As early as 1914, moreover, Crowley had called for the birth of a new kind of "natural religion," a more this-worldly form of spirituality based not on abstract deities but on the primal forces of the sun, moon, and earth: "The time is just ripe for a natural religion," he wrote. "People like rites and ceremonies and they are tired of hypothetical gods. Insist on the real benefits of the sun, the Mother-Force, the Father-Force and so on. . . . Let the religion be Joy. . . . In short, be the founder of a new and greater Pagan cult."[3]

A second key figure in the birth of modern witchcraft and neopaganism was a British scholar named Margaret Murray (1863–1963). In 1921, Murray published an influential but controversial book entitled *The Witch Cult in Western Europe,* which made the bold argument that the witch trials in medieval and early modern Europe were based, not on mere paranoid fantasy, but on a real religious movement that dated back to pre-Christian times. According to Murray, long before the arrival of Christianity there had been an older pagan tradition of magic and Goddess worship, which was later misunderstood, demonized, and persecuted as witchcraft. Although Murray's account is not taken very seriously by most historians today, it would have a huge influence on the revival of neopaganism in the mid-twentieth century.

However, the most important figure in the development of modern pagan witchcraft was Gerald B. Gardner (1884–1964), a charmingly eccentric character who really sparked the modern Wicca movement. Gardner had spent his early career as a manager of tea and rubber plantations in South and Southeast Asia, but he also developed a strong interest in the occult, the supernatural, and mystical phenomena, reading widely in both Western esoteric traditions and Eastern traditions such as Hinduism and Buddhism. Gardner was strongly influenced by the occult works of Aleister Crowley, which he quoted extensively in his early manual of Wiccan rituals called the "Book of Shadows" (though, again, Crowley's influence was later downplayed by most Wiccans because of his scandalous reputation).

Gardner retired to London in 1936 and then moved to the area called New Forest two years later. It was here that he claimed that he was introduced to a mysterious figure called

Michael Dangler is a high priest in the Druid group ADF or Ár nDraíocht Féin and the leader of its Three Cranes Grove in Ohio. He is also a former major in religious studies and spent a great deal of time reading and studying various aspects of ancient religions before joining ADF. In this interview he talks about his background, the activities of ADF, and his understanding of how magic works.

I grew up in the United Church of Christ. My grandparents were Congregationalists, and we ended up in a UCC congregation for most of my formative years. But religion wasn't a real important thing in my family's life. It wasn't something that we did twice a week or three times a week. We went on Sunday. I was an avid reader, though, and I read a lot of fiction. I can account for most of my vocabulary coming from fantasy novels. But when we talk about the influence that fantasy novels or games like Dungeons and Dragons have, in my experience with other pagans, it's not the fantasy aspect of it; it's where people encounter for the first time this concept of magic or this concept of Druids or witches.

I encountered the word *Druid*, and I said, "That sounds really interesting." At the same time, I was taking a Latin class in high school, and we were translating pieces of Caesar's *Commentaries on the Gallic Wars*, and I ran into the word there as well. I did some reading, and you know Caesar is fairly gory in his descriptions of wicker men and people being killed in various ways. But what attracted me was not that piece in book 6 where he's talking about people being burned alive but where he's talking about Druids being philosophers and Druids being judges and Druids being healers, as well as magicians and spiritual leaders. So that was the piece that turned me on to it, this idea of the polymath, someone who is skilled, these natural philosopher types. I started reading everything that I could find on it. But it wasn't until I stumbled onto ADF that I found someone who was interested in looking at archaeology and at what the ancients actually did, what we could piece back together, and then moving from there to what it is that works for us.

Within ADF we keep eight high days at least. Groves are required to do public work on those eight high days; we can't do a private Beltane rite and call it our service to the community. It has to be a public rite, and the reason for that is that in the 1980s when ADF was formed there was the Satanic Panic and this notion that there are people out there trying to eat your children. What [ADF founder] Isaac Bonewits really wanted to do was to show that, no, pagans can be good neighbors too. They're not out to steal your kid away, they're not out here to hurt the community, they're out there to participate in the community. We do it at metro parks because they're cheap, and they're public. We haven't picked one metro park where we always do stuff because we want to move around the community, so that if you live in Reynoldsburg, two or three times a year we're doing a rite near you; if you live in Powell, two or three times a year we're doing a rite near you. We're trying to provide as much access to paganism as we can for those who want it.

I've always liked Crowley's definition of magic as changing reality to suit your will—as an art and a science. I tend to do what works, and I tend to change things around from different cultures and use them in a way that may not have originally been intended but fits what I want to do. And then I've also got this heavy streak of wanting to look at the old *grimoires* and the Greek magical papyri and try to see how well it works for me as a modern. The problem of course with the Greek magical papyri and ancient spells is that they involve things that I don't particularly care to do. We don't do animal sacrifice. I'm not going to go and dig the eyes out of a dove in order to follow a magical incantation specifically from one of those old texts. So I find ways to change and fit them into a practice that makes sense for modern folk.

To give you a good example: Earlier this year my wife and I had been trying to conceive for a while. So I went digging into these old spell books to see what I could find, and I came across this manuscript from the eighteenth century, a Germanic manuscript. It contains a very simple spell for getting someone pregnant. Every morning for several weeks while trying to conceive, the instructions say, "Carve this symbol onto a piece of cheese and give it to her to eat and she'll become pregnant." So we did that, and she ate a lot of cheese, and now we're expecting twins in October. It's one of these things where we didn't change anything else, we'd been working on it for months if not a year and a half at that point, and that's the only thing we changed. We did it with intent, we did it with a real desire to make something happen, and it worked.

There are several schools of thought on how exactly magic works. And not being able to explain it in purely scientific terms doesn't really bother a lot of pagans, and it doesn't particularly bother me. But I have the notion that, if it works for someone, and if it truly is magic, then if you give your script to somebody else and they do all the same steps, they should come out with the same end product. In some ways it is very much a scientific approach. But what actually does the work, in my mind, is the reciprocity and relationship with spirits. We're sitting here, and here's the cheese, and I'm writing instructions on the cheese to give to her to eat. To look at it in a really ancient way, there's some spirit that sees that, understands what that action is, and is able to take the appropriate action as a result. The theory that I tend to work with is that this stuff doesn't necessarily work free of those relationships. You have to have those relationships, especially if what you're doing involves calling on a deity. I don't like calling on those individuals cold. It would be like picking a random name from the phone book, calling them up, and saying, "You don't know me, but I'd really like

(continued)

a hundred bucks. Totally, I promise I'll pay you back." Most people wouldn't do that. I tend to think the spirits and the deities are the same. Some of them are willing to take a chance, but for the most part I think that they want a relationship as much as we do.

The majority of pagans tend to be female, educated, with college degrees, and between the ages of about twenty-five and forty-five. I've seen that borne out in ADF. We seem to have mostly women—I'd say about 60 percent—and we've got most between about the ages of twenty-five and forty-five. The fact that women can find roles of authority and ritual expertise that they wouldn't find in mainstream churches is a big part of it. It goes back to the idea of "power with instead of power over." Starhawk talks about that extensively in *The Spiral Dance*. There are roles for women in just about every pagan group. Generally speaking, men and women have very equal roles, and within Wicca you can find denominations that are entirely women.

I hate to generalize about other religions, but there is a comfort in having something written down that someone can tell you is always true and always correct, and paganism doesn't have that. It's religion with homework. For the most part, pagans like to read, they like to find out about the cultures that they're interested in, they like to find out where their gods came from, and they don't deal well with someone else telling them this is how it has to be. I think a lot of that has to do with the level of education that a lot of them have.

Old Dorothy—a woman he identified as a genuine witch belonging to an ancient tradition of pagan witchcraft that had survived secretly for centuries beneath the surface of Christian society—thus confirming Margaret Murray's thesis. It was Old Dorothy (later identified as Dorothy Clutterbuck, d. 1951) who allegedly initiated Gardner into her coven and introduced him to the ancient craft of magic.

Today there is a great deal of controversy surrounding the mysterious figure of Old Dorothy. Was she in fact a representative of some ancient form of witchcraft? Did she exist at all, or was she the figment of Gardner's own lively imagination? Was she really the person identified as Dorothy Clutterbuck—who was, ironically, a well-to-do and conservative woman, highly respected in the community? Or was this just the name he gave in order to distract attention from a *real* witch, whose identity he kept secret?[4]

But whether Gardner had really been initiated into an ancient tradition of witchcraft or had instead largely invented it himself, he did become the founder of a major neopagan revival through England, Europe, and the United States from the 1950s onward. Gardner claimed that he had first been given permission to represent some of the witch beliefs and practices in the disguised form of a novel called *High Magic's Aid* (1949); then, after the repeal of England's witchcraft laws in 1951, he was emboldened to publish these ancient secrets more openly in works such as his first major book, *Witchcraft Today* (1954).

Witchcraft Today offered a semihistorical narrative of Wicca—or what some call the "myth of Wicca"—which became widely accepted by many neopagans. As Gardner tells the story, Wicca (from the Old English term for a practitioner of magic or witchcraft) can be traced all the way back to the Stone Age, when a matriarchal culture flourished and women were the experts in the use of medicine and magic. The chief deity was the Goddess or Great Mother, with women as her priestesses, and her male counterpart was the God of the Hunt or the Horned God: "Historically, the matriarchal period had been tentatively dated from the middle of the ninth to the middle of the seventh millennium B.C., during which time caves, trees, the moon, and stars all seem to have been revered as female emblems. So the myth of the Great Goddess came into existence, and woman was her priestess. Probably at the same time the men had a hunter god who presided over the animals."[5] When Christianity spread across Europe and the British Isles, Gardner's narrative continues, this ancient Goddess tradition was pushed underground, matriarchy was replaced by patriarchy, the Horned God was turned into Satan, and women who practiced magic were persecuted as witches. However, this ancient tradition survived throughout the centuries of Christian rule and resurfaced in twentieth-century England.

Most historians today find Gardner's narrative of the origins of Wicca implausible. Even many practitioners today will acknowledge that neopaganism is not so much the literal continuation of an ancient Stone Age religion as a modern movement that looks for inspiration to ancient sources. And many others will argue that it simply doesn't matter. Rather, what matters is that the tradition exists now and is meaningful for people today, regardless of its precise historical origins. Indeed, even if it didn't exist in the ancient past, it needs to be invented today in order to protect the earth from widespread environmental devastation. As one Dianic priestess named Morgan McFarland put it, "At this point it doesn't matter whether or not it existed [in the ancient past]. . . . The people I know in the Craft are so desperate to bring back some balance of the Mother before she is totally raped and pillaged that we are, through that desperation, creating it or re-creating it."[6]

Regardless of the historical accuracy of Gardner's narrative of the origins of Wicca, he was the primary inspiration for a tremendous proliferation of new forms of paganism from the 1950s onward. In addition to Gardner's early Wiccan movement—often called Gardnerian or British Traditional Wicca—an enormous variety of other movements began to spread across England, Europe, and the United States. These include all women's groups such as Dianic Wicca, modern Druid groups such as ADF (Ár nDraíocht Féin, or "A Druid Fellowship"), Heathen groups that draw upon Germanic mythology, Reconstructionist groups that study and attempt to recreate ancient traditions, queer pagan groups such as the Radical Faeries and the Minoan Brotherhood, ethnic pagan groups that draw upon Celtic, Slavic, Italian, or other regional traditions, Wotanism or white supremacist paganism, and dozens of others. Finally, there are many solitary practitioners, who perform ritual and magic on their own without necessarily affiliating with any group.

NEOPAGAN BELIEFS, ETHICS, AND RITUAL: ORTHO-PRAXY RATHER THAN ORTHO-DOXY

Because of the sheer diversity of groups that fall under the label, it is impossible to describe a single neopagan "theology." In the Gardnerian Wiccan tradition, the emphasis is usually placed on the balance between the female and male deities. The female is typically identified as the Triple Goddess, who embodies the three phases of a woman's life as Maiden, Mother, and Crone and is represented by the three phases of the waxing, full, and waning moon. The male, conversely, is typically identified with the Horned God and the sun. Many neopagans, however, are polytheists, celebrating a wide array of gods and goddesses, drawn either from one traditional pantheon (Norse deities, for example) or from multiple pantheons (the full Indo-European spectrum, in the case of Druidry). Finally, at least one group, the Church and School of Wicca, is monotheistic and believes in one universal Deity called "God-ess," which includes but transcends both male and female aspects of the divine.

Most—though not all—neopagans also believe in some version of reincarnation, that is, the idea that we have lived multiple lives prior to this particular body and will take on many more after its end, undergoing a cyclical death and rebirth much like the cycles of nature. This is usually tied to some version of a belief in karma, or the idea that our actions have future consequences both in this lifetime and in future lives. And most—though, again, not all—neopagans abide by a basic ethical principle most famously embodied in the Wiccan "rede" or creed, which states: "An it harm none, do what ye will." This is in turn a reworking of Aleister Crowley's famous law of "Do what thou wilt," though it adds the important provision "if it harms none." In other words, do what makes you happy, as long as it doesn't injure anyone else or interfere with anyone else's happiness. As Gardner's chief student, Doreen Valiente, argued, this simple law is "the only moral code that really makes sense. If everyone lived by it, would not the world be a very different place? If morality were not enforced by fear, by a string of Thou-shalt-nots; but if instead people had a *positive* morality, as an incentive to a happier way of living?"[7]

In many ways, neopaganism is less a movement based on beliefs than a movement based on practice. Neopagans disagree widely on theoretical and metaphysical questions such as reincarnation, the number or nature of the gods, and even how exactly magic works, but they typically do agree that ritual practice is central to what neopagans do. Hence it may be thought of as a religion of "ortho-praxy" ("right practice") rather than "orthodoxy" ("right belief"). Most neopagans share a sort of symbolic vocabulary used in ritual practice. The most recognizable neopagan symbol is the pentacle or upward-pointing star, which is usually said to represent the four elements of earth, air, water, and fire plus the fifth element of spirit and is also identified with the four limbs and head of the human body. Most groups also use ritual implements such as the *athame* or short double-edged blade—typically identified with the male principle and the element of fire—and the chalice—usually identified with the female principle and the element of water.

Today, most neopagan groups follow a common ritual calendar organized around the solar calendar and the cycle of the seasons. The most widely used system is the Wheel of the

Year, which is oriented around eight key moments in the cycle of the earth's passage around the sun, marked by the two solstices, the two equinoxes, and the four midpoints between these solar events. These dates were widely celebrated in one form or another in most pre-Christian pagan communities in the British Isles and western Europe; hence modern neo-pagans claim to be either continuing or reviving these older pagan festivals. Although their names vary somewhat from one tradition to another, these eight festivals or *sabbats* are (1) Midwinter or Yule in late December, which marks the end of the shortening of daylight and the rebirth of the sun in winter; (2) Imbolc, which marks the first stirrings of spring for the year; (3) Ostara or the vernal equinox, the point when nights are no longer than days and nature begins to reawaken; (4) Beltane or May Day, which marks the transition from spring into summer; (5) Midsummer or Litha, which marks the summer solstice and the height of summer; (6) Lammas or Lugnasadh, which is the first harvest festival for the end of sum-mer; (7) the autumn equinox or Mabon, a second harvest festival when the lengths of day and night are equal again; and (8) Samhain or Halloween, which marks the end of the year and the time to pay respect to deceased ancestors, family members, and loved ones. Many pagans regard Samhain as the time when the boundary between the living and the dead is thinnest, and it is easiest to communicate with those who have left this world.

Most of these neopagan festivals either draw upon or revive much older pre-Christian traditions of Europe and the British Isles that gradually became melded into mainstream Christianity. For example, Yule logs, evergreen trees, and flying reindeer have little to do with Jesus Christ but were drawn from pagan traditions of northern Europe that were absorbed into mainstream Christianity as it spread and accommodated older folk traditions. Similarly, pumpkins and scary costumes have little to do with the holy day of All Saints, yet they were absorbed from folk traditions of the British Isles into the modern celebration of Halloween. And the name Easter itself is drawn from Ostara or Eostre, an old Germanic goddess associated with fertility and springtime. By building their sacred calendar around these older folk traditions, contemporary neopagans are both reminding us of the older pagan roots that we still see around us today and attempting to reconnect us to the cycles of nature.

Neopagan ritual can be performed for a wide array of purposes: it can, like mainstream Christian or Jewish worship, be used to honor a deity; it can be used to celebrate the chang-ing of the seasons, such as the transition from dark winter into early spring; or it can be used to harness spiritual energy toward some practical goal, such as protection or physical and psychological healing. It can be performed in the context of a massive festival, such as Star-wood, or by a small coven or even by a solitary practitioner in his or her home. Margot Adler—who was both a pagan practitioner and a respected journalist for National Public Radio—provides a useful overview of the basic elements found in most pagan rituals. The most common way of beginning a ritual is by casting a circle, or carving out a sacred space in which to work; within this space, various implements representing the elements of earth, air, fire, and water are used; and by means of these, the deity is invoked, and then the spiri-tual energy generated from the group and from the deity is directed toward some particular goal. In many neopagan groups, this is known as "raising the cone of power" or using ritual to generate spiritual and magical energy in order to focus it on some agreed-upon end:

> Craft ritual usually starts with casting and creating a magical space and ritually purifying it with the ancient elements: fire, water, earth, and air. The circle is cast with a ritual sword, wand or athame (a small, usually black handled and double-bladed dagger). Different covens have different symbolism, but often the sword represents fire, the wand (or incense burner) air, the cup water, and the pentacle—a round inscribed disk of wax or metal—earth. When the circle is cast, often the gods and goddess are evoked.
>
> Some covens use music, chanting and dancing to raise psychic energy within the circle. . . . The most common form of working is known as "raising a cone of power." This is done by chanting or dancing (or both) or running around the circle. The "cone of power" is really the combined will of the groups, intensified through ritual and meditative techniques, focused on an end collectively agreed upon. Usually a priestess or priest directs the coven; when she or he senses that it has been raised, it is focused and directed with the mind and shot toward its destination.[8]

In other rites, a particular deity may be invoked into the circle—including the Great Goddess or Triple Goddess herself. In the Wiccan ceremony of "Drawing Down the Moon," the Goddess is either invoked by the priest into the priestess or evoked by the priestess from within herself, who then becomes the vehicle and voice of the deity: "In some Craft rituals the priestess goes into a trance and speaks; in other traditions the ritual is a more formal dramatic dialogue, often of intense beauty, in which, again, the priestess speaks, taking the role of the Goddess. In both instances, the priestess functions as the Goddess incarnate, within the circle."[9]

NEOPAGANISM, RELIGIOUS FREEDOM, AND TOLERANCE IN CONTEMPORARY AMERICA: THE FORT HOOD CASE

From its origins, neopaganism has often been the subject of misunderstanding, bias, and intolerance—perhaps, above all, because it is frequently confused with Satanism by the popular media and by many conservative religious groups. Not surprisingly, neopagans' use of words such as *witch, coven,* and *sabbat* is often associated with devil worship in the popular imagination. Many conservative Christians, moreover, point to passages from the Bible such as Exodus 22:18, Leviticus 20:27, and Deuteronomy 18:9–12, which condemn the practices of sorcery, mediumship, and necromancy. A long history of horror movies, from early cult classics such as *Black Sunday* (1960) down to blockbuster films such as *The Blair Witch Project* (1999) and *The Book of Shadows* (2000), has helped solidify this popular image of witchcraft as evil and terrifying.

One of the most interesting examples of neopaganism's controversial role in American public life was the case of the Fort Hood military base in Texas. For years, Wiccan soldiers had been holding regular meetings and performing rituals on the base, and they were even authorized by the military to form a group called the Fort Hood Open Circle. In 1999, however, a photographer's published photos of the soldiers performing Wiccan rituals sparked a huge outcry from many politicians and Christian churches, calling for the group to be banned in the US military. Representative Bob Barr of Georgia attempted to amend a defense authorization bill in order to prohibit the practice of Wicca or any other form of neopaganism at Defense Department facilities. He was quickly joined by thirteen Christian groups and by conservative Christian leader Paul Weyrich, who described Wiccan rituals as "Satanic" and incompatible with the US military.

The Fort Hood case was even discussed as an issue in the 2000 presidential race between George W. Bush and Al Gore. When asked about the issue during the presidential debates, then governor Bush—well known for his conservative Christian beliefs—firmly expressed his opposition to the practice of Wicca at a US military base: "I don't think witchcraft is a religion, and I do not think it is in any way appropriate for the U.S. military to promote it." Then Vice-President Gore, on the other side, emphasized his strong commitment to the First Amendment and religious freedom but carefully dodged the actual question about Wicca at Fort Hood.[10] Despite Bush's victory in the 2000 election, the military has not reversed its position in favor of Wicca. Ironically, in 2007, under President Bush's own administration, the Department of Veteran's Affairs went even further by allowing the pentacle and other Wiccan symbols to appear on the headstones of fallen soldiers.

NEOPAGANISM, FEMINISM, AND ENVIRONMENTALISM

One of the most important reasons for the rapid growth of neopagan movements in the United States has been the close linkage between neopaganism and feminism since the 1960s and '70s. Obviously, not all neopagans are feminists—in fact, some forms of neopaganism are men-only groups. Yet just as Spiritualism often went hand in hand with the early women's rights movements of nineteenth-century America, so too Wicca and other new forms of paganism often went hand in hand with the new forms of feminism that emerged in the 1960s and '70s. From its origins with Gerald Gardner and his claim to have been initiated by the mysterious witch "Old Dorothy," modern Wicca has placed a great deal of emphasis on the authority of women as spiritual leaders, as well as on the central role of the Great Goddess or Triple Goddess as the female counter to the male Horned God. By the 1960s and '70s, throughout the United Kingdom, Europe, and the United States, Wicca and its various pagan offshoots had begun to blend naturally with the broader counterculture, including new strains of feminism that emerged out of these decades (feminism's so-called second-wave), particularly radical feminism. Whereas the early so-called first-wave feminists of the nineteenth century sought basic and practical goals, such as women's right to vote, the second-wave feminists of the 1960s and '70s strove for broader cultural goals, such as equal pay, equality in the workplace, and reproductive rights. With its central emphasis on the Goddess and the new roles of leadership and authority it offered to women, neopaganism made a natural fit with these feminist initiatives.

Feminist neopaganism has taken on a wide variety of forms—some of them quite extreme and aligned with the radical feminist movement of the late 1960s and some of them far more moderate. At the more radical end of the spectrum, one of the most outspoken early groups was WITCH, a collective founded in the late 1960s by women engaged in a kind of guerilla theater that mixed street performances with witch costumes and political activism. According to the group's manifesto from 1968,

> WITCH is an all-woman Everything. It's theater, revolution, magic, terror, joy, garlic, flowers, spells. It's an awareness that witches and gypsies were the original guerillas and resistance fighters against oppression—particularly the oppression of women down through the ages. Witches have always been women who dared to be: groovy, courageous, aggressive, intelligent, nonconformist, explorative, curious, independent, sexually liberated, revolutionary. . . . They bowed to no man, being the living remnants of the oldest culture of all—one in which men and women were equal sharers in a truly cooperative society, before the death-dealing sexual, economic, and spiritual repression of the Imperialist Phallic Society took over and began to destroy nature and human society.[11]

Of course, not all feminist neopagans are quite as radical or aggressive as WITCH, and most do not call for open war on the "Imperialist Phallic Society." Rather, many adhere to the more moderate definition of feminism as simply the "notion that women are human beings," as Cheris Kramarae famously put it—that is, the idea that women are as deserving of respect, recognition, and roles of authority as men are.

Two of the most influential figures in the early growth of neopaganism in the United States during the 1970s and '80s were Zsuzsanna (Z) Budapest and Starhawk. Born in Hungary in 1940, Z Budapest called herself a "hereditary witch" because she claimed to have learned her magic and spells from her mother and grandmother, who were part of a traditional witchcraft lineage that extended back to pre-Christian Europe. After coming to the United States at age nineteen and later moving to Los Angeles in 1970, Z Budapest became one of the most influential figures in the popularization of women's spirituality in America. As Z puts it, women have been systematically exploited and abused by the dominant patriarchal order, and it is now time for them to wake up and reclaim their rightful power: "Women's culture has been ripped off by the ruling class. . . . Most of the women in this world still suffer from this spiritual poverty."[12]

In 1975, Z Budapest became a controversial figure when she was arrested and charged with fortune-telling after giving an undercover policewoman a tarot card reading (at that time a violation of municipal codes in Venice, California). Outraged at the charge, she described herself as "the first witch to go on trial for my beliefs in 300 years." Declaring her-

FIGURE 8.3 Starhawk. Used with permission from Starhawk.org.

self to be a religious leader and high priestess, she demanded her freedom of belief under the First Amendment. Although the trial resulted in a $300 fine and a probation order, it did succeed in forcing many Americans to take paganism seriously as a growing new religious movement with a powerful appeal to women as leaders.

Z would also become controversial, even for some neopagans, because of her unique form of paganism known as Dianic Wicca. Unlike most Wiccans in the Gardnerian tradition, who honor the male and female deities equally and include both male and female members, Z is a lesbian separatist who teaches witchcraft as a pure women's religion, focused exclusively on the Goddess and organized as a women-only space. As Z argues, women need a space in which they can worship as and with women, free from the oppressive influence of men: "We have women's circles. You don't put men in women's circles. . . . Our goddess is life, and women should be free to worship from their ovaries."[13]

Starhawk, on the other hand, represents a more moderate form of feminist paganism; neither a lesbian nor a separatist, she has been a powerful part of the women's spirituality movement since the 1970s (figure 8.3). Born Miriam Simos in 1951, she was raised in a Jewish family at a time when there were few opportunities for women to assume religious leadership and spiritual authority within most Jewish communities in the United States. She first encountered neopaganism in 1968—at the height of the countercultural revolution—while starting college at UCLA. Already an active feminist, she was immediately drawn to the Goddess-centered religion of witchcraft and instantly felt a "natural connection between a movement to empower women and a spiritual tradition based on the Goddess."[14] As she explained in her widely read book *The Spiral Dance*, she and other women were taking up the title of "witch" precisely because it had such a long history of negative connotations and had for so long been used to oppress women. By reclaiming the label "witch," she hopes to use it as a reminder of the power and magic of women's spirituality: "The word 'Witch' carries so many negative connotations that many people wonder why we use the word at all. Yet to reclaim the word 'Witch' is to reclaim our right, as women, to be powerful; as women, to know the feminine within as divine. To be a Witch is to identify with nine million victims of bigotry and hatred and to take responsibility for shaping a world in which prejudice claims no more victims."[15] During the same period in which she began to embrace neopaganism, Starhawk was strongly influenced by the work of environmentalists and ecofeminist philosophers, such as Carolyn Merchant's widely read book *The Death of Nature* (1980).

In 1980, Starhawk formed a group called the Reclaiming Collective, founded on the belief that contemporary witchcraft was "reclaiming" the ancient Goddess religion for a new era. According to the *Reclaiming Newsletter*, their mission was to create a "center for feminist spirituality and counseling. . . . We reclaim the Goddess, the immanent life force, the connecting pattern to all being; we reclaim the creative and healing power of women."[16] Reclaiming became involved in direct political and environmentalist action in 1981, when they joined other activists to engage in a large nonviolent civil disobedience demonstration at Diablo Canyon, California, to stop the opening of a nuclear power plant. They were arrested along with several thousand other activists and members of a wide range of alternative spiritual, political, and environmentalist groups. This was the first time the group had engaged in ritual magic in an explicitly political context and the first time the group had joined with other political movements such as the anarchist community. In turn, members of other leftist political movements began to take Reclaiming classes and to become involved in neopaganism.

The neopagan worldview, Starhawk argues, is a key ally for environmentalist political causes and a much-needed corrective to the patriarchal traditions of Judaism and Christianity. In her view, patriarchal religions reinforce the domination of humans over nature just as they reinforce the domination of male over female, which has resulted in a long history of exploitation of both women and the environment: "Estrangement is the culmination of a long historical process. Its roots lie in the Bronze-Age shift from matrifocal earth-centered cultures whose religions centered on the Goddess and Gods embodied in nature, to patriarchal urban cultures of conquest, whose Gods inspired and supported war. Yahweh of the Old Testament is a prime example, promising His Chosen People dominion over plant and animal life. . . . Christianity deepened the split, establishing a duality between spirit and matter that identified flesh, nature, woman and sexuality with the Devil."[17] The neopagan worldview, conversely, sees the entire natural world as filled with divine energy that flows through the human body as well as through the external environment, binding all living things together in a complex magical web: "The world itself [is] a living being, made up of dynamic aspects, a world where one thing shape-shifts into another, where there are no solid separations. . . . Magic teaches that living beings are beings of energy and spirit as well as matter, that energy—what the Chinese call *chi*—flows in certain patterns throughout the human body."[18]

Thus the image of the Goddess is central to Starhawk's larger social and political agendas. For it gives her—and all women—a sense of connection with the Great Mother and the eternal feminine force that runs through all of creation. By participating in rituals, women are able not only to connect intellectually with the Goddess but to discover the Goddess within themselves and to realize their own identity with all of nature: "We are all the Goddess in her multitude of forms . . . a Maiden, a Mother, a Crone. We are all Persephone dragged into the underworld by the forces of patriarchy."[19] As such, the Goddess offers women a radically new way to experience their own bodies and all of nature: "This symbolism of the Goddess has taken on an electrifying power for modern women. The rediscovery of the ancient matrifocal civilization has given us a deep sense of pride in women's ability to create and sustain culture. It has . . . given us models of female strength and authority. . . . She is the vaginal passage through which we are reborn."[20]

Finally, in more practical terms, Starhawk's interests in spirituality, environmentalism, and social justice come together in her practice of permaculture. First developed by two Australians named Bill Mollison and David Holmgren in the 1970s, permaculture is a branch of ecological design and environmental engineering that seeks to create self-sustaining and regenerative habitats and agricultural systems based on natural ecosystems. As Starhawk explained the idea in a lecture at the Harvard Divinity School in 2013, permaculture is the natural application of her long-held belief that the earth is sacred and that humans need to exist in a harmonious spiritual relationship with the natural environment: "[Permaculture is] a whole system of ecological design that [is] based on the idea that, if we can observe nature, and figure out how nature is working, and work in the same way that nature works, we can actually create systems that will meet our human needs while actually regenerating the environment around us instead of destroying it. I got very interested in that and thought, 'This is the practical application of the idea that the earth is sacred.'"[21]

This emphasis on the links between neopaganism and environmentalism is not unique to prominent witches such as Starhawk. In her interviews with a wide range of neopagans, Margot Adler found that "a reverence for the earth and nature" was one of the few common bonds among pagans, despite their tremendous diversity and disagreements on almost every other issue. As one priestess named Morgan McFarland put it, "A Pagan world view is one that says the Earth is the Great Mother and has been raped, pillaged, and plundered and must once again be celebrated if we are to survive. Paganism means a return to those values which see an ecologically balanced situation so that life continues and the great Mother is venerated again. . . . If you're not into ecology, you really can't be into Paganism."[22]

However, Adler also found that there was some ambivalence among neopagans as to what exactly should be done about the environment. While most affirmed the idea of respecting nature, not all were sure what should be done about our mounting environmental crises. As one priestess from Ohio named Roberta Ann Kennedy put it, "I see people in the Craft talking about ecology, but not living it. I believe there's a problem, but until it gets a lot worse nobody's going to do anything about it."[23] At least in this respect, neopagans may not be entirely different from most other nonpagan Americans.

"MEN ARE FROM THE SUN, WOMEN ARE FROM THE MOON"? DEBATES OVER NEOPAGANISM, FEMINISM, AND ENVIRONMENTALISM

Despite their broad influence, the attempts to link neopaganism, feminism, and environmentalism have raised some important debates and critical questions. As we saw above, Starhawk and Z Budapest were part of the so-called second wave of feminism that began in the 1960s and '70s and introduced a wider range of cultural issues into feminist discussions. However, by the 1980s and '90s they had come under criticism from a later wave of feminists (so-called third-wave feminists and postfeminists). Among other things, more recent feminists have argued that Starhawk and others are burdened by the problem of "essentialism," or the assumption that there is a single, universal, and essential female nature. By identifying all women with "the Goddess" or with universal symbols such as the Moon, witches such as Starhawk risk lumping all women into one monolithic category and overlooking the tremendous diversity of women's experiences. Moreover, by identifying women with figures such as the Triple Goddess, "Maiden-Mother-Crone," they ironically reinforce the idea that women are primarily associated with their reproductive cycle and motherhood, rather than with some other quality (their intellect, their leadership skills, etc.).[24]

Thus many recent feminist critics have wondered whether this form of neopaganism is not ironically *reinforcing* gender stereotypes and traditional ideas of femininity rather than challenging them. In other words, by identifying women with the Goddess and men with the Horned God, are witches such as Starhawk simply putting a more positive spin on the same old gender binaries? Are they simply substituting "men are from the Sun, women are from the Moon," for the usual "men are from Mars, women are from Venus" idea that dominates popular American views of the sexes? While they may be giving women's roles a far more positive interpretation, are the Goddess-centered pagans also reinforcing these old gender roles more strongly than ever by giving them a divine and metaphysical status?[25]

These criticisms and debates have emerged not only in academic circles but within contemporary neopagan communities themselves. In the last few decades, a huge number of new movements have emerged that challenge traditional gender stereotypes, often in quite creative new ways. Today, there are dozens of lesbian, gay, bisexual, and transsexual pagan groups, such as the Radical Faeries, the Minoan Brotherhood, the Minoan Sisterhood, and the Brotherhood of the Phoenix—all of which draw upon neopagan symbolism but reject traditional gender stereotypes and experiment with a wide array of alternative sexual orientations. As one Radical Faery named Jody put it, both men and women need to break free of oppressive gender roles, and paganism should allow men to explore stereotypically "feminine" qualities and women to explore stereotypically "masculine" qualities: "Finally we have the ability to play. Men who are stuck in the role model of the stern, mature adult never truly engage in creative play."[26] Particularly at pagan festivals today—such as Starwood and others—one sees quite a lot of this fluid play with gender roles. Cross-dressing, gender bending, and experimentation with alternative sexual identities are all common phenomena within the space of the festival, which allows for a kind of "serious play with the self."[27]

A similar debate has emerged around the links between neopaganism and environmentalism. By identifying femininity with nature and the earth, witches such as Starhawk may be seeking to undo the history of exploitation of both women and nature; but, ironically, they risk reinforcing the very old gender binaries and stereotypes of women versus men, earth versus heaven, nature versus culture, and so on. As critics such as Anne Archambault argue, this actually undermines their own larger feminist agenda: while they want to celebrate the sanctity of both women and nature, by identifying the two they repeat and reinforce the traditional stereotype that women are closer to nature, closer to biology, and closer to reproduction: "The claim that women are biologically closer to nature reinforces the patriarchal ideology of domination and limits ecofeminism's effectiveness."[28] More recent feminist environmentalists have therefore rejected the essentialist view of earlier 1970s-era ecofeminists. As the theologian Rosemary Radford Ruether argues, women may have historically been identified with "nature," and both nature and women may have been exploited for similar reasons, but this is a social construct, not an essential quality of their being. Today, she writes, "most ecofeminists . . . reject an essentializing of women as more in tune with nature by virtue of their female body. They see this concept of affinity between women and nature as a social construct that both naturalizes women and feminizes nonhuman nature. . . . Women may also suffer more due to the abuse of the natural world . . . but this is a matter of their experience in their particular social location, not due to a 'different nature.'"[29] In any case, despite these internal debates over women, nature, and essentialism, many neopagans such as Starhawk continue to work toward a new vision of a human relationship with the environment that weaves together spirituality, ecology, and political activism.

QUESTIONS FOR DISCUSSION AND DEBATE

1. Why do you think neopaganism emerged when and where it did—in the middle of the twentieth century in England, Europe, and the United States? What did it offer that many well-educated people found so appealing as an alternative to mainstream religions?

2. Does it seem strange that a tradition based on *magic* should have not only emerged but become hugely popular in the twentieth and twenty-first centuries, even as our society has become increasingly technological and scientific? And how do we account for the popularity of magic in more popular media such as

the Harry Potter novels or films such as *The Craft, Hocus Pocus,* and countless others?

3. Gardner claimed that Wicca was an ancient pre-Christian tradition of Goddess worship that had survived underground for millennia and had finally resurfaced in the modern world. Do you find this narrative plausible? Or does it even matter? Does a religious movement *need* to have an ancient history to be persuasive, or is all that really matters the fact that it exists and is meaningful to practitioners today?

4. What do you make of the debates over neopaganism, feminism, and environmentalism? Do you agree with authors such as Starhawk that the women's movement and environmentalism need the Goddess and pagan spirituality today? Or do you agree with more critical feminists who argue that this appeal to the Goddess is a form of essentialism and more of a hindrance than a help to these other social movements? Does an environmentalist movement need spirituality at all—or is the appeal to something outside science more of a distraction from than an aid to the effort to protect the environment and address ecological crises?

SUGGESTED CLASSROOM ACTIVITY

Critically examine the question of Wiccan rituals being performed at the Fort Hood military base, which was a key issue in the 2000 US presidential debates (the candidates' responses can all be viewed online, for example on the Religious Tolerance.org website: www.religious tolerance.org/wic_pres.htm). Why did this particular question involving a small new religious group in Texas become such a polarizing and divisive political issue at the national level? And why did the various candidates address it in the ways they did (for example, why did Bush firmly reject it, while Gore dodged the question?)? And what larger interests were at stake in the possibility of granting or not granting Wiccans the right to perform ceremonies on a US military base?

SUGGESTED FILM

Read, Donna, director. *Women and Spirituality: The Goddess Trilogy.* Alive Mind, 2008.

SUGGESTIONS FOR FURTHER READING

Adler, Margot. *Drawing Down the Moon: Witches, Druids, Goddess Worshippers, and Other Pagans in America Today.* New York: Penguin, 2006.

Farrar, Janet, and Stewart Farrar. *The Witches' Bible: The Complete Witches' Handbook.* Blaine, WA: Phoenix, 1996.

Gardner, Gerald B. *The Gardnerian Book of Shadows.* London: Forgotten Books, 2008.

———. *Witchcraft Today.* 1970. Reprint, New York: Citadel Press, 2004.

Hutton, Ronald. *Triumph of the Moon: A History of Modern Pagan Witchcraft.* New York: Oxford University Press, 1999.

Pike, Sarah M. *Earthly Bodies, Magical Selves: Contemporary Pagans and the Search for Community.* Berkeley: University of California Press, 2001.

Ruether, Rosemary Radford. *Integrating Ecofeminism, Globalization, and World Religions.* Lanham, MD: Rowman and Littlefield, 2005.

Salomonsen, Jone. *Enchanted Feminism: Ritual, Gender and Divinity among the Reclaiming Witches of San Francisco.* New York: Routledge, 2002.

Starhawk. *Dreaming the Dark: Magic, Sex and Politics.* Boston: Beacon Press, 1982.

———. *The Spiral Dance: A Rebirth of the Ancient Religion of the Great Goddess.* 1979. Reprint, New York: HarperOne, 1999.

Urban, Hugh B. *Magia Sexualis: Sex, Magic, and Liberation in Modern Western Esotericism.* Berkeley: University of California Press, 2006.

Valiente, Doreen. *Witchcraft for Tomorrow.* Blaine, WA: Phoenix, 1978.

NOTES TO CHAPTER 8

1. "Overview," Starwood Festival, July 8–14, 2014, www.rosencomet.com/starwood/2014/.
2. Margot Adler, *Drawing Down the Moon: Witches, Druids, Goddess Worshippers, and Other Pagans in America Today* (New York: Penguin, 2006).
3. Aleister Crowley to Charles Stansfeld Jones, December 23, 1914, quoted in John Symonds, *The Great Beast: The Life of Aleister Crowley* (New York: Roy, 1952), 194–95. See Ronald Hutton, *Triumph of the Moon: A History of Modern Pagan Witchcraft* (New York: Oxford University Press, 2001); Hugh B. Urban, *Magia Sexualis: Sex, Magic, and Liberation in Modern Western Esotericism* (Berkeley: University of California Press, 2005), chap. 4.
4. Hutton, *Triumph of the Moon,* 209–11.
5. Gerald B. Gardner, *Witchcraft Today* (1970; repr., New York: Citadel Press, 2004), 31–32.
6. Adler, *Drawing Down the Moon,* 89.
7. Doreen Valiente, *Witchcraft for Tomorrow* (Blaine, WA: Phoenix, 1978), 41.
8. Adler, *Drawing Down the Moon,* 41.
9. Ibid., 19–20; see also Gerald B. Gardner, *The Gardnerian Book of Shadows* (London: Forgotten Books, 2008), 3–4.
10. "Presidential Candidates and Religious Freedom: 2000 Election," Religious Tolerance.Org, 2000, www.religioustolerance.org/wic_pres.htm. See also Hanna Rosin, "Wiccan Controversy Tests Military Religious Tolerance," *Washington Post,* June 8, 1999, A1.

11. Adler, *Drawing Down the Moon,* 179.

12. Z Budapest, interview by Cheri Lesh, "Goddess Worship: The Subversive Religion," *Twelve Together,* Los Angeles, May 1975.

13. Z Budapest, interview for *The Occult Experience,* produced for Channel 10, Sydney, Australia (1985), and released on Sony Home Video.

14. Jone Salomonsen, *Enchanted Feminism: Ritual, Gender and Divinity among the Reclaiming Witches of San Francisco* (New York: Routledge, 2002), 37.

15. Starhawk, *The Spiral Dance: A Rebirth of the Ancient Religion of the Great Goddess* (1979; repr., New York: HarperOne, 1999), 7.

16. Salomonsen, *Enchanted Feminism,* 40.

17. Starhawk, *Dreaming the Dark: Magic, Sex and Politics* (Boston: Beacon Press, 1982), 5.

18. Starhawk, *Truth or Dare: Encounters with Power, Authority and Mystery* (San Francisco: Harper and Row, 1987), 15, 24.

19. Starhawk, *Dreaming the Dark,* 152.

20. Starhawk, "The Goddess," in *A New Creation: America's Contemporary Spiritual Voices,* ed. Roger S. Gottlieb (New York: Crossroad, 1990), 213–14.

21. Starhawk, "Permaculture and the Sacred: A Conversation with Starhawk," Harvard Divinity School, March 7, 2013, https://www.youtube.com/watch?v=zV-MsQYrWog.

22. Adler, *Drawing Down the Moon,* 399.

23. Ibid., 401.

24. For a discussion of these debates, see Urban, *Magia Sexualis,* 184–89.

25. For a critique of Starhawk, Carol Christ, and others, see Helene P. Foley, "A Question of Origins: Goddess Cults, Greek and Modern," in *Women, Gender and Religion: A Reader,* edited by Elizabeth A. Castelli (New York: Palgrave, 2001), 216–36. For a critique of essentialism in feminism more broadly, see Judith Butler, *Gender Trouble: Feminism and the Subversion of Identity* (New York: Routledge, 1989).

26. Adler, *Drawing Down the Moon,* 348.

27. Sarah Pike, *Earthly Bodies, Magical Selves: Contemporary Pagans and the Search for Community* (Berkeley: University of California Press, 2001), 182–218.

28. Anne Archambault, "A Critique of Ecofeminism," *Canadian Women's Studies* 13, no. 3 (1993): 20.

29. Rosemary Radford Ruether, *Integrating Ecofeminism, Globalization, and World Religions* (Lanham, MD: Rowman and Littlefield, 2005), 93. See also Carol J. Adams, ed., *Ecofeminism: Feminist Intersections with Other Animals and the Earth* (New York: Bloomsbury Academic, 2011).

NINE

The Church of Satan
and the Temple of Set

Religious Parody and Satanic Panic

On April 30, 1966—the night of Walpurgisnacht, or the traditional European spring festival—an American occultist named Anton Szandor LaVey shaved his head and proclaimed the formation of the Church of Satan (CoS). Declaring this "Year One, Anno Satanis," LaVey quickly generated a great deal of media attention by performing the first Satanic wedding in 1967 and then enacting the first modern "black masses" in the basement of his Victorian San Francisco home, called the Black House. With LaVey draped in a mock devil outfit, complete with billowing black robes, clerical collar, and horned skullcap, surrounded by masked figures and a naked woman serving as the altar, these early black masses were clearly as much burlesque parody as religious ritual. Throughout his writings (such as *The Satanic Bible*) and his colorful ritual performances, LaVey often walked a fine line between serious religion and comical satire, exploiting the power of performance art as much as the power of occult philosophy and magic. Yet he did help give birth to modern Satanism as a new religious movement that has had a widespread influence not just on American spiritual life but on popular culture, music, and film.

Today, the Church of Satan is the best-known Satanic movement in the United States, and it has certainly been the focus of the most media attention and sensationalism. However, there are now numerous other Satanic groups operating throughout the United States, England, and Europe, many of them more "serious" and less parodic than LaVey's church. In this chapter we will also look at two movements that emerged out of the Church of Satan and moved in a more radical direction, usually called the "Left Hand Path": the Temple of Set (ToS), founded by Michael Aquino in 1975, and the Setian Liberation Movement, founded by LaVey's daughter Zeena and her husband Nikolas Schreck.

However, perhaps the greatest influence of modern Satanism has been not on contemporary American spirituality but on music, particularly hard rock and heavy metal. Since the late 1960s, a variety of folk and rock bands such as the American group Coven had begun making serious use of Satanic imagery and lyrics; by the 1970s, bands such as Black Sabbath (while not particularly "Satanic" themselves) helped popularize Satanic themes, combined with down-tuned guitars and dissonant, minor, and atonal chords. By the 1980s and 1990s, a huge variety of new genres had emerged, such as black metal, death metal, doom, and others, that made extensive use of Satanic themes and often Satanic performances on stage.

Not surprisingly, the emergence of new Satanic movements such as CoS and ToS, combined with the growing influence of Satanic themes in popular music, helped give rise to a widespread paranoia throughout the American media in the 1980s, often called the Satanic Panic. The panic was in turn part of a broader anticult paranoia in the United States that dates back to at least the 1960s and that rapidly intensified after the Charles Manson murder spree in 1968 and then after the Peoples Temple suicides in 1978 (see chapter 12 below). While most of the charges later proved to be imaginary, a powerful narrative spread throughout the mainstream media that Satanic groups were whisking children away to be sexually abused and subjected to all manner of bizarre ritual perversions. Ironically, the Satanic Panic and the hysteria about "Satanic ritual abuse" probably only encouraged the black metal bands and other groups to employ Satanic imagery, since it lent even more power, fear, and awe to the idea of Satanic ritual and its threat to mainstream society.

THE SECRET LIFE OF A SATANIST: ANTON LAVEY AND THE BIRTH OF THE CHURCH OF SATAN

Neither the concept of Satan nor the idea of a black mass was new in the late 1960s, of course. When Anton LaVey began his new church and performed his first Satanic rituals, he was drawing upon a very long tradition of belief, folklore, superstition, literature, and popular imagination surrounding the devil and devil worship in Western history. With a few notable exceptions, however, virtually all of the stories about Satanic worship and black masses from the last 2000 years have been imaginary—largely the product of cultural hysteria, paranoia, and fantasies of a "world turned upside down." Virtually every group that was labeled as heretical by the mainstream Christian Church was accused of black magic, devil worship, and usually obscene rituals. From early Christian heresies such as Gnosticism down to medieval sects such as the Cathars and military orders such as the Knights Templar, marginal religious groups were commonly accused of engaging in corrupt, inverted, and perverted rituals and worship of dark forces. These fantasies culminated in the late Middle Ages and the early modern period with the witch trials and the execution of thousands of people—particularly women—on suspicion that they were engaged in witches' sabbaths, interactions with demons, and other evil rites.[1]

Documented cases of actual black masses being performed prior to the twentieth century are few and far between. Perhaps the most famous was the case of the so-called Guiborg Masses

FIGURE 9.1 Anton LaVey. Photo by Nick Bougas. Courtesy of the Church of Satan.

at the court of French King Louis XIV in the seventeenth century. The priest performing the rites was Abbé Étienne Guiborg (1610–86), a Catholic priest and occultist who became involved with the king's mistress, Madame de Montespan. Fearing that the king was losing affection for her, Madame de Montespan first sought out a witch known as La Voisin, who performed a series of rites that involved calling upon the devil and killing and taking the blood from a newborn infant. In 1666, Montespan went still further by enjoining the Abbé Guiborg to perform a black mass over her nude body in a ritual that also involved an infant sacrifice. While it is unclear how many of these black rites actually took place and how many were imagined, they would become a central part of the larger narrative of the black mass in modern times. In the late nineteenth century, French novelists such as J. K. Huysmans would help popularize the idea of the black mass in widely read works such as *Là-bas* (Down there; 1891), which explores the occult underworld and culminates in a sensational account of a secret black mass in Paris.[2]

When he formed his own new Church of Satan in the late 1960s, Anton LaVey drew upon all of these historical and imaginary narratives of the black mass. But he also creatively reworked them in the new context of modern America, amid the new circumstances of the sexual revolution and the rise of a wide range of alternative spiritual movements.

Like the biographies of other new religious leaders, LaVey's life story is a complex mixture of history, embellishment, and sometimes fantastic elaboration (figure 9.1). Most of what we know of LaVey's life is derived from his own personal accounts from Blanche Barton's "official" biography, *The Secret Life of a Satanist* (1990), but the details in these official narratives are often at odds with the findings of more skeptical journalists and scholars, and even LaVey's own daughter Zeena would later denounce much of his biography as "a catalogue of lies" and "self-serving bullshit."[3]

According to the legendary narrative as told by Blanche Barton, the story goes something like this: LaVey was born in Chicago in 1930 of French, Alsatian, Russian, and Romanian descent, though he also claimed to possess gypsy blood and to have learned about vampires from his grandmother. Brought up in San Francisco, LaVey was the proverbial boy who ran off to join the circus, leaving his family and school at age sixteen to work in amusement parks, first as a roustabout and then as a cage boy with big cats. He also worked as a musician, playing calliope and organ, performing for both the provocative carnival dancers and the Christian tent revivals—an experience that, he claimed, proved to him the hypocrisy of Christianity and the deeper reality of carnal desire: "On Saturday night I would see men lusting after half naked girls dancing at the carnival and on Sunday morning when I was playing at the other end of the carnival lot I would see these same men sitting in the pews with their wives and children asking God to forgive them. . . . I knew then that the Christian Church thrives on hypocrisy and that man's carnal nature will out!"[4]

Another formative experience in his early life, LaVey claimed, was his time working as a criminal photographer for the San Francisco Police Department, where he regularly saw examples of horrible cruelty and bloodshed. If his organist days proved to him the reality of carnal desire and the hypocrisy of religion, his time as a police photographer proved to him the violence of human nature and the nonexistence of God.

During the 1950s and '60s, LaVey developed an interest in the occult and parapsychology, investigating reports of ghosts, UFOs, and other unusual phenomena. Eventually he would begin holding classes on esoteric subjects, attracting a number of people interested in occultism, spirituality, and the supernatural, including science fiction author Forrest Ackerman and filmmaker Kenneth Anger. LaVey also read widely in Western philosophy, particularly the works of the German philosopher Friedrich Nietzsche and the Russian-born American author Ayn Rand, which helped form the basis of his highly individualist and anti-Christian ideology. During the late 1960s, LaVey made his headquarters in an old house on California Street in San Francisco, which became known as the Black House because he had painted it entirely black. This became the home for his new Church of Satan, formally announced in 1966 at the dawn of his new Anno Satanis, the Age of Satan. As LaVey later recalled, the late 1960s in America was exactly the right time to launch a new Satanic movement: "The Satanic Age started in 1966. That's when God was proclaimed dead, the Sexual Freedom League came into prominence, and the hippies developed the sex culture."[5]

Many of the details of Barton's biography have been challenged by later authors and journalists. For example, LaVey's claim to have worked for the San Francisco Police Department has been found to be completely unsubstantiated; he also claimed to have had an affair with the young Marilyn Monroe while playing the organ at burlesque houses in Los Angeles, and this also appears to have been imaginary. Yet regardless of the truth of his official biography, LaVey's reputation as the high priest and "Black Pope" for a new age of sensual religion spread rapidly. In 1967, a year after the founding of the Church of Satan, LaVey began to attract tremendous media attention, first by performing a Satanic wedding for radical journalist John Raymonds and New York socialite Judith Case and then by performing the first Satanic baptism for his daughter Zeena. Also in 1967 Ira Levin published his popular Satanic horror novel *Rosemary's Baby.* When director Roman Polanski decided to turn the novel into a film, LaVey seemed a natural choice to serve as the technical adviser and even to appear as the devil in the film's surreal impregnation scene. By 1969, LaVey had published his *Satanic Bible,* and his reputation as the devil's spokesman was well established.

LAVEY'S SATANIC PHILOSOPHY

LaVey's Satanic worldview is founded on a complete rejection of all existing religious and moral systems, which are in his view bankrupt, hypocritical, and irrelevant. His own new creed is based on the fundamental acceptance that all religions are human creations, that all moral codes are relative, and that we may as well create a new religion that we can enjoy rather than feel guilty about: "No creed must be accepted upon authority of a 'divine' nature. . . . No moral dogma must be taken for granted—no standard of measure deified. There is nothing inherently sacred about moral codes. Like the wooden idols of long ago, they are the work of human hands, and what man has made man can destroy."[6]

LaVey's philosophy is perhaps best described as a kind of radical materialism and hedonistic individualism that celebrates the human body, ego, and sensual pleasure. It is, in sum, "a system based on rational self-interest, sensual indulgence, and the constructive use of alienation."[7] While LaVey's writings greatly resemble those of earlier authors such as Aleister Crowley, Nietzsche, and Rand, LaVey clearly marketed his philosophy for a new generation of sexual freedom and individualism in 1960s' America. The main point for LaVey is that Satanism does *not* mean the worship of some actual deity named Satan who is the opposite of some imagined God. Rather, it is the rejection of *all* gods altogether and the worship of one's own individual self. Here Satan—literally "the adversary"—is merely the symbol of the individual human ego, with all its desires and passions, which should be embraced, not repressed.

LaVey made no secret of his disgust for Christianity, which he saw as a religion of weakness, repression, guilt, and hatred of the body. Christianity, in his view, is largely the root of our present misery, since it has taught us to repress and deny our true physical desires rather than to embrace and celebrate them. Yet he was no less harsh in his criticism of the various forms of neopaganism and feminist witchcraft that had become so popular in the wake of Gardner's Wiccan revival. All of that nature worship and naked dancing in circles was merely so much "namby-pamby ethicalism" mingled with "sanctimonious fraud" and "exoteric gibberish."[8]

What humankind needed today, LaVey argued, was a religion based not on hypocrisy or sentimental morality but rather on the worship of the individual human being as a carnal beast with desires that need to be fulfilled. As he put it in an interview in 1970,

> Well, it had occurred to me for many, many years that . . . no religion had ever been based on man's carnal needs or his fleshly pursuits. All religions are based on abstinence rather than indulgence, and all religions therefore have to be based on fear. Well, we don't feel that fear is necessary to base a religion on. The fact that religions for thousands of years have been telling people what they should do or shouldn't do according to the basic whims of the person who might be running the show is very understandable. We're realists, we Satanists. But we also feel that a person has to be good to themselves before they can be good to other people. So we feel that the greatest sin is self-deceit. This is a very selfish religion. We believe in greed, we believe in selfishness, we believe in all of the lustful thoughts that motivate man, because this is man's natural feeling. This is based on what man would naturally do.[9]

This "carnal" philosophy is embodied in the "Nine Satanic Statements" that constitute LaVey's response to the Jewish and Christian Ten Commandments. Deliberately turning the latter on its head, LaVey proudly declares,

1. Satan represents indulgence instead of abstinence!
2. Satan represents vital existence instead of spiritual pipe dreams! . . .
5. Satan represents vengeance instead of turning the other cheek! . . .
8. Satan represents all of the so-called sins, as they all lead to physical, mental or emotional gratification![10]

In many ways, LaVey's Church of Satan could be said to represent the dark side of the 1960s, the sexual revolution, and the American counterculture. The church emerged at the epicenter of the counterculture—in San Francisco in the late 1960s—and it embraced many elements of the counterculture, such as individualism, opposition to religious and political establishments, freethinking, and sexual liberation. But LaVey also openly despised many aspects of the hippie movement and drug culture blossoming all around him in San Francisco during the 1960s. "I found the hippie movement distasteful on a personal level," he recalled. "Suddenly the ingestion of lysergic acid made every man a king. It made nincompoops self-assured . . . and my beloved San Francisco became engulfed by the movement."[11] Perhaps more than anything, LaVey rejected the new forms of feminism that emerged in the 1960s, along with the more androgynous style of dress and hair adopted by both men and women. For LaVey—a self-described "misogynist"—women should look "like women" (i.e., curvy and feminine) and men should look "like men" (strong, aggressive, masculine), and the hippie blending of gender roles was a disaster. On August 8, 1969, LaVey even held a special ceremony called the Rising Forth in which he launched a terrible curse on the hippie movement: "Beware you psychedelic vermin! Your smug pomposity with its thin disguise of tolerance will serve you no longer! . . . Our steeds await and their eyes are ablaze with the fires of Hell!"[12]

SATANIC RITUAL: CEREMONY, MAGIC, AND DRAMATIC PERFORMANCE

Though LaVey rejected the idea of Satan as an actual being existing outside the individual, he did believe in the power of ritual, and he developed a wide repertoire of rites and ceremonies for the church. As he put it in an interview, dramatic performance is as important to Satanism as it is to the Catholic mass: "Drama and melodrama are very meaningful. Bombast has its place in Satanism—in some ways, Satanism takes up where Catholicism leaves off."[13] Shortly after forming the Church of Satan, LaVey began to attract widespread media attention for performing the first Satanic wedding and then the first Satanic baptism (of his daughter Zeena). In 1972, LaVey published a collection of practical techniques entitled *The Satanic Rituals,* which also explains the philosophy behind the seemingly paradoxical idea of performing rituals for a being who does not exist outside oneself. As LaVey explains, the rituals of other religions are designed primarily to control and subdue followers, but the rituals of Satanism are designed to liberate the individual and empower him or her to accomplish real goals in the world: "The religious rites of Satanism differ from those of other faiths in that fantasy is not employed to control the practitioners of the rites. The ingredients of Satanic ritual are not designed to hold the celebrant in thrall but rather to achieve his goals. Thus, fantasy is utilized as a magic weapon by the individual rather than by the system."[14] Despite not believing in an external deity, LaVey believes in the power of magic, which can have real effects in the world by generating emotional intensity and directing that toward some desired end.

The most infamous of LaVey's rituals was the black mass, first performed in San Francisco in the late 1960s. Although LaVey would downplay the importance of black masses, they did help solidify his reputation as the "Black Pope." One of them was recorded in 1968, and many of its elements became standard format for performances of the rite throughout America and Europe. LaVey's early black mass ritual was performed with an almost absurdly demonic drama. It opened with dramatic chords from an organ and the appearance of LaVey, wearing a horned cap and a long cape, and surrounded by black-robed worshippers; on the wall was the Sigil of Baphomet (a goat's head superimposed onto an inverted pentagram), and beneath it was a naked female body serving as the ritual altar. Extending a long sword in the four directions, LaVey invoked Satan, Lucifer, Belial, and Leviathan and then passed around a chalice (according to LaVey's *Satanic Rituals,* the chalice should be filled not with wine but with some other beverage of one's choice, such as bourbon).

The text of LaVey's black mass is a mixture of a Latin parody of the Catholic mass and English and French prayers to Satan. Several paragraphs of the text are drawn directly from

Huysmans's famous literary account of the of the black mass in his novel *Là-bas,* including the following ironic Satanic prayer to Jesus: "Thou, thou whom, in my quality of Priest, I force, whether thou wilt or no, to descend into this host, to incarnate thyself into this bread, Jesus, artisan of hoaxes, bandit of homages, robber of affection, hear! Since the day when thou didst issue from the complaisant bowels of a virgin, thou hast failed all thy engagements, belied all thy promises. Centuries have wept, awaiting thee, fugitive god, mute god!"[15]

LaVey's mass also contains various instructions for the desecration of the ritual and the sacred Host by means of bodily fluids and sacrilegious acts. For example, the nun lifts her habit and urinates into the font, after which a ritual implement analogous to one used in Catholic services to sprinkle holy water is dipped into the urine and shaken in the four directions. The wafer, which is to be made of turnip or coarse black bread, is placed between the exposed breasts of the woman who serves as the altar, then touched to her vaginal area, and finally trampled by the priest, deacon, or subdeacon.

Clearly, much of this ritual is aimed at an explicit, exaggerated, even ridiculous inversion of the Catholic mass. LaVey himself more or less acknowledged as much, suggesting that the early Church of Satan had to use such extreme displays of Christian inversion in order to awaken the American public and make itself known to the world: "Any ceremony considered a black mass must effectively shock and outrage, as this seems to be the measure of its success."[16] Once the original shock had worn off, however, these theatrical performances of the black mass would no longer be necessary, and Satanists could move on to attacking other "sacred cows."

OTHER SATANIC AND LEFT-HAND MOVEMENTS: TEMPLE OF SET, WEREWOLF ORDER, AND SETHIAN LIBERATION MOVEMENT

While the Church of Satan is the most famous modern Satanic group, it is by no means the only one. Just a few years after LaVey founded his church, a variety of other Satanic groups, such as the Cathedral of the Fallen Angel and the Church of the Satanic Brotherhood, spread across the United States, the United Kingdom, and Europe. By the mid-1970s, LaVey's own church had also begun to develop internal tensions and finally splintered into a variety of new groups. Among other things, many members were unhappy with LaVey's increasing focus on money and finances rather than the philosophy and practice of Satanism. In 1975, LaVey began marketing the degrees of initiation within the church; higher degrees could now be obtained by contributions in cash, real estate, or valuable pieces of art. As LaVey himself acknowledged, he never had any illusions that the Church of Satan was somehow above the practice of business and the need to make money: "Satanism as mass culture is great. . . . There's a great advantage in mainstreaming and I'd be a hypocrite to dislike it."[17]

Many of his early supporters saw this as a sign that LaVey had allowed a blatant commercialism to creep into and undermine the church. One of the most prominent figures to leave the CoS at this time was Michael Aquino, a former high-ranking officer in US military intelligence, who held a PhD in political science and had served in Vietnam. Aquino joined the church in

1969 but already by the mid-1970s was beginning to feel that LaVey's movement was attracting the wrong sort of crowd. It had become, in his view, "a carnival of freaks," composed of "sexual inadequates ogling the naked altar, social misfits looking for an identity, intellectual poseurs." The leadership had meanwhile fragmented into "petty squabbles over titles, ranks and privileges."[18] However, Aquino was even more appalled by LaVey's policy of selling degrees, which he saw as the same sort of hypocrisy that Satanists had been attacking in the mainstream Christian churches: "If there had been a single factor that had brought us to Satanism, it was the church's stand against hypocrisy. So when we learned of this policy, our reaction to it was that LaVey was . . . betraying everything that he had worked for for so many years."[19]

In 1975, Aquino broke from the church and founded his own new order, the Temple of Set. During the summer solstice of June 21–22, 1975, in Santa Barbara, California, Aquino undertook a "Greater Black Magical Working," which resulted in a text called *The Book of Coming Forth by Night*. Aquino presented the text as an inspired work, generated by some power other than his own hand but working through him. The title is a reference to and an inversion of the famous Egyptian Book of the Dead, which is also known as the Book of Coming Forth by Day. In the text, the Egyptian god Set declares himself to be the ancient and powerful deity called Satan by the Hebrews, now revealing himself for a new age following the decline of LaVey's Church of Satan:

> The Equinox has succumbed to my Solstice, and I, Set, am revealed in my majesty. The time of the Purification is past. . . .
>
> I am the ageless Intelligence of this Universe. . . . All other gods of all other times and nations have been created by men. This you know from the first Part of my Word, and from my Manifest semblance, which alone is not of Earth. Known as the Hebrew Satan, I chose to bring forth a Magus, according to the fashion of my Word. He was charged to form a Church of Satan, that I might easily touch the minds of men in this image they had cast for me. In the fifth year of the Church of Satan, I gave to this Magus my Diabolicon, that he might know the truth of my ancient Gift to mankind, clothed though it might be in the myths of the Hebrews.[20]

Just as LaVey before him had announced the new Age of Satan, Aquino announced the dawn of a new era, the Aeon of Set.

For ToS, Set is the god who always opposes the status quo and conformity, the god who slays conventional social norms and patterns of thought just as he slew Osiris in Egyptian mythology. Ultimately, Set points the way for human beings to become "gods" themselves, to achieve an immortal and all-powerful state of divinity. As a former high priest of the temple, Don Webb, explains,

> Set, the Egyptian god of Darkness, is the Divine origin of the Word. Set's name ultimately means the "Separator" or "Isolator." His chief enemies are the gods of Stasis and Mindlessness. The first of these is Osiris, Death himself. Set's slaying of

Osiris has a twofold significance. . . . Firstly this represents the slaying of old thought patterns; the dethroning of those internal gods that we have received from society. On a second level this was the act by which Set, alone of all the gods of ancient Egypt, became deathless. The Left Hand Path is a quest to Become an immortal, potent and powerful Essence.[21]

The key word used to convey Setian philosophy is the Egyptian verb *Xeper* (pronounced "Khefer"), meaning "I have come into being." As Webb explains, *Xeper* refers to the experience of an individual becoming aware of his or her own existence and deciding to develop that existence through his or her own actions. It represents the freedom and possibility that we have to move forward into a divine state, into godhood—"an immortal, potent and powerful Essence." Setian practice is thus a "Left Hand Path," set in contrast to the "Right Hand Path" of most traditional religions. While the "Right Hand" is a path of submission and denial (submission to an external deity or denial of physical desire), the "Left Hand" is the path of *self-deification* achieved through the *embrace* of the desires, pleasures, and pains of existence. Its goal is, in short, that of "becoming a god while still alive": "The tradition of spiritual dissent in the West has been called Satanism, but more universally the Left Hand Path is a rationally intuited spiritual technology for the purpose of self-deification. We choose as our role model the ancient Egyptian god Set. . . . As part of our practice we each seek the deconstruction of the socially constructed mind, so we begin in rebellion. . . . We do not worship Set—worshiping instead only our own potential."[22] The verb *Xeper* thus captures the Setian idea of both eternal being and eternal becoming—that is, "being" an eternal part of the cosmos forever and "becoming" in the sense of an ever-changing process of evolving and self-refining.

A second and even more extreme current within modern Satanism evolved out of LaVey's church through the work of his daughter Zeena LaVey and her husband Nikolas Schreck. Zeena served as the high priestess of the Church of Satan from 1985 to 1990 and had actually been the church's chief spokesperson against allegations of Satanic ritual abuse. In 1990, however, she and Schreck left her father's church and began to explore other, more radical forms of Satanism.

The first of these was the Werewolf Order, a movement based on the idea that mythical figures such as werewolves and vampires are actually archetypal models for the next step in human evolution, toward higher, superhuman existence. A flyer for the Werewolf Order describes this as "the frontline of the demonic revolution" aiming to "unleash the beast in man," and features a figure wearing a pointed hood with an image of a snarling werewolf behind him presiding over a congregation of hooded figures. The flyer goes on to proclaim the werewolf uprising against Judeo-Christian society and the return to a pagan heritage: "We are the shock troops of a youth uprising against the Judeo-Christian tyranny; the focus of a return to the ancient pagan/satanic tradition that is the birthright of Western European men and women. Like Faust, we have made our pact with the mighty powers of darkness. No boundary can halt our quest for dominion."[23]

Don Webb served as the high priest in the Temple of Set from 1993 to 2002 and is still extremely active in the Setian movement. He is also the author of several books on magic and the occult, such as Mysteries of the Temple of Set *and* Aleister Crowley: The Fire and the Force, *as well as numerous mystery, fantasy, and science fiction novels. Here he recounts how he first came to be involved in the Temple of Set, his views on "Satanism," and the connection between his magical practice and his fictional writings.*

In 1988 I was commissioned to write a short story about the Salem witch trials. . . . I worked a little chart for my reference about how the hysteria spread—suspicions about child care, spectral evidence, et cetera. I took a break from my work and flipped on the television. There was the Geraldo Rivera special on Satanism in America. What a circus. I listened to the "experts" talk. After a few minutes I picked up my chart and started crossing off the schema I'd just written. Human superstition was alive and well. I noticed this Vulcan-looking guy representing Satanism. Jeez, another freak. After one of the "experts" claimed to have huge files on Satanic crime, the Vulcan said, "Well then, why don't you arrest them?" I actually cheered. This was the first logical statement made in the show. The next night I mentioned to a few friends that I wish I could send that "Aquino guy" a fan letter. One of my friends kept eyeing me strangely. She pulled me aside and said that if I wished I could give the letter to her because she was seeing Aquino next week at the international Conclave of the Temple of Set.

I had been attracted to the occult and the mysterious all my life, but I had always found occultists a few tacos short of a combination plate. They are overwhelmed by the symbol systems they seek to manipulate. Yet here was a college-educated middle-class person with a real job who held a senior position in a cult. Not what I was expecting.

I sent a letter off to Dr. Aquino praising his coolness on the show but telling him that I had serious doubts that a group could work toward individuality. I threw in a couple of remarks about Set in history so I would look smart. He wrote back and said that folks in the Temple didn't know why it worked either and that maybe I should join and explain it to them.

I researched the group. I read all of the negative press. I read the scant information I could find on the group. I talked to my friend's husband, Dr. Stephen Flowers. The mixture of antinomianism and Neoplatonism appealed to me, so in 1989 I joined. Maybe I could explain it to them. Seven years later I was high priest and began writing books on Setian practice.

Fiction is magic. Magic is the art of changing the subjective universe so that a proportional change occurs in the objective universe according to the desire and precision of the

(continued)

magician. Fiction guides the reader through changes in her subjective universe. Is anyone the same after reading *To Kill a Mockingbird, One Hundred Years of Solitude,* or "The Call of Cthulhu"? Human imagination is the "place" where imagination takes place. The Temple has a couple of full-time (i.e., more successful than me) fiction writers in it.

Now this does not mean that I use my fiction to further the Temple's goals, other than in the broadest sense of increasing Mystery in the world. Fiction written for initiation often falls very flat. Magic lies in enchanting your audience, whether in a ritual chamber or not—it does not lie in preaching to them. In fiction one willingly applies one's imagination, for the sake of pleasure. Fiction is the opposite of conventional religion.

"Satanism" is a label for spiritual rebellion in a host culture ruled by the Abrahamic faiths. For self-change to occur, the self must first be isolated. Then after luminal experiences (magic), the self must reintegrate into the world. I feel that "Satanism" fails in the third step of the process. The Temple has moved beyond that label—let's face it, real antinomianism lies in acting against media-constructed reality. Satan lost a lot of his power when he became a way to sell music. *Left Hand Path*—the process of self-deification through a mixture of antinomianism and experience of the direct and mysterious effect of the psyche on the world—is a better term. We are the Western version of certain [Hindu] Shaivists—however, we value the aspect of reintegration more highly than carrying our skull cups and smearing ourselves with ashes. . . .

The "Satanic Panic" of the '80s led to Setians adopting the term *Satanist* more dearly. Like the early Christians taking on the derogatory term *Catholic,* or homosexuals have embraced the term *queer.* One of the ways to work your will on society is to use their dark side to your advantage.

Schreck has been particularly controversial (probably deliberately so) because of his open admiration for some of history's greatest villains, including Hitler, Nazi SS commander Heinrich Himmler, and serial killer Charles Manson. In 1989, Schreck released a documentary film entitled *Charles Manson Superstar,* which presents Manson as the victim of demonization by a sensationalist media, and in 2011 he published a book entitled *The Manson File: Myth and Reality of an Outlaw Shaman.* In the mid-1980s Schreck's band Radio Werewolf, which combined dark, violent music with experimental performance art, generated criticism for songs that focused on serial killer John Wayne Gacy and an imagined former Nazi commander and employed imagery of vampirism and necrophilia.

In addition to the Werewolf Order, Zeena and Nikolas formed a Satanic group called the Sethian Liberation Movement (SLM) when, after briefly joining Aquino's Temple of Seth, they left it over religious and organizational differences. The SLM, also a "Left Hand Path" group, draws heavily not only on Egyptian mythology but also on ritual and magical techniques drawn from India, such as Hindu and Buddhist Tantra. In their book *Demons of the Flesh,* Nikolas and Zeena describe their Left Hand Path in deliberately transgressive and provocative terms, as a path that unveils the secrets of "Sadomasochism, Orgies, Taboo-breaking, Fetishism, Orgasm prolongation, Sexual vampirism, Ritual intercourse with divine and demonic entities, Awakening the Feminine Daemonic."[24] Here we see that, even after parting ways with LaVey's Church of Satan, they have continued his goal of attacking all existing sacred cows through the power of shock, transgression, and the overstepping of all conventional boundaries.

SATANISM AND POPULAR CULTURE: THE DEVIL IN FILM AND MUSIC

While Satanism's influence on modern American religious life has been limited, its influence on modern popular culture has been significantly greater. In the American film industry, Satanic themes had appeared in Hollywood since its origin, beginning with *The Devil's Darling* in 1915 and *The Devil's Assistant* two years later. The same director who had made the influential American film *The Birth of a Nation* in 1915 also highlighted John Milton's romantic figure of Lucifer in his 1925 film *The Sorrows of Satan.* In the 1930s and '40s, Satanic themes entered the emerging genre of horror film in movies such as *The Black Cat* in 1934, starring Boris Karloff, and *The Seventh Victim* in 1943, which tells the story of a devil-worshipping conspiracy on the loose in Greenwich Village.

However, it was really in the late 1960s—in the larger atmosphere of the counterculture, the sexual revolution, and cult paranoia—that Satanic film really began to flourish. One of the classics of this genre is the 1968 British film *The Devil Rides Out,* which was based on a popular occult novel of the same name by Dennis Wheatley. The story features a diabolical Satanic priest named Mocata, who is loosely based on the infamous British occultist Aleister Crowley and his circle of devil worshippers. The climax of the film is a "sabbat" held in the English countryside that culminates in the invocation of Satan himself and a kind of bacchanalian drunken orgy among the congregants.

That same year, director Roman Polanski would make what is arguably the greatest Satanic film of all time, *Rosemary's Baby.* Based on a 1967 novel by Ira Levin, the film is the story of a young couple who move into a New York City apartment building that happens to be inhabited by a group of Satanists. The young wife, Rosemary (played by Mia Farrow), is drugged by the Satanists while at a dinner party and falls into a dream state filled with bizarre and frightening psychedelic images. Under the influence of the drug, she is raped by the devil himself—played by none other than Anton LaVey. At the end of the film, she learns that the baby's father is not her husband but Satan, and she is urged to join the cult.

While *Rosemary's Baby* may be arguably the finest example of Satanic horror in film, it was surely not the last. Other Hollywood blockbusters quickly followed, playing upon Satanic themes, such as *The Exorcist* in 1973, *The Omen* in 1976, and many others. In 1999, Polanksi returned to the Satanic horror genre with the apocalyptic thriller *The Seventh Gate,* starring Johnny Depp, which revisited many of the earlier Antichrist themes explored in *Rosemary's Baby*.

SATANISM AND ROCK 'N' ROLL

Even greater than Satanism's influence in film has been its influence—both real and imaginary—in music, where it has inspired artists working in genres from folk to hard rock and of course various forms of heavy metal. Ironically, many of the bands most often associated with and accused of Satanism—such as Black Sabbath, Blue Oyster Cult, and AC/DC—had little or no real Satanic influence, while some of the most important and serious Satanic bands received little attention in the popular media.

One of the first and most dedicated early Satanic groups was the American folk band Coven. Today Coven is best remembered for their recording of the popular antiwar song "One Tin Soldier," which was also featured in the soundtrack of the film *Billy Jack*. However, in addition to their lighter pop recordings, Coven recorded a number of explicitly Satanic albums, beginning with their first record in 1969, *Witchcraft Destroys Minds & Reaps Souls*. Featuring a thirteen-minute track of prayers and chanting entitled "Satanic Mass," the album also included a black mass poster with the members of the group making the sign of the horns as they surround the body of a naked woman on an altar. In fact, this is the first photographed use of the horned salute, which would later become a ubiquitous feature of heavy metal from the 1980s onward. Interestingly enough, although Coven recorded their "Satanic Mass" at roughly the same time as LaVey performed his own black mass, the two appear to have developed independently and suggest the existence of a wider underground Satanic subculture during the late 1960s.

The imagery of Satanism and the black mass was widely popularized in the 1970s through early heavy metal bands such as Black Sabbath. In their first self-titled album, Black Sabbath used the imagery of a Satanic mass to cultivate an atmosphere of horror, fear, and dread (though certainly not worship or reverence), a theme that was continued on their 1973 album *Sabbath Bloody Sabbath*. But the band also included many pro-Christian songs and never really embraced Satanism as anything more than a powerful and provocative trope.

Satanism did not really enter the heavy metal genre until the 1980s and 1990s, particularly in England and Europe. With the rise of new trends such as black metal, death metal, and doom metal, many bands began to explore far more explicitly anti-Christian, aggressive and violent themes, along with a far more open embrace of Satanism as a philosophy. The first wave of black metal began with British bands such as Venom and European bands such as Bathory, Hellhammer, and Celtic Frost; and by the 1990s a second, even more aggressively Satanic wave had spread particularly in Norway through bands such as Mayhem, Darkthrone, and myriad others. Featuring very fast rhythms, aggressive double bass drumming, heavily distorted guitars, and raspy snarling vocals, black metal embraced the anti-Christian, nonconformist, and radically individualistic ideology of Satanism, sometimes adding elements of racism and anti-Semitism.

Although a huge number of black metal bands emerged from Norway and other parts of northern Europe in the 1990s, one of the most influential and controversial is Gorgoroth. Taking its name from the realm of darkness and evil in the land of Mordor as imagined in Tolkien's *Lord of the Rings,* Gorgoroth is best known for its aggressive mixture of dark fantasy, explicit Satanism, and extremely fast, dissonant, and distorted music. Much like LaVey's Church of Satan and its burlesque performance of the black mass, Gorgoroth is very much a performative act that takes the themes of devil worship and Satanic violence to their most exaggerated extremes. From its demo first recording, "A Sorcery Written in Blood," and first studio album, *Pentagram* (1993), to its most recent *Instinctus Bestialis* (2012), Gorgoroth has been at the forefront of a vast pack of bands vying to outdo one another in their use of violent, demonic, and aggressively anti-Christian themes, both in studio recordings and on stage, in highly dramatic Satanic live shows.

One of the best examples of this performative aspect of black metal was Gorgoroth's 2004 concert in Krakow, Poland. The event featured a massive bloodbath of eighty liters of sheep's blood, an array of sheep's heads spitted on stakes, and three naked models covered in blood and arrayed on crucifixes across the stage. Adorned in bloody corpse makeup, inverted crosses, and armbands bristling with nails, the band launched into its opening song, entitled—appropriately enough—"Procreating Satan," an explicit call to rise up and greet the Dark Lord:

I awake
The raging blasphemy
Rise all to hell
Procreating Satan
Satan!
Whenever demons fornicate
Shout the purified beliefs
Sacrificial lambs
Procreating Satan
Our master is coming
The one wants to return
Take place up high
Throne of god
Our masters return
Praise Satan, Praise Satan.[25]

As a result of this hugely controversial event, the band was investigated for religious offense and cruelty to animals, and the concert organizer received a large fine. Ironically, however, the publicity from the event only catapulted Gorgoroth into international celebrity, making the band far more popular than ever before, and the footage from the infamous concert was released as a DVD entitled *Black Mass in Krakow, 2004.*

Between 1992 and 1996, the Norwegian black metal subculture also gained international attention from a series of over fifty church burnings carried out by fans and musicians. The cover of the band Burzum's album *Aske* (Ashes) even featured a photo of a church after its destruction, and the band's leader, Varg Vikernes, was suspected of being behind the arson. In 1994, Vikernes was found guilty in the burning of three other churches and in the murder of fellow black metal musician Euronymous, for which he was sentenced to twenty-one years. While some musicians in the black metal scene condemned the church burnings as attention-seeking acts by misguided fans, others praised them. One of the most outspoken and controversial figures during this period was Gaahl, lead singer of Gorgoroth, who publicly embraced Satanism in interviews and defended the need for this attack (or in his view, counterattack) on Christianity. When asked what were the primary ideas that fueled Gorgoroth's music, he answered simply, "Satan," who in his view embodied "freedom." When asked about the church burnings, he replied quite frankly: "Church burnings and all these things are, of course, things that I support 100 percent and it should have been done much more and will be done much more in the future. We have to remove every trace from what Christianity and its Semitic roots have to offer this world."[26]

In the American heavy metal scene, Satanism typically entered in a more eclectic and less violent way. Perhaps the most famous artist to speak publicly about the influence of LaVey in his work is Marilyn Manson, another artist who is well known for his highly dramatic, often over-the-top performances and open embrace of Satanic themes, particularly in his 1996 album *Antichrist Superstar*. The back cover of the album, for example, features a red symbol consisting of a downward-pointing lightning bolt surrounded by a circle and Hebrew letters spelling "Leviathan," drawn directly from the Church of Satan's goat-head pentagram symbol. In interviews, Manson has been quite frank about the fact that the Church of Satan is one—though only one—of many influences on his thinking and music. As he put it in an interview in 1997, "Over the years I've spent a lot of time interested in religion, and I've read into all different dimensions, whether it was Judaism or . . . Christianity. And Satanism is one that particularly appealed to me. So I struck up a friendship with Anton LaVey. . . . But Satanism is really just, in my view, a philosophy, not unlike Nietzsche or Darwin, an idea of man and his self-preservation, man being his own God. And the word Satan, which tends to scare a lot of people, represents the ultimate rebellion against the mainstream."[27] But Manson was also quick to cite the many other influences on his thought, including Jesus Christ. Of course, this would not prevent many religious leaders and politicians for blaming Manson for tragedies such as the 1999 Columbine school shootings, which were carried out by two students who were fans of his music.

Like Gorgoroth, Marilyn Manson has often played upon the most outlandishly dramatic and performative aspects of Satanism. In his live shows during the 2001 Guns, God and Government tour, for example, Manson appeared behind a prop that seemed to be a cross between a political podium and a priest's lectern, which was adorned with a cross made of a rifle and two guns. Manson's outfit, meanwhile, was a mixture of Nazi and sadomasochistic imagery, with a black SS-style hat and a leather corset and garter belts.[28] Much like

LaVey himself, Manson appeared in these shows to be enacting an exaggerated, even absurd, parodic inversion of dominant symbols and ideals; in this case, however, Manson's performance was an inversion and satire not only of Christianity but also of the American political system, now mocked on stage with authoritarian chants, crosses made of guns, and Nazi imagery.

"FAR BEYOND TEENAGE OBSESSION": THE SATANIC PANIC OF THE 1980S

By the 1980s, Satanism came to be seen as far more than a small fringe group of alternative religious movements such as CoS and ToS. Indeed, throughout the American popular media, tabloid newspapers, and daytime TV shows, it began to be imagined as a vast underground secret conspiracy linked to child abuse, human sacrifice, bizarre pornography, and various other atrocities. Thus, on May 16, 1985, the popular news show *20/20* aired a program called "The Devil Worshipers" that claimed to reveal a host of "perverse, hideous acts that defy belief," including "suicides, murders, and ritualistic slaughter of animals and children," often accompanied by cannibalism, eating of human hearts, and drinking of urine, feces, and blood.[29] Although virtually all of these claims turned out to be completely imaginary, they helped create a widespread Satanic paranoia throughout the United States and a broader fear of new religious groups in general that continues to have lingering implications today.

The reasons for the rapid spread of the Satanic Panic in 1980s America are multiple and complex. In many ways, this was a continuation of the cult paranoia and the anticult movement that had already been growing in the United States since the 1960s, following the rapid growth and spread of new religions, particularly among young people. Particularly after the grisly murders carried out by Charles Manson's quasi-religious group the Family in 1968, and then after the mass suicides of over nine hundred members of Peoples Temple in 1978, there were widespread fears that deviant cults might be brainwashing young people and manipulating them into carrying out other heinous acts.

A second reason was the rise of new forms of socially and politically conservative Christianity during the 1970s and '80s through groups such as the Christian Coalition, the Moral Majority, and Focus on the Family. Reacting against the liberalism and permissiveness of the 1960s, these groups warned of America's loss of a moral compass and saw the alleged spread of Satanism as a telling example of that dangerous trend.

Finally, a third reason was the spread of numerous stories of children involved in abusive and often bizarre Satanic rituals, allegedly uncovered by social workers during child protection investigations. The most famous reports began with Kee MacFarlane, who joined a network of child protection workers in Los Angeles and claimed to have uncovered vast numbers of abuses, perversions, and "bizarre rituals involving violence to animals, scatological behavior," and black magic among the children she examined.[30] Although these allegations later proved to be fabrications generated by coercive and leading interviewing techniques, they had a huge impact on popular awareness and even inspired Congress to double its budget for child protection programs. They also helped popularize the idea that adults might suddenly uncover repressed memories of childhood ritual abuse. As the rumors of Satanic abuse began to spread wildly, some individuals in therapy sessions began to claim that they had unlocked buried memories from their early years, often in outlandish detail.

One of the first and most influential accounts of Satanic ritual abuse appeared in the book *Michelle Remembers* in 1980. Based on a long series of therapy sessions between Michelle Smith and psychiatrist Lawrence Pazder, MD, the book claims to uncover and present the childhood memories of forced involvement in a secret Satanic organization and its violent, sexual, and abusive rituals. With her doctor's help, Michelle claimed to have dredged up memories beginning from age five when she was forced to participate in a Satanic cult, which involved being smeared with the blood of slaughtered babies, being buried in a grave as part of a "rebirth into evil," and participating in an eighty-one-day black mass called the Feast of the Beast. Michelle also recalled seeing Satan himself, whom she described as a huge, hideous figure made of shifting, fiery blackness: "His face is more like fire. You think you see it, and by the time you look hard, it's already changed. . . . His legs are long, and he has funny toenails. There's lots of hair on his legs. . . . Sometimes all you see are huge legs, and then a minute later you can just see a clawlike hand. And other times, he's just a dark space with glistening eyes. You never see him all at once—he's always distorted and not quite substantial, more like a vapor."[31] Those who have seen *Rosemary's Baby* will probably notice that this description sounds very similar to the dreamlike rape scene in Polanski's movie, where the devil appears only in fragmentary, shifting images, with glistening eyes and hairy, clawed hands.

By the late 1980s, accounts of Satanic abuse had begun to appear in truly outlandish and sensational ways in the American popular media. One of the most infamous examples is an episode of Geraldo Rivera's talk show that aired on October 22, 1988, entitled "Devil Worship: Exposing Satan's Underground." Mixing all the most sensational tropes of sexual perversion, drug abuse, and heavy metal, Geraldo described this as nothing less than a "nationwide network of Satanists" working secretly underground to prey upon vulnerable teenagers and entice them into violent and depraved rituals:

> Satanism is more than a hodge-podge of mysticism and fantasy, more than a Halloween motif. It's a violent impulse, it preys upon the emotionally vulnerable, often teenagers, alone and lost. . . . It attracts the angry and the powerless . . . possessed by an obsessive fascination with sex and drugs and, yes, heavy metal rock and roll. . . . Satanism goes far beyond teenage obsession. Today there are cults that worship the devil, engage in secret ceremonies, believe in ancient or bizarre theologies, all of it constitutionally protected, as long as no laws are broken. . . . The other face of adult Satanism is violent and fiendish, centered on sexual ritual and too frequently descending into the vilest crime of all, sexual abuse of children.[32]

Members of the actual Church of Satan, however, did not remain silent on the issue. In their view, the Church of Satan represented a legitimate religious movement that had been grossly misrepresented by an irresponsible media and thus wrongfully associated with these fanciful narratives of Satanic ritual abuse. At the time, Zeena LaVey was still serving as the public spokesperson for CoS. Delivering a scathing critique of sensationalistic television journalism such as Geraldo Rivera and 20/20, Zeena argued that religious minorities such as CoS had been made an easy and convenient scapegoat for other social anxieties:

> The average person these days looks to the television for comfort. And we liken the television to the new god. . . . The media now is that comfort source for the more ignorant of our society. And what Satanists are experiencing now is the result of that ignorance and what that god has created. . . . We are the last scapegoat, we're the last minority, we're the last religion that always requires somebody to define what we are. . . . We're the only thing that the media can toss our name around . . . indiscriminately with no regard for whose lives it affects. And the fact of it is that many Satanists' lives and their families have been completely destroyed, and it's because of this ignorance.[33]

In sum, the Satanic Panic of the 1980s adds a new twist to the theme of performance and spectacle that runs through modern Satanism from the late 1960s onward. While the early Church of Satan had made a point of performing shocking and provocative ritual spectacles such as the black mass, the American media of the 1980s made a spectacle of their own, by sensationalizing and exaggerating the power of Satanism in the modern world.

In the twenty-first century, Satanism seems far less sensational as either a religious movement or a popular spectacle, since today all kinds of religious extremism, terrorism, and violence can draw the mainstream media's attention. However, the questions that it raises concerning religious performance, social and moral transgression, and religious violence remain central ones that we continue to grapple with to this day.

QUESTIONS FOR DISCUSSION AND DEBATE

1. Can a movement that involves a strong element of religious parody and inversion—as we see in the early black mass and LaVey's deliberately silly costumes, complete with devil's horns, cape, and tail—be taken seriously as "religion"? Or should it be viewed more as theater, performance art, or satire? And what is the point of this sort of religious satire? Is it just an ironic game, or is there a more serious philosophical and spiritual point behind it?

2. Why do you think the Satanic Panic was such a powerful and widespread phenomenon during the 1980s? What other social, cultural, historical, and religious forces might have helped give rise to the remarkable paranoia that

gripped the United States, with widespread fears of Satanic ritual abuse, animal and human sacrifice, the influence of Satanic themes in rock and heavy metal music, and so on?

3. How would you approach a case such as that of Michelle Smith and her claims to recall elaborate details of Satanic abuse? Can she be dismissed as simply an attention seeker or possibly mentally ill? Or does she reflect in more complex ways the larger social, cultural, and religious context of the United States during this period?

4. Defenders of the Church of Satan such as Zeena Schreck argued that this religious minority had been made a convenient scapegoat for the mainstream media, which is interested more in titillating sensationalism than serious information. Yet at the same time, the work of LaVey and others does seem to have helped inspire acts such as the string of church burnings in Norway during the 1990s. So is CoS completely innocent in these cases of serious criminal activity? Or should we hold it accountable in some sense for the violent acts that some individuals have carried out in its name?

SUGGESTED CLASSROOM ACTIVITY

Critically examine an example of a Satanic "performance," such as LaVey's black mass in San Francisco or Gorgoroth's musical drama in Krakow. How would you analyze these performances in terms of their sociological function, their psychological impact, and their religious significance? Is it possible for a radically iconoclastic and rebellious performance like this also to be a "religious ritual," filled with sacred meaning and value for its participants? How would you compare these performances to more mainstream religious performances, such as a Christian "passion play" about the trial and death of Jesus, or a Hindu drama about the life and activities of Krishna (among myriad other examples)? Does the "Satanic" nature of this performance make it fundamentally different from other examples of religious drama, or is it just another example of people using dramatic forms to enact larger religious ideas?

SUGGESTED FILM

Laurent, Ray (director). *Satanis: The Devil's Mass.* Something Weird Video, 2003.

SUGGESTIONS FOR FURTHER READING

Aquino, Michael. *The Temple of Set.* San Francisco, 1975. https://xeper.org//maquino/nm/TOS.pdf.

Baddeley, Gavin. *Lucifer Rising: Sin, Devil Worship and Rock 'n' Roll*. London: Plexus, 1999.

Barton, Blanche. *The Secret Life of a Satanist: The Authorized Biography of Anton LaVey*. Los Angeles: Feral House, 1990.

Drury, Nevill. *The History of Magic in the Modern Age*. New York: Carroll and Graf, 2000.

Frankfurter, David. *Evil Incarnate: Rumors of Demonic Conspiracy and Satanic Abuse in History*. Princeton, NJ: Princeton University Press, 2006.

LaVey, Anton. *The Satanic Bible*. New York: Avon, 1969.

———. *The Satanic Rituals*. New York: Avon, 1972.

———. *The Satanic Witch*. Los Angeles: Feral House, 1989.

Schreck, Nikolas, and Zeena Schreck. *Demons of the Flesh: The Complete Guide to Left-Hand Magic*. New York: Creation Books, 2002.

Smith, Michelle, and Lawrence Pazder, MD. *Michelle Remembers*. New York: Congdon and Lattes, 1980.

Urban, Hugh B. *Magia Sexualis: Sex, Magic, and Liberation in Modern Western Esotericism*. Berkeley: University of California Press, 2005.

Victor, Jeffrey. *Satanic Panic: The Creation of a Contemporary Legend*. Chicago: Open Court, 1993.

Webb, Don. *The Seven Faces of Darkness: Practical Typhonian Magic*. Smithville, TX: Runa-Raven Press, 1996.

———. *Uncle Setnakt's Essential Guide to the Left Hand Path* (Smithville, TX: Runa-Raven Press, 1999.

Wright, Lawrence. "Sympathy for the Devil: It's Not Easy Being Evil in a World That's Gone to Hell," *Rolling Stone*, September 5, 1991.

NOTES TO CHAPTER 9

1. See Hugh B. Urban, *Magia Sexualis: Sex, Magic, and Liberation in Modern Western Esotericism* (Berkeley: University of California Press, 2005), chap. 1.
2. See ibid., chap. 7.
3. Zeena Schreck to Michael Aquino, December 30, 1990, quoted in Urban, *Magia Sexualis*, 201.
4. Blanche Barton, *The Secret Life of a Satanist: The Authorized Biography of Anton LaVey* (Los Angeles: Feral House, 1990), 39–40.
5. Anton LaVey quoted in Urban, *Magia Sexualis*, 201.
6. Anton LaVey, *The Satanic Bible* (New York: Avon, 1969), 31.
7. Blanche Barton, "About the Author," in Anton LaVey, *The Satanic Witch* (Los Angeles: Feral House, 1989), n.p.
8. LaVey, *Satanic Bible*, 21.
9. Anton LaVey, interview in *Satanis: The Devil's Mass*, dir. Ray Laurent (Something Weird Video, 2003).
10. LaVey, *Satanic Bible*, 25.

11. Anton LaVey, interview by Gavin Baddeley, in Baddeley's *Lucifer Rising: Sin, Devil Worship and Rock 'n' Roll* (London: Plexus, 1999), 66.
12. Ibid., 67.
13. Ibid., 76.
14. Anton LaVey, *The Satanic Rituals* (New York: Avon, 1972), 15.
15. Ibid., 49.
16. LaVey, *Satanic Bible*, 101.
17. LaVey, interview by Baddeley, in Baddeley, *Lucifer Rising*, 133.
18. Michael Aquino, interview by Gavin Baddeley, in Baddeley, *Lucifer Rising*, 100.
19. Michael Aquino, quoted in Nevill Drury, *The History of Magic in the Modern Age* (New York: Carroll and Graf, 2000), 196.
20. Michael Aquino, "The Book of Coming Forth by Night," n.d., http://cd.textfiles.com/thegreatunsorted/texts/txtfiles_misc/TEMP/BOCFBY.TXT.
21. Don Webb, "Xeper: The Eternal Word of Set," 2012, Xeper.org, https://xeper.org//pub/pub_dw_xeper.html.
22. Don Webb, *Uncle Setnakt's Essential Guide to the Left Hand Path* (Smithville, TX: Runa-Raven Press, 1999), 105–6, and *The Seven Faces of Darkness: Practical Typhonian Magic* (Smithville, TX: Runa-Raven Press, 1996), 5.
23. Ministry of Propaganda and Public Enlightenment, "Werewolf Order: To Unleash the Beast in Man," flyer, Los Angeles, n.d.
24. Nikolas Schreck and Zeena Schreck, *Demons of the Flesh: The Complete Guide to Left-Hand Magic* (New York: Creation Books, 2002), back cover advertisement.
25. Gorgoroth, "Procreating Satan," from *Twilight of the Idols* (Nuclear Blast, 2003). See also Gorgoroth, *Black Mass in Krakow, 2004* (Metal Mind, 2008).
26. Gaahl, interview, in *Metal: A Headbanger's Journey*, dir. Sam Dunn (Seville Productions, 2005).
27. Marilyn Manson, interview, CMJ Music Marathon, New York, 1997, www.mansonwiki.com/wiki/Interview:1997_CMJ.
28. Marilyn Manson, *Guns, God and Government*, DVD (Eagle Rock Entertainment, 2002).
29. "The Devil Worshipers," *20/20*, ABC News, May 16, 1985.
30. David Frankfurter, *Evil Incarnate: Rumors of Demonic Conspiracy and Satanic Abuse in History* (Princeton, NJ: Princeton University Press, 2006), 57.
31. Michelle Smith and Lawrence Pazder, MD, *Michelle Remembers* (New York: Congdon and Lattes, 1980), 201.
32. "Devil Worship: Exposing Satan's Underground," *The Geraldo Rivera Show*, October 22, 1988.
33. Zeena LaVey, interview on KJTV, 1990, www.youtube.com/watch?v=cDNwdcKdboQ.

TEN

ISKCON (Hare Krishna)

Eastern Religions in America and the "Brainwashing" Debate

Perched high up in the mountains of West Virginia, surrounded by beautiful forests, stunning views, and peaceful farmlands—including its own cow protection farm—lies Prabhupada's Palace of Gold. Originally intended to be a home for Swami Prabhupada (figure 10.1), the founder of the International Society for Krishna Consciousness (ISKCON), the palace is now a shrine to the Swami, who died in 1977 before it was finished. Complete with twenty-two-carat gold leaf, an award-winning rose garden, peacock-shaped stained-glass windows, and live peacocks running around the grounds, the Palace of Gold is in many ways an especially clear example of the ISKCON movement as a whole. Advertised as "America's Taj Mahal," the palace combines Indian themes with Italian marble, Persian onyx, antique Chinese vases, and life-sized effigies of Prabhupada himself. As such, it is in many ways emblematic of ISKCON's own unique blend of Indian and American styles and its global presence throughout South Asia, Europe, the United Kingdom, and the United States. This blend of Eastern and Western themes can be seen both in ISKCON theology—which is rooted in ancient Hindu sacred literature but is also presented in notably "Western" terms—and in its colorful artwork—which combines traditional Indian religious themes with styles drawn from Renaissance and Baroque painting.

Just down the hill from the Palace lies a lively temple, where frequent celebrations attract thousands of attendees, ranging from ISKCON members, to first- and second-generation South Asian Hindus, to various American young people who enjoy the scenery, the lively chanting, and the free food. During a visit to the temple in the summer of 2013, for example, I witnessed a "twenty-four hour *kirtan*," a large celebration in which thousands of devotees and visitors perform public chanting (*kirtan*) accompanied by cymbals, drums, and

harmonium. With its rich mix of South Asian Hindus, American devotees, and dreadlocked young people, the event resembled a cross between a traditional Indian festival and a Phish concert.

Since its beginnings in 1960s America, ISKCON has been at once the most successful of the many religious movements to come from India to the United States and also the most controversial. When he arrived in New York City in 1966, Prabhupada quickly began to attract a large following of American young people, appealing to a 1960s generation that was thirsting for alternative spirituality but growing disillusioned with the counterculture of drugs and sex. By the end of the 1960s, Prabhupada would also attract some of the most famous celebrities in the world, including Beatle George Harrison, who first encountered ISKCON in 1969 and remained an enthusiastic supporter until his death.

Yet at the same time, almost from its origins, ISKCON was also often singled out as a dangerous mind-control cult that led vulnerable young people away from their homes and families to adopt a foreign, vegetarian diet and a seemingly "un-American" monastic lifestyle. Particularly during the 1970s and '80s, as a result of several high-profile lawsuits, ISKCON became a central part of the larger debates over "brainwashing," raising much larger issues about conversion, free will, and religious expression that have had implications not just for Eastern-based movements but for alternative spiritual groups more broadly.

ISKCON is only one of many India-based religions that have arrived in the United States since the late nineteenth century. Already in the mid-1800s American philosophers such as Ralph Waldo Emerson and Henry David Thoreau had begun to show a serious interest in Eastern religious thought, which they recognized as equal to or perhaps even more profound than the most sophisticated Western philosophical traditions. One of the most important early events in the transmission of Indian religions to the United States was the World Parliament of Religions Conference held in Chicago in 1893. Bringing representatives of the world's major religions to speak at a huge global expo, the World Parliament was one of the first events to introduce Americans to religions from Asia. The individual chosen to represent Hinduism at the conference was Swami Vivekananda, who preached a very monist or nondualist ("all is one") version of Hinduism that was particularly attractive to a modern American audience and helped spawn the Vedanta Society in the United States. In the early twentieth century, various other forms of Hinduism began to spread to the United States, including many forms of yoga, such as the now hugely popular forms of Hatha Yoga that focus primarily on the physical postures.

During the 1960s, however, a whole new wave of South Asian religions began to reach the shores of America. One reason for the new interest in South Asian religions was surely the larger counterculture movement and the search for new spiritual alternatives to mainstream Christian and Jewish traditions. At the same time that young people of the 1960s began to challenge the dominant cultural, domestic, and sexual norms of their parents, so too they began to experiment with new forms of spirituality and new states of consciousness, sometimes through drugs and sometimes through meditation and yoga. Another reason was the civil rights movement. Just as there was a growing consensus that African Americans deserved rights equal to those of other citizens, so too there was a growing acknowledgment that Asians and minority religious groups also deserved basic rights and recognitions. However, perhaps the most important reason for the new interest in Eastern religions was the change in US immigration laws following the Hart-Cellar Act of 1965. From the mid-1920s until the mid-1960s, the United States had very strict immigration laws for those coming from Asia, which were largely reversed under the Hart-Cellar Act. This legal shift opened the doors to a huge number of immigrants coming from India and other parts of South and East Asia.

Swami Prabhupada, in fact, arrived in the United States that same year. Although ISKCON can usefully be understood as a "new" religious movement, it is also the continuation of a much older tradition of devotional religion that began in India in the sixteenth century. The inspiration for the modern revival was a saint from Bengal (northeast India) named Shri Chaitanya (1486–1534). Believed by his disciples to be the dual incarnation of the god Krishna and his female consort Radha in one human form, Chaitanya began a hugely popular revival of devotion to the Hindu deity Krishna (figure 10.2), which spread across north

FIGURE 10.2 Krishna and Radha. Photo by Ilya Mauter. GNU Free Documentation License; Creative Commons Attribution 3.0.

India for the next five centuries. The simple method of worship that Chaitanya taught was the Hare Krishna mantra, or the chanting of the simple prayer "Hare Krishna, Hare Krishna, Krishna Krishna, Hare Hare; Hare Rama, Hare Rama, Rama Rama, Hare Hare." Based on two names for god, Krishna and Rama, this simple mantra was said to be the easiest and fastest means to spiritual liberation in this degenerate modern age and is still the primary chant used by the ISKCON movement today.

Prabhupada himself came from a line of gurus in the Bengali tradition descended from Chaitanya. He was born with the name Abhay Charan De in Calcutta (the modern city of Kolkata), in northeast India in 1896. Receiving a European education from the Scottish Church College, he made his early living as the owner of a pharmaceutical business and raised a family. In 1922, Abhay Charan met his spiritual master, Bhaktisiddhanta Sarasvati Thakura, who gave him the task of spreading the message of Chaitanya in the English language. Eventually he was recognized with the titles Bhaktivedanta (from *bhakti* for devotion and *vedanta* for the fulfillment of the Veda, sacred scripture) and Prabhupada (meaning "one who has taken shelter at the feet of the Lord"). In 1959 he became a renunciant, living in a monastery and devoting himself full time to the study and translation of sacred scripture.

Finally in 1965, at the remarkable age of sixty-nine, Prabhupada decided to fulfill his master's instruction to spread Chaitanya's message to the English-speaking world by traveling to the United States. Leaving home with nothing more than a suitcase, an umbrella, some dry cereal, several boxes of books, and eight dollars in Indian currency, he boarded a freighter and set out to bring Krishna consciousness to America.

Despite its humble beginnings, Prabhupada's movement took off very quickly. In many ways, this can be explained by its being in just the right place at just the right time—in New York City and then San Francisco and London in the mid- to late 1960s, at the height of the countercultural revolution and amid an intense new interest in Eastern spirituality. ISKCON arrived and spread across the United States at the very same time that the anti–Vietnam War movement was intensifying, at the height of the civil rights movement, amid a fresh wave of new alternative spiritual ideas and a general suspicion of all established institutions, whether political, social, or religious. In many ways, the message of a peaceful Indian guru speaking about love and joyous worship was exactly what many young people wanted to hear.

A key part of Prabhupada's message is that the Hare Krishna path is the simplest, most natural, and most immediate way to achieve spiritual liberation in the modern world. In the current age (called the Kali Yuga, or the last and worst period in the cycles of time, according to Hindu mythology), human beings need an easy and direct way to union with God, and the Hare Krishna lifestyle is a universal path open to anyone from any social status in any part of the world. As Prabhupada wrote in his translation of the key Hindu text, the Bhagavad Gita or "Song of God,"

> Anyone from any walk of life can attain the Supreme. One does not need highly developed intelligence. . . . Anyone who accepts the principle of *bhakti-yoga* and accepts the Supreme Lord as the *summum bonum* of life, as the highest target, the ultimate goal, can approach the Lord in the spiritual sky.
>
> In this present day, man is very eager to have one scripture, one God, one religion, and one occupation. So let there be one common scripture for the whole world—*Bhagavad-gita*. And let there be one God only for the whole world—Sri Krsna. And one *mantra* only—Hare Krsna. . . . And let there be one work only—the service of the Supreme Personality of Godhead.[1]

After spending a short time in a family's home in Pennsylvania and then in a yoga studio in Manhattan, Prabhupada eventually set up a small temple in a loft in the Bowery district on the Lower East Side. At that time one of the roughest parts of New York, this area was a skid row of homeless alcoholics, but it also offered ample loft space for young artists, musicians, and bohemians. News of the Swami in the Bowery soon spread quickly by word of mouth, and young people began to come to the temple to chant and study with him. Many of the first generation of followers attracted to his message were experimenting with various other offerings of the 1960s counterculture, including not just yoga, meditation, and Eastern philosophy but also LSD and other psychedelic drugs. Prabhupada, in fact, helped guide several young people away from drugs as a means of exploring higher states of consciousness, suggesting that the Hare Krishna mantra and the lifestyle of a *sannyasi* could provide a higher and more permanent state of transcendental awareness than any drug.

Formally established in July of 1966, the International Society for Krishna Consciousness clearly represented a more austere and ascetic alternative to the sexual freedom and drug use of the American counterculture. The ISKCON lifestyle was in many ways a stark contrast to the culture of sex, drugs, and rock 'n' roll, prohibiting meat, alcohol, gambling, and illicit sex. Yet remarkably, despite its ascetic nature, the ISKCON lifestyle proved to be an attractive alternative for many young people of the late 1960s and '70s, and the movement grew at a remarkable rate for the next decade.

Prabhupada's next stop in his "journey through the West" happened to be another major center of the American counterculture, the Haight-Ashbury district of San Francisco, where he established a second ISKCON center in 1967. This was, of course, the same year as the "Summer of Love," one of the most famous moments of the 1960s, when as many as one hundred thousand young people converged on the Haight-Ashbury neighborhood to celebrate the larger cultural, sexual, and political shifts of the hippie revolution. Despite their ascetic lifestyle, the Hare Krishnas became an important part of the larger festive spirit of the Summer of Love, adding their own boisterous, high-energy chanting to the scene of thousands of other young people playing music, dancing, and experimenting with all manner of new spiritual, philosophical, and social ideas. ISKCON in fact flourished in this environment, drawing in and converting hundreds of hippies who were, often quite literally, right at the devotees' doorstep. The early movement made an explicit appeal to this generation of seekers, offering them a permanent bliss that no worldly substance could provide. Indeed, just below the "Hare Krishna" sign outside the San Francisco temple door was a smaller sign that read "Stay High All the Time, Discover Eternal Bliss"[2]—a phrase that became a kind of second mantra of the early movement. As one young devotee put it, "Everybody's trying to get high and stay there. Everybody's looking for an exalted state of consciousness. . . . But there's something bringing you back to the same old routine. Not in this. This has a snowballing effect. You can chant your way right into eternity."[3]

HARE KRISHNA, MUSIC, AND THE BEATLES

One of the most important factors in ISKCON's rapidly growing popularity in the late 1960s was the endorsement from the Beatles—at that time by far the biggest band in the world, with a staggering cultural influence that is really difficult to measure by twenty-first-century standards. The members of the Beatles had been briefly attracted to another Indian-based new religious movement, Transcendental Meditation (TM), and had all traveled to India in 1968 in order to stay at the ashram of the movement's founder, Maharishi Mahesh Yogi. However, the Beatles quickly became disillusioned with TM and explored various other Indian spiritual options, including ISKCON. References to the Hare Krishna mantra made their way into several songs, including the Beatles' "I Am the Walrus" (1967), Ringo Starr's solo recording "It Don't Come Easy" (1971), and George Harrison's "My Sweet Lord" (1970).

In September 1969, John Lennon, Yoko Ono, and George Harrison met with Prabhupada and had a long conversation about the soul, reincarnation, chanting, and various spiritual matters, which was later published in the book *The Search for Liberation*. During their discussion of meditation, Lennon asked Prabhupada about the significance of the Hare

Krishna mantra and its relation to other forms of chanting: "If all mantras are just the name of God . . . it doesn't make much difference, does it, which one you sing?" As Prabhupada explained to Lennon, the Hare Krishna mantra is the best of all names of God, because it is the one recommended for this particular cosmic age: "It *does* make a difference. For instance, in a drug shop they sell all types of medicines for curing different diseases. But still you have to get a doctor's prescription in order to get the particular type of medicine. . . . Similarly, in this age of Kali, the Hare Krsna mantra is prescribed."[4]

Of the four Beatles, however, only Harrison would become a serious follower of ISKCON, which he supported strongly up until his death in 2001. Harrison had been fascinated with Indian spirituality and culture since 1965, when he first encountered the sitar during the making of the film *Help!* (a film that also included many Indian religious themes, though in a rather distorted and satirical form). Harrison produced a recording of the Hare Krishna mantra, which reached the charts in twenty countries and helped make the chant famous worldwide. In 1969, Harrison was also the co-signer of the lease for the Radha Krishna Temple, which has served as the UK center for ISKCON ever since. Hare Krishna themes pervaded Harrison's music throughout his solo career. Not only did the Hare Krishna mantra itself serve as the chorus for his huge hit single "My Sweet Lord," but Indian philosophical ideas recur throughout his recordings from "All Things Must Pass" in 1970 until his final album in 2002.

In 1970, Harrison wrote the introduction for Swami Prabhupada's book *Krsna: The Supreme Personality of Godhead,* in which he explains his understanding of ISKCON philosophy and the meaning of the Hare Krishna mantra. In Harrison's rather inclusivist and universalistic view, Krishna is just one of many names for God, alongside Jesus, Buddha, Allah, and others, and the message of Hare Krishna really boils down to the Beatles' own simple message of "All you need is love":

> Everybody is looking for KRISHNA. Some don't realize that they are, but they are.
>
> KRISHNA is GOD, the Source of all that exists, the Cause of all that is, was, or ever will be. As GOD is unlimited HE has many Names. Allah-Buddha-Jehova-Rama: All are KRISHNA, all are ONE.
>
> . . . If there's a God, I want to see Him. It's pointless to believe in something without proof, and Krishna Consciousness and meditation are methods where you can actually obtain GOD perception. You can actually see God, and Hear Him, play with Him. It might sound crazy, but He is actually there, actually with you.
>
> There are many yogic Paths—Raja, Jnana, Hatha, Kriya, Karma, Bhakti—which are all acclaimed by the MASTERS of each method. SWAMI BHAKTIVEDANTA is as his title says, a BHAKTI Yogi following the path of DEVOTION. By serving GOD through each thought, word, and DEED, and by chanting HIS Holy Names, the devotee quickly develops God-consciousness. By chanting:
>
> *Hare Krishna, Hare Krishna—Krishna Krishna, Hare Hare*
> *Hare Rama, Hare Rama—Rama Rama, Hare Hare*

one inevitably arrives at KRISHNA Consciousness. (The proof of the pudding is in the eating!) . . .

ALL YOU NEED IS LOVE (KRISHNA)[5]

Perhaps even more than Prabhupada's own writings and translations, it was Harrison's powerful endorsement of the movement that helped ISKCON to grow into the largest and most successful of all the various Indian religious imports to the United States. As we see in this quote, his universalistic equation of Krishna with Jesus and other names for God helped young people accept ISKCON as a spiritual worldview that was compatible with and complementary to Christianity rather than some strange import from the exotic Orient.

Harrison's involvement with ISKCON continued until his death in 2001. On his final album, *Brainwashed,* he not only incorporated Indian philosophy but also made an ironic commentary on the whole "brainwashing" debate itself. As he sang in the title track for the album, most ordinary people living in modern society are perhaps far more "brainwashed" by television, advertising, and consumerism than members of ISKCON or other alternative religious movements: "Brainwashed in our childhood, brainwashed by the school, brainwashed by the teachers, and brainwashed by all their rules. . . . Brainwashed by the Nikkei, brainwashed by Dow Jones, brainwashed by the FTSE, Nasdaq and secure loans," he sings, concluding the track with a long Hindu chant in Sanskrit.[6]

ISKCON PHILOSOPHY

ISKCON is deeply rooted in much older traditions of Indian thought dating back to the oldest known scriptures in South Asia, the Vedas (1500–400 BCE), which are the basis for all later forms of Hindu religion and philosophy. However, ISKCON philosophy also has several unique features that help distinguish it as a unique and in many ways "new" religious movement rather than simply another variation of ancient Hindu traditions. While most Hindus today typically regard all the many Hindu deities as just the many various manifestations of one supreme being, ISKCON regards one deity in particular—Krishna—as the ultimate divinity or "supreme personality of Godhead." According to the various narratives of his life and activities, Krishna is portrayed as a beautiful, adorable, yet mischievous baby during his infancy and later as an incredibly handsome young man during his adolescence and adulthood. At once playful and silly, yet also powerful and sometimes frightening, Krishna is both irresistibly attractive and often awesomely majestic. Most Hindus today consider Krishna to be one of the many avatars ("descents" or incarnations) of the god Vishnu, the deity who upholds the cosmic order and periodically appears in a physical form in this world in order to combat evil or set the cosmic order aright. However, ISKCON regards Krishna not simply as an incarnation of Vishnu but rather as the highest, original, and true personification of the Godhead, of which all other deities are mere reflections and manifestations.

Another unique feature of ISKCON philosophy is that it is essentially a dualist worldview. Many other forms of Hindu philosophy are "monistic," that is, based on the belief that there is only one Reality—God or Brahman (the impersonal Absolute or Supreme Being)—and that everything from souls and bodies to material objects is inherently one with that divine. This is the worldview that we see in modern Hindu movements such as the Vedanta Society and in new religions influenced by Indian thought such as the Theosophical Society, which we mentioned in chapter 4. ISKCON, by contrast, is based on a dualist philosophy, insofar as it sees God or Krishna as ultimately superior to and distinct from the human soul. When we achieve spiritual liberation, we can have a loving relationship with Krishna, as his consort Radha does, but we never become identical with God. In this sense, ISKCON philosophy is much closer to most forms of Christian theology, which also typically maintain a distinction between the soul and God.

The concept of Krishna as the incarnation of God in human form also had obvious intersections with Christian beliefs. This parallel between Christian and Indian beliefs was highlighted not only in ISKCON publications such as the book *Christ and Krishna* (1987) but also in scholarly works such as Geoffrey Parrinder's *Avatar and Incarnation* (1997). Of all the various forms of Indian spirituality to come to the United States, ISKCON arguably has the most obvious philosophical and even ritual intersections with Christianity, which probably in part helps explain its general success in this still predominantly Christian nation.

ISKCON LIFESTYLE: AN ANCIENT MONASTIC ORDER IN THE CONTEMPORARY UNITED STATES

Perhaps the primary reason that ISKCON has been controversial in the United States is the highly austere monastic lifestyle that it requires of its full-time members, which typically involves a marked change in dress, diet, daily routine, and community. Prabhupada recommended four regulative principles as the foundation of spiritual life: no eating of meat, fish, or eggs; no illicit sex (meaning complete celibacy outside marriage and sex only for reproduction inside marriage); no gambling; and no intoxication (including alcohol, caffeine, tobacco, and recreational drugs).

Full-time ISKCON members are also clearly marked by dress and hairstyle: male devotees have shaven heads except for a small topknot at the back of the skull; the men wear traditional Indian dhotis (white for married men and saffron for unmarried men), while the women wear saris; all members carry a sack with a rosary containing 108 beads, and they aim to recite sixteen rounds of 108 Hare Krishna mantras each day. Those who live in ashrams (monasteries or spiritual retreats) generally wake very early in the morning and follow essentially a monastic lifestyle divided into periods of work, ritual, and chanting. ISKCON also maintains several of its own farms, which operate largely autonomously and independently from mainstream society, much as the Amish and other religious communities do. Thus many Americans have regarded ISKCON not simply as an alternative belief system but as a fairly radical alternative to American social, family, and communal life altogether.

In addition to offering an alternative lifestyle for adult members, ISKCON has opened its own schools from primary to secondary and advanced education around the world. These

Jagannath (figure 10.3) is an American ISKCON devotee who first became introduced to the movement in 2005. When I spoke with him in 2013, Jagannath had just returned from Mayapur, India, where he had begun an intensive course of Sanskrit language study. He talked with me about how he was first introduced to ISKCON and the basics of ISKCON lifestyle.

Ever since I was a kid, I used to be really sensitive about killing animals. My big brother would like to swat flies and crush them with his sock, and I would cry. I can remember it still. I maintained that kind of temperament throughout high school. I was interested in being morally concerned for nonhumans. But I didn't get a lot of feedback for that belief. So I felt isolated, lonely. Gradually I thought more deeply about this, and when I was about sixteen or seventeen years old, I came to the point where I phrased it that "I love every living entity." That may have been sentimental, but it was important to me. I couldn't turn it off. It wasn't a belief; it was an experience. It continued with me as I went to college. I came here for art college at CCAD [Columbus College of Art and Design]. I met a couple of friends there who could kind of get it, but still I was alone, I didn't have many people to associate with.

My parents were open-minded and spiritual, appreciating all kinds of spiritual culture from around the world and even things in science—just genuinely inquisitive and open-minded people. They were socially religious, and we would go once or twice a year, the whole family went. We were Catholic. I always liked the Catholic Church. I just liked how beautiful the stained glass was, the incense—superaesthetic.

By the time I was in college, I felt that I still just couldn't relate with people. I got depressed, because I was saying, "I love every living entity," but I had no practical way to help. So imagine a point with centrifugal circles around it. The point is you, then beyond you there is like your social network and then your family, your society, then all of humanity, then beyond would be animals, then beyond that plants. The farther I went out on that line, the less practical I could do anything to help. It just became talk. And so there was a mismatch. I felt I wanted to help every living entity. That's what I meant by love. I wanted to serve and love and benefit them. But I had no ability to do it. So that was frustrating. And I couldn't turn off the feeling. It was real and important to me.

I was agnostic. I wasn't convinced whether or not there was any God. So I prayed, "Dear God, if you exist, please help every living entity so I can stop worrying about it." A few days later, I met one of the devotees who was distributing books on my campus. He had a Bhagavad Gita. I saw him standing there with a stack of books. On CCAD campus people don't stand around with a stack of books. It's a more colorful and dramatic, kind of flamboyant atmosphere. I thought, "Wow, he looks philosophical." So I went over to him and asked, "Excuse me, do you know about God and whether he can

FIGURE 10.3 Jagannath Dasa. Photo by the author.

help every living entity?" So he was pleasantly surprised. He paused for a second. And he said, "Yes." He showed me a verse: "*Bhoktaram yajna tapasam / sarva loka mahesvaram / suhrdam sarva bhutanam / jnatva mam santim rcchati.*" He showed me the word-for-word translation. "*Suhrdam sarva bhutanam*" means that God is the best friend of every living entity. And I thought, "Wow, that is so relevant." So I asked him about the temple. He told me that there's something here on Eighth Avenue you can go visit. I've been visiting ever since.

My mother was supersupportive. It was interesting for her. She got a book in 1977, *The Teachings of Lord Kapila, the Son of Devakuti,* in an airport, though she never interacted with devotees by going to a temple. But she had such a favorable impression of that interaction that she was really happy to know that devotees still exist. She didn't know that there was such a thing as Hare Krishna anymore after the 1980s. My mother is still supportive.

I go to sleep early and wake up early—that's one big difference from before I met devotees. This is the situation for anyone who's living in a temple. There are regular deity worship services that take place in the morning. The morning is important for spiritual activity, so that's why we use that. Because you're fresh at that time—there's no phone calls and distractions. It was tough to go to sleep early—that's the hardest thing.

I learned how to cook. And I learned how to play music; with an artistic temperament, that's been a stabilizing force in my spiritual practice. It's part of our regular daily routine. We sing every morning, and gradually if you want to participate in the program you have to learn how to play this stuff. It's an immersion thing, just like

(continued)

learning a language. If you hear it every day you'll figure it out. So you figure out *kartals*, the little hand cymbals, and the *mrdanga* drum. It just comes. I agree with St. Thomas Aquinas about the primacy of will in learning. If you really like something, it becomes easy to get it.

If people ask me, "What religion are you?" I would say, "Hare Krishna." But I also qualify it almost every time, because the notion of "What religion are you" carries with it the assumption that religions conflict with each other and are mutually exclusive. I don't want to reinforce that. So I tease it out and explain that our position is that, as long as you love God, it's all right if you call him by one name or another.

range from small primary schools associated with local temples all the way to large centers for the study of Sanskrit literature and philosophy, such as the Mayapur Institute in northeast India and the Bhaktivedanta Institute in Mumbai and Berkeley. ISKCON's central focus on education has been a cause of both its success and its controversies: while its schools have clearly been part of its strength and global presence as a new religious movement, there have also been numerous cases of child sexual abuse at ISKCON-run schools, which, as we will see below, were part of a larger scandal surrounding the movement in the 1970s and '80s.

ISKCON has not only full-time members who live in monastic communities but also a large and now growing lay population. Particularly today, now that the movement is almost fifty years old, fewer members live in temples and more live ordinary family lives in their own homes, simply visiting the temple periodically for worship or socialization. Another shift that has taken place as the movement has matured is a growing appeal to second- and third-generation South Asian Hindus living in the United States. As ISKCON temples have become increasingly accepted and "mainstreamed" over the decades, they have become attractive places for all varieties of Hindus to worship. In Columbus, for example, I have Hindu friends from Bangladesh who cannot easily get to the more distant Hindu temples, so they have used the local ISKCON Krishna house for basic religious services, such as the first feeding with rice ceremony for their infant daughter. Overall, the movement has shifted from a largely monastic community of individuals who withdraw from the world and live full time in ashrams to a more publicly engaged community that interacts with a broader lay audience, both American and South Asian.

ISKCON AND THE BRAINWASHING DEBATE

One of the most important issues raised by new religions such as ISKCON is the debate surrounding the idea of "brainwashing" or "mind control." Can a member of a religious (or political or ideological group) actually become "brainwashed," that is, lose her or his own ability to think and choose freely, effectively becoming an uncritical and passive member of a community that thinks and chooses for her or him? Or is the concept of "brainwashing" an outdated relic of the Cold War that is far too simplistic to account for the many complex reasons that individuals become deeply involved in alternative spiritual groups?

The concept of brainwashing, or "thought reform," first began to be discussed during the Korean War, when a large number of US soldiers defected to the North Korean side, allegedly because of the influence of Chinese mind-control techniques. The term *brainwashing* was then popularized by the American psychiatrist Robert Jay Lifton in his widely read book *Thought Reform and the Psychology of Totalism* in 1961, and also in blockbuster films such as *The Manchurian Candidate* (1962, remade in 2004).

However, the concept of brainwashing was quickly applied to the growing number of new religious movements that began to proliferate during the 1960s and '70s. As more and more young people began to join alternative spiritual groups during these volatile decades, the concept of brainwashing offered a convenient explanation for why so many Americans were turning away from traditional religious and family structures to join new religious movements. The murder spree led by Charles Manson and his group of young followers, "the Family," in 1969 only generated greater paranoia about dangerous cults that might brainwash vulnerable teenagers. By the 1980s, the idea of brainwashing had become a central part of the larger "cult scares" that swept through the American media, fueling the fear that deviant religious groups were stealing away our youth and undermining society.

Charges of brainwashing have been leveled at many new religious movements in the United States, such as the Church of Scientology, Peoples Temple, the Unification Church, and Heaven's Gate. However, ISKCON is an especially important example because the accusations of brainwashing in this case actually went all the way to the US Supreme Court and generated a much larger national debate surrounding new religions, young people, and the law. With their seemingly exotic Indian clothing, vegetarian diet, communal living arrangements, and alternative educational system, the Hare Krishnas were widely attacked by journalists and anticult activists as the epitome of the brainwashing religious group.

This stereotype was only reinforced by a series of crises and scandals within the movement during this same time period. First, accounts of child sexual abuse at ISKCON facilities began to emerge in the 1980s, with accusations of abuse going back to the 1970s. Indeed, a report published by the movement's own publication, the *ISKCON Communications Journal*, documented numerous cases of sexual abuse at its schools in both the United States and India between 1971 and 1986,[7] and ISKCON leadership itself took action to acknowledge, address, and clean up the serious problem with the movement. ISKCON was eventually sued by ninety-five people, and the suit forced the movement into chapter 11 bankruptcy in order to work out a $9.5 million settlement.

A second scandal that helped buttress the brainwashing accusations took place at the Palace of Gold and the New Vrindaban community during the 1980s, when it was under the leadership of a devotee named Swami Kirtanananda. In 1987, Kirtanananda was expelled from ISKCON because of his unorthodox (and apparently illegal) activities and founded his own rival organization centered in West Virginia. In 1990, Kirtanananda was indicted on eleven counts of racketeering, fraud, and conspiracy to commit murder. The government claimed that Kirtanananda had illegally amassed $10.5 million and had ordered the murder of two opponents within the community to cover up his sexual abuse of minors. Although he was initially convicted of all counts, his lawyer convinced an appeals court to throw out the charges, and Kirtanananda was released. However, he lost his control of the New Vrindaban community, which was reintegrated into the main ISKCON movement.

But the most important allegations of brainwashing began in California during the mid-1970s. In 1974, a fourteen-year-old girl named Robin George began to visit the ISKCON temple in Laguna Beach, California, attending the free feasts and chanting. According to her testimony during the trial, Robin had initially been given permission by her parents to practice the religion of her choice, but at some point her parents rejected that choice and destroyed her altar, books, and other ISKCON materials. She then ran away from home and became an ISKCON devotee, moving from place to place (San Diego, Louisiana, and Ottawa) in order to outrun her parents. In October 1975, her parents finally tracked Robin down and promptly filed a lawsuit against ISKCON for false imprisonment and emotional distress. Their daughter, they argued, had not joined ISKCON freely but had been brainwashed and kidnapped by the group. Robin herself later claimed that she had been pressured into becoming a devotee, frightened with the idea that she would be reincarnated as "a worm in stool" if she didn't join. She also later alleged that she had been forced to collect money under false pretenses, telling people she was collecting donations for some other worthy cause and concealing her ISKCON identity: "They told us to say anything at all to get a donation. . . . Sometimes we said we were feeding starving people. The attitude was that we were doing the *karmis* [nonbelievers] a favor by taking their money."[8]

During the suit, a psychologist named Margaret Singer served as an expert witness. A part-time adjunct professor in the Department of Psychology at the University of California, Berkeley, Singer also served on the board of an anticult group called the American Family Foundation and later wrote the book *Cults in Our Midst* (1996). Singer developed a model of brainwashing that draws upon and adapts Robert Jay Lifton's famous model of thought reform, identifying six conditions that she believes are needed to make mind control possible by systematically increasing the restrictiveness enforced by the cult: first, keep the person unaware that there is an agenda to control or change the person; second, control the person's time and physical environment (including the person's contacts, information, and so on); third, create a sense of powerlessness, fear, and dependency; fourth, suppress old behaviors and attitudes; fifth, instill new behaviors and attitudes; and finally, put forth a closed system of logic. The end result of these six conditions, Singer argued, is that the individual will undergo a kind of invisible social adaptation, becoming silently converted into a completely new way of thinking, believing, acting, and socializing—in effect a whole new identity and self—without even realizing that a profound transformation is taking place.[9]

Invoking theories of brainwashing that she had used in previous cases involving new religious movements, Singer helped persuade the jury that the ISKCON lifestyle employed sleep deprivation, a restrictive diet, long hours of chanting, and indoctrination in order to effect a form of mind control: "It's my opinion that she was not at that point freely using her own will and volition, but being influenced and manipulated and made to comply with the wishes of the various Krishna organization representatives."[10] Singer further testified that George suffered from three mental disorders—atypical dissociative disorder, post-traumatic stress disorder, and an identity disorder—as a result of her time spent in the Krishna organization. George would, in Singer's opinion, require "prolonged psychological or psychiatric treatment by persons who are familiar with and have worked with people who have been exposed to similar types of trauma."[11]

Singer and the Georges' lawyers also highlighted the fact of Robin's age—at fourteen to fifteen, clearly a minor—as a sign that ISKCON had taken advantage of a vulnerable young woman who should have been under the legal protection of a parent or guardian. Even ISKCON's own lawyer, Bhutatma Das, conceded this point, stating, "Certainly, we should have sent her back to her parents. And, admittedly, today we would only allow a minor into ISKCON with written permission from their parents."[12]

In June 1983, an Orange County jury awarded Robin and her mother $32.5 million in actual and punitive damages—a figure that shocked even the Georges' lawyer, who had asked for only half that amount. While the judge later reduced the amount to $9.7 million, it was still the largest award of its kind against a new religious movement. The case, however, continued to be debated, and the amount was further reduced to $2.7 million by the California appeals court. The California court, moreover, threw out the most overt allegations of "brainwashing" made by the plaintiff.[13] Finally, the US Supreme Court was asked to grant review of the George case, which the National Council of Churches dubbed perhaps "the most important single religious liberty case ever filed in this Court."[14] The Court issued a stay on executing the judgment and ruled that ISKCON would not have to sell its temples in order to satisfy the judgment. Eventually in 1993, ISKCON reached an out-of-court settlement with the Georges for an undisclosed amount of money, and the lawsuit was dropped.

Although the charges of "brainwashing" were ultimately never accepted by the higher courts, the Robin George case does raise the much larger and deeply contested question of mind control in new religious movements. Psychologists, anticult activists, and scholars of religion have mounted heated arguments on both sides of the debate. On one side some sociologists, such as the Canadian scholar Stephen Kent, have argued that certain alternative spiritual communities do in fact involve a form of "systematic, scientific, and coercive elimination of the individuality of the mind of another." In Kent's view, this can in some cases be extreme enough to be described as a process of brainwashing.[15] While Kent's analysis in this case was focused on the Church of Scientology, other authors have made similar charges regarding ISKCON and a wide array of other new movements.

On the other side, perhaps the majority of scholars of new religious movements are far more skeptical of the brainwashing narrative. As authors such as Catherine Wessinger, Lorne Dawson, and others argue, the concept of brainwashing is far too simplistic and generally far too biased to account for the real complexity of an individual's involvement in a new religious movement. As Wessinger argues, "The term obscures the fact that people adopt alternative beliefs because those beliefs make sense to them, and that people join groups because those groups offer them benefits."[16] Moreover, all religions old and new involve some degree of shaping, reshaping, and transforming the thoughts and habits of their adherents; as Dawson notes, "Religions have been in the business, throughout the ages, of emotionally prompting and physically and socially supporting the abandonment of old habits of thought and word and deed and inducing new ones."[17] So it seems unfair to single out new religions and their conversion tactics as a form of "brainwashing."

Rather than relying on a simple account such as brainwashing, many scholars prefer to use more neutral language such as "socialization procedures." As Wessinger suggests, all of us, whether members of new religions or not, are socially conditioned in various ways from birth, through family, school, media, and legal and political systems, as well as religious organizations (and many members of new religions—such as George Harrison—also regard the rest of mainstream society as "brainwashed" in a way). Smaller and newer movements such as ISKCON, Scientology, or Peoples Temple might involve socializing procedures that are more intensive than, but perhaps not inherently different from, the sort found in other, more "mainstream" religions.[18]

Although it has usually focused on fairly small alternative spiritual communities, the brainwashing debate raises philosophical, legal, and religious questions. On the philosophical side, it forces us to ask whether individuals really can lose free will: Can one become so dominated by a community that one loses the ability to think and decide freely? Or is the question of free will and social conditioning far more complex than the brainwashing model suggests? On the legal side, however, it raises a more difficult question: Can or should the state ever intervene in lives of individuals—such as Robin George—who have joined a controversial new religious movement? And in what ways does the fact that she was a minor complicate the question? Even if not "brainwashed," was she arguably more susceptible to the socialization procedures of ISKCON than an adult would have been?

Today, ISKCON has largely weathered the storm of the brainwashing controversy and the other scandals that surrounded it in the 1970s and '80s. It is now arguably the most successful new religious movement to have emerged from India, not just in the United States but globally. But these larger questions of free will, thought reform, and social conditioning in alternative spiritual communities continue to be debated with many other new religions, such as Heaven's Gate, the Branch Davidians, Scientology, and numerous others.

QUESTIONS FOR DISCUSSION AND DEBATE

1. Why do you think ISKCON, of all the many forms of Indian spirituality, became the most popular Indian-based religion in the United States? Does it seem

ironic that a movement that advocates a fairly austere and monastic lifestyle would become successful in modern America, or does that make a certain kind of sense? Can you imagine reasons why a young American (such as a typical college student) would be attracted to ISKCON?

2. Some of the first people in the United States, the United Kingdom, and Europe to become attracted to Indian religious movements were musicians, artists, and entertainers such as the Beatles. Why would musicians tend to be more attracted to Eastern and new religious movements, particularly movements such as ISKCON (whose ascetic lifestyle seems the opposite of the "rock star" lifestyle)? Do you think ISKCON could have become as important a new religious movement without the support of hugely influential celebrities such as George Harrison?

3. Does "brainwashing" or "thought reform" seem like a useful way of making sense of new religious movements such as ISKCON? Is it a useful concept at all, or is it—as some scholars argue—too simplistic and biased to be of any help in the interpretation of new religions? Is the kind of socialization that is involved in new religions such as ISKCON really inherently different from the kind of socialization involved in any religious lifestyle or in secular institutions such as sports or the military?

4. Does the fact that Robin George was a minor complicate the brainwashing debate? Are minors more susceptible to social conditioning or the pressure of a religious community than adults would be? Does the concept of brainwashing make more sense in the case of a minor, or is it still a flawed model?

SUGGESTED CLASSROOM ACTIVITY

Enact a courtroom trial based on the Robin George case. Appoint lawyers for the George family, lawyers for ISKCON, anticult witnesses such as Margaret Singer, and scholars of new religions such as Catherine Wessinger or Lorne Dawson. Again, make sure that the debate is not a simple "either/or," that is, "Brainwashing is real or brainwashing is not real," but a more complex debate that highlights the free will involved in membership in new religions as well as the seemingly "brainwashing" aspects of mainstream religions and secular institutions. For example, is boot camp basic training in the US military a form of "brainwashing?" Is entry into ISKCON really different from entry into other recognized "mainstream" religious orders, such as the Benedictine, Franciscan, or other Catholic monastic orders, or into major Buddhist or Jain monastic traditions? If we abandon the idea of "brainwashing," then how do we still deal with cases of real physical and psychological harm in in new religious movements, such as the child sexual abuse that occurred at New Vrindaban under Swami Kirtanananda?

SUGGESTED FILM

Hare Krishnas: Hiders or Seekers? Vanguard Cinema, 1998.

SUGGESTIONS FOR FURTHER READING

Barker, Eileen. *The Making of a Moonie: Choice or Brainwashing?* London: Basil Blackwell, 1984.

Beck, Guy, ed. *Alternative Krishnas: Regional and Vernacular Variations on a Hindu Deity.* Albany: SUNY Press, 2005.

Bhaktipada, Swami Kirtanananda. *Christ and Krishna: The Path of Pure Devotion.* Moundsville, WV: Bhaktipada Books, 1985.

Bromley, David G., and Larry Shin, eds. *Krishna Consciousness in the West.* Lewisburg, PA: Bucknell University Press, 1989.

Dawson, Lorne. *Comprehending Cults: The Sociology of New Religious Movements.* New York: Oxford University Press, 2006.

Ellwood, Robert S. *The Sixties Spiritual Awakening: American Religion Moving from Modern to Postmodern.* New Brunswick, NJ: Rutgers University Press, 1994.

Hinduism Today. "Robin George vs. ISKCON." *Hinduism Today,* January 1984. www .hinduismtoday.com/modules/smartsection/item.php?itemid=1133.

Kent, Stephen. "Brainwashing in Scientology's Rehabilitation Project Force." Interior Ministry, Hamburg, Germany, 2002. www.solitarytrees.net/pubs/skent/brain.htm.

———. *From Slogans to Mantras: Social Protest and Religious Conversion in the Late Vietnam War Era.* Syracuse, NY: Syracuse University Press, 2001.

Lifton, Robert Jay. *Thought Reform and the Psychology of Totalism: A Study of Brainwashing in China.* New York: Norton, 1969.

Prabhupada, A. C. Bhaktivedanta Swami. *Bhagavad Gita As It Is.* 1972. Reprint, Los Angeles: Bhaktivedanta Book Trust, 1986.

———. *Krsna: The Supreme Personality of Godhead.* Boston: ISKCON Press, 1970.

Rochford, E. Burke. "Child Abuse in the Hare Krishna Movement, 1971–1986." *ISKCON Communications Journal* 6, no. 1 (1990). http://content.iskcon.org/icj/6_1/6_1rochford .html.

———. *Hare Krishna Transformed.* New York: New York University Press, 2007.

Rosen, Steven J. *Vaisnavism: Contemporary Scholars Discuss the Gaudiya Tradition.* New York: Folk Books, 1992.

Singer, Margaret Thaler. *Cults in Our Midst.* San Francisco: Jossey-Bass, 1995.

Tweed, Thomas, and Stephen Prothero, eds. *Asian Religions in America: A Documentary History.* New York: Oxford University Press, 1999.

Zablocki, Benjamin. "The Blacklisting of a Concept: The Strange History of the Brain-washing Conjecture in the Sociology of Religion." *Nova Religio* 1, no. 1 (1997): 96–121.

NOTES TO CHAPTER 10

1. A. C. Bhaktivedanta Swami Prabhupada, *Bhagavad Gita As It Is* (New York: Collier Books, 1972), 27, 28.
2. E. Burke Rochford, *Hare Krishna Transformed* (New York: New York University Press, 2007), 12.
3. Irving Shushnick, "Save Earth Now!" *East Village Other,* October 15–November 1, 1966, 11.
4. Thomas Tweed and Stephen Prothero, eds., *Asian Religions in America: A Documentary History* (New York: Oxford University Press, 1999), 247.
5. A. C. Bhaktivedanta Swami Prabhupada, *Krsna: The Supreme Personality of Godhead* (Boston: ISKCON Press, 1970), www.harekrsna.de/artikel/looking-for-krishna_e.htm.
6. George Harrison, "Brainwashed," from *Brainwashed* (Capitol Records, 2002).
7. E. Burke Rochford, "Child Abuse in the Hare Krishna Movement, 1971–1986," *ISKCON Communications Journal,* 6, no. 1 (1990), http://content.iskcon.org/icj/6_1/6_1rochford.html.
8. Carl Arrington, "In a Landmark Case Ex-Krishna Robin George Sues the Cult and Wins Big," *People,* September 12, 1983, www.people.com/people/archive/article/0,,20085897,00.html.
9. Margaret Singer, *Cults in Our Midst* (San Francisco: Jossey-Bass, 1995), 61–67.
10. Margaret Singer quoted in David Bromley, "Hare Krishna and the Anti-Cult Movement," in *Krishna Consciousness in the West,* ed. David G. Bromley and Larry D. Shin (Lewisburg, PA: Bucknell University Press, 1989), 276.
11. Bromley, "Hare Krishna," 286.
12. "Robin George vs. ISKCON," *Hinduism Today,* January 1984, www.hinduismtoday.com/modules/smartsection/item.php?itemid=1133.
13. George v. International Society for Krishna Consciousness, No. D007153, Court of Appeal of California, Fourth Appellate District, Division 1, 213 Cal. App. 3d 729; 262 Cal. Rptr. 217; 1989 Cal. App., August 30, 1989.
14. Umapati Swami and Jayadvaita Swami, "The $5 Million Brainwashing Case," *Back to Godhead* 25, no. 1 (1991), http://backtogodhead.in/the-5-million-brainwashing-case-by-umapati-swami-and-jayadvaita-swami/.
15. Stephen Kent, "Brainwashing in Scientology's Rehabilitation Project Force," Interior Ministry, Hamburg, Germany, 2002, www.solitarytrees.net/pubs/skent/brain.htm. See also Benjamin Zablocki, "The Blacklisting of a Concept: The Strange History of the Brainwashing Conjecture in the Sociology of Religion," *Nova Religio* 1, no. 1 (1997): 96–121.
16. Catherine Wessinger, *How the Millennium Comes Violently: From Jonestown to Heaven's Gate* (New York: Seven Bridges Press, 2000), 6.
17. Lorne Dawson, *Comprehending Cults: The Sociology of New Religious Movements* (New York: Oxford University Press, 2006), 115.
18. Wessinger, *How the Millennium Comes Violently,* 6–7.

ELEVEN

Channeling and the New Age

Alternative Spirituality in Popular Culture and Media

In 1987, ABC Television aired a five-part miniseries entitled *Out on a Limb,* which starred Shirley MacLaine and was based on the actress's best-selling autobiography of the same name, published in 1983. The story follows MacLaine as she navigates a troubled romance and then encounters a wide array of alternative spiritual ideas and practices through her friend David. Among other things, MacLaine explores the ideas of reincarnation, psychic phenomena, aspects of Eastern religions, astral projection, UFOs, and trance channeling. The miniseries even featured real-life channels playing themselves and entering into trance states, where they transmitted messages from a variety of spiritual entities. Although most of these ideas had been around in American culture for at least two decades, the airing of MacLaine's series was the first time they were made instantly available to millions of ordinary TV viewers and really marked a key moment when previous "esoteric" alternative spiritual ideas reached a mass consumer audience. In many ways, the airing of *Out on a Limb* signaled the culmination and popularization of New Age spirituality, which had begun in the 1960s and had come to national attention by the 1980s.

By the twenty-first century, New Age ideas had become pervasive throughout American popular culture. They could be seen regularly, for example, on daytime TV shows such as *The Oprah Winfrey Show,* where New Age self-help guru Deepak Chopra was a frequent guest. Formerly a practitioner of Transcendental Meditation, Chopra is the author of best-selling New Age books on health and well-being, such as *Timeless Mind* (1993), and he reached a massive audience through his friendship with Michael Jackson and his appearances on *Oprah* and other TV shows. More recently, New Age ideas have also been popularized through major films such as *What the Bleep Do We Know* (2004), which featured the famous channel JZ Knight and combined alternative spirituality with aspects of quantum physics. Produced by followers of JZ Knight's movement, Ramtha's School of Enlightenment, the film interviews Knight as she channels the ancient being called Ramtha and explains the intricacies of both New Age philosophy and quantum theory.

As we saw in chapter 1, the term *New Age* does not refer to a singular or homogeneous movement. Rather, it is a broad label that covers a wide array of alternative spiritual beliefs and practices, ranging from the use of crystals and aromatherapy, to speculations about UFOs and astral projection, to selected elements drawn from Eastern religions. Yet despite their remarkable diversity, most forms of New Age spirituality do tend to share a few features. First, in contrast to new religious movements such as Mormonism or Scientology, the New Age has no clear boundaries between insiders and outsiders and no real organization; it is a highly individualistic and eclectic movement that allows the spiritual seeker maximum freedom to create his or her own personal worldview drawn from a vast array of religious, philosophical, and psychological ideas and practices. Second, in contrast to neopagan groups, which generally look back to ancient pre-Christian sources, the New Age is on the whole quite forward looking, imagining a coming era of spiritual harmony and well-being that will transcend this current age of violence and strife. As Kathryn Lofton observed in her book *Oprah: The Gospel of an Icon,* New Age really refers to "an eclectic mix of world religious traditions, pop psychology, quantum physics, and occult practices" that were rather esoteric prior to the 1970s but were quickly introduced to a mass audience in the 1980s and '90s; what the various phenomena called New Age do tend to share, however, is "an optimistic view of the future, a rejection of any form of authoritarian doctrine or hierarchy, an ethic of self-empowerment, an eclecticism of beliefs and practices, and a press to use science for spiritual ends."[1]

Because the various spiritual phenomena lumped under the label "New Age" are so vast and diverse, it would be impossible to do justice to this complex movement in a large encyclopedia, much less in a short book. So for the purposes of this chapter we will focus on just one aspect of New Age spirituality that shows its continuities with earlier religious movements: the practice of trance channeling. In many ways the modern successor to nineteenth-century Spiritualism, channeling continues the Spiritualist belief that particular individuals—"channels"—can enter altered states of consciousness and serve as the voice or vehicle of a spiritual entity from another plane of existence. Like nineteenth-century Spiritualists, channels tend to use the language of technology to describe the process of spirit communication—in this case, the language of TV and radio channels rather than the nineteenth-century language of the telegraph. Like the earlier Spiritualists, channels are very often women, and they raise many of the same questions of female empowerment and/or exploitation that we discussed in chapter 4.

In this chapter we will examine three key examples of channeling that have entered American popular culture since the 1960s: Jane Roberts, the channel for an entity named Seth; JZ Knight, the channel for an entity named Ramtha; and actress Shirley MacLaine, who is not a channel herself but helped popularize channeling and other New Age ideas through her best-selling book *Out on a Limb* (1983). In many ways it was through these figures that New Age ideas really entered American culture in a big way, particularly after JZ Knight's appearance on daytime TV shows such as *The Merv Griffin Show* in 1985 and Shirley MacLaine's TV miniseries in 1987. From the mid-1980s onward, many previously "esoteric" ideas such as trance channeling, astrology, reincarnation, clairvoyance, and other psychic phenomena became part of everyday conversation and a commonplace part of American popular culture.

One of the key issues that channeling and New Age spirituality as a whole raise is the question of the commercialism and commodification of spirituality. In the eyes of skeptics and critics, the New Age simply takes the exotic spiritual offerings from many cultures (Native American, Asian, Chinese, African, etc.) and transforms them into marketable trinkets in the vast shopping mall of religions. For those who are more sympathetic to New Age spirituality, conversely, this is a profoundly democratic movement that highlights the best aspects of American spirituality: liberty, choice, individualism, and freedom of religious expression. In either case—whether we see it as consumerist or democratic—the New Age is a deeply "American" form of spirituality.

CHANNELING AND THE NEW AGE

As we saw in the Introduction, many of the key ideas in the New Age movement are actually not particularly "new" at all but have deep roots in a long tradition of alternative spirituality, often called the Western esoteric tradition, that dates back to the early centuries of the Common Era. These ideas include the concept of correspondences or the hidden connections that are believed to exist between all levels of the cosmos and the human body; the idea of living nature, or the belief that the universe is a living organism animated by its own vital energy or soul; belief in the existence of a chain of intermediary beings or spiritual entities between the human and the divine; and the experience of transmutation, or the practical manipulation of the physical world through magic, alchemy, and other arts. Yet these much older traditions were articulated in new forms in the twentieth and twenty-first centuries, refracted through aspects of the modern world, such as new forms of science, technology, and popular culture. The New Age practice of channeling is a clear example of this transformation of esotericism, taking much older ideas of communication with the spirit realm and reworking them in the language of modern physics, new technologies such as radio and television, and aspects of consumer culture.

The phrase *New Age* was used as early as 1804 by the English poet, painter, and mystic William Blake (1757–1827). In the preface to his great prophetic poem *Milton,* Blake described the coming of a new era of artistic and spiritual transformation: "When the New Age is at leisure to Pronounce, all will be set right & those Grand Works of the more ancient & consciously & professedly Inspired Men will hold their proper rank & the Daughters of Memory shall become the Daughters of Inspiration."[2] However, the phrase was not really used in its contemporary sense until over a century later, particularly with the rise of new religious movements such as the Theosophical Society. As we saw in chapter 4, the first use of the phrase as we understand it today appeared in Alice Bailey's book *Discipleship in the New Age,* where it refers to the transition from the astrological sign of Pisces to the sign of Aquarius. This astrological shift was believed to be linked to a larger historical shift from an age of strife to a new era of spiritual growth and harmony: "The New Age is upon us, and we are witnessing the birth pangs of a new civilization. That which is old and undesirable must go and of these undesirable things, hatred and separateness must be the first to disappear."[3] But the real flowering of the New Age as a movement and a popular phenomenon began in the 1960s and '70s, when it was inspired by new centers of an alternative spirituality such as the Esalen Institute in California, by the many new forms of Eastern spirituality entering the United States, and by the general countercultural movement of these decades. By 1967, New Age ideas had burst into popular culture and music with songs such as "The Age of Aquarius," which opened the hit Broadway production of *Hair: The American Love-Rock Musical.*

Although just one of the many phenomena associated with New Age spirituality, channeling is in many ways emblematic of the movement as a whole. Though clearly rooted in older esoteric ideas such as correspondences, spiritual intermediaries, and transmutation, channeling makes heavy use of the language of modern technology. It is also a deeply individualistic and decentralized phenomenon, which relies not on fixed dogmas, priestly hierarchies, or rigid institutions but rather on individual channels who have their own personal relations with the spirit realm.

Like New Age spirituality as a whole, channeling is an extremely varied and heterogeneous phenomenon. While generally rooted in nineteenth-century Spiritualism, it is performed in many different ways and is used to articulate a great variety of spiritual and philosophical ideas. Many of the most famous channels serve as the voice or vehicle of a single entity, with whom they form a close and long-term spiritual relationship. For example, in 1969, Pat Rodegast began to channel a spirit named Emmanuel who came to her during her Transcendental Meditation practice; in 1977, Mary-Margaret Moore encountered an entity called Bartholomew during a hypnosis session; former insurance salesman Jach Pursel encountered a being of love and light called Lazaris in 1974 during his daily meditation session; and British-born channel Alison L. James serves as the medium for none other than the wizard Merlin from Camelot. Other channels, however, give voice to multiple entities, serving as the vehicle for two, three, or even hundreds of different spirits. For example, in central Ohio I met Cindy Riggs, a channel and psychic who has served as the vehicle for a wide array of spirits, entities, and deities ranging from Jesus, Muhammad, and Buddha to Osiris, Vishnu, and Quetzalcoatl. Channels also vary widely in how they describe the process of trance channeling. Some explain that they have little or no memory of what has transpired in the trance state and that their normal consciousness is largely displaced by the channeled entity; others explain that they are aware of most of or everything that transpires and that their consciousness has simply stepped to one side to allow the entity to speak through them.

Despite their diversity, most channels do emphasize a few common themes that are also core themes in the broader New Age movement as a whole. Most channels suggest that

Cindy Riggs is a professional channel, psychic, and healer who offers a variety of services in central Ohio. She is also the author of a book based on her encounter with the Hindu deity Vishnu. In her interview, she talked about her first encounter with spirit guides, the process of channeling, and her healing practices.

My religious background was Presbyterian—pretty normal, Christian. I got to a point in my life where I was pretty unhappy, depressed, a victim, and I was starting to seek out something different. So I let all that go from the past and said, "I'm just going to start out fresh." I took a Reiki class. When I got that first attunement, I started to hear things and see things. I started to get messages in the middle of the night, always at 3:15 a.m. I was starting to write them down, and I realized that I probably wasn't making that stuff up. So one night I finally said, "Who is talking to me?" And he said, "We are light beings, like you." That's when I realized something else really was talking to me.

Soon after that, I met one of my spirit guides in a dream, an Aztec woman. Then not long after that I met another guide who is a shape-shifter; he's a hawk and a man, sometimes he appears as a man, sometimes as a hawk. It was the Aztec woman who started teaching me how to receive messages from her and relay them to other people, and it was one word at a time at the beginning. I was a little afraid of this stuff. I wasn't sure what was happening or if I was crazy. So I decided that I always want control over this. I said, "I always want to be aware of what's happening, and no one can merge with me unless I allow them to. I'm in control." I know some channelers go completely unconscious, and I do not. I allow the being to come to me wherever they come in. Sometimes they come in my crown or my heart, but usually it's just everywhere now. When they complete the integration, I actually step myself out. But I am conscious. And people who see energy have actually seen me standing over here, beside myself.

I've read many channelers' books, and I thought, "Who am I going to channel, who is going to be my one spirit?" People are familiar with Jane Roberts and Seth, and I thought, "Well, maybe one of these days, I'll meet the one who I'm supposed to channel all the time." That's never happened. It has always been different beings, and I've literally met thousands of beings. They appear to me. Vishnu, for instance —I didn't know who that was. I had channeled Ganesha, Shiva, Hanuman. I was interested in Hinduism but I didn't know all the gods and goddesses. I just went into a trance and waited for the being to appear. I saw this saffron color, and then I heard the name Vishnu. And that blew me away, that energy was massive. Then he asked if he could work with me on a daily basis, with my energy field. So I merged with him during my morning meditations. Then he said, "We're writing a book," and I asked, "How are we doing that?" He said, "I'll give you a chapter a day." And he did. He said, "Here's the outline," and I actually made myself get up at 5:00 a.m. I sat down with my laptop and my candles and incense. I merged with him and then typed what he was saying.

I believe that channeling is a skill that can be learned, but I think everyone will do it a little bit differently. My process is going into a trance state, which takes me only seconds now, waiting to see who wishes to speak to either my group or my client, and allow[ing] them to approach me. Then I allow them to merge with me. In the beginning it was into my crown. Then it moved onto my heart one night. This being said, "Now you're going to merge with us through your heart." Most recently in the past two years, I've been channeling the Oneness, which is all of the light beings in the universe at once, or the "All that Is." That absorbs into me like I'm a sponge, all directions. Usually I will speak with my own voice. But it will be a little bit higher or a little bit lower, people have noticed. People have also pointed out that when I'm channeling the Egyptian god or goddess, my feet will go into a position like the statues.

Once in a while, I will encounter something that is not "of the light." But it doesn't matter who approaches; I always ask them if they're from the light, because the dark side can disguise themselves as guides and angels. But they just leave. It seems that when they're confronted with that question, they can't lie. They just dissipate.

Much of my worldview comes from what these spirits have taught me through the process of channeling over the past sixteen years now. I believe that there is a conscious creative force of all that is, that is the consciousness behind every subatomic particle, that is everything and nothing. I believe in a divine creative force which permeates every subatomic particle and is the consciousness behind that. I describe our soul as a power strip, and we're plugged in over here in this lifetime. If we died in another lifetime and we didn't cross over, we're still plugged into the power strip, and so that current can possibly be negatively affecting us now. If it was a traumatic death—which it usually is when somebody doesn't cross over—I can close myself and see a person's past lives and have a conversation to help them cross over.

I help people get to happy. So I am helping to remove things that may be blocking them or remove things that may be interfering with their energy. That could be a spirit attaching, or it could be a pattern of belief that they have created throughout their lifetime. We use some hypnosis; I do a lot of energy body working; and I do sessions I call defragmenting, because they're kind of like a soul retrieval session. But it could incorporate any of the tools that I use. So it could be some psychic reading, it might be some channeling, it might be some energy work. I also do past life readings and past life clearings, I can do a past life regression, where I would put you under hypnosis and you could maybe see your own past life.

I've had a three-year-old in here and an eighty-five-year-old. I would say probably more women than men. It's probably 75 percent female, 25 percent male. Most are seeking something. They're seeking some kind of spiritual understanding for

(continued)

(Interview with Cindy Riggs, continued)

themselves that's not traditional religion. Or they're looking for something that traditional medicine has not helped them with. People sometimes just say, "I came across your website, and I felt like I was supposed to call." But the main thing is they're not content, they're not happy, they're trying to discover their truth—like everybody.

I believe that every belief system or religion has merit or it wouldn't exist. It's benefiting someone. Originally the goal was all the same, which is to reconnect with Source or God or whatever you call that. I call it Source. Yet throughout the ages things have become way too dualistic in nature, way too much fear. I believe that to reconnect with Source, we need love, not fear. We don't need to be scared into it. We need to remember that it's natural for us. But it becomes taken over by duality and ego and power and trying to control people. When I've talked to Jesus, he says, "I never intended for people to worship me. I really was just trying to introduce some new concepts to empower people and show them that if it was possible for me, it's possible for them." I see all of us as divine. We are at our core an aspect of the divine creative force. I see the master Jesus as one who was enlightened while in the physical body and came as the archetype of teacher. He says, "You are all masters, you are no different than I."

humanity is entering some kind of new era or approaching a historic turning point in which we have the opportunity to leave behind the destructive patterns of our past and enter a higher phase of spiritual evolution. Most also teach a highly democratic and individualistic message, suggesting that we are all in some sense divine and that God is found within rather than outside the self. Most emphasize healing (in the complete sense of physical, mental, and spiritual healing). And perhaps most importantly, most channels teach that we all "create our own reality"—that is, that the world we perceive, either positively or negatively, is a projection of our own consciousness and that we can transform our reality for the better by transforming ourselves internally.

JANE ROBERTS AND "SETH"

One of the first and most important figures in the development of New Age channeling was Jane Roberts (figure 11.1). Born in Saratoga Springs, New York, in 1929 and spending her early years as a housewife and an author of poetry and children's stories, Roberts emerged as perhaps the most influential channel of the 1970s. Her writings and filmed speeches helped launch an era of nationwide awareness of channeling and helped form the identity of the emergent New Age movement.

Roberts claimed to have first come into contact with a supernatural entity in December 1963 while she and her husband were experimenting with a Ouija board. The being they contacted later identified himself as Seth and soon began dictating messages directly

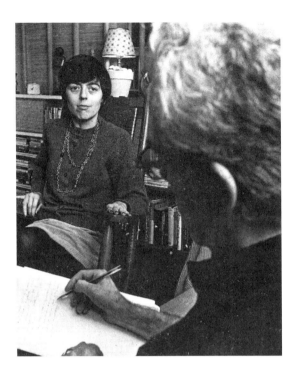

FIGURE 11.1 Jane Roberts. Used by permission from the Seth Learning Center.

through Roberts without the aid of the Ouija board. Although Roberts also claimed to have channeled several other beings, including psychologist William James and painter Paul Cézanne, Seth was the being she channeled consistently until her death in 1984.

Among her other contributions to New Age spirituality, Roberts is an especially clear example of both the continuities and the discontinuities between nineteenth-century Spiritualism and twentieth-century channeling. In many ways, Roberts has much in common with nineteenth-century mediums and their Spiritualist message. As we saw in chapter 4, early Spiritualism was closely identified with both women and the domestic sphere. Because women were imagined in nineteenth-century discourse to be inherently passive, humble, receptive, and open to the spiritual realm, they made natural mediums for otherworldly influences. Spiritualists, we saw, tended to use the new language of science and technology to describe communications with the unseen world—particularly the language of electricity and the telegraph to explain the instantaneous transmission of messages from one world to the other. Finally, Spiritualism was very much a religion of the domestic sphere, bringing mediumship, planchettes, and Ouija boards into the home and allowing middle-class families to communicate with spirits from other worlds in their parlors and living rooms.

Almost one hundred years later, Jane Roberts and her channeled entity Seth continued many of these Spiritualist themes, but with some important transformations for a twentieth-century audience. Like her Spiritualist predecessors, Roberts played the role of a largely passive female receptacle for a higher masculine spiritual entity; and like female Spiritualist mediums, she found in that role a powerful new voice and authority that she had otherwise not found through her poetry or short stories. She also found in the domestic sphere a new space to receive a spiritual message that would eventually reach a massive popular audience through her numerous books and recorded speeches.

Finally, much as Spiritualists had drawn on the imagery of the telegraph, Roberts made explicit use of language drawn from the new medium of television. As one of the very first modern mediums to use the term *channeling*, Roberts made extensive use of the metaphor of TV channels to describe her contact with Seth's unseen realm. Indeed, as Roberts described her first encounter with Seth's spiritual world, it was as though her brain was a "receiving station" now being bombarded with transmissions from a wholly new source of broadcast information: "Between one normal minute and the next, a fantastic avalanche of radical, new ideas burst into my head with tremendous force as if my skull were some sort of receiving station, turned up to unbearable volume. Not only ideas came through this channel, but sensations, intensified and pulsating. I was turned in, turned on . . . *connected* to some incredible source of energy. . . . It was as if the physical world were really tissue paper thin, hiding infinite dimensions of reality."[4]

Throughout the early Seth materials, Roberts elaborates on the metaphor of TV transmissions, describing human consciousness as a kind of receiver that can tune in to one or more channels of information. As Seth explains, most of us in the ordinary world are like TV sets without all the channels working properly: "There are aspects of my identity with which you are not acquainted. . . . All the channels are not yet working on this set, you see."[5] Hence, becoming aware of higher dimensions of reality requires that we open our minds to other channels of information, changing from the waking channel to a trance channel where we receive knowledge from transcendent beings: "The waking state . . . is as much a trance state as any other. Here we merely switch the focus of attention to other channels."[6] Listening to the messages from a supernatural being is thus a matter of switching stations, turning from the ordinary frequency of the mind to a new one. We can, in short, "change the channels" of our awareness, thereby accessing other conscious selves.

On some occasions, Seth used the metaphor of a tape recorder to describe the nature of consciousness. The self is like an audio recording device with multiple channels, which, through contact with supernatural dimensions, can be opened to new and potentially infinite channels of information. On other occasions, however, Seth made explicit use of the language of television and the channels of the TV screen. Seth even compared his human channel to a kind of "television screen," which could broadcast either a live performance or a prerecorded performance of his message:

"So now see Rubert [Jane Roberts] as my television screen. . . . It makes no difference whether or not I am myself speaking within Rubert now . . . or whether I did this last night in his sleep and tonight is a film or playback.

"Again: the medium is the message in the Spacious Present," Seth said smiling, "and whenever the time for the program arrives, I am here in your present. . . . I may prepare my film in advance."[7]

But perhaps most importantly, Roberts repeatedly emphasized the idea that we have the power not simply to tune in to different channels of awareness but to *change* reality. For Roberts, as for virtually all later New Age channels, reality as we perceive it is largely a projection of our own minds—for good or for ill. Therefore, by changing our consciousness, we can actively change our perceptions and ultimately change our reality for the better. As Seth explains, using the metaphor of a motion-picture film projector, "The eye projects and focuses the inner image (idea) onto the physical world in the same manner that a motion-picture camera transfers an image onto a screen. . . . Actually the senses are the channels of creation by which idea is projected into material expression."[8]

This notion that we project and therefore can change our own reality is one of the most important themes throughout virtually all of the channeling literature and the New Age movement as a whole. In its most ambitious forms, this idea is tied to the belief that the human self is in fact divine, godlike, or even identical to God. Just as God creates, maintains, and transforms this world through divine creative power, so too we each have that same creative potential within ourselves, because we each are ultimately one with God: "You are always and you always will be," Seth asserts. ". . . The God that is, is within you, for you are a part of all that is."[9] In sum, we are each potential channels for the divine transmission of our own inherent godliness. As Seth declared in a videotaped session in June 1974 (now available on YouTube): "You give the message to your self, for you are the message. . . . If only we can show yourselves, then you will trust yourselves to explore those dimensions of your own greater reality."[10]

Jane Roberts died in 1984. However, her husband continued to promote Seth's teachings, compiling Roberts's works and donating them to Yale University Library, which still maintains a large collection of her writings. Through groups such as the Seth Learning Center, her work continues to have a profound impact on contemporary channeling, and she is often cited as the spiritual teacher who launched the New Age.

JZ KNIGHT AND RAMTHA

If Jane Roberts helped develop the theology of channeling as a new spiritual medium, then JZ Knight helped bring it to a mass public audience (figure 11.2). Far more than Roberts, Knight emerged as a channel who appealed directly to ordinary Americans, presenting herself as simply a suburban housewife who had spontaneously come into contact with an exotic warrior from an ancient civilization. It was Knight's commercial success, however, that contributed to the skeptical view of New Age channels as mere charlatans out to dupe a gullible public with pseudometaphysical jargon.

As she recounted in her best-selling book *A State of Mind*, JZ Knight first came into contact with Ramtha at her home in Tacoma, Washington, in 1977. Before meeting Ramtha, she described herself as a happy housewife and mother whose husband delighted in her good cooking and homemaking. During these years, the loose blend of alternative spiritualities known as the New Age movement was just beginning to seep into American popular

FIGURE 11.2 JZ Knight. Photo courtesy of Ramtha's School of Enlightenment.

consciousness, and one of the most pervasive New Age trends was the idea of "pyramid power." Thanks to the best-selling 1976 book *Pyramid Power*, by Max Toth and Greg Nielson, pyramids were believed to have the power to do everything from preserve foods to sharpen razor blades, and Knight and her husband began, half-jokingly, to build and play around with a wide array of pyramids in their home. In a fit of silliness in the middle of her kitchen floor, Knight placed one of the pyramids on her head and was immediately stunned by the dramatic appearance of Ramtha:

> In jest, I grabbed one of the rejects off the floor, held it over my head and proclaimed, "Attention, attention please, you are now about to witness a miracle . . ."
>
> I placed it on my head, and through peals of laughter . . . mumbled "I sure hope it works." . . . Laughing so hard that tears were streaming from my eyes, I caught the glimmer of a bright light at the other end of my kitchen. . . . I blinked, and to my utter shock and amazement, there stood a giant man at the other end of my kitchen. . . .
>
> This . . . thing . . . was made all of light, like golden glitter dropped through a ray of sunlight. His shoulders came to the top of the door, and it was as if the ceiling had disappeared to make room for his head. It was beautiful. His robe seemed to be of purple light. A dazzling display of color and crystal against the

strangeness of immense human form. . . . His face . . . it was the most beautiful face I had ever seen . . . eyes that shone like ebony stones with copper flashes . . . skin, if that is what it was, the coloring of olive, bronze, illuminated and a fine chiseled nose and a broad jaw line and smile that would rival any Hollywood star's. My eyes went glassy, like those of a sleepwalker.[11]

Several aspects of Knight's first encounter with Ramtha are worth noting here. First, like her nineteenth-century Spiritualist predecessors, Knight has an encounter that is very much *domestic,* taking place in the kitchen (the "woman's domain") and also clearly *gendered:* the blonde, petite housewife meets a giant, handsome warrior with chiseled nose and jaw. Second, Knight likens the Lemurian warrior to a Hollywood star, suggesting that he is not simply handsome but movie star gorgeous.

Initially, Knight had no clear understanding of her relationship with this handsome being from ancient Lemuria. However, after visiting a Spiritualist named Lorraine and reading various books about Hindu avatars, Madame Blavatsky, and Edgar Cayce, Knight came to realize that she was a channel for Ramtha. As Lorraine explained, there is a fundamental difference between a medium in the nineteenth-century Spiritualist sense and a channel such as Knight. For a channel is one who allows herself to "die" temporarily, to become wholly taken over and *used* by the channeled entity: "A channel leaves her body, as in death, and allows the entity to express his own personality. A medium only serves as a bridge between dimensions but does not entirely leave her body. It is a rare phenomenon for one to allow herself to be used like that."[12]

Knight's domestic encounters with Ramtha continue throughout her narrative in *A State of Mind,* where he frequently appears in her living room or kitchen. In some cases, these encounters combine the sublime with the ridiculous—intentionally, it would seem—as Ramtha repeatedly appears to Knight while she toils through her housewifely chores. Ramtha is even willing to materialize spontaneously to help clean up after her kids' sloppy breakfast when their spilled Cheerios become stuck to her kitchen floor:

I got the good doctor off to work, my two ideal children off to school, and after my cup of tea, I started in on the housework. . . . I did the dishes and then started to mop the kitchen floor. I was in a hurry, so when three Cheerios that had become glued to the floor wouldn't come up with the mop I threw the mop to the side and tried to pry them loose with the toe of my shoe. They refused to budge, so I . . . dropped to my knees and began to chisel the little suckers off with a butter knife. At that moment, the Ram appeared in front of me by the sink, but I was too engrossed in my war with the Cheerios. He stooped down, put his hands on the floor, and came eye level with me and the O's. . . . He didn't say a word, just put one of those long cinnamon fingers on one stubborn O and it lifted off with the greatest of ease. . . . I dropped my head in my hands and muttered, "Thanks, the next time I need a helping—glowing—hand, I'll call ya."[13]

Having won the war with the stubborn Cheerios, Knight goes on to make the beds, while she and Ramtha engage in a lengthy discussion of religion, God, and interreligious conflict.

Despite the seemingly mundane domestic venues in which Ramtha chose to appear to Knight, his message was ultimately one of profound metaphysical significance. Echoing Seth's words that "the medium is the message" and that the individual self is divine, Ramtha repeatedly proclaimed the central channeling belief that each one of us is a god if we simply recognize our own true nature. Thus when Knight asked Ramtha, "You are a god?" he promptly replied, "Indeed! Beloved entity, so be you God also. The only difference between that which be you and that which be I, is that I know that I am and you, beloved woman, do not."[14]

The message that we are each "sleeping gods" was also the central theme of Ramtha's first television appearance on *The Merv Griffin Show* in August 1985. Already well known with a large following, Knight had filled the studio audience with Ramtha enthusiasts who lined the sidewalk for blocks outside waiting to get in. Here on daytime TV, the viewer could clearly see the striking juxtaposition between Knight—the self-described housewife and suburban mom—and Ramtha—the thirty-five-thousand-year-old divine being proclaiming the godhood of each individual. Knight's self-presentation was mild, self-effacing, and extremely "feminine." Ramtha's, in contrast, was loud, assertive, and extremely "masculine." However, their central message was one that is at the heart of New Age spirituality, the central idea that we are all divine and creative beings. Even before Knight spoke, Merv played an earlier videotape of Ramtha, in which he proclaimed the godhood of every human being: "My advent on this plane . . . is to bring to you an understanding of you. . . . What I teach and manifest is the personal self. Because only when you go inward are you going to understand 'behold God.'"[15] Ramtha then reiterated this central message. God is not without but within, he repeated. Ramtha is a God; JZ is God; Merv Griffin is God; the viewers are God. Medium, message, and audience are one: "That which is termed . . . God, which has been misunderstood, which has been taught to live outside of your being, is within your being. And that that which is called Christ is within your being, and that which is called life is the grand experience, that it is where the kingdom of heaven is located, entity. When know you that that which is termed you are God, that that which emanates within you is divine, you will find joy."[16]

Like other channels, Knight also discusses the idea of a coming "New Age" or a major transformation toward a future era of love, peace, and harmony. However, she interprets the New Age less in literal terms—as a kind of mass social or political change—than as an inner awakening within the individual. The second coming of Christ, as she describes it, is not a literal descent of God from heaven but a new awareness that we all bear Christ or divinity within ourselves. As Ramtha told Merv Griffin,

To that which is termed a new consciousness, it is coming forward. What was always longed for as the destruction of the world will never happen. To that which is termed the coming of Christ, that will come before the end of this your time flow, the next decade. . . . Know you what the Son of God is? . . . The coming of Christ is the awakening of that principle of that divinity in all people. 'Tis not one entity, but the whole of the world, master, comes into the Christ, into that understanding. That is what is meant by the prophecy.[17]

When Merv then asked Ramtha about the popular ideas of the "Aquarian Age" or New Age and the hope for a millennium of universal peace, he replied, "Once the consciousness has been acclaimed here, it shan't end with two thousand years, because that which is called your scientists will have conquered time and space. To that which is called peace shall be an ongoing thing. The primeval war, entity, will die before the end of the next decade."

Ramtha's television presence was by no means limited to *The Merv Griffin Show*. Indeed, the ancient Lemurian has a vast televised history, both positive and negative, ranging from network exposés to numerous talk show appearances to thousands of hours of video now accessible online. Not long after her Merv Griffin appearance, Knight was made the subject of a major *ABC 20/20* exposé, which aired January 22, 1987. Among the many charges leveled against her, *20/20* claimed that JZ was essentially a fraud; that she had duped her followers financially; that she had falsified the details of her autobiography; that she was getting rich from a vast confidence scheme; and that she was ultimately a power-driven cult leader who taught dangerously immoral ideas.[18] Ironically, the *20/20* exposé probably did as much good as harm to JZ's channeling career, generating so much media attention that she became the object of countless other television shows, newspaper reports, and magazine articles.

Knight's television presence has continued well into the twenty-first century, as she has appeared on major programs such as CNN's *Larry King Live*. As she reiterated the central message on King's show in 2008, we are all divine beings who have not just the possibility but the obligation to take charge of our lives and create our own new realities: "Instead of being a reactive person, to be a master of the reality, even our house, even our family, our workplace, our greater place of enjoyment. That instead of reacting in the old ways, that we absolutely cultivate the ability to create new realities."[19] Thought, she explained to King, has the power to create any reality we choose, from greater happiness to more wealth to youthful health:

> Thought is there in your brain to construct reality. It is important what we think. . . . We learn to make a small list. It's important. And the small list says, "This day, I'm going to create my day. This day I have always been filled with joy." Not that I will be—but that I've always been filled with joy. . . . Your body hears every thought in your brain. You begin to heal yourself—"This day I've always been fabulously wealthy," "this day I am 30 years younger." . . . You are affirming a new reality.[20]

Although Ramtha is most famous for his appearances on television, he also made a film debut in the 2004 movie *What the Bleep Do We Know?* Conceived and directed by three

Ramtha students—William Arntz, Betsy Chasse, and Mark Vicente—the film attempts to connect aspects of quantum physics with New Age spirituality. A relatively low-budget independent production, the film spread widely to theaters across the United States before being picked up by a major distributor and eventually grossed over $10 million. Centered on the plot of a deaf photographer on a journey of self-discovery, the film weaves interviews with physicists, philosophers, and New Age enthusiasts with footage of Ramtha himself, all to assert the basic message that mind creates reality. Now projected on a movie screen rather than a TV screen, Ramtha repeats the same basic theme he stated on Griffin's show twenty years earlier: it is the divine power of the mind that creates the reality we experience. This power of mind over matter can be observed everywhere from the quantum realm to the most mundane phenomenon of a man's overly active imagination giving him an erection: "It only takes one sexual fantasy for a man to have a hard-on. In other words it only takes one thought here for a man to have an erection in his member. And yet, there was nothing outside of him that gave him that. It was within him that gave him that."[21] This same power of thought is also the power that creates and transforms our reality. In short, even when presented in the medium of film rather than TV, Ramtha's message repeats the central channeling theme that we are both the source of our own reality and the truth of our own creative godhood.

Today, Knight is arguably the most famous and financially successful channel in the United States, if not the world. The center of her movement is Ramtha's School for Enlightenment, based at her eighty-acre estate near Yelm, Washington. Knight herself lives in a massive 12,800-square-foot French chateau-style mansion on the estate and leads the courses next door. The classes offered at the school range in cost from $400 for a beginner's online course up to $1,500 for longer events at the Washington campus. To maintain a "current" status, students of the school are required to attend two retreats a year, which cost about $1,500 each.

However, if Knight is America's most successful channel, she is also surely the most controversial. Not surprisingly, many skeptics have found the claim that Ramtha is an ancient warrior from Atlantis to be implausible and contrary to what most scientists say about the earth of thirty-five thousand years ago. As scientist Carl Sagan wrote in his book *The Demon-Haunted World,* "The simplest explanation is that Ms. Knight makes 'Ramtha' speak all by herself, and that she has no contact with disembodied entities from the Pleistocene Ice Age." Sagan goes on to note that Ramtha never tells us anything concrete about life in prehistoric times but only offers "banal homilies" and New Age jargon.[22] The film *What the Bleep Do We Know?* has also been widely criticized by scientists because of its poor explanation of quantum physics and its misleading comparisons between contemporary science and Ramtha's New Age ideas.

Meanwhile, Knight has been denounced as a fraud and a charlatan. Her own former husband, Jeff Knight, has accused his ex-wife of running a simple "farce of a teaching that is just a money-making business for her." In a 1992 interview, he warned that the students at her School of Enlightenment are engaged in a dangerous and evil form of mind control that is "all for one purpose, and that's for the lady who runs it."[23] Other ex-members and former employees have described the movement as a manipulative "cult" and Knight as simply putting on an act to extract money from gullible followers. As one former student, Nancy Barr-Brandon, told the *New York Times* in 1992, she spent eight years and over $100,000 at the School of Enlightenment before deciding that Knight was a fraud. In her opinion, Knight was a manipulative charlatan who "would frequently rip off other people's ideas from books and movies."[24] As we will see, this controversy over Knight's wealth and the large spiritual business empire that she created is part of a larger controversy surrounding the commercial aspects of New Age spirituality as a whole.

SHIRLEY MACLAINE AND CHANNELING FOR PRIME TIME

If JZ Knight helped bring channeling and New Age ideas to a daytime TV audience, it was really Shirley MacLaine who helped bring them to the American public on a mass scale through her best-selling books and her hugely successful TV miniseries. While not a channel herself, MacLaine helped transmit, communicate, and translate—in short, in her own way, "channel"—the ideas of Ramtha and others to a much broader general audience that might never otherwise have heard of reincarnation, UFOs, lost worlds, or the divinity of the individual self.

By the early 1980s, MacLaine was already a hugely successful actress. She had just won an Academy Award and a Golden Globe Award for best actress in the 1983 film *Terms of Endearment,* and she was preparing for a one-woman Broadway show. That same year, she also published *Out on a Limb,* her autobiographical narrative of self-discovery, which became an instant best seller. Described by critics as "a stunningly honest, engrossing account of an intimate journey inward," the book recounted MacLaine's story of personal growth through her acting career, passionate love affairs on several continents, and exploration of New Age philosophy.

Both *Out on a Limb* and the follow-up book, *Dancing in the Light* (1985), contain numerous accounts of channeling through MacLaine's encounters with a variety of channels, including JZ Knight. Indeed, MacLaine describes Knight's channeled entity Ramtha as the most remarkable and powerful being she ever encountered. Much like Jane Roberts, JZ made explicit use of the language of TV and "tuning in" to explain the phenomenon of channeling to MacLaine. We all have the potential to tune in to the spiritual realm, she explained, but the channel has a unique ability to get the signal, as it were: "When you're tuned in, you're tuned in. . . . A psychic is just a little more tuned in to the knowingness of his or her higher self."[25] Ramtha's advice to MacLaine ranged from the metaphysical to the mundane, covering everything from her own divine nature to the details of her diet, exercise, and acting career: "He spoke of the vitamins I needed, the kind of exercise I should have . . . and even gave me an evaluation of the scripts I was reading. I asked questions relating to everything from the personal life of Jesus Christ to whether I would ever meet my soul mate in this incarnation."[26]

While her paperbacks sold several million copies, it was her prime-time TV miniseries that reached a truly mass American audience. MacLaine was the first to really bring the phenomenon of channeling—along with astral projection, UFOs, and other New Age ideas—to a major prime-time channel and to millions of ordinary viewers. One of the most striking scenes in the miniseries was the appearance of real-life channel Kevin Ryerson. Ryerson's gift of channeling had already been described in the book version of *Out on a Limb,* which recounted his arrival at the actress's home in Malibu. As MacLaine described him, Ryerson seemed like a strange combination of a medieval anachronism and a 1980s pop star: "He seemed to swing back and forth between the Knights of the Round Table and the rock generation."[27] Unlike most channels, Ryerson had the unique ability to channel not just one but multiple supernatural entities. To use Jane Roberts's metaphor, he could change multiple channels on the receiving set of consciousness. As Ryerson explained, these entities ranged from the profound to the ridiculous, from an otherworldly metaphysician to a petty Irish thief:

> Two, three of maybe four spiritual entities use me to channel information. The first who usually comes through to greet people calls himself John. . . . He speaks in a biblical lingo that is sometimes hard to follow. . . . If you prefer . . . another entity comes through. He calls himself Tom McPherson because his favorite incarnation was that of an Irish pickpocket a few hundred years ago. He can be very amusing. . . . Then there's Dr. Shangru, a Pakistani of a few hundred years ago, well versed in medical matters, and Obidaya, whose favorite incarnation was that of a Jamaican who understands modern-day racial problems.[28]

While Ryerson's appearance in MacLaine's book was fascinating, his appearance on her TV miniseries was even more remarkable. Playing himself in the series and reenacting the same scene described in the book, Ryerson actually went into a trance and channeled John and the pickpocket before the camera. In other words, he rechanneled his original channeling episode for TV, in order to be rebroadcast for the viewing audience on MacLaine's miniseries.

The central message of MacLaine's various channels throughout her journey, however, remained essentially the same as the one articulated by Seth and Ramtha: God is within, we are all divine, and we create our own reality. In Ryerson's words, the self "*knows the Divine truth because the self is itself Divine.*"[29] Interestingly enough, however, MacLaine also described the ways in which she worked this basic philosophy of self-deification into her acting profession. While preparing for her one-woman Broadway show, she began to use a series of affirmations that reminded her of her own divinity as she rehearsed her dancing, singing, and stage moves. Thus she repeated a series of affirmations such as "I am God," "I am God in action," "I am God in health," "I am God in happiness," and so on: "It worked in a remarkably simple manner. I trusted what I can only describe as my higher unlimited self. . . . The higher unlimited superconsciousness can best be defined as one's eternal unlimited soul. . . . It knows and resonates to God because it is a part of God."[30]

If Jane Roberts made explicit use of the metaphor of the TV screen to explain the phenomenon of channeling, MacLaine made explicit use of the metaphors of acting, film, and performance to explain her spiritual quest and personal philosophy. Following the New Age dictum that mind creates reality, MacLaine concluded that life itself is "an illusion—just like the movies" but that this insight also means we have the divine power to transform the illusion of our lives, to enact our lives in new ways, to create new realities. We are not bound to the single script of a movie but rather have infinite possibilities to rewrite the scripts of our lives. This central message of channeling was perhaps mostly famously enacted in the key scene of *Out on a Limb,* as Shirley and her New Age guru David were discussing deep metaphysical questions on the Malibu beach. David offered to teach her "a good exercise that helps us get in touch with the realization that we have God inside of us," which culminated in the two of them leaping up and down joyously before the glimmering ocean, shouting, "I am God! I am God!" While it was by then a fairly standard trope in most New Age literature, this message of divine self-realization was probably a fairly radical one for most American viewers of prime-time television in 1986.

In this sense, MacLaine might best be understood as a kind of second-order medium for the channeling movement—not a channel herself but a kind of metachannel for figures such as Knight and Ryerson, transmitting their message to a much wider audience of spiritual seekers in a new media age.

KEY ISSUES AND DEBATES: "NEW AGE CAPITALISM"?

One of the key questions raised by the New Age is the role of consumerism and capitalism in contemporary spirituality. As we have seen throughout this chapter, New Age spirituality is usually presented as "alternative," nonmainstream, and often countercultural; yet it also often participates in the most mainstream forms of consumer culture, such as New Age bookstores, websites, Expos, and even "metaphysical department stores" that sell all variety of spiritual wares, ranging from crystals and aromatherapy kits to books, DVDs, and food, to a vast array of spiritual services. Anyone visiting New Age centers such as Sedona, Arizona, for example, can browse through hundreds of stores selling every imaginable form of spiritual merchandise, including crystals, jewelry, incense, clothing, books, music, and videos, as well as a vast array of spiritual services, such as psychic readings, chakra balancing, Reiki, massage, and of course channeling.

Ramtha School of Enlightenment is a particularly good example of a New Age movement that has become a huge commercial business, offering a wide array of services such as workshops, seminars, and retreats as well as products such as books, videos, apparel, and other merchandise. As some critics have argued, the New Age has evolved into a lucrative market and a billion-dollar business that has allowed "Eastern" and other non-Western traditions to be "coopted by Western capitalism" and commodified for an American public. For many critics, this represents a kind of "New Age capitalism" and a "silent takeover of religion" by the capitalist marketplace, which really reflects the broader infiltration of consumerism and privatization into all aspects of modern culture, including the religious domain. As Jeremy Carrette and Richard King argue, "From feng shui to holistic medicine, from aromatherapy candles to yoga weekends, from Christian mystics to New Age gurus, spirituality is big business. . . . Spirituality as a cultural trope has also been appropriated by corporate bodies and management consultants to promote efficiency, extend markets, and maintain a leading edge in a fast-moving information economy."[31]

On the other hand, however, one could argue that this sort of commodification of spirituality is by no means unique to the New Age but has been part of American religious life from the very beginning. As we saw in chapter 1, the United States has been a diverse and thriving "spiritual marketplace" since at least the nineteenth century, with countless new religious groups and denominations competing side by side in an unusually free new spiritual atmosphere. Moreover, the transformation of religion into a highly lucrative business is surely not a phenomenon that we see only in New Age channels such as JZ Knight. If anything, the Ramtha business empire is fairly small potatoes when compared to that of Christian televangelists such as Pat Robertson or Joel Osteen, or megachurch preachers such as Rod Parsley. So is it really fair to single out New Age spirituality for adopting the language and logic of the marketplace? Or is it simply an easy target because it is still largely a nonmainstream and marginal movement?

QUESTIONS FOR DISCUSSION AND DEBATE

1. What is gained and what is lost when previously "esoteric" ideas become available to a mass consumer audience, as we see in New Age spirituality? Should we lament this as a kind of watering down and cheapening of older religious traditions for a general public? Or should we celebrate it as a kind of democratization of these traditions that makes them more widely accessible to ordinary people? Or is it more complicated?

2. How would you compare the role of female channelers such as Roberts or Knight with that of nineteenth-century Spiritualists such as Cora Hatch? Do gender roles, femininity, and spiritual authority seem to work in similar ways, or are they very different in the modern American context?

3. When we see channeling performed on TV, as on *The Merv Griffin Show* or in Shirley MacLaine's TV miniseries, does that make it more difficult or less difficult to take it seriously as a "real" spiritual phenomenon than, say, a Pentecostal church service where people speak in tongues or a Santeria ceremony where people become possessed by spirits? Explain your reasoning.

4. As we saw above, some critics see a tension or contradiction between the "alternative spirituality" of New Age practices and the fact that so many of these practices have become commodified and turned into products for a market

economy (as we see, for example, at New Age conventions such as the Universal Life Expo or at stores such as the Crystal Palace in Sedona). Do you think this is a fair criticism of New Age spirituality? Or could similar critiques be made of more or less all religious life in the twenty-first century? After all, don't Catholics and Evangelicals sell a lot of books, DVDs, jewelry, and other merchandise too?

SUGGESTED CLASSROOM ACTIVITY

View a clip of either Jane Roberts or JZ Knight as they become channels for the entities Seth or Ramtha (both readily available on YouTube). Note the changes in body language, accent, mannerisms, and other physical attributes before and after the channel has begun speaking via the channeled entity. Discuss the ways in which channeling is similar to or different from other forms of religious communication with the divine (prayer, for example, or most forms of ritual). In what ways does twentieth- and twenty-first-century channeling seem similar to and different from the nineteenth-century Spiritualist mediumship discussed in chapter 4?

SUGGESTED FILMS

Out on a Limb. ABC Television, 1987.

What the Bleep Do We Know? 20th Century Fox, 2004.

SUGGESTIONS FOR FURTHER READING

Albanese, Catherine L. *A Republic of Mind and Spirit: A Cultural History of American Metaphysical Religion.* New Haven, CT: Yale University Press, 2007.

Brown, Michael F. *The Channeling Zone: American Spirituality in an Anxious Age.* Cambridge, MA: Harvard University Press, 1999.

Carrette, Jeremy, and Richard King. *Selling Spirituality: The Silent Takeover of Religion.* New York: Routledge, 2004.

Ferguson, Marilyn. *The Aquarian Conspiracy: Personal and Social Transformation in the 1980s.* New York: Houghton Mifflin, 1980.

Hanegraaff, Wouter J. *New Age Religion and Western Culture: Esotericism in the Mirror of Secular Thought.* New York: SUNY Press, 1997.

Heelas, Paul. *The New Age Movement: The Celebration of the Self and the Sacralization of Modernity.* London: Blackwell, 1996.

Knight, JZ. *A State of Mind: My Story (Ramtha: The Adventure Begins)*. New York: Warner Books, 1987.

Kripal, Jeffrey J. *Esalen: America and the Religion of No Religion*. Chicago: University of Chicago Press, 2008.

Lau, Kimberly J. *New Age Capitalism: Making Money East of Eden*. Philadelphia: University of Pennsylvania Press, 2000.

Lewis, James R., and J. Gordon Melton, eds. *Perspectives on the New Age*. Albany: SUNY Press, 1992.

Lofton, Kathryn. *Oprah: The Gospel of an Icon*. Berkeley: University of California Press, 2011.

MacLaine, Shirley. *Out on a Limb*. New York: Bantam Books, 1983.

Melton, J. Gordon. *Finding Enlightenment: Ramtha's School of Ancient Wisdom*. Hillsboro, OR: Beyond Words, 1998.

Ramtha. *Voyage to the New World: An Adventure into Unlimitedness*. New York: Ballantine Books, 1987.

Roberts, Jane. *The Seth Material*. Englewood Cliffs, NJ: Prentice Hall, 1970.

———. *Seth Speaks: The Eternal Validity of the Soul*. New York: Bantam, 1974.

Schmidt, Leigh Eric. *Restless Souls: The Making of American Spirituality*. Berkeley: University of California Press, 2012.

NOTES TO CHAPTER 11

1. Kathryn Lofton, *Oprah: The Gospel of an Icon* (Berkeley: University of California Press, 2011), 79. See also James R. Lewis and J. Gordon Melton, eds., *Perspectives on the New Age* (Albany: SUNY Press, 1992). As Lewis and Melton suggest in the introduction to their book, New Age spirituality tends to have the following features: an emphasis on healing; a desire to be modern and use scientific language; eclecticism and syncretism; a monistic and impersonal ontology; optimism, success orientation, and a tendency to evolutionary views; and an emphasis on psychic powers (7).
2. E. R. D. Maclagen and A. G. B. Russell, eds., *The Prophetic Books of William Blake: Milton* (London: A. H. Bullen, 1907), 2.
3. Alice A. Bailey, *Discipleship in the New Age* (New York: Lucis, 1944), 74.
4. Jane Roberts, *The Seth Material* (Englewood Cliffs, NJ: Prentice Hall, 1970), 10.
5. Ibid., 271.
6. Ibid., 66.
7. Ibid., 271.
8. Ibid., 12.
9. Ibid., 3.
10. Jane Roberts, videotaped session, June 4, 1974, YouTube, www.youtube.com/watch?v=ZRG-IR3aqec&feature=related.

11. JZ Knight, *A State of Mind: My Story (Ramtha: The Adventure Begins)* (New York: Warner Books, 1987), 10–11.

12. Ibid., 324.

13. Ibid., 343.

14. Ibid., 290. See also Steven L. Weinberg, ed., *Ramtha* (Eastsound, WA: Sovereignty, 1986), 101.

15. JZ Knight on *The Merv Griffin Show,* August 1985.

16. Ibid.

17. Ibid.

18. J. Gordon Melton, *Finding Enlightenment: Ramtha's School of Ancient Wisdom* (Hillsboro, OR: Beyond Words, 1998), 139–41.

19. JZ Knight, on *Larry King Live,* CNN, August 2, 2008.

20. Ibid.

21. William Arntz, Betty Chasse, and Mark Vicente, directors, *What the Bleep Do We Know?* (Twentieth Century Fox, 2005).

22. Carl Sagan, *The Demon-Haunted World: Science as a Candle in the Dark* (New York: Ballantine Books, 1997), 204–5.

23. Jeff Knight, interview by Joe Szimhart, 1992, www.youtube.com/watch?v=KM45obLdDEI.

24. Timothy Egan, "Worldly and the Spiritual Clash in New Age Divorce," *New York Times,* September 25, 1992, www.nytimes.com/1992/09/25/us/worldly-and-the-spiritual-clash-in-new-age-divorce.html.

25. Shirley MacLaine, *Dancing in the Light* (New York: Bantam Books, 1985), 123.

26. Ibid., 127.

27. Shirley MacLaine, *Out on a Limb* (New York: Bantam Books, 1983), 178.

28. Ibid., 182.

29. Ibid., 208.

30. MacLaine, *Dancing in the Light,* 111.

31. Jeremy Carrette and Richard King, *Selling Spirituality: The Silent Takeover of Religion* (New York: Routledge, 2004), 1. See also Kimberly Lau, *New Age Capitalism: Making Money East of Eden* (Philadelphia: University of Pennsylvania Press, 2000).

TWELVE

Peoples Temple

Mass Murder-Suicide, the Media, and the "Cult" Label

On November 18, 1978, more than nine hundred people died in a series of murders and suicides in Guyana, South America, most of them members of an American-born religious movement called Peoples Temple. Founded by the Reverend James Warren (Jim) Jones (figures 12.1–3), Peoples Temple was for a time one of America's most innovative, progressive, and successful religious movements, blending charismatic Christianity with a powerful message of social justice and racial integration. However, the group and its leader faced intense criticism from the American media, politicians, and anticult groups, and so relocated to Guyana in 1977 in order to build a progressive agricultural project based on racial harmony and a form of Christian socialism.

Peoples Temple also had a powerful streak of Christian millenarianism, or the expectation of the imminent end of the world (informed in part by the Cold War threat of nuclear holocaust and in part by the growing persecution the community faced). The group had in fact been preparing for some sort of cataclysmic end, going through several "practice suicides" in the 1970s. However, the final tragic events were triggered when California congressman Leo Ryan flew down to Jonestown on behalf of a group called Concerned Relatives in order to bring any members of the group who wished to leave back to their families. While Jones initially allowed several members to leave voluntarily, gunmen from Peoples Temple ambushed the group at the airstrip, killing the congressman and four others. Then, back at Jonestown, Jones gave his community the order to commit an act of what he called "revolutionary suicide," protesting an inhumane and intolerant world that would not leave them in peace to pursue their communal ideal. Most members died by drinking Flavor-Aid mixed with cyanide, Valium, and chloral hydrate—though not all did so voluntarily, and many were reportedly injected with the poison (leading some to call this a mass murder rather than a

FIGURE 12.1 Jim Jones and children, Redwood Valley. Photo courtesy of the Jonestown Institute, http://jonestown.sdsu.edu.

FIGURE 12.2 Jim Jones, Jonestown, 1978. Photo courtesy of the Jonestown Institute, http://jonestown.sdsu.edu.

FIGURE 12.3 Jim Jones in Guyana.
Photo courtesy of the Jonestown
Institute, http://jonestown.sdsu.edu.

mass suicide).[1] Meanwhile, a radio communication was sent to another Temple member, Sharon Amos, in Georgetown, who killed her two youngest children and then, together with her oldest daughter, took her own life. Overall, the deaths represent the largest mass murder-suicide in modern history and the largest loss of American civilian lives in a deliberate act prior to the terrorist attacks of September 11, 2001.

While the Jonestown tragedy of 1978 is the most spectacular example of a self-destructive new religious movement in modern times, it is by no means the only one. The final decades of the twentieth century and the years leading up to the new millennium witnessed a proliferation of end-times movements, such as Heaven's Gate (discussed in chapter 1 above), the Order of the Solar Temple (an apocalyptic movement originating in Geneva, whose members committed mass suicide in 1994), the Branch Davidians (whose members had a violent showdown with the Bureau of Alcohol, Tobacco and Firearms in Texas in 1993, which we will discuss in the following chapter), Aum Shrinrikyo (a Japanese group that spread sarin gas in Tokyo subways in 1995), and many others.

The idea of an approaching end times or apocalypse is obviously not unique to contemporary new religious movements. Indeed, it is deeply embedded in the much older Christian concept of the "millennium" (literally, a thousand-year period) and is first mentioned in the book of Revelation or Apocalypse of St. John, which describes a millennium after Satan is defeated and the righteous will reign with Christ for a thousand years. Throughout Christian history—particularly during the late medieval and early modern periods—there have been a number of millenarian movements, such as the Free Spirit, the Münsterites, and many others. During the 1840s, a huge millenarian movement called the Millerites spread across the northeastern United States, inspired by William Miller's calculation that the Second Coming of Jesus would occur sometime in 1843–44. However, it does seem that the final decades before the year 2000 inspired a fresh wave of religious groups anticipating the catastrophic end of the world and the transition to something radically new.

In this and the subsequent chapters, we will look at just a few examples of millenarian movements—two that ended in violent tragedy (Peoples Temple and the Branch Davidians) and one that has a more optimistic view of the coming millennium (the Raëlians). Because of its catastrophic end, Peoples Temple raises a number of profound issues and debates for the study of new religions and of religion more generally. Perhaps most importantly, it raises the debate surrounding the "cult" label, which, as we have seen, has often been applied to many new religious and alternative groups from the Mormons onward. Dubbed "the Cult of Death" by *Time* magazine in 1978, Peoples Temple became the media poster child of a dangerous, murderous cult and has informed much of the popular representation of new religions ever since. As the *Time* article put it, "The Jonestown story, like some Joseph Conrad drama of fanaticism and moral emptiness, has gone directly into popular myth. It will be remembered as an emblematic, identifying moment of the decade: a demented American psychopomp in a tropical cult house, doling out cyanide with Kool-Aid. Jonestown is the Altamont of the '70s cult movement."[2]

As we saw in chapter 1, most scholars in the United States today reject the term *cult* in favor of more neutral terms such as *new religious movement*. However, this still leaves us with the question of how to talk about and make sense of groups that might be violent or self-destructive. How can we examine such groups both sympathetically and critically in ways that will take them seriously as genuine quests for religious meaning, while at the same time also seriously analyzing their more problematic and self-destructive elements?

JIM JONES AND THE FORMATION OF PEOPLES TEMPLE

Like those of other new religious leaders we have discussed so far, the biography of Jim Jones is difficult to write, since there are relatively few sources, and the few that we have tell very different stories about the man. According to some accounts, he was a "bad seed" and a troublemaker from his childhood onward, known as the local "Dennis the Menace,"[3] but others describe him as a spiritually gifted young man with an innate calling to the church.[4] However, at least the basic facts do seem to be generally agreed upon.

James Warren Jones was born on May 13, 1931, in Crete, Indiana, and then moved with his family to the small town of Lynn, Indiana, three years later. Struggling in the midst of the Great Depression, the Jones family was poor. The family farm failed shortly after Jim's birth, his father was largely disabled from a war injury, and his mother worked various jobs to support them. At the time, this was a part of the country that was not only deeply divided by racial segregation but also pervaded by Christian fundamentalism. Although his family was not particularly religious, Jones became interested in various local churches as a young man and was quickly drawn to the lively and charismatic services of the Pentecostal Church. Pentecostalism would leave a lasting impression on his own preaching style and the later Peoples Temple, particularly its vibrant, expressive worship, manifestations of the Spirit, faith healing, and communal ideal of mutual sharing and support. By age sixteen, Jones had already begun preaching on his own, traveling to predominantly African American neighborhoods to spread a message of revival and brotherhood.

In 1949, while attending Indiana University–Bloomington, Jones married Marceline Baldwin. Marceline came from a Methodist background, and although Jones was critical of Methodism as an organized church he found that reading the Methodist social creed was a life-changing experience. Here was a church that believed in real issues of social justice, such as alleviating poverty and promoting free speech, prison reform, and racial integration. At the same time, he was repelled by the racism and intolerance that he encountered in places such as Bloomington, which was a center of Ku Klux Klan activity and, in his view, "besieged by redneck mentality from the South."[5] Thus Jones developed two passions that would drive him for the rest of his life: racial integration and socialism.

In 1954, Jones set up his own church, called Community Unity, in Indianapolis. With his charismatic, energetic preaching style, he began to attract a growing congregation and also the interest of local Pentecostal church elders. However, his insistence that his congregation be racially integrated was both unusual and controversial among the racially divided churches of Indianapolis. In 1955, he moved his community to a larger building in the city and took the new name Peoples Temple; then in 1959, the congregation voted to affiliate itself with the Disciples of Christ, a mainline church already known for its commitment to progressive issues and social justice.

"A BLACK CHURCH": RELIGION AND RACE IN PEOPLES TEMPLE

Perhaps the most remarkable aspect of Peoples Temple was its attitude toward race, which was in many ways radical and well ahead of its time. Several of the movements we have discussed in this book were racially separatist—including the Nation of Islam and early Rastafari—calling for blacks to have their own homeland in Africa, free of white oppression. Jones's vision was quite the opposite. At a time when most churches in the United States were still segregated, Jones's commitment to social justice was closely tied to an ideal of a racially integrated congregation, and he actively sent missionaries out into black communities to draw in new members. In turn, many African Americans were drawn not simply by his charismatic preaching style but also by his fiery message of justice and unity. While its leadership remained largely white, Peoples Temple was, in many ways, a "black church"—that is, its preaching style, energetic worship, music, and commitment to social and political ideals had much in common with African American churches. In the words of Rebecca Moore, a religious studies scholar and relative of former Peoples Temple members, "Peoples Temple really was a black church. It was led by a white minister, but in terms of the worship service, commitment to the social gospel, its membership, it functioned completely like a black church."[6] The exact demographics of Peoples Temple are a bit uncertain, but various sources state that it was between one-fifth and one-half black by 1960.

Tim Carter joined Peoples Temple in 1972 and was one of the few members who survived the tragedy in Jonestown. In this interview he talks about what drew him to the community, his reflections on Jim Jones as a person, and how he was able to move on after the events of 1978. Carter served in the military in Vietnam and then explored a variety of spiritual, social, and political ideas in the early 1970s. He found many of his own spiritual and political views embodied in the unique community of Peoples Temple.

As soon as I walked into the Temple, I was home, and I knew it. It felt like I had known those people forever. We've all experienced that, where you meet somebody and it just feels like you've known them for a long time, even if you've only known them for an hour. I hadn't met Jim Jones, I had no idea who he was, I had no idea really what the Temple was about. I had no concept of joining the Temple or living with them. But I knew that I had found a home for me. It felt like a synthesis of everything that I believed in spiritually and politically. One of the first things that Jones talked about was the Sermon on the Mount, which resonated with me.

There was no color. That was a thing you could feel and literally see in the Temple—*there was no color.* From my experience in Vietnam, I was one of the few whites that was totally accepted by the brothers over there. But there weren't that many of us. There were race deaths in Vietnam. Race deaths were real. Racism always has been real, but it was very real in Vietnam. So the contrast of that with the Temple was there.

One of the first things I heard Jones say was "Be still and know I am God," which is from the book of Psalms. A lot of people interpreted it as "*He* is God." Maybe that's what he meant, but I never interpreted it like that. I interpreted it as "I am" equals God, Universe, Source, whatever that is. Later on in the meeting they started passing around the bucket, and I had very little money. I was working whatever jobs I could find. In the Redwood Valley, I spent two days chopping wood so I had money to date with. The plate came around, and I put in my last sixty-eight cents. I leaned over to my sister and said, "I hope you got smokes, because that was all my money." About ten minutes later, Jones pointed to the balcony where my sister and I were sitting, and he said, "You who just gave your last 68 cents, that means more than these people who have a hundred dollars and only gave ten." I thought, "Wow, this guy is legit in terms of being psychic."

In terms of why people stayed in the Temple and what attracted them to the Temple, I do believe that there was a huge dichotomy between the younger and the older members. The younger members, both black and white, were much more politically oriented. I think that for the older black folks and white folks it was more religious, even though in the Temple religious faith meant helping other people, putting into action the Sermon on the Mount. That was an incredibly powerful thing for

(continued)

me. I could actually see with my own eyes that we were making a difference in the community. The Temple was helping people. For a lot of my liberal friends, it was a lot of talk and not a lot of do. And I felt good about the "do" part.

Jim Jones was brilliant, he was charismatic, he was a genius—and that's not an exaggeration. He was the best speaker that I ever heard in my life to this day. He was better than Jesse Jackson when Jesse was at his best. He was also manipulative, he was cunning, he was controlling. If I had seen all those things when I was first there, I probably wouldn't have ended up in Guyana. My reason for staying in the Temple for the last two years was my loyalty to the people. That was genuine and is genuine. It didn't have to do with following Jim Jones, because I hated the son of a bitch for about the last year and a half. I really did not like him, but I believed in what we were doing. And if you take away Jim Jones, I believe in my heart that Jonestown would still exist in some form or fashion. It might only be two hundred people, but I think it might be two thousand people or five thousand. I'm almost certain that it would still be in existence today.

I didn't know he was a drug addict. From what I've learned since, he was doing drugs back then. He was doing speedballs. I also learned that he was actually giving out bennies (Benzedrine) to some folks. There was a clear devolution in his personality, although I did not know that it had to do with drugs. The person that existed as a being when I first joined the Temple was not the same person that existed when everything came down. Was he a good man gone bad, was he a bad man gone worse? The light and the darkness existed equally. It's just that we only saw that which was more of the light.

People want to focus on Jim Jones. But the story of Peoples Temple is the people. It's not Jim Jones. He's a part of it. He added them all together. But what made the Temple dynamic and successful and *mainstream* was the people—because we were as mainstream as it could get in terms of the progressive movement in the Bay Area. We were not freaks. We were not cultists. We were mainstream. When the focus is on Jones, then all we are is "cultists." We are "them." For anybody to actually begin to learn anything about Peoples Temple, it has to become a "we."

There are a lot of people who feel that Jonestown really was just a concentration camp and nothing more, and others who feel that it was a real opportunity. Both realities are true, and that's one of the mind-fucks of Peoples Temple, is that everything about it is *contradictory*. The more I learn about what went on in Jonestown, though, the more I get sick to my stomach.

If the only story that somebody focuses on is that, well, there was this underground sensory deprivation chamber, and people had to work twelve hours a day, and the diet was horrible, and people couldn't leave—well, that's an accurate image. Is it the whole image? No. For everything in the Temple there are contradictions. At the same time that that's going on, we were building a city in the middle of the jungle. I saw kids that were sociopathic in the States. One of them was a black albino kid. He was out of place everywhere. He had been teased and given a hard time to the point where he was torturing animals. There was another kid who had watched his mother's brains blown out by his father. He was an angry kid. When I got to Jonestown I could see that these were completely different human beings—and I'm not talking about robot automatons. One of them was in charge of the animals; the same kid that had been torturing animals had a great relationship with them.

There were things that make me want to swell my chest with pride. Then I think, what difference did it make? Everybody died. If you look at the ending as suicide, then it really was a waste. But if you look at the ending as *murder,* then some of the things that we did do still have meaning.

They knew that people didn't want to die. There might be some, but most didn't. So they actually created the means to murder everybody. But it's one of those concepts that is so insane that even if you're there, you, and it looks like it's a threat, you ignore it because it's so crazy. It's like nuclear war—neither side fired the shot, thank God; it doesn't make any sense to destroy everything, because you gain nothing.

People say, "How did you survive?" And I say, "I survived, number one, because I know that there is a Source that is more than this physical realm, that nothing is lost in God or the Universe, whatever appellation you want to apply to that Energy." But mostly it was just that I willed myself to survive. I just don't believe in suicide. I don't know if it was because of my Catholic upbringing, or because of whatever Jewish genes I still have left in me. Everything that I have ever read spiritually says that whatever lessons you were supposed to learn in this life, you're going to be back in that position to learn them again. I thought to myself, I can't ever go back again to that blackness that was Jonestown on that final day. Maybe that was a selfish reason, but it kept me going.

For me, personally, it was all about not putting my faith in anybody but myself. Now, if the Dalai Lama walked into my house I would be thrilled, and I would sit and listen, and it would be wonderful. I would consider him a teacher—but not *the* teacher. So for me, it was not putting faith in anybody else. Am I still spiritual? Extremely. But in terms of putting my energy into any specific group? No, I can't do groups anymore, including the church.

Much of Jones's style and message was directly influenced by one of the most charismatic black preachers of the twentieth century, Father Divine, and his Peace Mission. As early as the 1930s, Father Divine had begun an interracial community in New York, preaching a message of racial integration and self-help for blacks and whites alike. Jones visited the Peace Mission several times in the 1950s and was so impressed by the church that he wrote a short booklet praising its principles of "cooperative communalism," which would become central to the vision of Peoples Temple.[7] Like Father Divine, Jones would encourage his congregation to call him "Father," and he began a housing and feeding program modeled on the Peace Mission. After Father Divine's death in 1965, Jones attempted to take over the organization, and while he failed to do so, Peoples Temple members did recruit many from the Peace Mission.

COLD WAR NUCLEAR ANXIETIES AND CHRISTIAN SOCIALISM

In many ways, Peoples Temple was a complex mixture of a highly optimistic form of Christian socialism and a darker anxiety about the imminent end of the world. From at least the early 1960s, Jones had deep concerns about a coming Armageddon—concerns that were neither unique nor very surprising considering the Cold War context of the movement, at a time when many Americans were building bomb shelters and preparing for nuclear war. In 1962, Jones read an article in *Esquire* magazine that recommended "Nine Places in the World to Hide" in order to survive nuclear war. Following the article's advice, Jones moved his family to Brazil and lived there during 1962–63—during the very period when the Cuban missile crisis occurred, confirming his belief that the world was on the brink of nuclear holocaust. After returning to the United States, Jones also had a vision in which he saw a nuclear flash hitting Chicago. In 1965, Jones and about seventy of his followers relocated to the Redwood Valley in California—another site mentioned as a safe haven in the *Esquire* article. As Jones put it in a sermon in 1973, mixing biblical passages with nuclear fears: "So we have to be prepared to take our flight to the valley in the case of great desolation or Armageddon that would spring forth in a nuclear hell, as Peter said, when the elements melt with a fervent heat."[8]

In California, the community began to draw a mix of young, college-educated whites who were attracted by its progressive spiritual and political mission and lower-income blacks who were drawn by the church's urban ministries in San Francisco and Los Angeles. Peoples Temple also engaged in a wide range of social services, establishing nine residential homes for the elderly, six homes for foster children, and a forty-acre ranch for the mentally handicapped. By the mid-1970s, Jones's social service programs had begun to attract very positive media attention. Thus he was named one of the nation's one hundred outstanding clergymen by *Religion in Life* magazine in 1975; he won the *Los Angeles Herald*'s Humanitarian of the Year award in 1976; and he was one of four recipients of the annual Martin Luther King, Jr., Humanitarian of the Year award at Glide Memorial Church in San Francisco in 1977.

However, Jones's religious beliefs and teachings appear to have evolved significantly over time. From his early roots in Pentecostalism, Jones began to preach ideas that departed more and more from mainstream Christianity. After his contact with Father Divine, he increasingly began to emphasize his own divinity and godlike powers—not simply as a pastor but as a prophet or even a newly anointed being. As Jones described himself in a sermon delivered in San Francisco, he was not simply a man but really a manifestation of the "Christ Principle" or "Christ Revolution." Embodying the same egalitarian love as Jesus himself, Jones claimed the same power to heal and perform miracles:

I have put on Christ, you see. I have followed the example of Christ. When you see me, it's no longer Jim Jones here, I'm crucified with Christ, nevertheless, I live yet not I, but Christ that lives here. Now Christ is in this body.

You will not get Christ's blessing in Jim Jones' blessing until you walk like Jim Jones, until you act like Jim Jones. . . . *I* am no longer a man, but a Principle. I am the Way, the Truth, and the Light. No one can come to Father but through me.[9]

Jones's divine claims appear to have been accepted by many in the Peoples Temple community. As Harold Cordell put it in a letter of 1965, "Jones is certainly a deliverer and the same anointed Spirit or Christ Spirit that we know resided in Jesus. . . . [He is] one of the greatest prophets and messengers that have ever appeared on this earth."[10] Faith healings were often a key feature of the church's services, as Jones claimed to restore sight to failing eyes, remove pain, and allow the crippled to walk.

At the same time, Jones's sermons progressively incorporated a more socialist message—or rather, a kind of Christian communalism. At a time when the United States was still very much in the grip of the Cold War and communism was widely perceived as the ultimate enemy of the American way of life, Jones was remarkable for his outspoken criticism of American capitalism and his embrace of socialism. Jones was also critical of traditional Christianity, which he dismissed as a kind of "fly away religion" based on a vague faith in a "Sky God." Instead, Jones taught a form of Christian socialism based on the more practical goal of liberating and uplifting all people—particularly women and people of color—here on earth. American capitalist culture was, in his view, an "irredeemable Babylon" and an "Antichrist system" that was bound to destroy itself through nuclear war. In contrast, Jones offered the hope of creating an egalitarian, racially integrated society and a kind of "socialist millennial" vision of a new Eden. As he put it in a sermon delivered in San Francisco in 1973, "If you're born in capitalist America, racist America, fascist America, then you're born in sin. But if you're born in socialism, you're not born in sin."[11] Peoples Temple was thus presented as a kind of "apostolic socialism," a nonviolent revolution that would sweep the world like a hurricane:

I am the only fully socialist. I am the only fully God. . . .

We could invite people then into other main services and up in our valley, beautiful projects and our senior homes, and let them see what we've done through cooperative, *non-violent*, true *apostolic* socialism, as an alternative to totalitarian fascism. . . .

I am going to establish a *hurricane*. I'm going to shake the whole nation with my spirit and my mind socialism. I'm going to *shake* the whole creation.[12]

In other sermons, Jones launched a scathing attack on mainstream Christian churches and their imaginary "Sky God." At times, Jones even attacked the Bible itself, which in his view had been used throughout history to support and reinforce rather than to fight racism, slavery, genocide, and other social injustices. As he put it in another sermon from 1973, this book had become another idol, and a dangerous one at that:

> Never in the history of mankind has a black book done so much infamy as this book. It brought blacks back in chains, it murdered the Indians, till there's not one hardly left. Their tribes are done. Their religion is gone. . . . The Mexican people, their whole nation was *robbed* from them . . . in the name of this black book. It is a paper idol. It's a destroyer. It's a *killer.* . . .
>   Your Bible is *full* of lies. Your Skygod makes no sense. If he was all-perfect, why doesn't he heal 'em all?[13]

In place of the dead letter of the Bible, with its vain promise of a distant heaven after death, Jones promised the more immediate rewards of divine socialism—food, shelter, comfort, and community here and now on this earth.

GROWING TENSIONS FROM WITHIN AND OUTSIDE PEOPLES TEMPLE

Peoples Temple had in many ways two very different sides to it—a popular public face and a more complex and darker internal dynamic. Publicly it was seen as a compassionate, caring, socially engaged church concerned with poverty, integration, and social justice, but inwardly it had a more authoritarian and disciplinary structure. Members were kept in check by a system of rewards and punishments and by catharsis sessions that focused heavily on sexuality and confession of sexual transgressions. After the move to Guyana, the disciplinary nature of the community became even more intense. Members who tried to flee were beaten, humiliated, or sentenced to heavy labor; some who broke rules were placed in sensory deprivation chambers; and finally, some were kept sedated with drugs.[14]

Jones himself had an extremely active and complicated sexual life. Not only did he often control and arrange the sexual lives of members—by deciding who would marry whom and who would be encouraged to procreate—but he also made himself the primary object of the members' sexual desires. While still married to Marceline, he had numerous relationships with both female and male members and fathered two sons with other women. Various observers have interpreted Jones's sexual life in rather different ways. Some scholars such as Catherine Wessinger offer a fairly generous interpretation of Jones's sexual relations, viewing them as an important part of the social dynamics of this religious community, and particularly as a means of offering women new roles in the church hierarchy. As she suggests, this was a means of "empowering them as his delegates to perform administrative duties . . . in the establishment of their ideal socialist community."[15] Others, however, see Jones's sexual affairs as primarily a matter of power and a way of asserting control over every facet of members' lives and all levels of the community as a whole. As Rebecca Moore concludes, "Sex was an important way Jim Jones controlled individuals. . . . Jones' management of relationships was not about sex, but about power, and he used his power to control all aspects of life inside the Temple."[16]

THE MOVE TO GUYANA: BUILDING JONESTOWN AS HEAVEN ON EARTH

Despite the success of Peoples Temple in California and the recognition that Jones received as a humanitarian leader, the church faced increasing pressure from all sides. Because of its racially integrated community, the church was targeted by white racists and threatened by neo-Nazis, who sent hate mail and slashed members' tires. At the same time, Peoples Temple became the target of a number of extremely negative news stories concerning its "cult-like behavior" and investigations by various federal agencies. In 1972, the *San Francisco Examiner* published a series of articles attacking Jones's messianic pretensions and the authoritarian structure of the movement; and in 1977, *New West* magazine published an exposé suggesting that Peoples Temple should be investigated for financial misdealings, coercive practices, and questionable involvement in San Francisco politics.

Finally, the movement also came under attack from former members, who had begun to speak out publicly against Jones in the early 1970s. Perhaps the most vocal opponents were Grace Stoen, who left Peoples Temple in 1976, and her husband Timothy Stoen, who left in 1977. The Stoens were a particular problem for the community because they were fighting for custody of their young son, John Victor Stoen, who was under Temple guardianship. Together with other ex-members and parents of members, the Stoens formed a group called the Committee for Concerned Relatives, which saw Peoples Temple as a "dangerous cult that had to be dismantled."[17] Later in 1977, Jones learned that the allegations of ex-members had helped prompt an investigation by the Treasury Department, and he feared that Peoples Temple might also be scrutinized by the IRS, as many other new religious movements had been during the 1970s.

Feeling himself attacked on all sides, and already deeply critical of American-style capitalism, Jones began to look for a new home for his church outside the Babylon of the United States. Jones had already visited Guyana in 1973, and in 1975 he stationed fifty members of the church there to begin clearing the jungle and building houses. As pressures in the United States escalated, Jones began to refer to Guyana as a "promised land" and a "socialist paradise" for the exodus from America; here they would attempt to bring their vision of an egalitarian, integrated socialist community to fruition in the new city of Jonestown. As former member Tim Carter recalled, the United States seemed to them to be a place of "creeping fascism" and intolerance where they were no longer at home: "It was apparent that corporations, or the multinationals, were getting much larger, their influence was growing within the government, and the United States is a racist place." Jonestown, conversely, "was a place in a black country where our black members could live in peace."[18]

By September 1977, nearly one thousand members had been transferred to the new site, which was imagined as a kind of heaven on earth, a paradise in the jungle where racism, sexism, and classism would be eliminated and where people who had been discriminated against in America could live in peace and freedom. As Harriet Tropp argued in a radio broadcast in defense of Jonestown, Peoples Temple was an amazing "democratic socialist cooperative," with a long list of valuable accomplishments: it had eliminated class distinctions, achieved a socialist lifestyle based on cooperation and sharing, and established successful medical, educational, and agricultural projects.[19] For many participants in Jonestown, this utopian vision would be valued up until the very end of the experiment. In the words of Annie Moore, who was apparently the last person to die at Jonestown,

> Jim Jones showed us all this—that we could live together with our differences, that we are all the same human beings. Luckily, we are more fortunate than the starving babies of Ethiopia, than the starving babies of the United States.
>
> What a beautiful place this was. The children loved the jungle, learned about animals and plants. There were no cars to run over them; no child molesters to molest them; nobody to hurt them. They were the freest, most intelligent children I had ever known.[20]

Despite this tremendous optimism and hard work, however, Peoples Temple faced a number of serious challenges in their new location. First, a large percentage of the population at Jonestown—about half of the over nine hundred members—were either elderly or children, which meant that the able-bodied adults had to struggle to provide material support, health care, and education for the entire population. At the same time, there were growing suspicions that, even after leaving the United States, the community was still under scrutiny by the US government. Residents were convinced that the CIA was watching them and working to undermine the community; in fact, the heavily excised documents released by the CIA do indicate that agents were working in Guyana, and the agency was the first to notify the US Defense Department of the deaths. However, this is not particularly surprising, given that this was an American movement espousing socialism and criticizing the United States—all in the midst of the Cold War and the larger paranoia about communism, cults, and brainwashing.[21]

Jones himself, meanwhile, declined rapidly during the period in Guyana, both physically and mentally. In addition to mental exhaustion, Jones developed serious health problems by mid-1978, including high fever and a fungal disease in his lungs. At the same time, he appears to have been using large amounts of drugs, which increasingly impaired his ability to lead the community. Embassy officials who visited Jones in May and November of 1978 stated that he was clearly on drugs, noting his slurred speech, erratic behavior, and mental confusion.[22] After the murder-suicide, the autopsy report would show that Jones had toxic levels of pentobarbital in his system. Overall, as Jones's physical and mental state declined, the morale of the Jonestown community appears to have declined rapidly as well.

PRACTICE SUICIDES, WHITE NIGHTS, AND THE END OF JONESTOWN

The final tragic events of November 1978 were not the first time Peoples Temple had discussed the idea of mass suicide. Even as early as 1973, Jones appears to have suggested the idea that the leadership might need to take their own lives. In 1976, Jones ordered a suicide drill, in which members of his inner circle were asked to drink wine and were then informed that they had consumed poison that would kill them within forty-five minutes. Finally, when no one questioned the decision or rebelled, he informed them that it had simply been a test. As one former member, Bonnie Thielmann, recalled, collective suicide was seen by many members as the logical and necessary alternative to dehumanizing, self-destructive, and increasingly fascistic American society: "We expected to move to a safe haven in another country before America collapsed, but if we didn't, we all agreed that, yes, we'd commit suicide."[23]

Another suicide drill took place in Jonestown in February 1978. In this case, members of the community were given a drink they were told was a mixture of juice and potent poison. As one member, Edith Roller, recalled in her journal from this period, there was little protest as the members of the community lined up for the drink. While she didn't personally believe that the current situation called for such a radical decision, she also reflected that she "had to die sometime."[24] Other members even wrote publicly about their willingness to die for Jonestown. According to a letter sent by Pam Moton to all members of the US Congress in March 1978, it is evident "that people cannot forever be continually harassed and beleaguered by such tactics without seeking alternatives that have been presented. I can say without hesitation that we are devoted to a decision that it is better even to die than to be constantly harassed from one continent to the next."[25]

As real and perceived threats from both within and without the community mounted, Peoples Temple began to prepare for attack. Jones used the term *White Nights* to refer to moments of "severe crisis within Jonestown and the possibility of mass death during, or as a result of, an invasion."[26] While White Nights had taken place earlier in California, they became far more intense after the move to Guyana. For example, in September 1977 the attorney of former member Timothy Stoen traveled to Jonestown to serve court papers to Jones and then persuaded a Guyana court to issue an arrest warrant. Believing that the community was threatened, members armed themselves with farm implements and stood waiting on the periphery of the compound for days, ready for an attack. In January 1978, Jones announced another White Night, claiming that they were under attack from the Concerned Relatives and the CIA. On this occasion—an eerie foreshadowing of the final suicides—members of the community lined up to take poison in order to prevent their children from being taken and tortured. Before anyone actually died, however, Jones announced that the crisis was over.

November 18, 1978, was the final White Night. When Congressman Ryan arrived in Guyana to meet with Jones and members of Peoples Temple that day, he was initially received very politely and was even allowed to take fourteen members who wished to leave along with him to the airplane. Shortly after Ryan and most of his party were gunned down on the airstrip, however, Jones announced that this was the time to end this social experiment, and a large batch of Flavor-Aid mixed with cyanide, valium, and chloral hydrate was prepared for the community. In Jones's final words, this was not to be a mere suicide but a kind of revolutionary act, a protest against an intolerant, racist, and inhumane world. It was in his view preferable to the persecution they would face from the US government and an act of defiance against a society that would not leave them in peace:

> We're not committing suicide—it's a revolutionary act. We can't go back; they won't leave us alone. They're now going to tell more lies, which means more congressmen. There's no way, no way we can survive. . . .
>
> They'll pay for it. This is a revolutionary suicide. This is not a self-destructive suicide. So they'll pay for this. They brought this upon them.
>
> It's been done by every tribe in history. Every tribe facing annihilation. All the Indians of the Amazon are doing it right now. They refuse to bring any babies into the world . . . because they don't want to live in this kind of a world. . . .
>
> We said . . . we don't like the way the world is. Take our life from us. We laid it down. We got tired. We didn't commit suicide, we committed an act of revolutionary suicide protesting the conditions of an inhumane world.[27]

At least some of the members on the final day seemed to agree with Jones. In the words of one woman, recorded on the same tape with Jones as the suicides began, "This is nothing to cry about. This is something we could all rejoice about. . . . They always told us that we could cry when you're coming into this world. So we're leaving it, and we're leaving it peaceful. . . . I have been here one year and nine months, and I never felt better in my life. . . . I had a beautiful life. We should be happy."[28]

However, these recordings from the final hours of Peoples Temple reveal that not all of the members were in agreement that the situation was entirely hopeless. Some challenged Jones's decision, suggesting that it was senseless to throw away all of their hard work and the amazing community they had created. "I look at all the babies, and I think they deserve to live," one member, Christine Miller, said to Jones, asking if it was too late for the movement to follow a proposed plan to move to Russia for safe haven.[29] But she was quickly shouted down amid the escalating rhetoric. Moreover, not every member of Peoples Temple chose to drink the Flavor-Aid willingly; and at least five who were meant to be poisoned survived by hiding, pretending to be dead, or fleeing the scene. Tim Carter, who fled Jonestown but only after watching his own wife and infant son die, recalls that many were either injected with poison or forced to drink the Flavor-Aid at gunpoint. As we will see in more detail below, Carter argues that this was not a "revolutionary suicide" at all but largely an act of mass murder, in which hundreds of children, seniors, and adults were executed against their will.

KEY ISSUES AND DEBATES: DESTRUCTIVE NEW RELIGIONS AND THE MEDIA—"CULT," "REVOLUTIONARY SUICIDE," OR "MASS MURDER"?

As we saw in chapter 1, one of the key problems in the study of new and alternative religious groups has been the "cult" label. Many of the movements discussed so far in this book—such as ISKCON, the Church of Satan, and the Church of Scientology, in particular—were regularly branded as cults in the mainstream media, becoming part of a larger "cult scare" that spread across American during the 1970s and '80s.[30] Yet Peoples Temple arguably became the most infamous poster child for the popular stereotype of the dangerous, destructive cult.

Literature on cults had been around long before Peoples Temple, dating back at least to the 1920s, with books such as Gaius Atkins's *Modern Religious Cults and Movements* (1923). But the real flood of anticult publications began in the 1960s and '70s—not surprisingly the very period in which the American spiritual marketplace was growing rapidly and providing a variety of new religious offerings—with books such as Jan Van Baalen's *Chaos of the Cults* (1962) and Walter Martin's *The Kingdom of the Cults* (1965). By the late 1960s, anticult paranoia combined with the growing fears about the alleged phenomenon of brainwashing during the Cold War, which we discussed in chapter 10. This paranoia was only exacerbated by the media sensation of the Charles Manson family and its murder spree in 1969, leading to widespread fears that destructive groups were waiting to capture the minds of vulnerable young people and lead them to commit heinous acts. And by the 1970s, the fear of new religions had blossomed into a widespread "cult scare" and given rise to a wide array of anticult groups—the Individual Freedom Foundation, Love Our Children, the Citizens Freedom Foundation, the Spiritual Counterfeits Project, Cults Exodus for Christ, and the Cult Awareness Network, among many others—dedicated to saving America's youth from dangerous mind-control groups. These cult anxieties were clearly tied to a wide range of other anxieties, tensions, and obsessions of post-1960s America—not simply the fear of communism spreading on US soil but also the countercultural movement, the civil rights movement, the sexual revolution, experimentation with mind-altering drugs, shifting gender roles, and radical new social experiments.

With its explicitly socialist rhetoric, its radical racial politics, its complex sexual dynamics, and its catastrophic end, Peoples Temple became the quintessential cult in the American popular imagination. Major publications such as *Time* and *Newsweek* burned the image of Jonestown into American's collective consciousness with cover stories such as "The Cult of Death" and luridly detailed descriptions of the suicides. As we saw in chapter 10, many new religions such as ISKCON had been described as dangerous "brainwashing" groups, and Peoples Temple quickly became the poster child for the idea of mind control—a movement so total in its domination of members' minds that it could lead them to self-destruction. As *Time* magazine put it immediately after the deaths in Jonestown, "In an appalling demonstration of the way in which a charismatic leader can bend the minds of his followers with a devilish blend of professed altruism and psychological tyranny, some 900 members of the

California-based Peoples Temple died in a self-imposed ritual of mass suicide and murder."[31] In its analysis of the psychology of Peoples Temple, the *Time* article draws upon well-known "cult experts" such as Margaret Singer, whom we encountered in our discussion of ISKCON and the brainwashing debate. Once again, the members of Peoples Temple are portrayed as mind-controlled dupes who have become entangled in the cult's poisonous web and have given up all free will to the powerful, seductive cult leader:

> Why did they join an organization like the Peoples Temple? And why did they stay in it? . . . Social scientists who have studied these groups agree that most cult members are in some sort of emotional trouble before they join. Says Dr. Margaret Thaler Singer, a psychologist at Berkeley: "About one-third are very psychologically distressed people. The other two-thirds are relatively average people, but in a period of depression, gloom, being at loose ends." Such people are vulnerable to well-planned recruitment techniques. These usually involve displays of effusive affection and understanding, or "love bombing," as one psychiatrist puts it. Once recruits start going to meetings, they are frequently subjected to various drills and disciplines that weary them both physically and emotionally, producing a sort of trance.
>
> Cut off from family and friends, the new member gets repeated infusions of the cult's doctrines. The lonely, depressed, frightened and disoriented recruit often experiences what amounts to a religious conversion. . . . At this point, the cultist's life is no longer his own. Personalities change from the lively and complex patterns of normality to those of an automaton reciting what he has been taught. The usual problems of living have been replaced by a nearly childish existence in which the cult and its leaders supply all rules and all answers.[32]

In sum, Peoples Temple is portrayed as the epitome of a deadly mind-control group at the terrifying intersection between spirituality and madness: "Religion and insanity occupy adjacent territories in the mind; historically, cults have kept up a traffic between the two."[33]

Today, Jonestown is a kind of cultural reference point for the stereotype of the "crazy cult," to which we repeatedly return in popular discourse. Thus "drinking the Kool-Aid" has become common slang for someone who has given up rational thought and adopted a group mentality and/or a crazy idea (even though the beverage consumed at Jonestown was actually the knock-off brand Flavor-Aid, not Kool-Aid). Jim Jones's face with his large dark sunglasses now adorns T-shirts, lunchboxes, album covers, and other pop culture material. And virtually every subsequent movement that has been thought to be potentially dangerous or self-destructive has been described in the popular media as "another Jonestown" waiting to happen. As such, Peoples Temple is a particularly acute example of the problem of the "cult" label and the question of how we *should* describe movements that have such a history of destructive and ultimately self-destructive behavior.

For most scholars of religion today, as we saw in chapter 1, the term *cult* is so biased and loaded with negative connotations as to be largely useless in the serious academic study of these controversial movements. As Rebecca Moore put it in her study of Peoples Temple, "Cult is never a value-neutral word, since it always carries an implicit criticism. We do not call Baptists or Catholics or Jews cultists; we only call religions of which we disapprove cults."[34] Most often, the cult label is used for groups that challenge or reject mainstream social norms by changing their dress and hairstyle or living in alternative communal or family arrangements or dropping out of school or jobs: "One thing they all seemed to have in common was a rejection of the lives their parents led, discarding worldly success and traditional markers of middle-class achievement such as careers, families, homes."[35]

As an alternative to the cult label, more sympathetic scholars have tried to humanize Peoples Temple by taking it seriously as a legitimate religious movement and placing it within the broader framework of American history and comparative religion. As John Hall suggests, Peoples Temple was not just some weird aberration from mainstream society but in many ways a deeply *American* movement. With its commitment to the Social Gospel, its charismatic worship, and its progressive politics, Peoples Temple was very much a reflection of American religious life, particularly during the volatile decades of the 1960s and '70s.[36]

Going still further, other scholars such as David Chidester suggest that Peoples Temple and its tragic end need to be understood in the broader context of comparative religions. Mass suicide, Chidester points out, is by no means unheard of in the history of religions, and he cites numerous other examples of religiously sanctioned suicide, including *seppuku* or *hara kiri* in Japan, *sati* or widow's self-sacrifice in India, and the ritual suicides by the Cathar Christian sect in medieval France. After examining a variety of different traditions, Chidester identifies four main religious uses of suicide, all of which were found in Jonestown: (1) to *reinforce* the purity of the community in relation to the perceived defilement of the outside world; (2) to find *release* from a world of misery, suffering, and pain; (3) to exact *revenge* against a government, news media, and traitors to the movement who have provoked the final suicidal act; and (4) to enact *revolution* in the face of what members regard as a dehumanizing and intolerant larger society. In this sense, Chidester suggests, collective suicide might be not so much a bizarre result of cult "brainwashing" as a logical outcome of this community's religious worldview and its unique commitment to apostolic socialism.[37]

However, while Chidester's more sympathetic approach does help us understand Peoples Temple within the broader framework of the comparative study of religions, it seems perhaps less helpful for understanding the complex power relations and internal dynamics between Jones and his followers. Many religions may include the possibility of some form of ritual suicide, such as *hara kiri* in Shinto or *sati* in Hinduism; but not all of them involve the complex sexual relations, the severe discipline, and the drug abuse that we see in Peoples Temple. As we saw above, it is also not at all clear that all or even most of the members died voluntarily.

Others have therefore argued that the Jonestown deaths should not be called "revolutionary suicide" at all and were in fact largely an act of *mass murder*. Tim Carter was one of the few surviving members who witnessed the events firsthand, and he believes that by far the majority of those who died were killed involuntarily—by being either injected with poison or forced to drink the Flavor-Aid at gunpoint. By his count, 246 of those who died were children, who could not be considered to have committed suicide voluntarily; roughly 180 were seniors, who were unable to defend themselves; and somewhere around 125 were injected with poison, on the basis of the abscesses Carter claims that he saw on their bodies. In sum, in his words, "We were just fucking slaughtered. . . . There was nothing dignified about it. Had nothing to do with revolutionary suicide, nothing to do about making a fucking statement. It was just senseless waste, senseless waste and death."[38]

In Carter's view, the fact that Peoples Temple members were victims of murder rather than suicide is actually evidence that they were *not* brainwashed dupes in some mind-control cult. Rather than robot automatons under Jones's will, they were a group of individuals dedicated to working together and building a genuine spiritual community. The fact that most of them died against their will, in Carter's opinion, proves that they did not give up on this social and spiritual ideal but struggled for it until the end:

> People want to focus on Jim Jones. But the story of Peoples temple is the people. It's not Jim Jones. . . . What made the temple dynamic and successful and *mainstream* was the people—because we were as mainstream as it could get in terms of the progressive movement in the Bay Area. We were not freaks. We were not cultists. We were mainstream. When the focus is on Jones, then all we are is "cultists." We are "them." For anybody to actually begin to learn anything about Peoples Temple, it has to become a "we." . . .
>
> There were things that make me want to swell my chest with pride. Then I think, what difference did it make? Everybody died. If you look at the ending as suicide, then it really was a waste. But if you look at the ending as *murder*, then some of the things that we did do still have meaning.
>
> They knew that people didn't want to die. There might be some, but most didn't. So they actually created the means to murder everybody.[39]

To make sense of Peoples Temple, Carter suggests, we have to take seriously its complex and often contradictory nature; we have to examine *both* its darkest, most disturbing elements—its authoritarianism and violence—*and* its most positive elements—its often remarkable commitment to building a progressive spiritual community.

In sum, taking a movement such as Peoples Temple seriously as a legitimate "religion" rather than dismissing it as a "cult" does not mean that we should not *also* look critically at the more problematic aspects of the group. Calling something a religion does not mean that it is entirely good. After all, we can think of many examples of "mainstream" religions that have also been involved in horrible acts, from the Christian Crusades and Inquisition, to child sexual abuse in the Catholic Church, to acts of terrorism carried out by various Muslim, Christian, Hindu, and even Buddhist groups. As we saw in chapter 1, religious discourse is uniquely powerful, precisely because it involves an appeal to a transcendent, suprahuman, and eternal source of authority. As such, it can inspire acts of both great goodness and great evil. It can help lead movements of social justice (the civil rights movement, Gandhi's nonviolent resistance to British colonial rule, Mother Teresa's campaign to help the poor, etc.), but it can also be used to legitimate acts of violence and terror (flying airplanes into skyscrapers, justifying preemptive wars, covering up cases of pedophilia, etc.). So by taking controversial groups such as Peoples Temple seriously as "religions" rather than branding them as "cults," we are not thereby glossing over their negative, darker, or destructive aspects. Rather, we are simply saying: they are as capable of exploiting their claims to religious authority as adherents of "mainstream" religions.

Because Peoples Temple is such a complex and painful example of a religious movement that ended in tragedy, it highlights this point in a particularly acute way. It therefore deserves to be studied, examined, reflected upon, and taken very seriously, not simply reduced to a Jim Jones T-shirt or dismissed as just another weird anecdote from the 1970s. In the words of an anonymous letter, left by a member of Peoples Temple and found after the deaths: "To whomever finds this note. Collect all the tapes, all the writing, all the history. The story of this movement, this action, must be examined over and over. We did not want this kind of ending. We wanted to live, to shine, to bring light to a world that is dying for a little bit of love."[40]

QUESTIONS FOR DISCUSSION AND DEBATE

1. Where should we begin if we're trying to make sense of a movement as complex and tragic as Peoples Temple? Should we begin with a psychological profile of Jones himself? With an analysis of racial issues in America of the 1950s and '60s? With a sociological study of the members themselves?

2. Peoples Temple obviously had roots in mainstream Christianity, particularly in Pentecostalism and Methodism, yet it quickly went in a more radical and socialist direction, which included criticisms of the Bible and of the traditional Christian idea of God. Should it still be considered a form of "Christianity," or was it something else? Or could one argue that Jones was reasserting the radical socialist message inherent in the Gospels themselves?

3. Do you accept the argument of scholars such as Chidester that Peoples Temple should be viewed as a genuine religious movement that engaged in a form of "religious suicide" comparable to other examples in the history of world religions? Is it possible that these scholars might be bending too far over backward to portray Peoples Temple in a positive light—and thus perhaps are minimizing the fact that this was an extremely controlling and manipulative movement that ended in terrible tragedy?

4. What do you think of the arguments of former members such as Tim Carter, who believe that this was primarily an act of *murder*, not suicide? Do you find his argument persuasive? Also, what difference does it make—for survivors, family members, and students of religion—whether we call this a murder or a suicide?

SUGGESTED CLASSROOM ACTIVITY

Analyze the final audio recording of Jim Jones and Peoples Temple on November 18, 1978. How is Jones himself describing the decision to end this religious experiment by mass murder-suicide? What sorts of religious imagery is he using, what sorts of comparisons to other cultures and examples—and why? How are the other members of the community reacting? Does it seem as though there is general consensus, or confusion, or debate among the members? Finally, what should we call a document like this? A religious message? A suicide note? The ravings of a mentally disturbed individual?

SUGGESTED VIDEO

"Jonestown: The Life and Death of Peoples Temple." *PBS Frontline,* 2006.

SUGGESTIONS FOR FURTHER READING

Alternative Considerations of Jonestown and Peoples Temple. Department of Religious Studies, San Diego State University, 2014. http://jonestown.sdsu.edu/.

Chidester, David. *Salvation and Suicide: An Interpretation of Jim Jones, the Peoples Temple and Jonestown.* Bloomington: Indiana University Press, 1988.

Hall, John R. *Gone from the Promised Land: Jonestown in American Cultural History.* New Brunswick, NJ: Transaction, 1987.

Moore, Rebecca. *Understanding Jonestown and Peoples Temple.* Westport, CT: Praeger, 2009.

Moore, Rebecca, and Fielding McGehee III, eds. *New Religious Movements, Mass Suicide and Peoples Temple: Scholarly Perspectives on a Tragedy.* Lewiston, NY: E. Mellen Press, 1989.

Moore, Rebecca, Anthony B. Pinn, and Mary R. Sawyer, eds. *Peoples Temple and Black Religion in America.* Bloomington: University of Indiana Press, 2004.

Reiterman, Tim. *Raven: The Untold Story of Rev. Jim Jones and His People.* New York: Penguin, 2008.

Smith, Jonathan Z. "The Devil in Mr. Jones." In *Imagining Religion: From Babylon to Jonestown*. Chicago: University of Chicago Press, 1988.

Thielmann, Bonnie. *The Broken God*. Elgin, IL: David C. Cook, 1979.

Wessinger, Catherine. *How the Millennium Comes Violently: From Jonestown to Heaven's Gate*. New York: Seven Bridges Press, 2000.

NOTES TO CHAPTER 12

1. Tim Carter, "Murder or Suicide? What I Saw," in *Alternative Considerations of Jonestown and Peoples Temple*, Department of Religious Studies, San Diego State University, 2006, http://jonestown.sdsu.edu/?page_id=31976.
2. Lance Morrow, "The Lure of Doomsday," *Time*, December 4, 1978, 6.
3. David Chidester, *Salvation and Suicide: An Interpretation of Jim Jones, the Peoples Temple and Jonestown* (Bloomington: Indiana University Press, 1988), 2.
4. Rebecca Moore, *Understanding Jonestown and Peoples Temple* (Westport, CT: Praeger, 2009), 9–10.
5. Jim Jones quoted in Chidester, *Salvation and Suicide*, 3.
6. "Jonestown: The Life and Death of Peoples Temple," *PBS Frontline*, 2006. See also Moore, *Understanding Jonestown*, 15.
7. Moore, *Understanding Jonestown*, 16.
8. Jim Jones, 1973 Sermon, transcript Q 958, in *Alternative Considerations*, 2014, http://jonestown.sdsu.edu/?page_id=60665.
9. Jim Jones quoted in Rebecca Moore, *Sympathetic History: The Moore Family Involvement in Peoples Temple* (Lewiston, NY: E. Mellen Press, 1985), 155.
10. Moore, *Understanding Jonestown*, 20.
11. Jim Jones, "San Francisco Sermon," 1973, transcript Q1053, in *Alternative Considerations*, http://jonestown.sdsu.edu/?page_id=27318.
12. Ibid.; see also Chidester, *Salvation and Suicide*, 5.
13. Jim Jones, Sermon of 1973, in *Alternative Considerations*, 2014, http://jonestown.sdsu.edu/?page_id=60680.
14. Moore, *Understanding Jonestown*, 34; see Catherine Wessinger, *How the Millennium Comes Violently: From Jonestown to Heaven's Gate* (New York: Seven Bridges Press, 2000), 47.
15. Wessinger, *How the Millennium Comes Violently*, 35.
16. Moore, *Understanding Jonestown*, 35; see also Laurie Efrein Kahalas, *Snake Dance: Unraveling the Mysteries of Jonestown* (New York: Red Robin Press, 1998).
17. Wessinger, *How the Millennium Comes Violently*, 40.
18. Deborah Layton, *Seductive Poison: A Jonestown Survivor's Story of Life and Death in the Peoples Temple* (New York: Anchor Books, 1999), 111–16. See also Tim Carter, interview on *The American Experience*, Oregon Public Broadcasting, April 9, 2007.
19. Chidester, *Salvation and Suicide*, 149.
20. Rebecca Moore, *The Jonestown Letters: Correspondence of the Moore Family, 1970–1985* (Lewiston, NY: E. Mellen Press, 1986), 286.
21. Wessinger, *How the Millennium Comes Violently*, 42; Moore, *Understanding Jonestown*, 153.
22. Moore, *Understanding Jonestown*, 75.
23. Bonnie Thielmann, *The Broken God* (Elgin, IL: David C. Cook, 1979), 85.

24. Moore, *Understanding Jonestown*, 79.
25. Ibid.
26. Ibid., 75.
27. Jim Jones, transcript from November 18, 1978, in Jonathan Z. Smith's *Imagining Religion: From Babylon to Jonestown* (Chicago: University of Chicago Press, 1988), 127–34.
28. Ibid., 132.
29. "Jonestown: The Life and Death of Peoples Temple."
30. David G. Bromley and Anson D. Shupe Jr., *Strange Gods: The Great American Cult Scare* (Boston: Beacon Press, 1981); David G. Bromley and J. Gordon Melton, eds., *Cults and Religious Violence* (Cambridge: Cambridge University Press, 2002).
31. "Nightmare in Jonestown: A Religious Colony in Guyana Turns into a Cult of Death," *Time*, December 4, 1978, 4.
32. "Messiah from the Midwest," *Time*, December 4, 1978, 5.
33. Morrow, "Lure of Doomsday," 6.
34. Moore, *Understanding Jonestown*, 5.
35. Ibid., 4.
36. John Hall, *Gone from the Promised Land: Jonestown in American Cultural History* (New Brunswick, NJ: Transaction, 1987).
37. Chidester, *Salvation and Suicide*, 137–38.
38. "Jonestown: The Life and Death of Peoples Temple." See Carter, "Murder or Suicide."
39. Tim Carter, interview by the author, August 2014.
40. "Jonestown: The Life and Death of Peoples Temple."

THIRTEEN

The Branch Davidians

Millenarian Movements, Religious Freedom, and Privacy

While the case of Peoples Temple raises complex questions about how to label and make sense of new religious movements, other groups raise even more difficult questions about how law enforcement and government agencies should deal with new religions that might be violent or self-destructive. Just fifteen years after the tragedy at Jonestown, another millenarian religious movement, the Branch Davidians, became the focus not simply of media scrutiny but of a large armed raid by the Bureau of Alcohol Tobacco and Firearms (ATF) near Waco, Texas, in 1993. Acting on suspicions of weapons violations, the ATF obtained a warrant and sent heavily armed agents into the Branch Davidian compound, which in turn triggered an intense gun battle. After the ATF's failed raid, the FBI became involved and launched a fifty-one-day siege of the community, which ended with a tear gas attack and a massive fire on April 19, 1993. Although the cause of the fire remains a matter of some dispute, the flames engulfed the entire compound, killing seventy-six men, women, and children.

The tragedy at Waco has left us with a number of profound and troubling questions—not least of which is how scholars, journalists, and law enforcement should handle complex movements such as the Branch Davidians in ways that will not end in violence. On the one hand, many critics would argue that there were indeed aspects of the Branch Davidian community that were deeply problematic and warranted investigation by law enforcement. The group possessed large numbers of guns and was suspected of illegally converting semiautomatic weapons to fully automatic weapons. When combined with millenarian beliefs in a coming end of the world, it is perhaps not surprising that this alarmed many law enforcement officers. At the same time, there were allegations that the group's leader, David Koresh, had physically and sexually abused minors within the community.

On the other hand, however, the Branch Davidians argued throughout the standoff that their civil liberties had been grossly violated by law enforcement and that this religious community had been subjected to aggressive and unwarranted invasion. Many scholars have also argued that the community was unfairly targeted as a "cult" and that law enforcement was misled in its actions by ill-informed and biased anticult groups. If the ATF and FBI had listened to serious scholars of religions rather than to anticult activists, they might have had a better understanding of the Branch Davidians' millenarian religious beliefs and so avoided a violent showdown with the group.[1]

These questions of religious freedom, law enforcement, security, and surveillance have become all the more complicated in the wake of the 9/11 terrorist attacks, amid new fears of religiously motivated violence and ever more invasive forms of government surveillance. In the twenty-first century, we face not just the possibility of religious extremism and violence but also new concerns about the erosion of privacy and liberties in the name of national security. We now know that the FBI and various local police forces have been secretly monitoring mosques and other religious organizations; and with the series of revelations about the National Security Agency's secret wiretapping program in 2005 and 2013, we also know that the government has tremendous powers of surveillance over the phone and e-mail communications of ordinary citizens. All of this raises questions about how to balance the need for safety and security with the need to protect basic rights to privacy and freedom of expression, particularly for minority religious groups. Although the case of the Branch Davidians and the disaster at Waco preceded the 9/11 attacks by almost a decade, they foreshadowed many of these questions, which have only become more complex in a new age of terrorism and surveillance.

FROM THE MILLERITES TO THE BRANCH DAVIDIANS

The Branch Davidians were an offshoot of an offshoot of a Christian millenarian movement whose roots go back to the first half of the nineteenth century. As we saw in chapter 12, Christian history is full of millenarian groups who hold an expectation of the imminent Second Coming of Christ, and one of the largest ever to emerge in the United States was the Millerite movement. In 1833, the group's founder, William Miller, claimed that he had calculated the date of Jesus's second coming, which he believed would occur sometime between March 21, 1843, and March 21, 1844. When Jesus failed to arrive during that period, he recalculated the date to be April 18, 1844, and then again October 22, 1844. Although Miller briefly gathered a huge number of expectant followers looking forward to the appearance of Jesus, the movement quickly fell apart by the end of 1844, leading to what became known as the Great Disappointment. Out of the collapse of the Millerites, however, a new and more successful movement emerged called the Seventh-day Adventists, founded by Ellen G. White in 1863. While the Seventh-day Adventists also look forward to the second coming of Jesus, they refrain from assigning a particular date to the event and so have become a prosperous and increasingly "mainstream" church today, with over eighteen million members worldwide.

In 1929, another group splintered off from the Seventh-day Adventists called the Davidian Seventh-Day Adventists, led by a Bulgarian immigrant named Victor Houteff. According to Houteff's interpretation of the millennium, the mission of his new church was to gather 144,000 "servants of God" mentioned in the book of Revelation in order to prepare for the coming of Christ. While the main body of Seventh-day Adventists taught that the millennium would be a spiritual phenomenon in which they would spend eternity in heaven with Christ, Houteff understood the millennium to be a literal period of divine rule on earth, and specifically in the land of Israel. The name Davidian taken by his church referred to the ideal of restoring a messianic kingdom in Palestine like that of King David. In 1935, Houteff established the headquarters of the Davidians at the Mount Carmel center near Waco, Texas.

Finally, in the 1960s, yet another group splintered off from the Davidian Adventists, led by a couple from Texas named Ben and Lois Roden. Assuming control of the Mount Carmel property, the Rodens founded their own church called the Branch Davidians, referring to Jesus's saying that "I am the vine and you are the branches" (John 15:1–3). Like their predecessors, the Rodens believed in the imminent coming of Jesus and urged their followers to move to Israel to prepare for the final days.

In 1981, Vernon Howell (later David Koresh) joined the Branch Davidians at Mount Carmel (figure 13.1). As a young man, Howell had two great passions—the Bible (particularly the book of Revelation) and the guitar (in fact, he recorded some of his own songs, which focused heavily on biblical prophecy and millenarian ideas). Although he had been baptized in the Seventh-day Adventist Church just two years before, Howell was attracted by the prophetic teachings of the Mount Carmel Branch Davidians and became very close to Lois Roden. However, Howell's presence soon aroused the jealousy of the Rodens' son, George Roden, who saw himself as the rightful heir to Branch Davidian leadership and Howell as a rival. Roden also accused Howell of having sex with his mother—a charge Howell did not deny.[2]

The rivalry between Howell and George Roden culminated in one of the strangest incidents in the history of the movement. In November 1987, Roden dug up the body of Anna Hughes, a Davidian who had died at the age of eighty-four and had been buried on the Mount Carmel property for twenty years. Placing the casket in the chapel, Roden challenged Koresh to a contest to see who could raise the corpse from the dead. Instead of taking the challenge, Howell went to the police to file charges of corpse abuse, but the authorities refused to investigate the claim without proof. When Howell and seven armed companions tried to break into the Branch Davidian chapel to obtain photographic evidence of the corpse, a gunfight erupted and left Roden wounded. Howell was tried for attempted murder but was released after the jury failed to reach a verdict. Meanwhile, Roden was arrested several months later for attempted murder in an unrelated incident, and Howell and his followers moved into the Mount Carmel community. After assuming leadership of the community, Howell legally changed his name to David Koresh, taken from the names King David and Koresh, the Hebrew version of the Persian King Cyrus, who was also given the title of "messiah" or "anointed one."

Like other charismatic leaders discussed in this book—such as Jim Jones and Joseph Smith—Koresh had a complicated sexual life that helped reinforce his negative image as a

FIGURE 13.1 David Koresh. Photo used by permission from Sipa USA.

deviant and dangerous figure. While legally married to one wife, Rachel, he began to take multiple additional wives, many of them quite young. In 1986, he announced his marriage to Karen Doyle (age fourteen) and Michelle Jones (age twelve), and in 1987, he was married to Robyn Bunds (age seventeen), Nicole Gent (age sixteen), and Dana Okimoto (age twenty). Later in 1989, Koresh revealed a divine message called the "New Light" revelation, according to which all men in the community except himself were to remain celibate, while all women were to be his own wives. His children—both present and future—would in turn find an exalted status in the Kingdom of God, which would soon be established in Israel. According to Texas state law, Koresh clearly had sexual relations with minors and could therefore have been prosecuted with statutory rape; according to the Davidians' interpretation, however, Koresh was fulfilling the biblical role of the Lamb of God, offering his female followers the opportunity to be "sown with the light" and bear a child for Christ. As one member, Alisa Shaw, explained, "A central part of the message [of Revelation] is the marriage of the Lamb. That's the way to salvation. There are a few [women] who are worthy to be sown with the seed of God and produce children. It's considered an honor to have a baby for Christ. Not every woman is worthy of Koresh's loins."[3]

THE SEVEN SEALS AND THE MILLENNIUM: KORESH'S INTERPRETATION OF REVELATION

Much of Koresh's teachings centered on his unique interpretation of the book of Revelation and the events leading up to the Second Coming and the Last Judgment. In his words, "The servant of God will find as we continue in our searching of the scriptures that every book of the Bible meets and ends in the book of Revelation."[4] Following in the tradition of the Millerites and the Davidian Adventists, Koresh believed not only that the last days described in Revelation were coming soon but that they were intertwined with and reflected in contemporary world events. At the heart of this millennial worldview was his understanding of the "seven seals" described in the first eight chapters of Revelation. In the biblical text, St. John receives a vision in which he is taken before the throne of God; there he sees Christ, who holds a great scroll bound with seven seals. As each of the seven seals is broken open, a series of catastrophic events unfolds that heralds the dissolution of the present world and the creation of a new heaven and a new earth. Thus, when the first four seals are broken, four horsemen ride forth, bringing war, famine, plague, and death to the earth. When the fifth seal is opened, the souls who have been slain because of their testimony to the Word of God cry out, and they are each given a white robe while they wait for the rest of God's servants to be killed. When the sixth seal is broken, the entire cosmos begins to dissolve as a great earthquake shakes the ground, the sun turns black, the moon turns blood red, the stars fall from the sky, and the heavens are rolled up like a scroll. And when the seventh seal is broken, seven angels blow their trumpets, which unleash a rain of destruction as mountains are set ablaze and a third of all living creatures are slain.

Koresh understood his own role as a key figure in this narrative of the seven seals and the seven angels. Combining his interpretation of Revelation with the lineage of the Branch Davidian Church itself, Koresh saw himself as the final link in a line of prophetic figures going back to William Miller himself. Following the image of the seven angels who appear in the book of Revelation, Koresh saw Miller as fulfilling the roles of the first two angels; Ellen White, the founder of the Seventh-day Adventist Church, was the third angel; Victor Houteff was the fourth; Ben Roden and Lois Roden were the fifth and sixth; and Koresh was the seventh and final angel. As an anointed messiah, Koresh saw himself as a "suffering servant" who would help initiate Armageddon. There is some debate as to whether Koresh actually believed himself to *be* Jesus Christ or God; however, James Tabor and Eugene Gallagher make a persuasive case that Koresh never claimed to be *the* Christ but rather to be an anointed one (*christos,* like Cyrus and others) and that he understood himself to be the Lamb in Revelation who opens the scroll bearing the seven seals.[5]

Initially, Koresh believed that the role of the Branch Davidian community would be to move to Palestine and then fight on the side of Israel in an apocalyptic battle against the United Nations. However, his reading of history shifted after the 1991 Gulf War, and he concluded that this apocalyptic confrontation might in fact begin at home in Texas itself. The US federal government, in Koresh's view, represented an evil system identified in Revelation as "Babylon."[6] Preparing for a possible apocalyptic showdown in Texas, the Branch Davidians stockpiled food, weapons, and ammunition, along with a tank of propane in case of the loss of electricity.[7] Thus, when the ATF launched their raid on Mount Carmel on February 28, this seemed to Koresh to provide the ultimate fulfillment of his own reading of biblical prophecy, with the Branch Davidian community playing the role of those holy servants who are slain for the testimony to the Word of God. Ironically, the federal agents would fall right into Koresh's own prophetic narrative, playing the role of Babylon. Indeed, shortly after the raid began, Koresh announced that "We are now in the Fifth Seal," suggesting that humankind had entered that moment in the unfolding of the final days when God's loyal servants would be slain and the catastrophic events mentioned in the opening of the sixth seal would soon begin.[8]

THE ATF RAID AND THE FIFTY-ONE-DAY SIEGE

Like Peoples Temple, the Branch Davidians saw themselves as a persecuted religious community that was the target of repeated attacks from the government, the media, and ex-members. In 1989, a member named Marc Breault left the community because of his concerns about Koresh's multiple wives and sexual relations with minors. After moving to Australia, Breault dedicated himself to exposing Koresh as a false prophet and warning media and law enforcement about the Davidians' dangerous beliefs. He also worked with the Australian television program *A Current Affair* to make a documentary on the group and expose Koresh as a "cruel, maniacal, child-molesting, pistol-packing religious zealot who brainwashed his devotees."[9] In 1990, Breault began to warn other former members and Texas law enforcement agents that Koresh was planning to commit child sacrifice; later in 1992, he alleged that the Davidians were planning a mass suicide that would become "another Jonestown."

In the spring of 1992, the ATF began to investigate the Branch Davidians on the suspicion of possessing and trafficking illegal weapons. The Branch Davidians did in fact run a legal arms business called the Mag Bag, which purchased and sold guns and gun parts. Together with Paul Fatta and Mike Schroeder, Koresh attended large gun shows throughout Texas and sold weapons to support the community. However, the ATF became concerned that the group was stockpiling illegal arms as well. The bureau was first alerted when a UPS driver noticed that a torn package he was delivering to the ranch contained firearms and grenade casings. In July 1992, ATF agents visited the Davidians' gun dealer and then decided to set up surveillance of the compound from a house across the street for several months prior to the siege. In addition, the ATF sent in an undercover agent named Robert Rodriguez, who claimed to be interested in studying scripture with Koresh in order to gather intelligence on the community.

The actual search warrant for the raid, however, was not justified by any proof that the community possessed illegal weapons; rather, it was based on a suspicion that they might have been converting (legally obtained) semiautomatic weapons to fully automatic weapons. It is worth noting that the "Probable Cause Affidavit" used to secure the warrant described the Branch Davidians as a dangerous "cult" and its leader as a "power-mad, manipulative leader" who abused and raped young girls.[10]

On February 27, 1993, just one day before the ATF raid, the *Waco Tribune-Herald* ran the first installment of a series on Koresh, entitled "The Sinful Messiah." The article painted a particularly unflattering portrait of Koresh, largely informed by ex-members such as Breault and anticult activists such as Rick Ross. Special attention was given to Koresh's sexual relations with multiple minors and to the Davidians' stockpile of heavy weaponry: "If you are a Branch Davidian, Christ lives on a threadbare piece of land 10 miles east of here called

Mount Carmel. He has dimples, claims a ninth-grade education, married his legal wife when she was 14, enjoys a beer now and then, plays a mean guitar, reportedly packs a 9mm Glock and keeps an arsenal of military assault rifles, and willingly admits that he is a sinner without equal."[11] This was the image of Koresh that largely informed both government agencies and the national media in their coverage of Waco over the next several months.

THE BOTCHED RAID AND THE SIEGE

The ATF raid began at roughly 9:45 on the morning of Sunday, February 28. Almost from start to finish, however, virtually everything went wrong. Although the raid was supposed to be a surprise, the Davidians were alerted when a reporter for KWTX-TV was tipped off and then got lost on the way to the ranch. The reporter asked directions from a US postal carrier who happened to be Koresh's brother-in-law. Inside the compound, Koresh informed undercover agent Rodriguez that he knew a raid was coming, and the agent hurriedly left, surprised that his cover had been blown. Although the ATF knew that the Davidians had now learned of the raid, they decided to go ahead with it anyway—even though their plan depended on the community being unarmed and taken by surprise. Arriving in two cattle trailers, seventy-six heavily armed ATF agents surrounded the compound. It is unclear who fired the first shots, but heavy gunfire quickly broke out on both sides. Just minutes after the shooting began, a Branch Davidian called 911, begging them to call off the raid; nonetheless, gunfire continued for the next two hours, leaving five ATF agents and five Davidians dead and Koresh himself wounded.

After the failure of the ATF assault, the FBI took command of the siege, which dragged on in a fifty-one-day standoff. During this period, twenty-one children and fourteen adults exited the compound, while Koresh and bureau agents went back and forth on how to negotiate a peaceful resolution. At the same time, the FBI also employed a variety of extreme and at times surreal measures in the attempt to drive the Davidians out. These included inducing sleep deprivation by playing all-night recordings of loud and dissonant sounds, such as jet planes, Tibetan chanting, and even rabbits being slaughtered. Koresh, meanwhile, was outspoken in his critique of the siege, which he saw as a gross violation of his own civil liberties and an appalling assault on a religious community that posed no threat to anyone. As he put it in a conversation with FBI negotiators,

> And a lot of the things the FBI, or these generals, are doing is just kind of way beyond the scope of reason. They are not only destroying private property, they are also removing evidence. And this doesn't seem like these are moves that should be made by a government who says to a people that we're going to be able to take this up in a court of law. . . .
> And we're also Americans, and I think that America has a patronage [heritage] . . . of individual citizens who have a breaking point. The government has gotten this strong to where it can come on to something that we have worked for *hard*. . . .

And if this is the way our government is showing the world that its tactics are to get someone to do as they wish when realistically our rights have been infringed upon right and left.[12]

In late March and early April, two religious studies scholars named J. Phillip Arnold and James D. Tabor attempted to intervene in the siege. After learning that the FBI was planning a gas assault on the compound, Professor Arnold developed a plan to try to persuade Koresh that there were other ways of interpreting Revelation that would not necessarily lead to an apocalyptic martyrdom of the Davidians at the hands of the US government. Arnold called the FBI and left a message explaining that he was going to present a radio broadcast that would attempt to engage Koresh in a serious discussion of the Bible, and he urged the FBI not to undertake a violent attack on the community. Thus, on April 1, Arnold and Tabor held a radio discussion of the Bible on *The Ron Engelman Show,* offering an alternative interpretation of Revelation. In their reading, the text could be taken to mean that Koresh was not intended to die at that time but rather needed a longer period during which to spread his message of God's plan for salvation to the world. An audiotape of the discussion was taken into the Mount Carmel compound three days later, and attorneys told the FBI that the Branch Davidians would come out after Passover. On April 14, Koresh sent a letter explaining that he had been told by God to write down his interpretation of the seven seals. Once his completed manuscript was in the possession of his attorney and sent to Professors Tabor and Arnold, he claimed, he would come out peacefully. In fact, Koresh did complete a portion of the manuscript before the raid—his commentary on the opening of the first seal in Revelation—and there are indications within it that he may have been planning to lead his followers out peacefully: "Should we not eagerly ourselves be ready to accept this truth and come out of our closet and be revealed to the world as those who love Christ in truth and righteousness?" he wrote, which may have indicated that he was ready to lead the Davidians out of Mount Carmel.[13]

Apparently, this information was not passed on to Attorney General Janet Reno, who instead approved a plan to gas the Branch Davidian compound. Even though Koresh had requested a battery-operated word processor to complete his manuscript and announced that he had finished his interpretation of the first seal on April 16, the FBI's plans to engage in an aggressive assault moved forward. Finally, early on the morning of April 19, the FBI sent in tanks and used grenade launchers to hurl over four hundred rounds of CS gas into the buildings. Shortly after 12:00 p.m., after tanks had begun moving into the compound and knocking down walls, a fire broke out and quickly engulfed the entire complex, killing seventy-six of the remaining Davidians (figure 13.2).

The exact cause of the fire remains a matter of intense dispute. While the FBI claims that it was an act of suicide and a deliberate fire set by the Branch Davidians, others argue that it was more likely sparked by the CS gas grenades or by the tanks knocking over the kerosene lanterns the community was using after its power was cut off. Former US senator John C. Danforth was appointed special counsel to investigate the incident and issued a "Final Report" on November 8, 2000. Danforth's report concluded that the FBI assault did not

FIGURE 13.2 Mount Carmel ranch in flames. Federal Bureau of Investigation.

cause the fire and that all of the physical evidence and testimony pointed instead to the Branch Davidians setting the fire themselves. "The responsibility for the tragedy," Danforth declared, "rests with certain of the Branch Davidians and their leader."[14] However, even after the report, many critics continue to see the Waco tragedy as one of the worst law enforcement disasters in US history.[15] As such, it mirrors many of the debates surrounding the Peoples Temple murder-suicides at Jonestown. Those who want to read the fire as deliberately set tend to see the tragedy as "another Jonestown"—that is, another example of a violent "cult" committing mass suicide at the hands of a charismatic but dangerous leader. Those who want to read the fire as a result of the FBI's own aggressive assault, conversely, tend to see the tragedy as the victimization of a minority religious community on account of misunderstanding, prejudice, and unnecessary government persecution.

The repercussions of the Waco tragedy were felt for years to come and would also help inspire new forms of violence. During the siege, many defenders of the Branch Davidians arrived to show their support and voice their outrage at the federal government. Among them was Timothy McVeigh, a Gulf War veteran who had become increasingly disillusioned with the US government and suspicious of the growing power of federal agencies at the expense of the rights of ordinary citizens. While distributing progun materials and bumper stickers at the scene, McVeigh was interviewed by a student reporter. Like other defenders of gun rights, McVeigh warned that the Waco siege was only the latest example of a federal government that had become too powerful and was now squashing the freedoms of ordinary Americans: "The government is afraid of the guns people have because they have to have control of the people at all times. Once you take away the guns, you can do anything to the people. . . . I believe we are slowly turning into a socialist government. The government is continually growing bigger and more powerful, and the people need to prepare to defend themselves against government control."[16]

McVeigh became increasingly radicalized after the Waco siege and began distributing literature about the event, such as "Waco Shootout Evokes Memory of Warsaw '43" and

"U.S. Government Initiates Open Warfare against American People." Later, he would also compose a letter addressed to the ATF, whom he denounced as "fascist" tyrants, warning that "all you tyrannical mother fuckers will swing in the wind one day for your treasonous actions against the Constitution of the United States."[17]

Exactly two years after the fire at Mount Carmel, McVeigh launched his own assault on the federal government. Together with coconspirator Terry Nichols, McVeigh constructed a massive homemade bomb consisting of five thousand pounds of ammonium nitrate and nitromethane, loaded into the back of a Ryder truck. On the morning of April 19, 1995, McVeigh drove the truck to the front of the Alfred P. Murrah Federal Building in Oklahoma City and lit a two-minute fuse. The resulting explosion destroyed the entire north half of the building and killed 168 people, including nineteen children, while wounding another 450. This was the largest act of terrorism on US soil prior to the attacks of September 11, 2001.

KEY ISSUES AND DEBATES: NEW RELIGIONS, SURVEILLANCE, AND SECURITY BEFORE AND AFTER 9/11

One of the most complex and difficult issues raised by the Branch Davidian tragedy is the delicate balance between religious freedom and public safety. How do we simultaneously respect the rights to privacy and freedom of religious expression in these communities while at the same time addressing real concerns about potential abuse, violence, and illegal activities? In the case of the Branch Davidians, were law enforcement agents justified in their handling of the allegations of sexual abuse and weapons violations? Or did they overstep their bounds and violate the rights of this religious community? These were already difficult enough questions to grapple with back in 1993, but they have only become more contested in the post-9/11 world, amid new concerns about religiously motivated violence and ever more aggressive forms of surveillance wielded by federal and local governments.

At least in the field of religious studies, most scholars agree that the Waco siege is a particularly acute example of how *not* to handle a situation like this. As Catherine Wessinger forcefully argues, the ATF and FBI completely failed to understand the Davidians' millenarian religious views and so played directly into Koresh's own prophetic narrative that his community would die as martyrs at the hands of the Babylon government: "The Branch Davidian tragedy illustrates how law enforcement agents *should not* deal with armed catastrophic millennial groups. To avoid violence, law enforcement agents have to take seriously the group's religious views and avoid acting in ways that make them appear to be agents of Satan. . . . This was not done with the Branch Davidians, to a great extent because of the advice being given to law enforcement agents by anticult activists."[18] As James Tabor and Eugene Gallagher argue, the case of the Branch Davidians thus highlights in a particularly acute way the Free Exercise Clause of the First Amendment itself; and it suggests that law enforcement in this case acted in ways that fundamentally violate the Constitution: "If the purpose of the First Amendment is to protect religion from the state, rather than the state from religion, there is no constitutional basis for enlisting the power of the state in the campaign against so-called cults. . . . A wholesale government crusade against 'destructive cults,' such as that championed after Waco, is illegitimate and unconstitutional."[19]

On the other hand, however, there are cases of dangerous new religious movements where one could argue that law enforcement was not aggressive *enough* in monitoring and intervening in their activities. Perhaps the best example is the Aum Shinrikyo movement in Japan, which spread sarin gas in Tokyo subways in 1995, killing thirteen people and severely injuring fifty others. In that case, many would argue that the group was able to manufacture and deploy chemical weapons in part because of the Japanese government's more hands-off policy in dealing with religious movements after World War II: "Aum Shinrikyo had free reign . . . to develop weapons of mass destruction due to lack of scrutiny by law enforcement agents. In reaction to government abuses prior to and during World War II, Japanese law enforcement agents did not typically investigate religious organizations or conduct surveillance gathering by undercover work or wiretapping."[20] In this sense, the study of new religions must, in a way, steer "between Scylla and Charybdis"—between the danger of supporting government intervention at the expense of religious freedom and the danger of supporting religious freedom at the expense of security and public safety.

If this question of religious freedom versus government surveillance was already complicated after Waco, it has become far more so in the wake of the 9/11 terrorist attacks (and other subsequent attacks, such as the 2004 bombings in Madrid, the 2005 bombings in London, and the 2013 bombing in Boston). In the United States, the federal government has introduced aggressive new policies and methods of surveillance, such as the USA PATRIOT Act and the NSA's secret wiretapping program. Thus in 2002 changes were made to the Justice Department's guidelines in order to permit FBI surveillance of religious organizations. While this surveillance was initially directed primarily at Muslim organizations, it has opened the door to surveillance of many other religious groups: the FBI has also secretly monitored Quakers, Catholic peace activists, and various others who seemingly had nothing to do with terrorist activities.[21] In 2005 we learned that the NSA has been monitoring thousands—perhaps millions—of communications by US citizens, all without a warrant as required by the Foreign Intelligence Surveillance Act. And still more recently, because of the leaked information from former NSA contractor Edward Snowden in 2013, we learned that the NSA now has astonishing new powers to keep track of virtually all communications entering, leaving, or going through the country—including phone calls, text messages, e-mails, Google searches, and online activity. Indeed, Snowden's leaked documents revealed that the NSA was not only monitoring the communications of ordinary citizens but even tapping the phones of other national leaders such as German chancellor Angela Merkel. In Snowden's opinion, the NSA's staggering reach poses nothing short of "an existential threat to democracy."[22]

All of this has raised profound debates about freedom, privacy, security, and surveillance, with powerful voices on all sides of the issues. Some legal scholars have argued that an increase in security is necessary during times of national emergency, such as terrorist attacks or other violence, and that this will inevitably require some reduction in civil liberties. As Eric Posner and Adrian Vermeule suggest, this is simply the price we pay in the delicate balance between safety and freedom, and governments must be able to adjust the balance as conditions require at different moments: "There is a straightforward tradeoff between liberty and security," they write. "At the security-liberty frontier, any increase in security requires a decrease in liberty; a rational and well-functioning government will already be positioned on this frontier when the emergency strikes and will adjust its policies as the shape of the frontier changes over time. . . . If increases in security are worth more than the corresponding losses in liberty, government will increase security."[23]

Other legal scholars, however, have argued that the new measures put in place after 9/11 pose serious constitutional problems. As Georgetown law professor David Cole argues, the USA PATRIOT Act contains a number of new provisions that fundamentally undermine civil liberties and should make any citizen deeply uncomfortable. Among other things, the PATRIOT Act gives the government unprecedented power to detain noncitizens indefinitely; it allows the FBI to search citizens' homes or offices and to conduct surveillance of phone and Internet use without proving probable cause; it grants authorities the power to require bookstores and libraries to list the names of all books bought or borrowed; and it gives government agencies the authority to conduct so-called "Sneak and Peek" searches—that is, to search our homes or offices without even letting us know they've been there. As Cole argues, this represents a dangerous overreaction and overreach on the part of government: "In several critical areas, Congress gave the executive branch broad new powers that went far beyond the fight against terrorism and infringed on fundamental liberties. . . . The government overreacted in harmful ways, intruding on the liberties of thousands of people who had no terrorist ties whatsoever. It failed to show that many of the new powers it asserted were in fact necessary to fight terrorism."[24]

In Cole's opinion the NSA wiretapping program was even more problematic. The agency's massive data collection program, he suggests, was developed in secret and was never subjected to public scrutiny or judicial testing; as such, it "almost certainly violates the Fourth Amendment" (which prohibits unreasonable searches and seizures). Cole goes on to quote US District Judge Richard Leon, an appointee of George W. Bush, who voiced a scathing critique of the NSA program: "I cannot imagine a more 'indiscriminate' and 'arbitrary invasion' than this systematic and high-tech collection and retention of personal data on virtually every single citizen for purposes of querying and analyzing it without prior judicial approval. . . . I have little doubt that the author of our Constitution, James Madison, who cautioned us to beware 'the abridgement of freedom of the people by gradual and silent encroachments by those in power,' would be aghast."[25] Others have suggested that the NSA's new powers of surveillance rival or exceed anything that George Orwell imagined in his dystopian novel *1984*. According to James Bamford—the leading expert on the history and workings of the NSA—the new wiretapping and data-mining technologies wielded by the NSA are tools that "Orwell's Thought Police would have found useful."[26]

These debates are unlikely to be resolved any time soon, as new forms of religious violence proliferate and as ever more sophisticated forms of government surveillance continue to be developed on an almost daily basis. Defenders of the government's programs will probably argue that these are necessary precisely for monitoring potentially dangerous religious groups before they become violent, in order to avoid "another Waco." Critics, however, will argue that these aggressive new measures only create new problems by further undermining civil liberties and creating even more paranoia about an invasive and authoritarian federal government. In other words, they risk breeding even more fears of a government "Babylon" ready to assault religious minorities in the name of safety and security. Negotiating these difficult questions will surely be one of the greatest challenges of the twenty-first century.

QUESTIONS FOR DISCUSSION AND DEBATE

1. Scholars such as Wessinger, Tabor, and Gallagher argue that disasters such as Waco could be avoided if law enforcement paid more attention to what serious scholars of religion have to say and less attention to journalists and anticult activists. Do you agree? Or do you think this is giving too much credit to the scholarly community? After all, scholars of religion are not trained in law enforcement or the handling of potentially dangerous situations—any more than law enforcement agents are trained in the study of religion. Are there ways in which the two communities can work productively together? If so, how?

2. Many critics argue that the ATF overreacted in its response to the Branch Davidians' possession of weapons. After all, they made a living as gun traders, and many people in Texas have large numbers of guns. However, the charges of sexual abuse of minors seem more difficult to dismiss. Would sexual abuse have provided a justification for the raid even if weapons violations did not? Or was there no justification for such a raid at all?

3. If you agree with scholars such as Tabor, Gallagher, and Wessinger that law enforcement handled the case of the Branch Davidians very badly, then how do you think they *should* have handled it? What could have been done differently that might have avoided such a protracted standoff and catastrophic outcome?

4. Was law enforcement justified in setting up surveillance across the road from Mount Carmel or in sending in an undercover agent, Robert Rodriguez, to pretend to be interested in Bible study with Koresh? Should law enforcement be able to infiltrate and surveil any religious community at any time? Or are there limits? And should religious communities be given any special exemptions or protections from government surveillance, or should they be treated in the same way as any nonreligious organization?

SUGGESTED CLASSROOM ACTIVITY

Imagine that you are a group of religious studies scholars whose task is to advise law enforcement agencies about how to handle a group such as the Branch Davidians today, in a post-9/11 context. How would you explain this religious group's belief system and millenarian ideas to agencies such as the ATF and FBI, and what would you recommend that they do? What sort of intervention—if any—would be appropriate? Would undercover surveillance of the sort carried out by the ATF be warranted? Would an armed raid be necessary? Or would there be other ways of addressing the questions about child abuse and illegal weapons? Do you think the situation should be handled differently today, given the new fears of terrorism and new mechanisms of surveillance possessed by the government, than it was back in 1993?

SUGGESTED VIDEO

"Waco: The Inside Story." *Frontline*, PBS, 1995.

SUGGESTIONS FOR FURTHER READING

Barkun, Michael. "Religion and Secrecy after September 11." *Journal of the American Academy of Religion* 74, no. 2 (2006): 275–301.

Cole, David, and James X. Dempsey. *Terrorism and the Constitution: Sacrificing Civil Liberties in the Name of National Security.* New York: New Press, 2002.

Juergensmeyer, Mark. *Terror in the Mind of God: The Global Rise of Religious Violence.* Berkeley: University of California Press, 2000.

Moore, Carol. *The Davidian Massacre: Disturbing Questions about Waco Which Must Be Answered.* Franklin, TN: Legacy Communications, 1995.

Posner, Eric, and Adrian Vermeule. *Terror in the Balance: Security, Liberty and the Courts.* New York: Oxford University Press, 2007.

Reavis, Dick J. *The Ashes of Waco: An Investigation.* New York: Simon and Schuster, 1995.

Tabor, James D., and Eugene V. Gallagher. *Why Waco? Cults and the Battle for Religious Freedom in America.* Berkeley: University of California Press, 1995.

Wessinger, Catherine. *How the Millennium Comes Violently: From Jonestown to Heaven's Gate.* New York: Seven Bridges Press, 2000.

Wright, Stuart A., ed. *Armageddon in Waco: Critical Perspectives on the Branch Davidian Conflict.* Chicago: University of Chicago Press, 1995.

1. James D. Tabor and Eugene V. Gallagher, *Why Waco? Cults and the Battle for Religious Freedom in America* (Berkeley: University of California Press, 1995); Catherine Wessinger, *How the Millennium Comes Violently: From Jonestown to Heaven's Gate* (New York: Seven Bridges Press, 2000).

2. Tabor and Gallagher, *Why Waco?*, 41.

3. David G. Bromley and Edward D. Silver, "The Davidian Tradition: From Patronal Clan to Prophetic Movement," in *Armageddon in Waco: Critical Perspectives on the Branch Davidian Conflict*, ed. Stuart A. Wright (Chicago: University of Chicago Press, 1995), 59. See also Wessinger, *How the Millennium Comes Violently*, 83.

4. David Koresh, "The Seven Seals of the Book of Revelation," in Tabor and Gallagher, *Why Waco?*, 197.

5. Tabor and Gallagher, *Why Waco?*, 205, 50–51; Wessinger, *How the Millennium Comes Violently*, 88.

6. Tabor and Gallagher, *Why Waco?*, 4, 51.

7. Bromley and Silver, "Davidian Tradition," 61, 65–66.

8. Tabor and Gallagher, *Why Waco?*, 5; Wessinger, *How the Millennium Comes Violently*, 91.

9. Marc Breault and Martin King, *Inside the Cult: A Member's Chilling Exclusive Account of Madness and Depravity in David Koresh's Compound* (New York: Signet Books, 1993), 256–57; see Wessinger, *How the Millennium Comes Violently*, 97.

10. Wessinger, *How the Millennium Comes Violently*, 62.

11. Mark England and Darlene McCormick, "The Sinful Messiah," *Waco Tribune-Herald*, February 27, 1993.

12. Wessinger, *How the Millennium Comes Violently*, 106, 108.

13. Koresh, "Seven Seals," 203; see Tabor and Gallagher, *Why Waco?*, 205–11.

14. John Danforth, "Final Report to the Deputy Attorney General Concerning the 1993 Confrontation at the Mt. Carmel Complex, Waco, Texas," November 8, 2000, http://commons.wikimedia .org/wiki/File:Danforthreport-final.pdf.

15. Eric Lichtblau, "Report Clears Feds in Death of Davidians," *Los Angeles Times*, July 22, 2000, http://articles.latimes.com/2000/jul/22/news/mn-57442.

16. Brian Morton, "The Guns of Spring," *Baltimore City Paper*, April 15, 2009, http://www2.city paper.com/eat/story.asp?id=17888.

17. Kathryn S. Olmsted, *Real Enemies: Conspiracy Theories and American Democracy, World War I to 9/11* (New York: Oxford University Press, 2009), 197.

18. Wessinger, *How the Millennium Comes Violently*, 21.

19. Tabor and Gallagher, *Why Waco?*, 184.

20. Wessinger, *How the Millennium Comes Violently*, 150.

21. See Michael Barkun, "Religion and Secrecy after September 11," *Journal of the American Academy of Religion* 74, no. 2 (2006): 275–301; Jeff Stein, "FBI Misled Justice Department about Spying on Peace Group," *Washington Post*, September 20, 2010, http://voices.washingtonpost.com /spy-talk/2010/09/fbi_cover-up_turns_laughable_s.html.

22. Matt Smith, "NSA Leaker Comes Forward, Warns of 'Existential Threat,'" CNN, June 9, 2013, www.cnn.com/2013/06/09/politics/nsa-leak-identity/index.html; "Angela Merkel's Call to Obama," *Guardian*, October 23, 2013, www.theguardian.com/world/2013/oct/23 /us-monitored-angela-merkel-german.

23. Eric Posner and Adrian Vermeule, *Terror in the Balance: Security, Liberty and the Courts* (New York: Oxford University Press, 2007), 12.

24. David Cole and James X. Dempsey, *Terrorism and the Constitution: Sacrificing Civil Liberties in the Name of National Security* (New York: New Press, 2002), 174.

25. David Cole, "The NSA on Trial," *New York Review of Books,* December 18, 2013, www.nybooks.com/blogs/nyrblog/2013/dec/18/nsa-spying-leon-ruling/.

26. James Bamford, "The New Thought Police," *Nova,* PBS, January 2009, www.pbs.org/wgbh/nova/military/nsa-police.html.

FOURTEEN

The Raëlians

UFOs and Human Cloning

On the morning of December 13, 1973, a French sports journalist and musician named Claude Vorilohn (b. 1946) was visiting a secluded area inside a volcano near Clermont-Ferrand, France. Although he was uncertain why he had been drawn to this particular spot, Vorilohn claims that he looked to the sky and saw a flashing light, which turned out to be an extraterrestrial spacecraft, roughly seven meters in diameter, shaped like a bell, and made of shiny material. A staircase was lowered from the craft, and a small man with a greenish complexion, long hair, and a beard descended to speak with Vorilohn (figure 14.1). The message that the extraterrestrial brought to Vorilohn became the foundation of the Raëlian movement and was first recorded in the book *Le livre qui dit la verité* (The book that tells the truth) in 1974.

All life on Earth, the being told him, had been created by extraterrestrial "designers" called the Elohim who used advanced cloning technology to generate all of our species, including human beings. Because of our ignorance, we mistakenly regarded the extraterrestrials as gods—the Elohim of the Hebrew Bible—and described them in a confused but partially accurate way in our various religious scriptures. Now, however, human beings were sufficiently advanced intellectually and technologically to begin to receive the full message from the Elohim. Once we had built an embassy to welcome them, the Elohim would return, bringing us the means to establish a peaceful utopian civilization and to achieve immortality through the technology of cloning. Changing his name to Raël (Messenger of the Elohim), Vorilohn founded a new movement dedicated to spreading the teachings of the designers and building the community and the embassy to welcome them to Earth. Today the movement is known as the International Raëlian Movement or Raëlism and claims to have

FIGURE 14.1 Raël with UFO. Photo courtesy of Raël.org.

roughly sixty-five thousand members worldwide, including a large presence in the United States.

Although the Raëlian movement is today one of the largest UFO-based religions in the world, it is by no means the first or the only one. UFO religious movements have proliferated throughout the United States, the United Kingdom, Europe, and other parts of the world since the 1940s and became hugely popular during the decades of the Cold War. Much of the inspiration for these movements began immediately after World War II, particularly after the reports that a UFO had crash-landed near the US military base in Roswell, New Mexico, in 1947. Although the military later claimed that the crashed object had been a weather balloon and not a UFO, this incident immediately generated intense interest in the possibility of visitors from other worlds and a host of conspiracy theories that the government knew about extraterrestrials but was concealing their existence. Throughout the 1950s and '60s, a wide array of UFO religions emerged, such as the Aetherius Society, founded by George King in Los Angeles in 1955. Combining elements of Hinduism, Theosophy, and Cold War UFO beliefs, King believed that he had been contacted by alien intelligences and taught that nuclear war could be avoided if human beings embraced the teachings of Cosmic Masters (which included Jesus, Buddha, Krishna, and Mars Sector 6).

Public interest in UFOs was only intensified through classic films such as *The Day the Earth Stood Still* (1951), *Close Encounters of the Third Kind* (1977), and Shirley MacLaine's New

Age miniseries *Out on a Limb* (1987), making the idea of contact with beings from other worlds a basic feature of the modern popular imagination. In this sense, Raël's contact with the Elohim and his message from the designers is in perfect keeping with this longer tradition of UFO beliefs in the United States, the United Kingdom, and Europe since the 1940s.

Like other new religions that emerged in the late twentieth century, the Raëlians are in many ways a "millenarian" movement insofar as they look forward to a coming era of spiritual peace and harmony. Unlike other millenarian movements such as Heaven's Gate, Peoples Temple, or the Branch Davidians, however, the Raëlians are for the most part more optimistic in their expectations of the new era. Rather than an apocalyptic showdown with the US government, they anticipate the joyous welcoming of the Elohim. Moreover, their vision of the new era is not explicitly rooted in the book of Revelation or the Christian concept of the millennium. In fact, the Raëlians have been from their origins fairly hostile to Christianity, and particularly to the Catholic Church, which they regard as a backward institution based on the repression of human sexuality. The Raëlian vision of the coming "new age" is one in which humankind will welcome the Elohim and advance toward a more modern, scientific, and sex-positive world.

Most Americans today remember the Raëlians because of their stunning claim in 2002 that they had successfully cloned a human baby. According to Raël's message, all life on Earth had been created by the extraterrestrial designers through cloning, and we could achieve immortality by cloning ourselves and transferring our present memories into infinite future copies of ourselves. In 1997, Raël formed a company—now called Clonaid—to begin research into human cloning, and the company claimed to have developed a cell fusion device that assisted with human cloning. On December 27, 2002, Clonaid announced that it had cloned the first human child—named "baby Eve"—a claim that triggered an intense international debate surrounding the ethics, politics, legality, and religious implications of cloning. Although no child was ever actually produced, the claim generated numerous strong condemnations from political and religious leaders on all sides, ranging from President George W. Bush to numerous democratic congressmen. Among the most outspoken critics was Pope John Paul II, who described human cloning as a threat to the dignity of human life. Thus the Raëlians are yet another key example of the ways in which even small and obscure new religious movements help highlight much larger and more difficult questions, tensions, and debates in contemporary American society.

CLAUDE VORILOHN: FROM POP STAR AND RACE CAR DRIVER TO FOUNDER OF A UFO RELIGION

Before his encounter with the Elohim, Claude Vorilohn had already led a fairly colorful and eventful life. Born in Vichy in central France and then raised in nearby Ambert, Vorilohn ran away from his boarding school at the age of fifteen. After playing music on the streets of Paris for several years, he signed a recording contract and recorded a series of pop singles.

When his music career sputtered, he became a sports journalist with the dream of one day saving enough money to buy his own racing car.

Raël's first meeting with the Elohim on the volcano in 1973 was itself remarkable enough. However, a second and even more remarkable encounter took place in 1975, when Vorilohn claimed that he was actually taken aboard an Elohim spacecraft to visit their planet. This experience was described in vivid detail in his second book, *Extraterrestrials Took Me to Their Planet,* in which Vorilohn explained the inhabitants, flora, and fauna of the Elohim's planet, as well as the Elohim's philosophy, social structure, and plans for humankind. As Vorilohn described this planet, in elaborate, almost Technicolor detail, "Before me a paradisiacal landscape unfolded, and in fact I cannot find any words to describe my enchantment at seeing huge flowers, each more beautiful than the last, and animals of unimaginable appearance that were walking among them. There were birds of multicolored plumage, and pink and blue squirrels with the heads of bear cubs climbing in the branches of trees that bore both enormous fruits and gigantic flowers."[1] He then went on to meet the inhabitants of the planet, which included 8,400 people from Earth. Among them were the great spiritual teachers from Earth's history, such as Jesus, Moses, and Elijah, who had been granted immortality through cloning technology.

Shortly after receiving the first message from the Elohim, Vorilohn formed an organization dedicated to spreading their teachings, called MADECH. A double acronym, MADECH stood for both "Mouvement pour l'accueil des Elohim, créateurs de l'humanité" (Movement for the welcoming of the Elohim, creators of humanity) and "Moise a devancé Élie et le Christ" (Moses preceded Elijah and the Christ). By 1976, however, Vorilohn had changed his name to Raël and the name of his organization to the International Raëlian Movement (figure 14.2). Although the movement began in France, it quickly became a popular global organization, establishing a major center near Montreal in Canada and other centers in Japan, Korea, and parts of Africa. Up until 2001, the Canadian center featured a tourist site called UFOland, complete with its own life-sized spacecraft. The group also has numerous centers in the United States and plans to build a new UFOland, complete with a one-thousand-seat theater, a new UFO replica, and a museum in Las Vegas.

RAËLIAN BELIEFS AND PRACTICES

Raëlian philosophy is in many ways an odd combination of intense faith in modern science and technology with a form of creationism that, ironically, rejects Darwinian evolutionary theory. On the one hand, Raëlians largely adhere to a scientific and materialist view of the universe: they do not believe in gods, souls, or any "supernatural" entities, and they regard even the Elohim as physical beings just like ourselves. Their understanding of the infinite or the divine is simply the infinitude of the physical universe itself, which they believe extends endlessly in all directions and dimensions—infinitely large, infinitely small, infinitely old, and lasting infinitely into the future. Raëlians believe that DNA and the technology of cloning are both the source of life and the means to achieve our own immortality. As

FIGURE 14.2 Raël speaking during a seminar. Photo courtesy of Raël.org.

Raël put it, "Science is the most important thing of all for humanity. . . . Science should be your religion, for the Elohim created you scientifically."[2]

Today, in the twenty-first century, science is advancing so rapidly that it will bring about a radical transformation of our entire way of life, upending all traditional values and opening the way to a potentially limitless future: "The world today is stepping into the scientific age, where all that we take for granted and all our traditional values will be turned upside down by the technological revolution."[3] Ultimately, science will lead the way to genuine immortality through the technology of human cloning: "Cloning is an extraordinary goal to achieve since it concerns the conquest of the deadliest disease on earth, death itself. It is cloning that will make us equal to gods, as foreseen in the bible . . . since immortality is the privilege of the gods."[4]

Yet the Raëlians are very much creationists—indeed, as much as any committed Christian creationists—who reject the idea that species have evolved over millions of years and instead believe that all living species were created in their present form by the Elohim. Evolution, in the Darwinian sense, is simply a "myth"; the only evolution that has ever taken place has been the Elohim's advancement in cloning techniques that allowed them to fashion more complex and more sophisticated life forms on Earth.

Larry Abdullah, DDS, MHA, PhD, is a Raëlian guide, who explains how he was initially drawn to Raël's philosophy and its views on science, human society, and new technologies such as cloning.

The field of science has appealed to me since I was a young child, and when I learned of an organization that considered science to be a fundamental tenet of its religious philosophy, I was intrigued. I started to learn more about this group and discovered that its philosophy was completely compatible with my overall perspective of the meaning and purpose of human life on Earth. I have studied religious philosophy since I was very young, from firsthand involvement in Christianity and Islam to having a rich background in religious studies as a consequence of my formal education. Through these experiences, I had developed "my own" religious philosophy, and the Raëlian philosophy fits well with my personal religious beliefs. I primarily like the Raëlian philosophy because of its emphasis on meditation, science, and personal freedoms.

The Raëlian religious philosophy purports that all living things on Earth, including humans, were created by extraterrestrial scientists using their advanced knowledge of DNA. As is written in ancient Jewish scripture, we refer to these beings as "the Elohim," a plural noun that literally means "those who come from the sky." After the Elohim created us, they have continued to monitor and positively influence our development by periodically introducing guides and teachers that we have recognized as religious prophets, such as Buddha, Jesus, Moses, and Muhammad, to name a few. Each of these individuals espoused a message of peace and love. When humanity entered the Age of Apocalypse (meaning "revelation"), the Elohim decided to send us their last prophet, Maitreya Raël, for two specific missions: (1) to spread the message of their existence, which also contains teachings on how to blossom individually as well [as] a society, and (2) to construct an embassy on neutral territory where we can officially welcome them.

I especially appreciate the application of meditative practices during Raëlian get-togethers. The use of meditation generates a number of health benefits, including the positive changes to metabolism, blood pressure, brain activation, and reduction in stress and pain. Raëlian get-togethers incorporate a variety of meditation techniques. Overall, Raëlian get-togethers incorporate much diversity. The most common themes that link these activities would be the abundance of peace, love, harmony, and laughter. Our organization also supports many causes that promote human rights and human freedoms. This includes organizations such as Gotopless (www.gotopless.org), Clitoraid (www.clitoraid.org), Pro-Swastika (www.proswastika.org), Paradism (www.paradism.org), et cetera.

The members of the Raëlian movement come from all walks of life, and Raëlian chapters can be found in more than 104 countries around the world. Its representatives comprise many diverse social, educational, and ethnic groups. The central unifying theme between these individuals is a common desire to make the planet Earth a better place: a paradise where science is allowed to develop freely to solve the problems that plague human society (famine, pollution, etc.) and where violence is recognized as a disease, treated appropriately, and eventually eradicated completely from society.

The concept of cloning has intrigued me for years. I am particularly excited about the potential that it represents in fighting so many of the chronically devastating diseases that plague human health and life. Scientific studies have shown that diseases such as diabetes, Parkinson's, and Alzheimer's, spinal cord injuries, autoimmune diseases, just to mention a few, all have the potential to be eradicated completely through the processes of developing and expanding human cloning techniques. Its potential to create organs artificially cannot be underestimated. Ultimately, Raëlians look forward to the time when advances in cloning procedures will lead to life extension and eternal life.

The Raëlian philosophy offers a third explanation as to our existence as humans on Earth. Traditionally, the theories of evolution and supernatural creation have garnered the bulk of attention and have been given the closest scrutiny. At minimum, the concept of scientific creation deserves equal examination, analysis, and inquiry. Unlike the other two explanations for human life on Earth, the evidence and support for scientific creation has its basis in developmental, contemporary, and exploratory science, as well as in ancient, tribal, and traditional historical records.

One of the most interesting aspects of Raëlian philosophy is their reinterpretation of the world's existing religious traditions and scriptures. Essentially, Raël believed that the Bible and all the other scriptures of the world were partly correct insofar as they were generally describing the reality of extraterrestrials. But because human beings were at a less developed stage of civilization, they mistakenly imagined the Elohim to be supernatural beings rather than physical beings like ourselves. Thus Raël provides a detailed rereading of the Genesis narrative, explaining that the entire account of the creation of Earth and its various species is really a somewhat confused description of the coming of the Elohim and the cloning of all life on this planet. Likewise, the "end of the world" refers not to some sort of Second Coming and Last Judgment as in Christian theology but rather to the choice that humans now face at the turn of the millennium: either we will destroy ourselves through war and conflict, or we can embrace the message of the Elohim, build an embassy to welcome them to Earth, and, with their assistance, advance to a higher "intergalactic level of civilization."[5]

FIGURE 14.3 Raël
meditating. Photo courtesy
of Raël.org.

In this sense, Raëlism has much in common with New Age spirituality in that it looks forward to a coming era of personal and social transformation when humans will inherit the tremendous technology of the Elohim for a new civilization: "With the Elohim's guidance and humanity's right choices, this age holds marvelous potentialities: liberation, power, quasi-immortality, once the Elohim arrive to bequeath to their creations scientific knowledge."[6]

The Raëlians offer similar reinterpretations of other religious scriptures and myths, each of which reflects the message of the Elohim in a partial and incomplete form. For example, Raël is particularly interested in the Buddhist prophecy of a future Buddha, Maitreya, who will come to restore the Buddha's teaching for the end of this cosmic age. The future Buddha, it turns out, is none other than Raël himself, who is the true Maitreya and bearer of the final message for humankind in this age (figure 14.3).

All of this, however, has raised the question of whether Raëlism should be considered a religion. After all, it rejects the idea that there is a god or gods, since that is what we have mistakenly called the Elohim; and it rejects the idea of a soul, since immortality can be achieved not in heaven but in this universe through cloning our physical body. As is the case with Scientology, various countries have answered this question differently. In the United States, Raëlism has been recognized as a religion by the State Department and as a tax-exempt organization by the IRS. But in Canada its application for federal tax exemption as a "religious corporation" was rejected by the tax department because Raëlism did not meet the requirement that religions must believe in transcendent or immaterial beings.[7]

A LIFE-AFFIRMING AND SEX-POSITIVE RELIGION

In terms of its actual practice, Raëlism is on the whole an extremely life-affirming and sex-positive religious movement. Indeed, Raël's most intense criticism has been reserved for the Catholic Church, particularly because of its attitudes toward sexuality, abortion, clerical celibacy, and contraception. In 1992, the Raëlians launched Operation Condom, a widely publicized protest against the Montreal Catholic School Commission's decision to veto a proposal to install condom machines in its high schools. The Raëlians sent out a "condom mobile" to tour Quebec and Ontario, parking it outside Catholic high schools and distributing thousands of condoms to students.

The group has also engaged in a variety of other sex and body-friendly activities around the world. One is the organization GoTopless.org, which advocates women's rights to appear bare-chested in public. Arguing that women should have the same rights to appear publicly as men, the group has been involved in demonstrations in many countries and has organized an annual Go Topless Day. In my home city of Columbus, for example, a group of topless female Raëlians was prominent at our annual summer music and food festival, ComFest, as a major site on their national "Boob Map."

Another Raëlian initiative is Clitoraid, which is intended to help women who have been subjected to female circumcision (or female gender mutilation, as they call it). A nonprofit organization, Clitoraid promotes campaigns against female circumcision and works with doctors to rebuild the genitals of women who have undergone genital mutilation. The ultimate goal, according to Clitoraid's website, is to "celebrate sexual freedom and pleasure for all women of the world" by helping women to explore their sexuality and ideally "reach their first orgasm."[8] Like their Raëlian counterparts in the Operation Condom program, Clitoraid workers often combine a sense of humor with their political campaigns, for example by dressing up in giant clitoris suits for public demonstrations. However, the group also has more serious and more ambitious plans, such as the construction of a "Pleasure Hospital" in the city of Bobo-Dioulasso, Burkina Faso, West Africa, which will offer genital reconstruction surgery to women free of charge.

Raël recommends a variety of meditation and prayer techniques designed to help the individual come into harmony with the infinite universe and to reflect upon the meaning and message of the Elohim. However, one of the most popular Raëlian practices that really embodies their larger worldview is "Sensual Meditation." Rather than a form of asceticism or otherworldly denial of the senses, Sensual Meditation is a technique designed to use all of the body's senses in order to open the individual to the "Infinite" or the endless abundance of the universe.

The technique begins with the individual arranging a special meditation space, ideally surrounded with pleasurable sights, sounds, and textures. Raël recommends filling the space with works of art, beautiful music, pleasing scents, and comfortable furniture and rugs. Trays filled with food and drink should be on hand, and one or more close friends or lovers should be invited to come and share in the experience: "Then feed your senses together and open your bodies in order to open your minds in love and fraternity."[9] Finally, if two individuals feel a mutual attraction, they may also take the next step toward harmony with the Infinite through sexual union. By employing all of the senses together in a physical embrace, they can open themselves completely to the energy of the universe and so experience a kind of "cosmic orgasm" that unites them with the Infinite: "Together you can reach a sublime state of harmony, which will enable you to approach infinity by satisfying your five senses. To this state will be added the synthesis of all these enjoyments—the physical union of two individuals in total harmony and in the illumination of the act of love."[10] Such an experience goes well beyond the typical act of sexual union, for it is ultimately a joining of two bodies not just with one another but with the entire cosmos of which they are a part:

> Simultaneously reaching a conscious orgasm, felt by the whole body rather than just by the sexual organs, will be the reward of scrupulous preparation of this celebration of infinity, which could last a very long time and which will have nothing to do with what until now has been called "making love."
>
> The absolute symbiosis of two people finally becoming a bit of each other allows them to make love with the atoms which make them up and with the galaxies which they are part of, and thus to have what can be called a cosmic orgasm.[11]

RAËLIAN ORGANIZATION AND SOCIAL VIEWS: GUARDIANS, ANGELS, AND GENIOCRACY

The Raëlian movement is organized in a graded hierarchy or pyramid, with levels ranked 0 through 6. At the top of the hierarchy is level 6, the "guide of guides" or "planetary guide" (Raël himself), who is reelected every seven years by a council of bishops. Below this are level 5 ("bishop guides"), level 4 ("priest guides"), level 3 ("assistant priests"), level 2 ("organizers"), level 1 ("assistant organizers"), and level 0 ("trainees").

In addition to these levels 0 through 6, there are all-female orders within the Raëlian organization. In 1998, Raël announced that he had been ordered by the Elohim to create an Order of Angels, a new order exclusively for women, who would be trained to serve as hostesses, companions, and lovers for the aliens when they land. For the time being, while humanity awaited the arrival of the Elohim, they were to serve the needs of Raël himself and see to his comforts. Thus the order would be a "religious order encompassing women of the Raëlian religion who are legally of age. They will have the full-time responsibility of serving the Elohim, their Creators, and the great prophets . . . Moses, Jesus, Buddha, and Muhammad during their stay at the Embassy, seeing to their comfort at every level. Meanwhile, they will prepare themselves for this-long awaited day by being in the service of Raël the Last Prophet and attending to his well-being."[12]

In addition to preparing for the coming of the Elohim and attending to Raël's personal comforts, the Angels would serve as the Prophet's bodyguards. They had to be ready to sacrifice their lives for the Prophet—for example, by jumping in front of Raël to shield him if an assassin attempted to shoot him.

Apart from its advocacy of human cloning and free sexuality, one of the more controversial aspects of Raëlism is its vision of the ideal social order. From early on, Raël advocated a form of "Geniocracy," according to which the most intelligent members of society should be the ones in positions of power and decision making for the rest of humankind. As Yahweh explained to Raël during his first encounter, the cells of the foot do not make decisions for the rest of the body or tell the hand what to do; rather, the brain tells the rest of the body what to do, guiding the hands and feet as it sees fit. In the same way, geniuses, as the brains of society, should decide for the rest of humankind, guiding its government and economy:

> What kind of people allows humanity to progress? The geniuses. Therefore, your world must appreciate its geniuses and allow them to govern the Earth.
>
> The right to vote should be reserved for those people whose brains are more suited to thinking and finding solutions to problems—that is to say an elite group of high intelligence. . . . We are talking about placing the genius in power and you may call that "Geniocracy."[13]

Thus the Elohim recommend that only people whose intelligence can be measured as 50 percent above average should be eligible to stand for election, and only those whose intelligence is 10 percent above average should be allowed to vote. Accordingly, the geniuses should be given special genius-level educations, and the children of average intelligence should be given a normal education.

This ideal Geniocratic arrangement is reflected on the planet of the Elohim. While Yahweh's planet holds some seven billion inhabitants, its affairs are run by a small group of seven hundred elites who live entirely apart from the rest, do most of the work for the planet, and alone hold the privilege of being "eternals" (that is, cloned over and over again eternally).

Perhaps not surprisingly, the idea of Geniocracy has been viewed quite critically by many non-Raëlians. To some critics, this idea of a small elite of geniuses making decisions for the rest of society smacks of authoritarianism or worse. The criticisms of Raël's politics became even more intense when it was noted that the key symbol of the movement was a six-pointed star with a swastika in the center. In December 1977 French police raided Raël's house on suspicion of Nazi sympathies, and in 1978 a number of Raëlian guides had their homes broken into and were taken into police headquarters for questioning.[14]

The Raëlians themselves pointed out that the swastika was an ancient religious symbol that derived from the Sanskrit word meaning "auspicious sign" (*su-astika*) and could be found in early Hindu, Buddhist, Jain, and other Asian traditions. Nonetheless, when combined with the idea of Geniocracy, the swastika became a source of intense negative publicity for the Raëlians and was replaced by a swirling spiral. In fact, my own copy of Raël's *Sensual Meditation* book has the original swastika symbol on the front cover physically covered over by a sticker showing the less offensive spiral symbol.

Yet despite its bad publicity the Raëlians have apparently decided to once again embrace the swastika as a key symbol and to attempt to reclaim its ancient history from its Nazi uses. Today, the movement sponsors a group called Pro-Swastika, which aims to spread awareness of the ancient religious origins of the symbol; according to their website, "The Swastika is a symbol of peace for millions of Hindus, Buddhists and also Raëlians since it is their symbol of infinity in time." The group also generated a certain amount of controversy in 2014 when they flew an airplane over a crowded Coney Island beach carrying a banner that showed the swastika sign and the Raëlian symbol with the title "pro-swastika.org." While the Raëlians were apparently only trying to spread the word about the original religious meanings of the symbol, many bathers were outraged by the open display of swastikas flying overhead.[15]

KEY ISSUES AND DEBATES: THE ETHICS OF HUMAN CLONING

While the Raëlians have raised eyebrows because of their views on sexuality, Geniocracy, and the swastika, their position on human cloning has generated the most controversy and raised the most complicated ethical questions. The debate over human cloning was already well under way in the late 1990s—above all, after a sheep named Dolly was born on July 5, 1997, the first successfully cloned mammal and the first lamb to survive after 277 unsuccessful attempts. Dolly had not one but three mothers—one that provided the egg, one that provided the DNA, and one that carried the egg to term. Thus the DNA was removed from one body cell, placed into an egg whose DNA had been removed, and then planted into the womb of the birth mother. Dolly's birth also generated an intense interest in the possibility of cloning other mammals and led to the successful cloning of horses, bulls, and sheep as well as unsuccessful attempts at other large animals. However, it also triggered a fierce debate surrounding the ethical and religious implications of cloning and, above all, the possibility of human cloning. In the United States, a moratorium was placed on the use of federal funds for human cloning research, and President Clinton requested that private companies pass their own moratorium.

That same year, however, the Raëlian movement began a company to fund and research human cloning. Initially called Valiant Venture Ltd. Corporation, the company was later renamed Clonaid and its leadership was turned over to Raëlian bishop Brigitte Boisselier.

While other researchers such as those at Texas A&M were using up to $2.3 million to research the cloning of a dog, Clonaid claimed in 1998 that it could produce a human clone for a mere $200,000. In early 2001, the FDA investigated Clonaid's laboratory in Nitro, West Virginia. Although the agency found the lab's documentation to be inadequate, they did note the presence of state-of-the-art equipment, which had apparently been bought by former West Virginia state legislator Mark Hunt in the hopes of cloning his dead son. That same spring Clonaid announced that it had successfully impregnated a mother with a cloned embryo, and in December 2001 it announced the birth of baby Eve. Although Clonaid never produced the alleged baby Eve or any evidence that they had successfully created a human clone, the announcement did spark a media uproar and an intense religious and political debate.

More recently, the Raëlians have created a sister group to Clonaid called Stemaid, which is involved in therapeutic cloning research using embryonic stem cells. Therapeutic cloning is a procedure that begins in the same way as reproductive cloning, by removing the nucleus from an egg cell and replacing it with the nucleus of a body cell. However, in therapeutic cloning, stem cells are taken from the resulting embryo and used to produce tissue or whole organs that can replace sick tissue or organs in the donor's body. The cloned embryo in this case is destroyed rather than growing into a mature fetus. While many scientists worldwide are currently researching stem cells and therapeutic cloning, Stemaid claims to have already helped people who have suffered strokes, brain injury, cancer, and heart, kidney, and liver failure. But because its treatment is not approved by the FDA, it is located overseas.[16]

Both reproductive cloning of the sort pursued by Clonaid and therapeutic cloning of the sort pursued by Stemaid have raised profound ethical and religious questions. Not surprisingly, reproductive cloning or the duplication of an entire existing human has generated the most heated arguments. Supporters such as the Raëlians contend that it could be used to develop new fertility techniques that could extend existing techniques of artificial insemination. Cloning could be used to help sterile or lesbian couples have children together by using the DNA from one member and allowing the other to carry the fetus to term. Parents who had lost a child could replace it with one that was genetically identical.[17]

However, critics of the technique have raised a wide array of practical, philosophical, and religious objections. The first and simplest concern is that there is no guarantee that cloned humans would be normal. Cloned mammals have shown a number of disorders, some of which are not detectable by ultrasound and appear only later in life. At present, researchers are still unable to safely clone nonhuman primates, and critics argue that is it likely that experimentation with human cloning would produce numerous dead and dying babies.

Another widespread concern is that cloning could represent a fundamental threat to human dignity by undermining the precious uniqueness of each individual life and opening the possibility of creating new (perhaps disposable) carbon copies of human persons. Others worry that cloned humans would not have the same rights to self-determination as noncloned persons; that is, they might feel pressured to live a life that was already predetermined or that they were expected to live up to the expectations of the person from whom they were cloned. Perhaps a more serious concern is that wide-scale cloning would generate a large number of surplus embryos, in effect creating a business in which living beings or potential living beings were stored in deep freeze as human commodities.[18]

Finally, some religious leaders and organizations have offered a number of deep moral objections to human cloning. In the eyes of most prolife supporters, a fertilized human egg is already a full human person; removing the nucleus during the cloning process would in effect murder the person. Many prolife supporters believe that the soul enters the body at the moment when the sperm fertilizes the egg; since cloning does not involve a sperm, some worry that the cloned being might also lack a soul.[19]

Therapeutic cloning has generated perhaps less moral outrage than reproductive cloning, but it too remains controversial. Proponents list an array of possible benefits of stem cells, which could be used to provide genetically identical cells for regenerative medicine, as well as organs and tissues for transplantation. Cloned organs and tissues would not trigger an immune response and so would be much less likely to be rejected. Currently, research is under way in the use of embryonic stem cells to treat forms of brain degeneration such as Alzheimer's, brain and spinal cord injuries, heart disease, baldness, missing teeth, diabetes, and an array of other problems.

However, many critics maintain that even therapeutic cloning has serious ethical problems. Some conservative religious groups, in particular, have argued that it involves the creation of new life—a viable embryo—without a real father or mother and that it still results in the destruction of that new life. In 2013, a group of Catholic bishops issued a statement that called embryonic stem cell research "gravely immoral," claiming that no amount of good derived from therapeutic cloning can outweigh the evil of destroying a life:

> The false assumption that a good end can justify direct killing has been the source of much evil in our world.
>
> No commitment to a hoped-for "greater good" can erase or diminish the wrong of directly taking innocent human lives here and now. . . . In fact, policies undermining our respect for human life can only endanger the vulnerable patients that stem-cell research offers to help. The same ethic that justifies taking some lives to help the patient with Parkinson's or Alzheimer's disease today can be used to sacrifice that very patient tomorrow.[20]

Regardless of whether the Raëlians ever have produced or ever will produce a cloned human baby, their controversial ideas have sparked a much larger and more complex debate about the ethics of cloning and the larger religious, ethical, and philosophical implications of these rapidly advancing new technologies. Even if the Raëlians gradually fade as a new religious movement, the deep ethical questions they raise are unlikely to disappear in the twenty-first century.

QUESTIONS FOR DISCUSSION AND DEBATE

1. Many Americans dismiss UFO-based religions such as the Raëlians as silly and implausible. But is the idea of superior beings descending from another planet really that much more difficult to believe than the idea of angels or other supernatural entities descending from heaven, as described in the Bible and various other mainstream religious scriptures? Or is it in some ways perhaps *more* plausible, now that we know how many planets exist in our own galaxy that can likely support life?

2. Why did the announcement that Clonaid had successfully cloned a human baby generate such intense criticism, particularly from religious organizations such as the Catholic Church and the Christian Coalition? What uniquely *religious* questions or dilemmas does human cloning raise? Why haven't religious groups become quite as agitated by the successful cloning of other animal species, such as sheep or dogs?

3. Is the idea of achieving immortality through a modern technological means such as cloning more or less plausible than the idea of achieving immortality through older religious "technologies" such as prayer, meditation, ritual, devotion, or worship? Does the use of modern technology in the pursuit of immortality make the Raëlians appear less "religious" than mainstream traditions? Why or why not?

4. On the one hand, the Raëlians are very much advocates of modern science and technology and even represent a kind of "religion of science" in certain ways. Yet on the other hand, they are creationists who reject the idea of evolution and believe that all life was created directly by the Elohim. Is this a contradiction? Or is there a way in which it makes sense within the framework of the Raëlian worldview?

5. Could a Geniocracy possibly be the solution to all of humankind's political and social problems, as the Raëlians claim? Or does it seem like a totalitarian nightmare with fascist implications, as critics of the idea have argued?

SUGGESTED CLASSROOM ACTIVITY

Engage in a complex debate surrounding the practical, ethical, and religious implications of human cloning. Again, avoid making it a simple "either/or" debate and instead form groups that represent multiple nuanced positions. These might include a group of Raëlians, a group of conservative Christians, a group of scientists, a group of philosophers and ethicists, and so on. What are the major advantages and disadvantages, reasons for hope, and reasons for serious concern regarding human cloning? Each group should also make policy recommendations for lawmakers concerning the legality and regulation of human cloning.

SUGGESTED VIDEOS

The Encounter of December 13th, 1973. Rael.org, 2013. www.rael.org/videos.

Message from the Designers. Rael.org, 2013. www.rael.org/videos.

SUGGESTIONS FOR FURTHER READING

Brimah, Josephus. *The Ethics of Human Cloning.* Saarbrücken: Lambert, 2010.

Dean, Jodi. *Aliens in America: Conspiracy Cultures from Outerspace to Cyberspace.* Ithaca, NY: Cornell University Press, 1998.

Lewis, James R., ed. *The Gods Have Landed.* Albany: SUNY Press, 1995.

MacKinnon, Barbara, ed. *Human Cloning: Science, Ethics, and Public Policy.* Urbana: University of Illinois Press, 2001.

Palmer, Susan J. *Aliens Adored: Raël's UFO Religion.* New Brunswick, NJ: Rutgers University Press, 2004.

Partridge, Christopher, ed. *UFO Religions.* New York: Routledge, 2003.

Raël. *Geniocracy: Government of the People, for the People, by the Geniuses.* N.p.: Nova Distribution, 2008.

———. *Intelligent Design: Message from the Designers.* Vaduz: Raëlian Foundation, 2005.

———. *Sensual Meditation: Awakening the Mind by Awakening the Body.* Vaduz: Raëlian Foundation, 1987.

———. *The True Face of God.* N.p.: Raël Religion, 1998.

Reece, Gregory. *UFO Religion: Inside Flying Saucer Cults and Culture.* London: I. B. Tauris, 2007.

Robinson, Bruce. "Reproductive Cloning." ReligiousTolerance.org, 2004. www.religioustolerance.org/clo_intra.htm.

Wilmut, Ian. *After Dolly: The Uses and Misuses of Human Cloning.* New York: Norton, 2006.

NOTES TO CHAPTER 14

1. Raël, *The True Face of God* (n.p.: Raël Religion, 1998), 148.
2. Ibid., 189.
3. Raël, *The Maitreya: Extracts from His Teachings* (Vaduz: Raëlian Foundation, 2004), 119.
4. Ibid., 119–20.
5. Raël, *True Face of God*, 83.
6. Susan J. Palmer, "Raelian Movement International," in *Religions of the World: A Comprehensive Encyclopedia of Beliefs and Practices,* edited by J. Gordon Melton (Santa Barbara, CA: ABC-CLIO, 2010), 2362–63.

7. Susan J. Palmer, *Aliens Adored: Raël's UFO Religion* (New Brunswick, NJ: Rutgers University Press, 2004), 86.
8. "Why Clitoraid?," Clitoraid.org, n.d., accessed 2014, www.clitoraid.org/why-clitoraid.
9. Raël, *True Face of God*, 185–86; see also Raël, *Sensual Meditation: Awakening the Mind by Awakening the Body* (Vaduz: Raëlian Foundation, 1987).
10. Raël, *True Face of God*, 186; see also Raël, *Sensual Meditation*.
11. Raël, *Sensual Meditation*, 126.
12. Palmer, *Aliens Adored*, 135.
13. Raël, *True Face of God*, 85, 87; see Raël, *Geniocracy: Government of the People, for the People, by the Geniuses* (n.p.: Nova Distribution, 2008).
14. Susan J. Palmer, *The New Heretics of France: Minority Religions, la République, and the Government-Sponsored War on Sects* (New York: Oxford University Press, 2011), 89.
15. "Swastika Banner Flies over New York Beaches," *USA Today*, July 14, 2014, www.usatoday.com/story/news/nation-now/2014/07/14/swastika-banner-new-york-beaches/12618091/. See "Origin of the Swastika," ProSwastika.org, n.d., accessed 2014, www.proswastika.org/index.php.
16. "What Is Stem Cell Therapy?" Stemaid.com, n.d., accessed 2014, www.stemaid.com/index.php.
17. See, for example, Bruce A. Robinson, "Reproductive Cloning," ReligiousTolerance.Org, February 12, 2004, www.religioustolerance.org/clo_intra.htm#; Josephus Brimah, *The Ethics of Human Cloning* (Saarbrücken: Lambert, 2010); Barbara MacKinnon, ed., *Human Cloning: Science, Ethics, and Public Policy* (Urbana: University of Illinois Press, 2001); Ian Wilmut, *After Dolly: The Uses and Misuses of Human Cloning* (New York: Norton, 2006).
18. See Barbara MacKinnon, introduction to MacKinnon, *Human Cloning*, 1–17; Jorge L. A. Garcia, "Human Cloning: Never and Why Not," in MacKinnon, *Human Cloning*, 85–206; Wilmut, *After Dolly*, 223–71.
19. Robinson, "Reproductive Cloning."
20. Nancy Frazier O'Brien, "Embryonic Stem Cell Research Immoral, Unnecessary, Bishops Say," AmericanCatholic.org, n.d., accessed 2014, www.americancatholic.org/News/StemCell/.

Method and Theory in the Study of New Religions

In the preceding chapters, we have focused primarily on individual New Age, neopagan, and new religious movements themselves, and we have not always explicitly discussed theoretical and methodological questions in the study of these movements. All along, however, we have really been raising much larger issues that are all about "theory and method"— that is, about various ways of understanding, comparing, and making sense of these groups in a broader religious and historical context, rather than simply learning a bunch of facts about them. So we have already been "doing theory" throughout these chapters, and the point of this appendix is simply to make the theory aspect a bit more explicit and easier to put into application.

The English word *theory* comes from the Greek term *theoria*, which literally means a way of "looking" at something or a "way of seeing." Theory is in this sense just a kind of lens that we use to examine, compare, and interpret something—in this case, the tremendous variety of new religions—in order to try to explain why they have come to be and what roles they play in contemporary America.[1] In this short appendix, of course, we cannot possibly cover all the various theoretical approaches that have been used by modern scholars. For the sake of simplicity here, we will examine just six major approaches—sociology, ethnography, cultural studies, gender studies, psychology, and history of religions—along with one example of each and a brief discussion of the major pros and cons of these different models.

As I suggested in chapter 1, theoretical approaches can perhaps best be thought of as a useful set of tools, each of which might be appropriate when one is trying to make sense of different groups or different aspects of a particular movement.[2] In some cases, a sociological approach might be extremely valuable, while in others a historical perspective or a focus on gender and sexuality might be more appropriate. And in many cases we may want to make

use of a variety of perspectives at once in order to create as rich a picture of a given movement as possible. At the same time, each of these approaches has certain limitations or blind
spots, which means that it will ultimately be up to the reader to decide which ones might be
more or less useful in a given context.

A SOCIOLOGICAL APPROACH: THE MAKING OF A "MOONIE"

Much of the best scholarship on new religious movements has been generated by sociologists, who hope to understand the broader social and cultural contexts within which new
religions arise and the reasons why these become attractive alternatives for many individuals. While earlier literature had either ignored new religions or portrayed them as "deviant"
groups, sociologists during the 1980s and '90s began to take these movements much more
seriously as important, meaningful, and complex aspects of modern society.[3] For example,
one of the classic early works on new religions was *The Making of a Moonie: Choice or Brainwashing?*, by British sociologist Eileen Barker (1984). Barker began her project with the question of why someone would join the Unification Church (popularly known as "the
Moonies")—a new religious movement founded by Reverend Sun Myung Moon in South
Korea in 1954 that quickly spread worldwide during the 1970s and '80s. Particularly during
the "cult scare" of these decades, the Unification Church was widely regarded in the popular
media as a deviant mind-control group and was regularly charged with brainwashing its
new recruits in the United States and the United Kingdom.

Using a mixture of in-depth interviews, participant observation, and questionnaires, Barker's approach balances personal accounts and her own insights with empirical data and statis-
tics based on church workshops held in London. Although she worked closely with the church,
Barker never claimed to be a spiritual seeker, always making it clear that she was a scholar.
This "outsider" approach had both disadvantages and advantages. On the one hand, she was
not always given access to all aspects of the movement that a practicing member might have;
but on the other hand, she was allowed to ask more probing and sometimes uncomfortable
questions that no member would have presumed to ask one of her or his leaders.[4]

On the basis of her extensive study, Barker concluded that the decision to join the Unification Church could not be explained by the simplistic ideas of either "brainwashing" or pure
"rational, calculated choice." The brainwashing model is far too rudimentary to account for
the many complex external and internal influences that shape an individual's decision to join
an alternative religious group. At the same time, simple rational choice is also too easy an
explanation, since most members joined for reasons that may have been far more about the
intense emotions, sense of meaning, and feeling of community that they found in the movement—often in ways they could not clearly articulate themselves, other than that it simply
"felt right."[5] Ultimately, Barker suggests, the Unification Church and other similar new religions offer powerfully attractive alternatives to a confusing modern world that can often feel
like a "competitive, claustrophobic rat-race" devoid of community or meaning. For many who

find contemporary society alienating and isolating, new religions can provide both a new kind of family and a spiritual framework that gives life an ultimate value and purpose:

> The alternative which the Unification Church offers is one which seems both to recognize and to provide an explanation for the evils of the contemporary world. . . . It offers a clear direction, a clear leadership, which knows what to do and how to do it. It is, paradoxically, a movement which offers freedom from directionless choices. It offers a religious community within which God is at the centre of everyday life; God is a living Being with whom each individual can have a personal relationship. . . . It offers a loving, caring environment which gives its members not only warmth and affection but also a chance to love and sacrifice for others. . . . The Unification Church offers the potential recruit the chance to be a part of a Family of like-minded people who care about the state of the world, who accept and live by high moral standards, who are dedicated to restoring God's Kingdom of Heaven on Earth.[6]

Barker's sociological approach is valuable for many reasons. Not only does it avoid the biased and judgmental views of most earlier literature on new religions, but it also skillfully balances personal narratives and subjective accounts with hard empirical data. Thus Barker shows statistically that the majority of individuals who attend church workshops choose not to pursue the movement and that even most of those who become members leave after a short time—all of which makes it difficult to believe that members are being "brainwashed" or are in need of "deprogramming" by anticult experts. At the same time, however, her approach is by necessity limited. While she provides persuasive insight into the "making of a Moonie" in 1980s England, the small size and geographic limits of her study make it less useful for understanding the rapid global spread of a movement such as the Unification Church not just in the United Kingdom but throughout Asia, Europe, and North America.

AN ETHNOGRAPHIC APPROACH: CULTURAL ANTHROPOLOGY AND NEOPAGAN FESTIVAL CULTURE

Because new religions are "new" and exist in communities all around us in the contemporary United States, they often lend themselves to an ethnographic approach based on first-hand field research and insights drawn from cultural anthropology. One of the better studies of American neopaganism is Sarah M. Pike's *Earthly Bodies, Magical Selves,* a detailed ethnographic account of neopagan festival culture. Although Pike is not a neopagan herself and does not claim to present an "insider's view" of the movement, she does say that she was deeply affected and personally changed by her study of neopagan communities and now sees them in a more nuanced way than she had prior to her research: "I do not claim to be a neopagan or to represent this tradition as an insider might," as she put it, "but I have been transformed by my experiences in neopagan communities, and this transformation is surely reflected in the way I tell their stories."[7]

As we saw in chapter 8, neopagan festivals take place all across the United States, from Southern California to rural Ohio, from southwestern New York to central Michigan. Some of the best-known festivals that Pike studied include the Elf Fest and Wild Magick Gathering (held in southern Indiana), Starwood (held in New York and now in Ohio), and the Pagan Spirit Gathering (originally held in Wisconsin, then in Ohio, Missouri, and now Illinois). Neopagan festivals are typically extremely lively, very high-energy, and at times ecstatic events that involve all manner of colorful costumes, ritual performances, and dancing, as well as food, drink, commercial vendors, and good-natured socializing.

In her approach to neopagan festival culture, Pike draws upon several classic anthropological theories of ritual, such as the work of the French ethnographer Arnold van Gennep, and the British anthropologist Victor Turner. Using Van Gennep's terms, Pike describes the journey from the ordinary social world to the pagan festival world as a journey into a "liminal" space. Literally meaning a kind of "threshold" or transitional zone from one place to another, liminal spaces are typically characterized by a "suspension of the usual rules of living," a transcendence of the normal regulations of mainstream society, and in some cases certain kinds of "excesses," such as dance, ecstatic celebration, and sexual license.[8] Liminal spaces are also places in which the normal divisions between human beings are largely dissolved, and the participants experience a deep sense of oneness and solidarity—what Victor Turner called *communitas*. In contrast to the structured and regulated space of ordinary society, the liminal space is a realm of antistructure or connectedness with other members of the group that opens new possibilities for creativity and freedom.[9]

Pike sees neopagan festivals as classic examples of this sort of liminality and *communitas*. When neopagans make the trip to major festivals such as Starwood or Spiral, they often describe themselves as making a ritual journey from the ordinary, boring, workaday world to a kind of "Faerie" realm, a zone where magic is possible and the natural environment is still enchanted. Festivals are also places where neopagans can experiment—often wildly—with self and identity, by wearing all variety of costumes or ritual garb, playing with gender, and inhabiting different possible realms of the imagination. Through dancing, drumming, chanting, ritual performance, and a wide array of other means, neopagan festivals are places where not only ordinary identity but also ordinary modes of consciousness are left behind. At the same time, participants find a new kind of community with like-minded others—or rather, with equally marginalized others, creating a paradoxical sort of community of nonconformists: "Neopagans attend festivals to experience a sense of belonging to a community, but it is in part their experience of marginality that unifies them. Festivals become meaningful places as extensions of participants' own feelings of marginality. Many Neopagans see themselves as social outcasts and their Neopagan lifestyle as a rebellion against mainstream society. . . . At festivals, Neopagans who have felt ostracized celebrate their outcast status and make it into a defining identity in a space constituted as powerful because it is outside the ordinary, as they are."[10]

Finally, the neopagans in Pike's account say that they carry the liminal experience of the festival back home with them when they return to "mundania." They often recount experiencing a "new sense of self" uncovered at the festival that continues as they return to normal life, family, and jobs, bringing the deep "emotional and spiritual changes" they have experienced along with them as they are reintegrated into the nonliminal world of structure and social norms.[11]

Pike's ethnographic approach sheds valuable new light on both the experience and the larger spiritual implications of neopagan festival life. However, one could argue that it relies rather heavily on her own subjective reflections as a participant-observer and her own creative interpretation of neopagan festival culture, while lacking the more quantitative analysis provided by sociologists such as Barker. Pike's use of anthropological concepts such as liminality and *communitas* is fascinating and insightful, but it might leave some readers wondering: How many neopagans actually experience this sort of *communitas*, rather than just attending the festival for pure enjoyment or the party atmosphere? How many actually took this *communitas* experience back with them into their mundane lives? And how can we even measure that? What were the concrete demographics of these festivals in terms of age, gender, race, social class? In this sense, Pike's more interpretive ethnographic approach might provide a useful complement to more empirically based studies such as Barker's.

A CULTURAL STUDIES APPROACH: SIGNIFIERS, SYMBOLISM, AND SOCIAL RESISTANCE

While other approaches may emphasize the psychological, sociological, or historical dimensions of new religious movements, a cultural studies approach also examines their complex use of symbols and signifiers as they respond creatively to their social and historical contexts. Cultural studies as a field first developed in England in the 1960s, particularly at places such as the Centre for Contemporary Cultural Studies at the University of Birmingham, and then spread widely throughout England and the United States during the 1980s and '90s. Combining elements of Marxist materialist critique, literary criticism, and semiotics (the study of signs, symbolism, and communication), the Birmingham school of cultural studies paid particular attention to youth movements and subcultures in England during the 1970s and '80s.

One of the most famous works to come out of this movement was Dick Hebdige's *Subculture: The Meaning of Style* (1979), which examines a wide range of youth cultures in postwar England, such as punks, skinheads, Teddy boys, mods, rockers, and Rastas. Hebdige is especially interested in the ways in which individuals in these subcultures are able to appropriate ordinary aspects of culture and creatively transform them into powerful signifiers of social, economic, and political resistance. For example, punk rockers in the 1970s took simple everyday objects such as safety pins and, by piercing them through their cheeks or noses instead of using them in conventional ways, transformed them into effective signs of rebellion against the conventional social establishment.[12]

Hebdige examines the Rastafari movement similarly, exploring the ways in which Rastas were able to appropriate the most basic elements of the established religious and social institutions—such as the Bible—and transform them into often radical signs of social subversion and political resistance:

> The profound subversion of the white man's religion which places God in Ethiopia and the black "sufferer" in Babylon has proved singularly appealing to working class youth in both the ghettoes of Kingston and the West Indian communities of Great Britain. . . . Clothed in dreadlocks and "righteous ire," the Rastaman effects a spectacular resolution of the material contradictions which oppress and define the West Indian community. He deciphers "sufferation" . . . naming its historical causes (colonialism, economic exploitation) and promising deliverance through exodus to "Africa." He is the living refutation of Babylon (contemporary capitalist society) refusing to deny his stolen history. By a perverse and willful transformation, he turns poverty and exile into "signs of grandeur," tokens of his own esteem, tickets which will take him home to Africa and Zion when Babylon is over.[13]

As we saw above in chapter 6, the Rastas take the most basic aspects of the human body—hair, in particular—and transform them into signs of social resistance. By rejecting the fine, straight hair of the affluent classes and instead wearing long, matted dreadlocks, the Rastas are at once signaling their denial of mainstream social norms and embracing their blackness and African-ness. Likewise, by adopting an alternative diet (Ital), the Rastas are signaling their rejection of everything associated with Babylon at even the most basic level of food itself; and by making the smoking of ganja a religious rite, the Rastas reject not only the law but also the ordinary state of consciousness valued by the Babylon establishment.

Hebdige's semiotic interpretation of Rastafari offers a fascinating new way to think about the material culture of new religious movements—their clothing, hairstyle, and physical symbolism—and the ways in which these bodily markers can carry profound social and political significance. However, this approach is perhaps less useful for trying to understand the content of these groups as *religious* movements, which are concerned not only with social-political subversion and the playful use of bodily signifiers but also with questions of ultimate meaning and spiritual experience.

A FOCUS ON GENDER AND SEXUALITY: WOMEN IN NEW RELIGIONS

As we saw above in chapters 4 and 8, many new religious movements such as Spiritualism and Wicca offer women powerful new roles as authorities, mediums, and ritual specialists. More importantly, they have gone hand in hand with new social movements such as the early women's rights movement in the nineteenth century and new forms of feminism that emerged in the 1960s and '70s. Thus one of the most useful ways to gain insight into new religious movements is through the lenses of gender and sexuality studies, examining the gender roles, family arrangements, and sexual relations that many of these groups offer.[14]

One of the most comprehensive accounts of women in new religious movements is Susan J. Palmer's *Moon Sisters, Krishna Mothers, Rajneesh Lovers,* which examines a wide array of female roles in alternative spiritual communities. Although she focuses primarily on recent new religions such as ISKCON, the Unification Church, the Rajneesh movement, and the Raëlians, Palmer notes that this emphasis on new roles for women and new sexual relations has been a consistent trend in alternative religions since the nineteenth century. As we have seen in the case of the Mormons and the Spiritualists, radical new religious ideas often went hand in hand with new experiments in women's roles, marriage, sexuality, and family.[15] However, Palmer also suggests that women's roles underwent a profound shift in the decades after World War II, as traditional family arrangements were increasingly challenged and women began to enter the workforce in large numbers. In an ever more complex, changing, and demanding society, when women were expected to be not only mothers and wives but also breadwinners, the clearer and more defined female roles offered by new religions could be extremely attractive: "Is it surprising therefore that some women today might feel insecure as a wife, unimportant or undervalued as a mother, and stressed out as a worker-wife-mother-housekeeper? For women in this situation with religious sensibilities, the simple and valorized roles of 'sister,' 'mother,' and 'lover' within the setting of a religious commune might begin to exert an appeal."[16]

Palmer lays out a typology of three broad kinds of relationships within new religions, which she calls *sex complementarity, sex polarity,* and *sex unity. Sex complementarity* is the idea that each sex is endowed with different but complementary spiritual qualities, and it emphasizes the importance of marriage for uniting the two halves of the soul to form one complete being. A good example of a new religious movement that follows this model, Palmer suggests, is the Unification Church, which sees marriage between male and female as essential to restoring the harmonious spiritual unity that was lost when Adam and Eve fell from grace. *Sex polarity* is the idea that the sexes are spiritually distinct and largely irrelevant to each other's salvation. In groups that follow this model, men are often considered superior to women, as in ISKCON; but sometimes women may be considered superior to men, as in the case of the Rajneesh movement. Finally, the idea of *sex unity* is that the body and gender are superficial layers covering over the immortal and sexless spirit or real self. Groups that follow this model include Scientology—which sees the true self as the thetan, a spiritual entity that is beyond gender—and Heaven's Gate—which sees the true body of the Kingdom of Heaven as a perfectly genderless, sexless body.[17]

While Palmer discusses a broad array of women's roles in new religions, we can focus on just one for the sake of this brief appendix. One of the most successful but also controversial new religious movements to emerge in the second half of the twentieth century was the group centered on the charismatic Indian guru Bhagwan Shree Rajneesh (known in his later years as Osho). While it originated in India during the 1960s and '70s, the

Rajneesh movement came to the United States in the 1980s, where it established a huge and briefly successful utopian commune in Oregon called Rajneeshpuram. Throughout its history, the Rajneesh movement had a very sex-positive attitude, regarding sexuality not as a source of sin or weakness but as a means to mystical experience or "super-consciousness."

At the same time, the movement placed great emphasis on the power and authority of women. Like neopaganism, as we saw in chapter 8, the Rajneesh movement emerged during the same period as the new forms of feminism that grew out of the 1960s and '70s. And Rajneesh himself articulated his own "new vision of women's liberation." Women, in his view, were inherently superior to men because they were naturally in possession of greater sexual energy (*shakti*, or feminine power, according to traditional Indian yogic and Tantric philosophy). This was evidenced by the fact that "women are capable of multiple orgasms, man is not."[18] After centuries of male domination, it was finally time for the "new age of woman," when feminine energies had to be released. Thus women were also given a number of primary leadership roles within the movement. During the period in Oregon in the 1980s, the movement was run largely by female disciples, particularly Ma Anand Sheela (aka Sheela Silverman) and her female cohorts, often called the "Ma-archy."

As Palmer suggests, many of the women who joined the movement in the 1970s and '80s found this vision immensely appealing. Demographically, the Rajneesh community was predominantly female, with women outnumbering men by ratios of 3:1 to 3:2 at various times. Amid the larger cultural ferment of the sexual revolution and second-wave feminism, the Rajneesh movement offered a radical kind of spirituality where women could "throw off their shackles, discover their true strength, indulge their polyandrous tendencies, and, as the 'pillars of his temple,' assume positions of leadership to usher in the New Age of Woman."[19]

Overall, Palmer's approach is useful for understanding several aspects of new religions that are often neglected—above all, the central roles that women often play in these communities and the wide range of forms these roles might take in different movements. At the same time, however, it perhaps risks overlooking the *internal* diversity of women's roles within a single movement. After all, it seems unlikely that every woman who joined the Rajneesh community was interested in women's liberation or leadership roles; many were probably also attracted by the philosophy, the spiritual practice, or the sense of community. Similarly, it seems unlikely that every woman who joined ISKCON was interested in serving as a "Krishna mother," or that every woman who joined the Unification Church was interested in becoming a dutiful wife and half of a harmonious spiritual couple. This is true, of course, not just of new religions but also of mainstream religious and political institutions, where we find gays and lesbians supporting the Republican Party or the Catholic Church—institutions that typically discourage such sexual orientations. So there must be other—perhaps simply *religious*—reasons apart from gender and sexuality that lead women to join these movements. However, for identifying general trends and typologies in women's participation in these movements, Palmer's approach is extremely helpful.

A PSYCHOLOGICAL APPROACH: "PSEUDO-SOLUTIONS" OR "PSYCHIC RELIEF"?

One common way that many authors have attempted to explain the rise of new religions has been an appeal to psychological factors.[20] Some scholars, for example, have suggested that the founders of new religions may have had one or more unique psychological features that help account for their spiritual vision and charismatic appeal. Thus several scholars have suggested that the highly energetic and prolific Mormon founder Joseph Smith exhibited symptoms that could indicate bipolar (manic-depressive) disorder. Building on some insights of a Mormon psychologist, Lawrence Foster suggests that Smith's behavior during the last years of his life was very similar to the sorts of behavior associated with manic-depressive symptoms: "Although one could understand that an individual under the pressures Joseph Smith faced might experience substantial mood swings, in the Mormon prophet's case, those mood swings appear so severe that they may be clinically significant."[21] In particular, Foster suggests, Smith's practice of plural marriage and his large number of sexual partners might also be indicative of manic behavior: "If the initial systematic attempt to introduce the concept of plural marriage among his closest associates bespeaks of possible manic enthusiasm . . . his subsequent use of sexual activity with the fifteen or more women with whom he may have sustained sexual relations as plural wives . . . is even more suggestive of the hyper-sexuality that often accompanies manic periods."[22]

It would not be difficult to think of other leaders of new religions whom we might try to analyze through a psychological lens. For example, one could argue that Marshall Applewhite's long struggle with homosexuality, resulting in his own castration, was reflected in his spiritual worldview and religious practice, which included rigorous efforts to control all forms of sensuality and the physical body as a whole.

The problem with these kinds of psychological interpretations, however, is that they are almost always evaluations from a long distance. Can we really undertake a psychological analysis of Joseph Smith, who died over 150 years ago and left only his writings and the observations of others? Can we even evaluate more recent figures such as Applewhite without having the professional opinion of a qualified psychiatrist who could examine him firsthand? And of course, even if religious leaders such as Joseph Smith did have a diagnosable condition, that still would not account for the fact that millions of other people accepted his religious ideas and followed his new spiritual path. Various other authors have thus attempted to develop psychological explanations for those who choose to follow new religions.

One of the most widely read authors on the psychology of new religions is Marc Galanter, a medical doctor and a professor of psychiatry at New York University. Galanter has undertaken psychological studies of numerous religious, secular, and quasi-religious groups, such as the Divine Light Mission, the Unification Church, Peoples Temple, MOVE, and Alcoholics Anonymous, using a methodology based on detailed surveys among practitioners and long-term follow-up studies among both current and ex-members.[23]

According to Galanter's research, charismatic groups often have a particular appeal to young people. Because young people typically face challenges as they grow into adulthood, struggling to find new forms of identity, community, and meaningful work, charismatic movements can offer comfort and the hope of a positive transformation: "Charismatic groups appear to offer succor and the promise of resolution of many of these developmental conflicts, particularly in respect to identity and participation in a viable peer group."[24] While Galanter notes that sometimes the charismatic group may offer a kind of "pseudo-solution" for dealing with these problems, he does acknowledge that conversion to a new religious movement can have a positive and restorative function: it may bring "an enhanced sense of purpose and an improvement in their relations with peers" as well as a "potentially stabilizing effect," giving them new spiritual resources and feelings of calm and happiness: "The intense cohesiveness of the charismatic group in combination with its ability to influence members' beliefs can yield relief in psychopathology. The support of the group and the provision of routine and consistent tasks and role expectation may provide a measure of stability that socially alienated or mentally ill people desire."[25]

Some of Galanter's most extensive studies have been conducted on the Unification Church, which we discussed above. On the basis of his findings, Galanter argues that individuals who convert to and then have a long-term engagement with the Unification Church tend to have experienced some form of psychological distress and alienation before joining. Galanter suggests that the Unification Church exercises a great deal of social control over its members, which can be a source of psychological distress but also a source of tremendous psychological relief for those who ultimately comply with that control. The most famous example of the Unification Church's unique religious practices is its marriage ceremony, in which Reverend Moon himself selected the mates for almost all church members. The marriages often took place in mass gatherings, at which dozens, hundreds, thousands, or even tens of thousands of couples selected by Moon were married simultaneously. In Galanter's view, practices such as these mass weddings served at once to *generate* and to *offer the solution to* psychological distress. This is what he calls the "pincer effect": that is, the religious group would create psychological tension by requiring members to engage in "deviant" practices such as mass marriages, but at the same time it "provided relief when members complied and maintained their commitments to the group."[26]

Galanter's psychological approach is generally useful insofar as it provides a great deal of survey material that follows the mental well-being of members over long periods of involvement in groups such as the Unification Church. However, his approach is limited and arguably problematic in many ways. First, from the very outset, he approaches new religious movements through the lens of social "deviance," describing these groups as adopting "deviant life styles" and "the disruption of nuclear families."[27] But the concept of "deviance" is, of course, a relative one. Deviant in relation to what, we might ask? Many cultures practice arranged marriages, and many cultures have complex, often extended family arrangements that are not based on the American "nuclear" model. By calling these practices "deviant"

Galanter is implying from the very outset that they are not simply different but problematic, dysfunctional, or dangerous.

Second, it is not entirely clear that any of the conclusions he draws from new religions or charismatic groups could not *also* be drawn just as easily from a study of "mainstream" religions. Mainstream Christian and Jewish traditions also help young people deal with the transition to adulthood and the achievement of a stable, mature identity (through rites such as bar and bat mitzvahs, confirmation, marriage, and so forth); they also involve practices that both create and help resolve psychological tensions (for example, requiring celibacy before marriage but then encouraging sexual relations after marriage); they typically exert tremendous social pressure and social control (as in the case of Evangelical and Catholic condemnations of abortion and homosexuality); and so on. In short, it is not entirely clear that the psychological tensions and resolutions experienced in the Unification Church or any other new religious movement are significantly different from those experienced in any religious community.

A COMPARATIVE AND HISTORICAL APPROACH: ESALEN AND THE AMERICAN "RELIGION OF NO RELIGION"

One last approach to consider in this brief appendix is what we can call a history of religions or comparative religions approach, which roots new religious movements both in the longer history of American culture and in the broader framework of the world's religions outside the United States.[28] As we saw in the Introduction, many scholars have suggested that New Age and new religious movements are not so much "new" in themselves as continuations of a much older tradition of alternative spirituality that dates back to the early centuries of the Common Era. As Wouter Hanegraaff has argued, the New Age as a whole could be described as "esotericism in the mirror of secular thought": that is, New Age spirituality continues much older esoteric ideas such as correspondences, living nature, and transmutation, while rearticulating them in the language of modern science, rationality, technology, and consumer culture. In this sense, the newness of the New Age is not so much the content as the way in which this content has been adapted to the frameworks of evolutionary theory, modern science, technological innovations, and so on.[29]

Another excellent example of this comparative and historical approach is the work of the American scholar Jeffrey J. Kripal, who has written widely on new religions, alternative spirituality, mysticism, paranormal phenomena, and popular culture. In his book *Esalen: America and the Religion of No Religion,* Kripal focuses on one of the most important and influential centers of alternative spirituality in modern America, the Esalen Institute, located on the spectacularly beautiful coast of California near Big Sur. Founded in 1962 by Michael Murphy and Dick Price, the Esalen Institute combines elements of Western psychology such as Gestalt and personal growth therapy with elements drawn from Eastern traditions such as yoga and Buddhist meditation. In many ways, Esalen was really at the cutting edge of the exploration of alternative and non-Western spirituality during the 1960s and '70s and remains an epicenter of New Age practice in the twenty-first century.

In his study of Esalen, Kripal uses the tools of both the historian and the scholar of comparative religions. As a historian of religions, he traces the fascinating story of Esalen as it developed from the late nineteenth century, to the countercultural explosion of the 1960s, to its recent renaissance in the twenty-first century. In particular, he situates the rise of Esalen in the rich cultural ferment of the 1960s, amid the volatile yet creative energy that produced "the civil rights movement, the sexual revolution, and the definitive birth of feminist and gay consciousness in that still reverberating decade."[30]

Yet at the same time, as a scholar of comparative religions, Kripal shows the ways in which a variety of different influences from both East and West flowed into Esalen, from Buddhist meditation and yoga to humanistic psychology and 1960s psychedelia. In particular, Kripal sees many parallels between the spirituality of Esalen and the Hindu and Buddhist tradition of Tantra, which also places central emphasis on the role of the physical body, the senses, and sexuality in religious practice. Thus, Kripal suggests, Esalen was itself an experiment in comparative religion, mixing multiple religious and philosophical ideas to forge a unique sort of "American mysticism."[31]

Ultimately, Kripal argues, Esalen is a uniquely and even quintessentially "American" spiritual experiment. Grounded in the First Amendment's commitment to the free exercise of religion and in the separation of church and state, Esalen is a space in which any and all forms of religious practice can flourish, yet without any one of them becoming dominant:

> A religion of no religion is also deeply American. Like the constitutional separation of church and state, which effectively carves out a secular space in which almost any religious forms can find legal protection and so flourish within American society, Esalen's religion of no religion has no official alliance with *any* religious system. It can provide, like a kind of American Mystical Constitution, a spiritual space where almost any kind of religious form can flourish, provided—and this is crucial—that it does not attempt to impose itself on the entire community. . . . As an early Esalen motto put it, "No one captures the flag."[32]

In this sense, Esalen is in many ways the epitome of the New Age itself, with its eclectic blend of spiritual ideas from all corners of the earth and its anti-institutional faith in the power of the individual seeker to put these ideas together in his or her own meaningfully creative way.

Kripal's historical and comparative approach is extremely valuable for understanding the role of New Age and new religious ideas within the broader framework of both American history and religion more broadly. As Kripal persuasively shows, Esalen is best seen not as a flaky aberration from American culture but in many ways as the *epitome* of the American spirit of experimentation and borrowing from a wide array of different cultures.

At the same time, however, Kripal's approach might be said to be perhaps a bit *too* sympathetic and uncritical in its interpretation of Esalen and of contemporary American spirituality as a whole. As we saw in chapter 11, many critics have argued that the New Age movement could also be regarded as a form of commodification of spirituality, which appropriates exotic ideas from other cultures and markets them to a wealthy audience of American seekers. While the Esalen Institute is technically a "nonprofit" organization, it does charge fairly high prices for its various workshops, seminars, and other services. As of 2014, weekend seminars at the Institute such as "Strengthening the Heart with Compassion" and "Practical Intuition: Full Effectiveness Living" range between $405 and $1,750, while weeklong workshops cost up to $6,750.[33] Thus the kinds of individuals who are able to participate in Esalen's various activities are unlikely to be the poor and needy; rather, they are almost exclusively the wealthy who have both the leisure time and the resources to spend thousands of dollars on a weekend at this spectacularly beautiful spiritual resort on the California coast.

As we saw in chapter 11, many critics also argue that New Age spirituality of the sort that we find at Esalen tends to appropriate and transform non-Western traditions in problematic ways.[34] When Hindu yoga and Buddhist meditation are taken out of their cultural contexts by American practitioners and melded with contemporary Western psychology or New Age therapy, they may be changed in ways that make them unrecognizable—or possibly even offensive—to members of the original cultures.[35] None of this, we should note, invalidates Kripal's otherwise fascinating analysis, but it does raise some more critical questions that his approach leaves largely unasked.

Obviously, there are a great many other useful approaches to new religions that we could discuss here. We could, for example, employ a market-based model, examining the ways in which new religious movements emerge and compete with more established mainstream religions in the vibrant marketplace of contemporary spiritual life.[36] Or we could use insights drawn from contemporary neuroscience to examine what actually takes place in the brains of individuals who practice various techniques of meditation or prayer.[37] However, the approaches outlined here are merely intended to serve as a useful starting point and a basic toolbox for thinking about how to analyze, interpret, and make sense of new religious movements from a variety of different perspectives. Again, it should be left to the reader to decide which might be more or less useful in a particular context and which might be most helpful for the broader understanding of religion as a whole.

QUESTIONS FOR DISCUSSION AND DEBATE

1. Should the methods and theories we use in the study of New Age, neopagan, and new religious movements basically be the same ones we would use for the study of any other "mainstream" religions? Or does the study of new religions require alternative approaches in order to make sense of groups that seem "alternative" or outside the mainstream of American religious life?

2. Of the six approaches outlined in this appendix, which—if any—seem most persuasive or most useful to you? Which seem least helpful or most problematic?

3. What other approaches *not* discussed in this appendix might be useful? What other ways of making sense of new religious phenomena have we left out?

SUGGESTED CLASSROOM ACTIVITY

Take any of the movements discussed in this book—or another movement not discussed here and generated by the group—and analyze it through the lenses of the six approaches covered in this appendix. How would we interpret the Nation of Islam, for example, from the perspectives of a sociological, ethnographic, cultural studies, gender studies, psychological, or comparative religions approach? Which of these approaches seem most and least helpful in this particular case? And what other approaches not covered in this appendix can we come up with that might shed more light on this movement?

SUGGESTIONS FOR FURTHER READING

Barker, Eileen. *The Making of a Moonie: Choice or Brainwashing?* London: Basil Blackwell, 1984.

Cowan, Douglas E., and David G. Bromley. *Cults and New Religions: A Brief History.* Malden, MA: Wiley-Blackwell, 2007.

Dawson, Lorne. *Cult Controversies: The Sociology of New Religious Movements.* New York: Oxford University Press, 2006.

Galanter, Marc. *Cults and New Religious Movements: A Report of the American Psychiatric Association.* Washington, DC: American Psychiatric Press, 1989.

Hanegraaff, Wouter J. *New Age Religion and Western Culture: Esotericism in the Mirror of Secular Thought.* Albany: SUNY Press, 1997.

Hebdige, Dick. *Subculture: The Meaning of Style.* New York: Routledge, 1979.

Kripal, Jeffrey J. *Esalen: America and the Religion of No Religion.* Chicago: University of Chicago Press, 2008.

Lewis, James R., ed. *The Oxford Handbook of New Religious Movements.* New York: Oxford University Press, 2008.

Palmer, Susan J. *Moon Sisters, Krishna Mothers, Rajneesh Lovers: Women's Roles in New Religions.* Syracuse, NY: Syracuse University Press, 1996.

Pike, Sarah M. *Earthly Bodies, Magical Selves: Contemporary Pagans and the Search for Community.* Berkeley: University of California Press, 2001.

Stein, Stephen J. *Communities of Dissent: A History of American Alternative Religions.* New York: Oxford University Press, 2003.

Urban, Hugh B. *Tantra: Sex, Secrecy, Politics and Power in the Study of Religion.* Berkeley: University of California Press, 2003.

NOTES TO THE APPENDIX

1. For good, accessible, and brief overviews of theoretical approaches to religious studies generally, see Timothy K. Beal and William E. Deal, *Theory for Religious Studies* (New York: Routledge, 2005); Craig Martin, *A Critical Introduction to the Study of Religion* (New York: Routledge, 2012); Daniel L. Pals, *Eight Theories of Religion* (New York: Oxford University Press, 2006); Russell McCutcheon, *Critics Not Caretakers: Redescribing the Public Study of Religion* (Albany: SUNY Press, 2001).
2. I take this metaphor of the toolbox from Wendy Doniger O'Flaherty, *Women, Androgynes and Other Mythical Beasts* (Chicago: University of Chicago Press, 1980), 5–7.
3. See especially Lorne Dawson, *Comprehending Cults: The Sociology of New Religious Movements* (New York: Oxford University Press, 2006); Roy Wallis, *The Road to Total Freedom: A Sociological Study of Scientology* (New York: Columbia University Press, 1976); Lewis F. Carter, *Charisma and Control in Rajneeshpuram: The Role of Shared Values in the Creation of a Community* (Cambridge: Cambridge University Press, 1990); David G. Bromley and Anson D. Shupe, *"Moonies" in America: Cult, Church, and Crusade* (London: Sage Publications, 1979).
4. Eileen Barker, *The Making of a Moonie: Choice or Brainwashing?* (London: Basil Blackwell, 1984), 21.
5. Ibid., 254.
6. Ibid., 243–44.
7. Sarah M. Pike, *Earthly Bodies, Magical Selves: Contemporary Pagans and the Search for Community* (Berkeley: University of California Press, 2001), xvi.
8. Ibid., 20.
9. See Victor Turner, *The Ritual Process: Structure and Anti-structure* (Ithaca, NY: Cornell University Press, 1969), 94–165; Arnold van Gennep, *The Rites of Passage* (Chicago: University of Chicago Press, 1961).
10. Pike, *Earthly Bodies,* 31.
11. Ibid., 39.
12. Dick Hebdige, *Subculture: The Meaning of Style* (New York: Routledge, 1979), 18.
13. Ibid., 34.
14. See, for example, Ann Braude, *Radical Spirits: Spiritualism and Women's Rights in Nineteenth-Century America* (Boston: Beacon Press, 1989); Jone Salomonsen, *Enchanted Feminism: Ritual, Gender and Divinity among the Reclaiming Witches of San Francisco* (New York: Routledge, 2002); Hugh B. Urban, *Magia Sexualis: Sex, Magic, and Liberation in Modern Western Esotericism* (Berkeley: University of California Press, 2005); Susan J. Palmer, *Aliens Adored: Raël's UFO Religion* (New Brunswick, NJ: Rutgers University Press, 2004); Jeffrey J. Kripal, *Esalen: America and the Religion of No Religion* (Chicago: University of Chicago Press, 2008).
15. Susan J. Palmer, *Moon Sisters, Krishna Mothers, Rajneesh Lovers: Women's Roles in New Religions* (Syracuse, NY: Syracuse University Press, 1994), 4–5.
16. Ibid., 7.
17. Ibid., 10–11.

18. Ibid., 49.
19. Ibid., 51.
20. See, for example, Saul Levine, *Radical Departures: Desperate Detours to Growing Up* (San Diego: Harcourt Brace Jovanovich, 1986); John A. Saliba, "Psychology and the New Religious Movements," in *The Oxford Handbook of New Religious Movements*, ed. James R. Lewis (New York: Oxford University Press, 2008), 317–32.
21. Lawrence Foster, *Women, Family, and Utopia: Communal Experiments of the Shakers, the Oneida Community and the Mormons* (Syracuse, NY: Syracuse University Press, 1992), 162.
22. Ibid., 165.
23. Marc Galanter, "Cults and Charismatic Group Psychology," in *Religion and the Clinical Practice of Psychology*, ed. Edward P. Shafranske (Washington, DC: American Psychological Association, 1996), 269–98; Marc Galanter, *Cults and New Religious Movements: A Report of the American Psychiatric Association* (Washington, DC: American Psychiatric Press, 1989).
24. Galanter, "Cults," 271; Galanter, *Cults*, 56–57.
25. Galanter, "Cults," 281.
26. Ibid., 286; Galanter, *Cults*, 160.
27. Galanter, "Cults," 269; Galanter, *Cults*, 159.
28. For other examples of this approach, see Urban, *Magia Sexualis*; Hugh B. Urban, *The Church of Scientology: A History of a New Religion* (Princeton, NJ: Princeton University Press, 2011); David Chidester, *Salvation and Suicide: An Interpretation of Jim Jones, the Peoples Temple and Jonestown* (Bloomington: Indiana University Press, 1988); Catherine Wessinger, *How the Millennium Comes Violently: From Jonestown to Heaven's Gate* (New York: Seven Bridges Press, 2000).
29. See Wouter Hanegraaff, *New Age Religion and Western Culture: Esotericism in the Mirror of Secular Thought* (Albany: SUNY Press, 1997), 7.
30. Kripal, *Esalen*, 7.
31. Ibid., 6.
32. Ibid., 9.
33. "2014 Esalen Workshop Tuition," Esalen.org, 2014, www.esalen.org/page/2014-esalen-workshop-tuition-including-accommodations.
34. See Kimberly Lau, *New Age Capitalism: Making Money East of Eden* (Philadelphia: University of Pennsylvania Press, 2000); Jeremy Carrette and Richard King, *Selling Spirituality: The Silent Takeover of Religion* (New York: Routledge, 2004).
35. On this point, see Hugh B. Urban, *Tantra: Sex, Secrecy, Politics and Power in the Study of Religion* (Berkeley: University of California Press, 2003).
36. See R. Laurence Moore, *Selling God: American Religion and the Marketplace of Culture* (New York: Oxford University Press, 1994); Diane Winston et al., eds., *Faith in the Market: Religion and the Rise of Urban Commercial Culture* (New Brunswick, NJ: Rutgers University Press, 2002); Wade Clark Roof, *Spiritual Marketplace: Baby Boomers and the Remaking of American Religion* (Princeton, NJ: Princeton University Press, 2001).
37. See, for example, James H. Austin, *Zen and the Brain: Toward an Understanding of Meditation and Consciousness* (Boston: MIT Press, 1999); Clifton B. Parker, "Stanford Research: Compassion Aids Well-Being," *Stanford Neuroscience Institute News*, February 25, 2014, https://neuroscience.stanford.edu/news/stanford-research-compassion-aids-well-being.

Drew Ali, 92–94
Druids, 6, 157, 162–66

environmentalism, 22, 159–60, 169–76
Esalen Institute, 223, 309–11
esotericism, 11–13, 69, 85–86, 160, 222, 309;
    defined, 11–13

Fard, Wallace D., 94, 101, 104
Farrakhan, Louis, 103–4
Father Divine, 249–50
Federal Bureau of Investigations, 7, 9, 63, 93,
    150–51, 266, 271–75
feminism, 22, 68, 82–83, 87, 160, 169–76,
    184–85, 306
First Amendment, 7, 14, 22–23, 38–41, 56,
    59–60, 64, 149, 274–77
Five Percenters (Nation of Gods and Earths),
    90–91, 103–11
Fox sisters, 70, 83
Fundamentalist Church of Jesus Christ of
    Latter-day Saints, 46, 62–65. *See also* plural
    marriage

Gardner, Gerald, 159–65
Garvey, Marcus Mosiah, 92–93, 116–17, 121,
    127, 133
Ghost Dance, 29–30
Ginsberg, Allen, 2, 37
Gnosticism, 13, 85–86, 180
Gorgoroth, 193–94

Haile Selassie, 114–15, 117–20, 122–23,
    125–26, 128
Hanegraaff, Wouter, x, 309
Harrison, George, 202, 206–8
Hatch, Cora, 78–80, 82, 85, 238
Heaven's Gate, ix, 4, 15–19, 23–24, 213, 244,
    305
heavy metal, 179, 192–94
Hermeticism, 11–12, 86, 160
Hermetic Order of the Golden Dawn, 4, 160
Hinduism, 4, 9, 11, 15, 85–86, 110, 114, 117–18,
    161, 190, 201–4, 208–9, 212, 310
hip-hop, 90–91, 105–11, 127–29
Howell, Leonard, 114, 117–18
Hubbard, L. Ron, 5, 135–42, 144–47, 149–51
Huxley, Aldous, 36–37

Internal Revenue Service (IRS), 135–37, 149–53,
    253, 289
Internet, 18–19, 143, 148–49
ISKCON, 2–3, 15, 110, 201–19, 305–6; Krishna
    and, 203–9, 306; Swami Prabhupada and,
    2–3, 201–6
Islam, 9, 90–111; compared to Nation of Islam,
    109–10

Jesus Christ, 31–32, 36, 45, 48–49, 51–52, 55, 73,
    80, 114, 119, 121–22, 207, 209, 232–33, 235,
    244, 250–51, 266, 268–69
Jones, James Warren, 5, 242–64
Jonestown, 242–45, 249, 253–61, 270, 273

Kabbalah, 11–12, 85–86, 160
Knight, JZ, 5, 13, 86, 221–22, 229–35, 238–39.
    See also Ramtha
Koresh, David, 265, 267–72, 277
Kripal, Jeffrey J., x, 11, 309–11
Krishna, 203–9, 306

LaVey, Anton, 138, 179–87, 191, 193–94

MacLaine, Shirley, 5, 220–21, 235–38
magic, 160–64, 166–68, 179, 189–90, 302;
    defined, 161, 163, 189–90
Malcolm X, 90, 97–100, 111
Manson, Charles, 180, 195, 213
Manson, Marilyn, 194–95
marijuana, 15, 37, 115–17, 121, 124, 129–32; legal
    status, 129–32
Marley, Bob, 115, 120, 123–27, 131
McVeigh, Timothy, 273–74
meditation, 203, 289–90, 309, 311
Melton, J. Gordon, 3–4
Messiah, 80, 114, 118, 122, 126, 127, 267
millenarian movements, 242–45, 265–69
millennium, 233, 266–70
Millerites, 244–45, 266
Miscavige, David, 135, 144, 149, 151
Moorish Science Temple, 91–94
Mormonism, 5, 10, 13, 15, 21–22, 45–66, 68, 83,
    110–11, 137, 152–53, 221, 307
Muhammad, Elijah, 94–98, 101, 104–5,
    113
Muhammad, Wallace (Warith Deen),
    100–101, 103